MAN WITHOUT GOD

AN INTRODUCTION TO UNBELIEF

THEOLOGICAL RESOURCES is a series of books taking its impulse from the striking renewal of interest in theology to-day. That renewal is unique in theological history, because its impetus derives from all the churches and because evidence for it abounds in all countries. The contributors to the series have been chosen, therefore, for their suitability to particular subjects rather than for denominational uniformity. There are two General Editors, John P. Whalen, formerly acting head of the Catholic University of America, and Jaroslav Pelikan, a prominent Lutheran Pastor, at present the Titus Street Professor of Ecclesiastical History at Yale University.

In commenting on the current theological revival, the General Editors write—'this interest, vital though it is, stands in danger of being lost in superficiality and trivialized into a fad. The answer to this danger is greater depth. *THEOLOGICAL RESOURCES* is intended to supply that depth.'

JOHN REID

MAN WITHOUT GOD

AN INTRODUCTION TO
UNBELIEF

CORPUS OF NEW YORK

WESTMINSTER OF PHILADELPHIA

HUTCHINSON OF LONDON

CORPUS INSTRUMENTORUM

EDITORIAL OFFICES
110 East 59th Street, New York, N.Y. 10022

SALES & DISTRIBUTION
2231 West 110th Street, Cleveland, Ohio 44102

THE WESTMINSTER PRESS
Witherspoon Building, Philadelphia, Pa. 19107

Library of Congress Catalog Card Number: 72–110420
First Printing, 1971
MANUFACTURED IN GREAT BRITAIN

FOR MY SISTER, FLORENCE,
AND MY BROTHER, JERRY,
WITH LOVE.

Contents

Editors' Foreword

When some future historian of theology comes to describe the development of Christian thought in the second half of the twentieth century, one phenomenon that will undoubtedly bulk large in his account is one theological discovery of atheism. There have always been men who lived without a consciousness of God, and at least since the fourteenth Psalm believers have commented on their existence. But today for the first time theologians feel the obligation to take unbelief seriously as a philosophy of life and to hear the questions it addresses to a faith which they have too long taken for granted.

Man Without God breaks out of the smugness and condescension of traditional theism to ask why it is possible for admirable men to live their lives not only without admitting the presence of God but in denying it. When Dostoevsky said that the choice was 'either God or murder', he was voicing a widespread Christian conviction that only theistic belief (preferably of an orthodox variety) can restrain the beast in man from taking over. The exemplary lives of many of our unbelieving contemporaries are a refutation of that conviction—a refutation with which theology must somehow come to terms.

The chief danger to Christianity in the growing atheism that surrounds it is that the Churches may refuse to take it seriously. The chief danger to the atheist in the midst of a growing atheism is that he develop a smugness and condescension toward traditional Christianity. For the motivation that persuades one to be a practising Christian and a convinced atheist is much the same: to find value and meaning in human life. The Christian finds this value because

ix

of his belief in the revelation that God has become man. Thus he shares with the atheist two fundamental commitments: that no creature deserves to be worshipped as divine, and that human life could be more humane. If the Christian finds these two commitments bound together in a Christ who is divine and human, he must also respect a view of the world that proceeds from radically different premises to striking similar conclusions. But the atheist, for his part, must ask—or be asked—whether his view of the world and of man can perpetuate itself without a transcendent point of reference; in short, whether it is finally possible to be human without the divine.

Before such an exchange can take place, however, both sides need to know much more about each other than they do now. It is one of the strengths of this book that it can help Christians to see atheism with understanding and atheists to look at Christianity with sympathy.

J.P.W.
J.P.

Introduction

This is perhaps the best and the worst of times in which to essay a study of unbelief. Interest in the problem and awareness of its manifold importance have reached unprecedented proportions and an immense amount of material has accumulated, on every aspect of a complex phenomenon, data and analyses which make the invitation to make one more contribution irresistible. If the contribution is an original one, pushing back the limits of present understanding of a specific facet of the question, it is self-justifying, and one can only wish such studies were not as rare as in fact they have been. Still, in many ways this is a period of rapid and significant developments, with which one can hardly keep pace, much less assimilate and properly assess. In defiance of this disconcerting situation I have tried to distil what seemed to me of superior and more permanent value in what has been thought and written on the subject of unbelief, but I could not hope to reproduce anything more recent than the next to the latest word, and I have, I confess, much more often reported someone else's word than expressed my own. Enough has been said and the discussion has reached a level of depth and maturity to warrant this kind of survey, and in any case the relatively pedestrian and unprestigious task of collecting, sorting out, and correlating a mass of information and interpretation has an intrinsic necessity and timeliness of its own.

In face of the extraordinary variety of themes touched by a sweeping overview of the problem of unbelief, I must assume, a priori, that mine has been the fragmented perspective of the fox rather than the concentrated vision of the hedgehog. It would be

arbitrary and unnatural of me to pretend to relate everything which
I have included in this volume to a single central and unifying theme,
a universal principle in terms of which the import and relevance of
the whole might be determined. The pursuit of unbelief as a factor
in human life and an intelligible object of concern to a number of
disciplines has led me onto many levels of experience and reflection,
so that I feel that I have plotted and mapped a diversified terrain
rather than fitted into position the pre-cut pieces of an immediately
recognizable mosaic. The variety of possible and legitimate approaches
to unbelief is reflected in the successive roles in which I have in my
own life encountered it, lived with it, and, unwittingly at first,
prepared to deal with it as I now have. I set aside the personal
struggle with unbelief that has been mine as faltering and faithless
believer and recall my experience as parish priest, with which I
began my ministry, and the shock of meeting real unbelief, of different
degrees, among those who professed what I would have thought was
the same faith as my own. Shortly after I began to teach philosophy
to undergraduates, I became intensely interested in Marxism and
pursued this interest in courses, seminars, and eventually a television
series which led to further personal study and the initiation of special
research in the area of Marxist thought. At Oxford my attention
shifted to the French Enlightenment but continued to focus on the
relationship of atheism to broader structures of thought and the
moving patterns of a social structure in the throes of imminent
upheaval. While at Oxford I was named a consultor to the newly
formed Vatican Secretariat for Non-Believers, an appointment
which provided the opportunity for the kinds of experience and
education without which I could not have attempted the broad pano-
ramic inquiry of which this book is the proximate outcome. A
year's leave of absence from my college has enabled me to share my
views and test them with the graduate students in theology at another
university.

Unbelief or atheism is a response, conscious or not, to the
reality of God, or at least to the assertion of His reality; the point
is that the investigation of, and meditation on, unbelief is essentially
a theological enterprise. It is at the same time, and this is obvious,
an exercise in anthropology in the sense of a sustained discourse on
the nature of man, for all talk about God is talk about man, as well.
Man the unbeliever is the proper and principal subject of the present
inquiry, which is thus located within the ambit of the human spiritual
condition.

A study that aims only to introduce the reader to its subject matter may have a much higher degree of originality than I have been able to achieve, but it will only with difficulty and by way of exception escape the limitations which I have been unable to avoid. My intention has been to organize, in a fashion which will display and articulate, the general features of unbelief, its causes, manifestations, and multiple significance. Unbelief is an extremely fertile field of research as well as a grave and obstinate pastoral problem; the possibilities of understanding and of action have guided the scope of my selection of material, which I hope is adequately expressive of these twin dimensions, theoretical and practical, of the problem. By using the best available resources, I have sought not only to make these materials generally available, if only at second hand, to a wider public, but also to open the field to those whose interest, concern, and competence may be applied to the resolution of the many outstanding issues which dot this area. Methods of digging out reliable information and of correlating it have yet to be seriously tested and proved; impressions are not yet firm and the subject is surrounded by opinion and conjecture more than with deep and solid penetration and a scientific grasp of what it is all about.

An introduction to this problem would fail in its purpose if it did not advert to the still halting and tentative character of much of our present understanding of man's attempt to live without reference to God. Dialogue is an ultimate goal and ought to be considered even now as an eventual response by believers to unbelievers, but the prospect of dialogue depends on the critical evaluation or acceptance and the accurate understanding of unbelief as a complex and elusive phenomenon. At this stage, enthusiasm for dialogue seems to be bounding ahead of the efforts at patient research and reflective appreciation which must sustain the most sincere and well-intentioned personal encounter. Unbelief, it will be seen, is not the closed preserve of a small band of professionals or experts but ought to be the concern of every Christian who feels himself touched by and responsive to the spiritual condition of his fellows.

When a topic is surveyed comprehensively and at a level suitable to introduce it to the inexpert, the treatment of various aspects tends to be potted, and there is a danger of oversimplification. The in-depth study of unbelief ought to be a joint venture, programmed or at least carried on as a concerted undertaking by theologians, philosophers, social scientists, and others. From the present work the reader should expect nothing more than the inclusive outline of the chief elements of the subject and suggestions for extending theological understanding as well as initiating a fruitful dialogue between believer and unbeliever. To move the understanding beyond its current imperfect and still inconclusive status will require the cooperation of those better informed, more perspicuous, and with greater synthesizing powers than I have at my command. I have felt especially limited by lack of consultation with other religious believers and perhaps even more by the spare occasion I have had to exchange views and profit by the insight and self-estimation of unbelievers. I have confined myself almost entirely to the unbelief of those who have never embraced religious faith in a serious or meaningful way, at a mature and reflective level. Those who have been believers in this sense, but have abandoned faith, present a particularly delicate and nuanced challenge, which I leave, with some misgiving, to the theology of faith. The problem of the lapsed believer has been neglected and calls for intensive study of the type which Maurice Bellet has conducted and of the same high caliber.

The unbeliever does not need or want sympathy; this would be offensive and indicate a value judgment which could interfere with the fair-minded respect and understanding to which he has a right. It is not clear to me that complete detachment would serve best the difficult phenomenological task of describing as accurately and completely as possible the complex and, in many respects, obscure fact which is contemporary unbelief. I write from belief but cannot stipulate that mine is pure and untainted by unbelief, probably latent or strongly affected by currents of thinking which presents a constant challenge to the stability and security of believing. The danger to faith derives not so much from factors which might lead to heterodoxy or approach it as from those spiritual and moral failures and aberrations which drain faith of its salvific value while, perhaps, leaving the outward profession of assent to dogmatic propositions intact. I can support the suggestion that an unbeliever could do a study on this subject of quite another color than mine and with insight and penetration beyond my competence. Interestingly enough, I was first asked by the publisher of this collection to write the volume on faith, and when I replied that my interest and research had been in the problem of unbelief, I was told that an atheist had been considered for this project. Thus I have, in fact, attempted what might better have given an unbeliever gainful employment, and the reader something quite different.

It would be difficult to situate the present work within the limits of any of the branches of theology recognized traditionally as occupied with the several offices of this discipline. A direct apologetics in the sense accepted until recently seems inappropriate in facing up to the major thrust of unbelief as a theological problem, certainly not as the primary or directive response. I do not flatly exclude the apologetic function, which is perfectly legitimate and indeed indispensable, in itself, but my own approach is something else again. I am concerned with defining unbelief as a multi-faceted reality, not an abstract category, with identifying the varieties and tracing the causes and effects of unbelief, personal and social, and with offering suggestions for a theological appraisal of the problem and the initiation of dialogue. I leave to others the point-by-point grappling with the difficulties and objections of the unbeliever, the defense of the faith, of its reasonableness and coherence with man's legitimate needs and aspirations (its transformation and transcendence of these is the subject, more properly, of other theological considerations). There is a difference between learning how to dialogue with unbelievers, an undertaking the formidable dimensions of which we are only just beginning to discern, and learning how most effectively to meet and answer the charges which unbelief brings against the reasonableness and probity of the believer as such. The two offices need not be kept apart in airtight compartments, and I should like to re-emphasize the absolute necessity and evangelical propriety of apologetics, which is not my direct concern for the present but to which I accord due honor and respect. The apologists have brought their art to the brink of disintegration, but it ought to be rescued from them and rehabilitated, not pushed over the abyss.

The unbeliever may find my presentation of his case seriously distorted or at least deficient in more than one important aspect, and in any case I do not propose to speak for him or in his stead. He can speak for himself; my aim has been to collect and report the arguments for rejecting theism and Biblical faith and for espousing varieties of secularist, atheistic humanism and to explore possible avenues leading to dialogue. My catalogue of evidences is an incomplete one, perforce, and other writings and events make it out of date even as it goes to press. I hope that the present work may aid the inexpert, for whom it is intended, to find their way about in a field changing and expanding rapidly. The believer will relate more readily, of course, to the canons of selection and inclusion as well as to the principles of interpretation and assessment and it is for him that I have written, rather than for the unbeliever, who will, understandably, find my perspectives strange and my preferences unacceptable. There are other approaches to the problem of unbelief —and it is a 'problem' for the believer and not, certainly not in the same sense, for the unbeliever. Practical experience, the heart of a vital pastoral of unbelief, is as urgently needed as it is widely lacking, and a theory of dialogue, such as I have outlined, is not the same as, or a substitute for, the actual undertaking. There are, lastly, the alternatives to dialogue, not necessarily excluded by or incompatible with the latter, and they are polemic and instruction, simple encounter and apologetic defense.

In a bibliographical note I have tried to indicate explicitly the authors to whom I feel I am most heavily indebted. Theology has supplied the bulk and the most important of the contributions, but other disciplines have provided indispensable materials for an essay as comprehensive as this one has tried to be. The systematic surveys and content analyses I have made, over a period of two years, have left me frustrated and not a little discouraged at the sheer enormity of what is being published; but one may chart courses and relate trends as they appear. Theology's function is to illuminate the major areas of human concern in the light of the Gospel, to spell out the implications of faith, to prepare the way for doctrinal declarations and resolutions, so far as these become possible, to understand the human predicament as faith discloses its meaning and import, and to recommend this understanding to the unbeliever and to the skeptic within. On the question of unbelief the great names in Catholic theology who emerged at the Council have all appeared in a steady stream of articles and monographs. The spate of light-weight paperbacks and journalistic pieces testifies to the interest in the problem of both professionals and the reading public, which is a welcome sign in spite of the attendant risk of debasing the theological currency. I have tried to rise above the level of theological journalism, to attain something approaching a systematic arrangement, an ultimate goal to which a great deal of preliminary work is prerequisite. With respect to the overall question of unbelief, theology has, until recently, suffered from insufficiency of data, an inadequate understanding of the situation, and a lack of recognition of particular problems. While theologians have shown increasing awareness of the needs in this area, churchmen have been caught unprepared and have had to assume positions at short notice and with unseemly speed.

Writing from faith to faith I must confess to a certain uneasiness, a suspicion that I have not been able completely to avoid a defective humanism that drains theological analysis of what should be its transcendent and Biblical inspiration. If the elaboration of a theology of man is our most imperative contemporary task, it must be a truly Christian humanism that we produce, a vision of man created and redeemed by God in Christ and called to new life in the Spirit. A theology of unbelief is one contribution to this urgent need, a right thinking (*recta sapere*) not only of the ways of living without God, but of the things of God as man experiences and tries to grasp them. It is a stunted naturalism which sees only in deeds, in external actions, the worship of God; reflecting seriously on the rejection of God can be a cultic act, in an attitude of mind that is Christian. The theology of unbelief can be an exercise in liberating truth from bondage to human whim and prejudice. In the text which follows the amount of space devoted to a specific question is not a reliable index of its intrinsic or topical importance, but I have sought to discover the *truth* of each question, as best I could.

My thinking is still fundamentally political in the matter of disengaging and appropriating the truth of God and of man in God, which is to say that I believe in the Church. It is a matter both of choice and of emphasis, and while I choose to situate belief within the community of those called to hear the word of God and celebrate His gifts, I do not intend to lend excessive weight to the powers, programs, or structures of the ecclesial institution. Belief-consciousness is a reality largely within a visible and operative social organization so that I have ventured to describe the varieties of unbelief over against the gathered, communitarian life of the believers. Much of present-day religious alienation and disaffection is, precisely, occasioned by and directed against what are thought to be the grave moral and spiritual vices of the Church as such. One might go further and say that it is the Church, in the first place, that is found to be incredible, totally and essentially, and beyond hope of repair, and that whatever the Church's message is, this too is not to be believed. Some churchmen sense this, but they are not deceiving any but themselves by defending their own vested interests as though these were inseparable from God's (as if God had any). A sense of the presence of God is not identical to a sense of conformity to traditional ecclesiastical forms and procedures but may indeed include a mighty protest against their very defects and limitations. Among believers today there has appeared a disturbing charge to the effect that the ecclesiastical hierarchy has arrogated to itself the symbols of Christian grace, assembled a gigantic collection of powers, and mythologized the institution beyond endurance. At this point there is an impressive measure of sympathy and concurrence on the part of the disaffected for the unbeliever, who finds not a witness to the reality of God but a self-serving establishment which has draped itself in the mantle of religion. Hence the importance of radical renewal, if the Church as such is to win the respect and eventually the confidence of those with whom it seeks to inaugurate dialogue.

The only effective and authentic response to unbelief as a challenge is a Christian life, whole and entire; but as a set of theoretical problems, unbelief raises issues for the rest of theology, all of it. Among the principal themes to be treated are those of faith in its many dimensions, epistemic and ethical, personalist and ontological. Others include theism, the reasoned movement of man to the sufficient if non-religious, knowledge of a transcendent, personal God, and religion in the most general sense, as a human and social phenomenon, as implicated, if only by its slight or the hostility toward it, in art and literature, the sciences and politics. The death of religion is a special theme, and there is religion in the classical sense, embracing paganism and pantheism, and the more sophisticated parareligious stances involved in deism and some types of agnosticism. Secularism readily suggests itself as touching the atheism phenomenon at several points, and beyond secularism the future of man in a world come of age but possibly seeking new ways of religious experience and faith. Unbelief today is inseparable from the shapes and thrusts of a dynamic and sometimes aggressive humanism, a direct repudiation of the Christian doctrine of salvation and reaching into the thorny thickets of human origins and the norms of morality. While pursuing these and other cognate questions, it is imperative to avoid the trap latent in Paul Tillich's principle of correlation, the narrowing of Christian answers to the scope called for by the unbeliever's objections. Creatively to confront a changing culture does not, in fact, reasonably demand returning, too quickly, easily, confidently, neat and definitive solutions to every question. To be concerned about a culturally prophetic faith, a Christianity which can speak in a contemporary idiom to the men of this time, is not to take the deliverances of the world as normative, much less as the source of ultimate truth.

In a subject as difficult, complex, and ultimately mysterious as that of unbelief, it is fairly impossible to develop a train of thought in a logically articulated, progressive, and consequential fashion. My first concern is to define the problematic of unbelief, to clarify terms, make working distinctions, locate the problem within a general framework, and lay down a program. Unbelief, it seems to me, is a slippery, imprecise, perhaps misleading category and has been interpreted too exclusively in terms of deviation from an institutionally determined norm and of cognitive options. A theological critique of unbelief is an evaluation and appraisal, as well as an objective examination and a search for positive insights and values. The theological significance of atheism is assessed in the light of God's word in the Scriptures, the faith and reflection of the Church and its hierarchical teaching authority. Unbelief is a public, social condition, but it is hidden in the overt faith of the believer, as well, and raises the acute question of salvation and the absence of faith. The penultimate word on unbelief must be critical, but finally one must face the unbeliever himself, the person and not merely his thinking, his decision and resolve detached from his concrete and unique condition. In view of this, an irenical, dialogal approach will respect other persons as persons and will seek ways of encountering them in their deepest convictions and most cherished aspirations. Dialogue, however, does not preclude the right and office of preaching, of presenting the Gospel as unequivocally and persuasively as possible to today's world.

My indebtedness to others is sufficiently, and perhaps embarrassingly, indicated in the bibliography. I had, indeed, thought of subtitling this work an introduction to *the literature on* unbelief. I am grateful to my publishers for their unfailing encouragement and patience and in a special way to the Reverend Doctor Jaroslav Pelikan, my editor. During the past year I have enjoyed a measure of leisure and freedom from academic duties, while visiting at the University of San Francisco and the San Francisco College for Women, which has enabled me to concentrate on the writing of this book. The President and Administrative Officers of Providence College have, in addition, granted me leave of absence for a year, to complete my research. My American colleagues, consultors to the Vatican Secretariat for Non-Believers, have inspired me with the conviction that the subject is well worth pursuing and the time is ripe. Lastly, Miss Eileen Walsh has supervised preparation of my manuscript and has my sincere thanks for her unfailing kindness and efficiency.

JOHN REID, O.P.

San Francisco

CHAPTER ONE

The Problem of Unbelief

Unbelief is inevitably a problem only for belief, and chiefly for Christian belief, or faith. For an unbeliever, unbelief is essentially something else; it is his deeply personal spiritual identity. To him it means life and decision and destiny, rather than something negative, certainly not a sheer privation or lack or reaction against another possible life choice. Historically, nonetheless, and logically, too, in some degrees, unbelief takes shape and acquires force largely in face of religious belief, and as such is specified by opposition to the latter. Believers, then, in virtue of this inescapable confrontation are concerned with, indeed, caught up in, the problem of unbelief.

In a way analogous to the condition of a mature faith, unbelief is a critical possibility only for those who have reached a certain level of cultural sophistication, or who live, at least, in such an ambience. As an expression of a distinctive spiritual attainment, unbelief takes on a striking, perhaps profound, human significance. One is born neither a believer nor an unbeliever, in the religious sense;* whether one becomes the one or the other is always one of the deepest and most consequential features of a man's life history. Whatever the case with faith, which poses peculiar theological

---

* In the present work, belief and believer, as well as unbelief and unbeliever, will be used in a religious sense, unless another meaning is clearly indicated. More specifically, since unbelief will be understood in the context of Western culture, the entire religious reference will be, ordinarily, to Christianity. The analysis and evaluation of unbelief is made, then, from the perspective of Christian faith, either formally and explicitly or by way of a rational, philosophical critique controlled by the revelation of God's word in Christ. The term faith will always designate man's response to this revealed word, but belief will at times be employed in a broader, not strictly theological sense.

1

perplexities, the possibility of unbelief is always, in the first place, a concrete, lived one. From this root in the logic and dynamics of vital experience, unbelief derives a great measure of its solidarity and seriousness.

To the unbeliever, unbelief is an achievement and, at the same time, a task to be fulfilled, a position reached and a burden to be borne. To his opposite number, the believer, unbelief is a challenge which summons up every available personal resource, intellectual and emotional, social and cultural, spiritual and religious. It is the purpose of the present work to examine the nature and causes of unbelief and to define the dimensions of the challenge it represents. Unbelief must be allowed somehow to speak for and justify itself, but without precluding absolutely a response of faith.

THE RESPONSE OF FAITH

That men actually deny and claim to live without God makes us startlingly aware of a fundamental truth, the bedrock of the Christian faith, and that is the infinite greatness of the God whom believers adore. Believers are struck by the assertion, often made by those who dismiss the reality of God, that they are unbelievers because they have never in any meaningful way experienced God. These include others besides the outspoken young cosmonauts who found nothing but empty space in their flight through the heavens. One must consider well that, even if 'the heavens declare the glory of God' (Ps 19.2), God Himself dwells in the universe as hidden and mysterious, 'all powerful, eternal, invisible and unchangeable.' The habitual and unreflective possession of faith can lead to an attenuation in one's grasp of a truth of the first importance: that God is always greater than ourselves, than our world, than any concept we can form of Him. Unbelief, especially when it assumes the proportions of a massive and systematic denial of God, forces the believer back to a more compelling realization of the utter transcendence of the God who is both accepted in faith and rejected in unbelief.

In the second place, the continuing and proliferating phenomenon of unbelief sharpens our appreciation of the price which God attaches to our freedom. God wants only the homage freely offered, the service and the consent freely given. He is totally other than an oppressive despot, a strangler of conscience, a manipulator or artful persuader. Faith, as a personal response, is no less free and unforced than unbelief, and to this sovereign liberty unbelievers bear a special witness, by refusing it and yet managing to exist without it. In this refusal the unique glory and greatness of man's freedom are unmistakably affirmed. Each man, in the secret of his heart, freely chooses for or against God and, in and by that choice, sets the seal on his future. This is why, in every pastoral and apostolic encounter with unbelievers, the inviolable freedom of man, which God Himself guarantees, must be scrupulously respected.

The third point is that unbelief, this above all, is man's undoing, his ultimate ruin. No worse disaster can befall man than for him to be without faith through his own guilty choice. The refusal to acknowledge and adore the living God is the downfall of men, individually and collectively. In respect to what is of supreme relevance to his well-being, man's private and social existence cannot be divorced from each other. This does not imply that faith enters the human scene as a kind of convenient idea, which may be invoked on behalf of all sorts of personal interests and aims. The fact is quite to the contrary. But if God is the infinitely free and loving Being, then belief in Him is inevitably bound up with man's life-long dialogue with reality, a reality which then assumes its deepest meaning and value precisely as the object of creation and sustenance by God. In his Christmas message for 1956, Pope Pius XII warned that: 'Theoretical atheism, or even the practical atheism of those who idolize technology or the mechanical development of events, necessarily ends by becoming the enemy of human freedom, because it treats man as the inanimate object of a laboratory.'[1]

The effort to understand unbelief and to take its measure with due care and concern will be strongly reinforced by an intense realization of these three key propositions of faith: how great must be the God who is beyond the comprehension and the utmost longing of His own creature; the value which God assigns to man's freedom, to the point where He allows man freely to blot out the very awareness of divine existence; and the unsurpassed tragedy of a life from which the reality of God has been deliberately and totally excluded.

The response of faith to the challenge of unbelief entails a theological concept of faith as a solid underpinning. The concept of faith must be articulated sufficiently to serve as a working model against and by which to measure the full impact of unbelief on human existence. For present purposes we are employing a theory of faith which has been worked out very much within the tradition central to Catholic theology. The approach is holistic, analytic and abstract, in part, and synthetic and concrete, for the rest.[2] The emphasis in this complex notion of faith is on the believer's personal relationship to God; the examination extends to both the subjective and objective elements of believing, and to faith as a unified whole, as it is actually given and exercised in one's spiritual life. Faith, understood as the act of believing, is radically personal and deeply personalizing. Three essential aspects of this highly personal self-engagement seem especially pertinent to its situating vis-à-vis unbelief: (1) God in Christ is the source of faith; (2) faith is a free response; and (3) there are successive dimensions or stages of faith: affirmation, union, witness, and transformation. After a brief sketch of each of these elements, we shall set faith and unbelief in explicit and mutual antithesis.

The objective principles of faith are all of the personal order: object, end, and guarantee are, singly and together, God Himself, as Creator and Redeemer, Father, Son, and Holy Spirit. The First Truth, revealing Himself, is not merely another one among intelligible objects, a logical rule and norm for an unparalleled and complex mental operation. Christian faith reaches out and, obscurely but unfailingly, fastens upon God Himself, in His very being and as the author of our beatitude. God speaks to men, in a unique and demanding fashion, through and in the voice of Christ and of His mystical body, the Church. Christ and His Church are living signs and bearers of God's word as true, personal in origin, and directed to a person. It is only through Christ that we attain to the Triune God, so that to speak of God's truth, accepted in faith, is to speak of Christ, God's true and faithful witness. Christ is, quite literally, God revealing Himself to men in their world. The grace of faith is, in sum, a wholly personal grace: the object, the end, and the guarantee of faith are all God Himself in Christ our Lord.[3]

The heart of faith as believing is a personal response of free men, the total giving of themselves to God, with trust in the efficacy of His word. The real contact established between God and the believer is a fruit neither of critical reasoning nor blind impulse, although both mind and feeling are, variously, involved. The act of faith, simple and without reservation, has an unmatched depth and richness which engages all of man's spiritual powers and brings them into a higher unity. Faith is a unique instance of concrete personal integration, realized on a plane that is supernatural and not entirely explicable in purely psychological categories. In the act of believing, knowledge and love together achieve a moment of fused personal inwardness, the gift of oneself to the Uncreated Being. I am certain in my faith because I am united with God, who sees, not because I see something as evident. A sacrifice of my precious autonomy is demanded. I must acknowledge its limits, its dependence upon and subordination to Him who alone is subsistent Truth and Freedom. Our inmost self, inviolable in its very creation, is opened and confided to Another. Humility and courage, the highest of human values, are engaged, and this precisely is what makes of faith a power of personalization. A style of life that is balanced, strong and fruitful is made possible, as the believer addresses himself to the earnest realization of himself as a person, the dislodging of raw emotion, morbidity, selfishness, whatever is finally irrational, illusory, self-defeating.

There are stages on the way of faith: a point of departure, of achievement, of further growth, and of consummation. Faith begins with an affirmation of the reality of God, a declaration of unqualified assent to God's self-witness, however weak or inadequate may be the formulas in which this assent is expressed. Once begun, this real movement of the believer towards God the rewarder provides a sufficient vehicle for continuance along the way of faith. Man is on his way in the order of grace and a new life is entered upon. This spiritual life which faith initiates and makes possible involves a purifying process whereby the believer, while he remains loyal to the summons of grace, becomes more and more like the God whom he is seeking. As it is assimilated and interiorized, the personalizing character of faith is accented increasingly in the life of the believer, uniting him more inimately, mind and heart, with the Triune God, the true ground and center of his being. The Christian believer is thereby constituted a witness; the power and joy given to him through faith shine forth, and an intense spiritual élan permeates and energizes his human material. Confirmation is the sacrament of Christ's commissioning the mature Christian personality as His witness. The world, everywhere with us, as Père de Lubac says, is always judging us, and in us it sees, or fails to see, the present reality of God in Christ.

Faith is brought to complete actuality through witness and in confrontation with others—this demand is made repeatedly in the Gospels. It is a question, primarily, not of what one does but of what one becomes and is. Further, faith is realized properly by entering into and persevering within the Church, the community of believers. To have faith in the plenary and explicit sense is to ask for (i.e., consent to) baptism; faith endures only as long as the will to remain effectively in the Church. When the Christian confesses to God: 'I believe in you,' he does not say it as an isolated unit, shut up in an exclusive intimacy with Christ. He professes his faith as a member of Christ, a fellow in the people of God, with all his brethren (Ephes 4.13–16).[4]

If the essential features of faith have been correctly delineated, how may unbelief be characterized? By way of contrast? There is normally in faith a state of questioning, a state which coexists with the assent that is given, and not withdrawn. The believer continues to accept God's grace and acknowledges His self-revelation. Henry Bars has illuminated the antithetical relationship of belief and unbelief by way of what he calls the aporiae of faith.[5] Faith, in his terms, is subject to a degree of tension which is intrinsic to the human condition, and as such inescapable, and emerges with apparently paradoxical qualities. These, if nothing else, disclose the difficulty and precariousness of believing, the pressures and temptations to which the believer is exposed, all of which contribute to the sources of strength available to unbelief. The aporiae of faith may be stated by contrasting the seemingly incompatible yet obscurely complementary conditions in which the believer is situated.

Faith concerns the most intimate and personal side of man's nature, yet is the content of an objective knowledge quite independent of him. It is bound up with a historical and ascertainable institution and yet is an invisible drama played out in the depths of each individual's conscience. Faith is a sacred deposit and a tree growing from a tiny seed, a hidden obedience and the principle of the most ambitious science (theology) of which man could dream. Believers are united by faith as they could be by no other agreement, even though believing commits a soul to the lonely adventure of the interior encounter with God. While faith is absolutely necessary for salvation and bestows a most stable certitude, no one can be sure of holding on to it, and the believer's supreme trial is to ask himself if he truly believes. There is not one faith for the learned and another for the unlettered, nor is faith ultimately vulnerable to either superstition or rationalism. In its less pure form, nevertheless, belief may often give the impression of being either a rationalism or a superstition. The act of faith consists in believing: how then can it be a possession of—a gift to—the newly born, who are incapable of placing the act? Faith is given absolutely in baptism, and still how many live as though they had never believed at all? There is no faith without credulity and none without rationality; faith is opposed to vision and yet is the beginning of it. It both sets the intellect free and puts it to the test. Faith, in fine, is word, knowledge, day; it is personal and incompatible with purely negative doubt; no less surely, faith is silence, ignorance, night; it is impersonal and the chosen place for doubt.

In the light of these overwhelming contrasts we may make a summary initial confrontation of faith and unbelief. Faith, the gift of God's grace, is something other than and quite different from belief in the minimal sense of strongly held religious opinion. Faith is more than belief; it is trust, word of honor, loyalty, obedience, and because of its uniqueness it cannot be encompassed in a psychology of belief. Every secular faith or belief is recognizable by its many potential contraries; divine faith has only one real alternative: unbelief in the sense of non-faith or anti-faith. Faith necessarily appears as one belief among others, but it alone is a grace, one which is converted into and remains a free act and which must mature as we ourselves progress (Rom 1.17). Christ is filled with astonishment when He finds a flawless faith, yet if faith were not so hard or so rare it would be worth that much less and could not achieve so much. From this point of view the Christian acquires a new awareness of his faith when he takes a close look at unbelief. He sees that belief is not 'natural,' even though, from another point of view, nothing seems more natural!

There are two kinds of credulity, one a necessary preliminary to faith, the other its parasite and false imitation. We are right in believing only because and to the extent that we are actually destined thereby to arrive at truth. Our intellect never adheres to a truth as though it completely possessed it or were possessed by it, because its capacity drives it inexorably towards Truth Itself. Reason will make no conquests without first taking a risk or without learning both that and how it can be mistaken or deceived. The inherent openness of reason cannot be utterly destroyed but it can be perverted in two ways, by rationalism and by a preference for triviality. Fear of being deceived will encourage an excessive and inhibiting esteem for reason's critical function, while, on the other hand, an obsession with safety will force a retreat to the tenets which can be comfortably held. Skepticism is just as much a shrinking from risk, from openness, as is that credulity which refuses to consider seriously or adhere to anything which threatens security. The action of critical and analytical reason is derivative, not primary; it presupposes the validity of what is basic, namely, intellectual quest and advance. Only a mature intellect, radiant with healthy *credulitas*, from the critical faculty can profit from depth—reflection on faith.[6]

Even when an adult is converted from unbelief to faith, his ultimate surrender is more like a total revolution than the conclusion of a strictly ratiocinative process. Belief, in other words, changes the meaning of everything. Only rarely, in fact, does apologetic play the preparatory role which theoretical analysis assigns to it. Certain ideas objectively incompatible with orthodoxy may persist in spite of genuine conversion; or, perhaps more frequently the case, an imprecisely grasped Christian sense of things may precede and even survive an explicit act of faith. It is a rather curious fact that instances of the acceptance of or return to faith (and, to a much lesser extent, of its loss) have been studied much more extensively than the actual life and development of faith in those who have kept it intact. Nothing lends itself to analysis less than what is constant, and this is true especially of the slow and almost imperceptible ripening in us of ideas and convictions received and held from our earliest years. But are we not all converts and is not our believing a continual turning away from incredulity? The unbeliever, in this connection, chides those who believe because, as he thinks, they have been conditioned or brainwashed since childhood.

The answer to the charge highlights the importance of a personal and unrelenting assimilation by the individual of what was originally the gift of God. It is true that faith is received, bestowed, and not appropriated through either intellectual acumen or moral endeavor. It is neither innate nor is it acquired solely by our own efforts. In this sense one who believes under the impulse (which is never a compulsion) of divine grace has not been left free either to have or have not this initial gift of grace. He must, nevertheless, still choose, freely and indeed repeatedly, for or against the power of faith which is implanted in him, and this until his last gasp, when he shall be required to make the final surrender of himself to God's mercy. The believer thus feels justified in rejecting decisively the unbeliever's distorted caricature of faith. Faith is emphatically none of the following: (a) some sort of charm or talisman; (b) a remedy for the inherent finiteness of human reason; (c) a Machiavellian device to have one's spiritual cake and eat it; or (d) a diplomatic gesture, to serve selfish and timely ends and interests. A formal and more thoroughgoing theological critique of unbelief, which we shall undertake in Chapter Two, will be based squarely on a theological concept of faith that takes into account the best in contemporary scholarship. What has been offered at this stage has been a rough working concept. Painstaking accuracy has not been an insistent demand; the aim was chiefly to anticipate a number of expected difficulties and distortions.

THE DIMENSIONS OF UNBELIEF

A man's heart is one thing; his manner of expressing it, of revealing his interior conviction and hope, may not be completely or clearly faithful. In this area things are sometimes better and sometimes worse than they appear; it is naive to expect that men are really exactly what they seem to be, in terms of what they themselves say. The statement that one is a believer or an unbeliever does not correspond necessarily or precisely to what in fact may be the case. There are several possibilities here, three of which may serve to underscore the complexity of the situation at hand.[7] The first is the reality of unbelief under the appearance of faith, and this is very likely to comprise a subtle and deep-rooted form of superstition actually masked by the very appearances. Emmanuel Mounier used to speak of 'unbelievers at heart' (*incroyants de l'intérieur*).

A second example of ambiguity of outward expression with respect to inner adherence is that of what may possibly be faith under the appearance of unbelief. How many upright men have declared themselves unbelievers largely because they came into contact only with sentimentally credulous believers, superstitious, craving for miracles, and addicted solely to devotional practices hoping to ensure success or favor. The self-confessed unbeliever, in contrast rejecting all of this, may yet be seeking absolute truth and goodness with all his heart. God knows what is at stake in the myriad external expressions and attitudes. Men can know the latter, what is seen and heard, but not what really lies behind all of this.

Lastly, apparent belief can conceal both a measure of unbelief and a genuine, if wounded and confused, faith. Neither faith nor superstition flourish invariably in stark purity; true and false religion may well be intermingled and confused. This is the sense in which P. Barthélemy interprets the incident of the golden calf, fashioned by the Hebrews and worshipped by them in the desert. 'Their idolatry,' he writes, 'is less simple and less primitive than one might perhaps suspect. Aaron had no intention of leading the people into apostasy but, conscious of his people's confusion, he set about only to furnish them with an object of worship more accessible to the human imagination than the thunder cloud in which the unbearable Presence hid Itself. Far from that of turning Israel away from Yahweh, the intent was, by the construction of a symbol, to give expression to the people's faith in the inaccessible God and thereby to avoid the apostasy of a disoriented and distracted people who no

longer knew what to believe in.'[8] Père Barthélemy goes on to explain
that the majority of the Israelites saw in Aaron's statue only an
image of Him who had led them out of Egypt. But it was just this
ambiguity in the image which God could not tolerate, because it
threatened the purity and authenticity of the faith which alone
was acceptable to Him. The image, like every symbol, was both a
transparent representation and an object in its own right; it could
point beyond itself to that for which it stood, but it could also be
itself the focus of attention and interest. What God insisted upon
was that all possible ambiguity be eliminated, given the simple-minded
literalness of a primitive people. Man is an idolater, then, when he
adores anything other than God, even if it be the idea which he
forms of God, so long as it is not God Himself and Him only.
Our worship is good and proper only when it is directed beyond any
particular representation we may fashion of the divinity.

Unbelief is an option, a fundamental moral decision.[9] It is not
a plainly evident or compelling necessity for reason, any more than
faith is—which is not to deny or ignore the differences between
the two with respect to canons of reasonableness. Unbelief is,
basically and in the concrete, a substitute for or the equivalent of
faith: one believes that there is no God. Through all of the rationalism, the hyper-cerebralism, of unbelief, there runs a deliberate
decision to refuse to accept or even to give a hearing to anything
which reason cannot demonstrate. The effective decision is gratuitous,
in that reason cannot prove that man should accept only what can
be demonstrated. In this decision, as in every serious personal
commitment, the place of the heart and the will is at least as great
as that of the mind and should not be overlooked.

It is even more important to realize that the distinction between
affectivity and intelligence is, in this connection, not a little arbitrary
and artificial. The two are, of course, distinct, but their cooperation
is constant and intense. What exists and functions, in reality, is the
intellect of this individual person, with his peculiar projects and
intentions, his desires and his longings. What counts, in estimating
the influences and pressures to which his options are subject, is the
fundamental thrust of his life, the radical intentionality of his concrete existence. This is far more significant and relevant than any
abstract or detached set of principles and convictions, theoretical
or practical, or any kind of reasoning process by which he has
managed, or at least attempted, to sort them out and establish their
respective coherence and viability. This is true indifferently of
believer and unbeliever. Ignace Lepp describes the essential bond

between one's fundamental option and one's intellectual position in his analysis of Marx's atheism: 'It is indisputable that the founder of communism did not become an atheist as a result of his philosophical or scientific studies, nor as a result of his political and social battles against the conservative and reactionary churches. In the light of the facts, it can be maintained with much more truth that it was, rather, Marx's ferocious atheism which played an important role in his political and philosophical formation.'[10]

What is primary and decisive in unbelief is not so much the doctrine or the rational construction; it is the more basic and more radical option. The varieties of unbelief will, therefore, in an important sense correspond to those of the fundamental options, i.e., the rejection of God will be common to all, but what is distinctive of each will be the human value or quality or condition which is chosen and is judged to be irreconcilable with the reality of God.

There is an interesting and instructive parallel between the rationalism which infects so many protestations of unbelief and the inverted rationalism which these often provoke in religious counter-statements.[11] Faith is, in itself, a response to an urgent summons of the living God; it is not properly the end product of a process of reasoning, however carefully wrought. It cannot be insisted with too much emphasis that the believer as such may be no more or no less rational, in the sense of attentive to experience, perceptive, and skilled at logic, than the unbeliever as such. This is not at all to admit that the reasons for faith are no better in any respect than those advanced for unbelief. This is a part of the ultimate mystery of unbelief: not the answers alone but the very questions about the meaning of life arise only within the framework of a decision, a position lived as well as reflected, an interior and practical attitude toward the world. All of which contributes, obviously, to the complexity and obscurity of unbelief as a human reality.

Unbelief: From Practice to Theory

The difficulties which present themselves in any attempt to define unbelief derive in great part from this same complexity and obscurity. One is well advised, all things considered, to mistrust the perfection of an excessively precise definition of terms as historically overladen as is unbelief. A working definition of faith has been proposed, by way of identifying what is essential to the act of believing, distinguishing the elements of which it is composed, and reconstructing the stages in the life which faith inspires. It is, however, not so simple a matter to forge even a single working definition of unbelief, as it were by analogy with, even though in opposition to, that of faith. It is hard, for example, to make sense out of expressions such as 'unbelief in' and 'unbelief that,' although both emphases are intelligible enough with respect to faith.[12] Unbelief is revealed on closer examination to be a highly original and positive act, or set of acts, not entirely explicable in terms of its obvious reference to the faith to which it stands in opposition. The reality of unbelief consists more substantially in what is affirmed and chosen than in the negative factor by which, grammatically at least, the personal attitude is denominated.

Martin Marty advises that caution be observed lest a projected definition of unbelief become prematurely fixed and inflexible. The same author suggests a useful and, I think, objectively sound distinction between unbelief and disbelief, in accordance with American usage.[13] Unbelief may be taken as a flat absence or non-positing of belief (thus, equivalent to non-belief); disbelief would then imply a positive rejection of what is stated or asserted, in some context, as religious truth. As a historical event on American soil, unbelief is not unrelated to or uninfluenced by non-belief, even where the two are not identical. Non-belief is characterized as lack of commitment, a refusal to become involved at all, or inveterate inattentiveness. In the present work, the term unbelief will be used, unless otherwise indicated, in a global sense embracing both disbelief and non-belief. When unbelief is evaluated in terms of moral fault, something for which an individual is culpably responsible, the stronger implication of disbelief will be invoked.

Belief encounters unbelief today not only in the stated convictions and lives of individuals and (this more rarely) groups, but as an almost palpable feature of much of organized social and cultural life. Not that unbelief is as yet extensively institutionalized among us, but it has reached the level of a visible historical development. The influence of unbelief is cast on the way people conceive of their most pressing problems and work towards their solution. Karl Barth reads this situation as evidence that unbelief is man's natural state and may be understood as a part of the world's secularizing of itself. its moving away from sacral categories to autonomy and self-direction.[14] Such a view, for which unbelief is an unfolding of man's natural potential, presupposes the radical opposition of man and God, a thorough depravity of nature apart from grace. It remains to be seen, then, whether or in what respects unbelief and secularization are mutually implicated.

This line of inquiry promises to clarify the problem of unbelief in virtue of the obvious interchange between the unbeliever and the secular society in which he flourishes and finds himself most securely at home. The most completely secular society in history undoubtedly includes people who live authentically by faith, but its motivating center can no longer be a reliance on religious doctrine or confessional loyalties and commitments. It will be necessary to locate unbelief in reference to the structure and dynamics of society as well as within the spiritual life of individuals.

It is worthwhile, as an initial effort, to unscramble the elements compounded in the general term 'unbelief.' The anatomy of unbelief and its counterparts is essentially a study of the analogy of unbelief.[15] Within the analogy, the distinctive features of the varieties of unbelief and the meaning of its counterparts emerge and give direction to an investigation of unbelief as concretely realized in history.

An unbeliever is a man who lives without God. Unbelief is both a way of life and an intellectual position. It turns directly upon an interpretation of the meaning and purpose of life and involves, therefore, a world outlook. The practical character of atheism, on the one hand, and its theoretical dimensions, on the other, provide a basis for a preliminary division of the subject. One may describe the effects of unbelief in human history and thus engage in a psychological and phenomenological approach. One may also approach the subject in search of its logical contours and ramifications, more explicitly as a metaphysical and theological problem. The two points of view complement each other; the total life-experience of the unbeliever helps to account for his beliefs, while the beliefs provide a partial explanation for his behavior.

Adapting a terminology borrowed from Jacques Maritain, the unbelief implicit in concrete existence, the pursuit of life and the facing of life's problems without faith, may be designated under three headings as: (a) practical unbelief; (b) unbelief with longing; and (c) unconditional unbelief.[16]

For the practical unbeliever, unbelief is the very style of life, more intimately an expression of his character and personality than any single physical or mental trait. For this man the specific and significant boundaries of human existence are determined solely by his own personal interests and endeavors. God simply does not enter into the consideration and concern of his day to day existence. Practical unbelief evidently entails a set of moral standards. A more or less original, completely naturalistic moral code will serve well as a guide, but only to the extent that the practical unbeliever finds

B

in it a ready justification for his desires. When this type of unbeliever is a Catholic, his utter disregard for the precepts of Christian morality is a sign and pregnant expression of inward abandonment of the faith he outwardly professes.

The second type of unbeliever denies and repudiates the gods which he knows other men to worship. He knows of no other god, none which he finds understandable or which he is prepared to love and serve. Yet in his heart he yearns for the manifest presence of the God of life and he may, without realizing what he is actually doing, search for years, drawing ever closer to this Unknown God. In the mind and intent of this type of unbeliever life without God is an inescapable alternative because He is nowhere to be found within the life-experiences and categories which are meaningful to him. The pseudo-unbeliever, as he has been called, has never sufficiently known the true God, whereas the practical unbeliever has chosen to ignore God and to eject Him effectively out of his thoughts and out of his life.

It is a cheap and facile apologetics that attempts to win a point by declaring that there are no absolute unbelievers and that every man who claims to be such is deceiving himself and others. This is to undervalue or even deny the seriousness of another man's most earnest affirmation about himself. Radical and absolute unbelief, a life from which God has been constantly and consistently excluded, is more than a mere possibility. This denial of God is regarded as the indispensable corollary of the positive affirmation of oneself. The good of humanity is focused and concentrated in the self and one's own person is made one's ultimate and solitary concern. The practical unbeliever almost never thinks of God and when he does his thoughts are characteristically fleeting and vague, without deep emotional impact. The absolute unbeliever, however, may think of God often, but only the more firmly and resolutely to shut Him out of his life and to confirm his attachment to those values which have usurped the place of God in his affections and strivings.

Absolute unbelief may and does grow out of and derive strength from the unreflective disregard of the practical unbeliever. The militant atheists are recruited as a matter of course from the camp of absolute unbelievers. In the struggle between those who blaspheme and those who adore the Lord, the practical unbelievers may seem to play a role of minor importance.[17] Their concern will narrow to standing up for man's right to blaspheme, without which their own right to ignore the divine might be in jeopardy.

It is an easier matter to describe, however dimly, recognizable types of unbelievers, according to the impact of unbelief in their lives, than it is to disengage from these types the intellectual components which lend to unbelief the status of a philosophy of life. The unbeliever may be as uncertain and as uneasy as the next person about many things, but unbelief in itself must comprise a final, definite denial of the reality of God. Theoretical unbelief may be largely negative or largely positive, depending on whether or not there is a lack of sufficient reflection on the question of God.

The negative unbeliever is in some respects similar to the practical unbeliever, in that neither gives serious or prolonged thought to God. The practical unbeliever, however, lives without reference to the God whom he has known and in whose supernatural revelation he may have believed. By definition, the negative unbeliever does not know God; his denial is the result of ignorance, a defect of the understanding, rather than of indifference, a defect of the will. This ignorance may be complete, if the thought of God has never been entertained in any meaningful way; or it may be partial, if the unbeliever has heard about God but has not sufficiently reflected on all that is implied in the concept, so that it remains extremely vague and incoherent.[18]

Positive unbelief involves the rejection of the reality of God by one who has reflected sufficiently on the evidence, i.e., the arguments and reasons for affirming His existence. The positive unbeliever knows who it is that he denies; the admission of a divine Being, a Creator and Lord to whom man owes all that he is and has, is for such a person absolutely intolerable. More than this, the positive unbeliever is prepared to defend his position and to challenge the faith of others together with the reasons to which they appeal. There is noticeable here a recurrence of traits characteristic of absolute unbelief, but transposed to the level of explicit awareness with a reflectively constructed rationale.

Three points may be emphasized in connection with positive unbelief: (1) sufficient knowledge of God—not perfect, even humanly speaking—but some familiarity with the reasons by which men feel justified in affirming the existence of God; (2) a subjective awareness of the position the unbeliever has adopted, including a reasoned grasp of the implications of unbelief and a reasoned rejection of theism; (3) the affirmation of a more or less original set of values, based on the denial of the divine order and the positing of man's complete self-autonomy.

The appetite of the positive unbeliever is not satisfied with the purely mental persuasion that God does not exist. This negation

releases in his innermost being an uninterrupted dialectic in which
the denial must be constantly reaffirmed in face of recurrent doubt
and faltering conviction. On the basis of this tension between persistent denial and disconcerting doubt, it is possible to distinguish
various degrees of positive unbelief.

The first degree includes a conviction impervious to any shadow
of doubt of the truth and validity of the position adopted, so that
there is no fear that the opposite may be true. The unbeliever is
self-assured that he has an accurate appreciation of the theistic
arguments, all of them and the best of them, and he rejects them to
his own satisfaction. He is likewise firmly convinced that the progress
of man depends on the rejection of religious faith.

The second degree of positive unbelief is mixed with occasional
doubts perhaps fears. There is the suspension of belief, or the
unbelief of unbelief. Unbelief remains substantially intact, but may
be pierced by the sharp point of a doubt too unsettling to ignore
altogether but not strong enough to penetrate deeply or leave an
open wound. The unbeliever who manages to sustain the shock
ascribes the waverings to the vestiges of superstition or human
stupidity, and makes even more vigilant efforts to immunize himself.

In the third degree of unbelief the inadequacy of his grasp of
what may be designated the doctrinal principles of unbelief may force
the unbeliever to suffer even for a lifetime the pangs of doubt and
confusion, arising both from within his concrete psychic condition
and from his experience of a world in which the impact of men's
belief in God cannot be evaded or easily dismissed out of hand.
Still, God must be absent and excluded from his life, if only because His presence is unbearable, but not because the unbeliever
has succeeded, through critical reflection, in establishing His
non-existence.

Counterparts of Unbelief

In a strictly and properly theological sense, unbelief is opposed
to faith; in a less strictly and improperly theological sense, unbelief
stands over against any form of theism or acceptance of God,
Creator and Lord of the universe. There are counterparts to unbelief
insofar as there are non-theistic attitudes and positions which,
however, do not go all the way in rejecting the very notion of divinity
or some sort of religious dimension. In all instances of these counterparts, faith is absent; God may or may not be denied, but the concept
of divinity is distorted, deficient, or held to be unattainable by reason.

Paganism

Whether primitive or refined, paganism identifies divinity with natural phenomena which are personified forces. Paganism is almost, but not entirely, identical with polytheism, the recognition and worship of a number of different beings distinct from and superior to man.[19] None of the pagan gods is endowed with the attributes of infinite perfection, absolute holiness or disinterested love for mankind. Several types of polytheism can be discerned; a survey of ancient and primitive religious expression discloses the tremendous variations and interminglings which the forms of paganism have undergone.

Nature worship expresses the pagan's incomprehension of the universe around him and awareness of his utter dependence on it for the necessities of life. In this respect nature worship is distinct from both idolatry, which constructs its own gods, and pantheism, which, besides denying a plurality of gods, completely identifies the divine with the universe as a whole. One of the most intriguing and widespread forms of polytheistic paganism, especially prominent in the culture of nomadic hunters, is totemism. This denotes belief in a peculiar kinship between a certain people and a certain animal species, which become its totems. Religious practice is reduced to mere external ritual and even to magical observances directed toward the interesting animals—or, alternatively, plants or stones. Magic is the effort to compel forces superior to man, by trickery or sorcery, to do his bidding. No clear-cut distinction can be drawn from anthropological data between magic and religion, since magic may represent one phase of the total body of debased religious beliefs and practices. The religious mood, however, common to most other forms of paganism is one of worship and a certain rapport between man and his gods, while the magic spirit is one of compulsion or cajolery. The polytheistic form of paganism is paralleled by another type, which acknowledges two great deiform powers, a benign and a hostile, and which believes that the forces of nature are alternately under the dominion of one or the other of these deities. This is dualism, a more refined type of paganism, which may allow of subordinate deities—demons, heroes, etc.—but which concentrates belief on two supreme and antagonistic beings, one good, the other evil.

Christian theological tradition, especially for the last one hundred years, has taken a less negative attitude than formerly toward paganism. The perversions of paganism are still uncompromisingly condemned and whatever of positive value it possesses has been outmoded by the higher truth manifested in Christ. Yet paganism

contains authentic religious values (Acts 14.16–17), and even de-
graded rites and doctrines show signs of genuine religion. The problem for theology is to detect and correctly appraise the values of
paganism. It may be that this necessary work cannot at present
be hopefully undertaken, for lack of a sound, well-articulated
theology of religion.[20] We shall confine ourselves here to a brief
analysis of the structure and dynamics of the principal forms of
paganism.

Each of the chief types of paganism has its counterpart today,
measurably more subtle and refined, perhaps, by the advance of
sophisticated thinking and technological progress, but nonetheless
pagan and tending toward atheism.[21] Naturalism, until yesterday
the leading philosophical tradition in America, rejects all 'bifurca-
tion.' It assumes that a sufficient explanation of experience is available
within the realm of nature itself, without appeal to a super- or
non-natural, principle or being of any kind. Scientific humanism
erects the products of human ingenuity—the works of technology
and industry as well as those of the liberal and fine arts—into
guideposts and basic sources of moral and spiritual inspiration. This
is idolatry in the contemporary mood; the idols are certainly more
complex, but on that very score the distorting of man's religious
sense is all the more unsettling. Extreme nationalism and all the
forms of racial pride and intolerance represent stubborn vestiges of
totemism in societies which had, supposedly, known hundreds of
years of Christian enlightenment.

The question of a relationship of paganism to unbelief is not an
idle or facetious one, in the light of the evidence of the gross absurdity
which characterizes pagan religious belief and practice. Pagan
concepts of God are so debased and distorted, as a matter of course,
that they scarcely stand up to comparison with theistic doctrine.
Atheism in one form or other is actually not infrequently a violent
reaction against the cruder and more revolting excesses of paganism.
The dispassionate mind, reflecting on the metaphysical shallowness
and spiritual poverty of paganism, and subjectively unable to rise
to the level of a pure theism, may in desperation take refuge in theism
or in some type of agnosticism.

And yet, in spite of its defects, paganism as such is not a species
of unbelief. The pagan feels after God but pictures Him faultily,
perhaps absurdly.[22] Polytheism is the malformation, originally, of
a soul that is instinctively religious but still primitive. It peoples the
cosmos with hierophanies, a distortion of the doctrine of God's
immanence and activity in the world. The deities are often arranged

hierarchically; the mistake, invariably, is to take all or some of the 'secondary gods' as divine. Some of the myths and rites of paganism bear traces of insight into or contact with divine realities, but even these faint echoes are drowned out in a chorus of polytheism, which lasted for thousands of years and can still be heard. The Christian may acknowledge countless presences, benevolent and malevolent (angels, saints, demons), but he never regards them as literally divine. The misadventures of pagans, more than anything else in man's religious history, provide solid, if indirect, evidence of a twofold truth: first that man is fascinated by whatever he regards as the revelation of God in the cosmos, but, and this is the second clue, lacking positive divine revelation, his mind easily falters and is deceived.

Pantheism

Pantheism identifies God with the universe, thus reducing to an absolute, entitative unity nature and God, the finite and the infinite. For the pantheist, reality is intelligible not in terms of a causal dependency of the finite on the infinite but as a fusion of their existence, eternal and indivisible. The complex pluralism of polytheism is repugnant to the pantheist, especially in its more mythical and fantastic implications.

Pantheism itself comprises two apparently divergent components: first, swallowing up the world of nature in God, whose reality is thus made to engulf all, to the point of negating what is not God; and second, banishing God from the world as a ridiculous and superfluous hypothesis. The component elements give rise to two distinct forms of pantheism, a materialist and a spiritualist. The first of these insists on a total immanence of the divine in the physical universe, to the point of identifying them. The second, in order to save the unique reality of the divine spirit, explains away the appearance of the visible world as so many manifestations of the unique divine Being. In either case one is very close to atheism, to the flat rejection of God as distinct from and Creator of the world of our experience.

One of the more remarkable characteristics of pantheism is the extraordinary way in which it has persisted in the history of thought.[23] Another is the amazing variety of forms it has assumed. St. Thomas Aquinas distinguished three types of pantheism, to one or other of which every historical expression can be reduced.[24] The first holds that God is the world-soul, the original vital principle infusing the entire universe with its motion and perfection and drawing it forward to more perfect existence. This was the error of some Neoplatonists, of which St. Augustine complained in many of his works. The second type, which has in recent times been called panentheism, makes of God the formal principal of all existent realities. The third is materialistic pantheism, which is literally an atheism and holds that God is the basic material stuff of the universe.

Pantheism is a radical monism, like naturalism, and cannot possibly be theistic: it makes no difference whether God be regarded as nature or nature as God. A spirit of pantheism, not clearly defined, pervades a great deal of modern Western literature, especially during periods of romantic sentimentalism.[25] One is thus thrust back to the frontiers of atheism by way of a secular mysticism and the attempted deification of nature.

Atheism and pantheism have this consequence in common: once the transcendent existence of God is denied, man has at least an ostensible claim to the sole mastery of his destiny. A total rejection of transcendence, which is essential to pantheism, logically entails a total adherence to immanence. There is nothing eternal in man; death means the total extinction of his being.

Pantheism is confused as to the representative function of the universe and impatient with the limits and imperfections to which man's mind is inherently subject. It seeks to surpass these limits, to overcome the imperfection by eliminating it. The outcome is obliteration of a real distinction between Creator and creature, a flat denial, indeed, of any basis for this distinction. For emanationist atheism, all things in the world are divine excrescences or overflowings. For evolutionary pantheism, all things in the world are in process of becoming divine.

Deism

Deism is one of two extreme views reached in an attempt to resolve the problem of the relation of the universe to God. One extreme, pantheism, identifies God and the universe. The other, deism, divorces God from the universe. Deism reacts vigorously to the pantheistic concept of divinity, positing a divine transcendence as extreme as the divine immanence of pantheism.

Deism recognizes the existence of God distinct from the world, possibly even conceived as personal, but it denies that God exercises providential care of man or of the rest of the universe. Whether or not God created the world, God has left it to itself, without intervening in any way in the course of nature or of human life. Deism requires a God in order to account for the order and reign of law in the world, perhaps also for its origin and existence. The first deists sought a basis in nature and reason for belief in a supreme Being which did not entail profession of faith in traditional religious creeds.[26] Deism is a rationalist faith, tinged with skepticism and in revolt against revealed religion. The deist speaks of 'nature and nature's God,' of God as the 'Author of nature,' or more simply of the 'Deity'; but whatever the name, his is a definitely limited and circumscribed God.

Deism conceives of the law of nature, immanent and immutable, as originally implanted by the Author of nature, but its actual operation in the world may be studied exhaustively without any reference to this Author. Man is then free to pursue his interests and build up the components of a life for himself which will secure his maximum happiness by conforming him to the laws of nature. In place of a doctrine of divine providence, deism substitutes reliance of man solely on his own understanding and mastery of the forces of nature, his ability to adapt himself to the world around him. Deism is, in this respect, a naturalism, and exaltation of the natural and a relegation of the supernatural to a realm that is questionable and, at best, irrelevant.

The deist restricts the scope and depth of man's relations to God, in which religion consists, no less severely than he does the relations of the universe as a whole to the supreme Being. God Himself is thereby limited in His dealings with men; the deist insists that a religion worthy of the name and of man, i.e., a religion wholly in harmony with reason, must confine itself to the fewest possible truths. No revelation is required to lay hold of these truths, so that infused faith is unnecessary. In any case, a positive or revealed religion is impossible because it would presuppose on the part of the Creator the suspension of His own natural laws, the disarranging of the order He had Himself imposed on the universe.

The deist rejects dogmas proposed by ecclesiastical authority as well as the works of grace by which God, on the one hand, sanctifies man and, on the other, confirms the supernatural character of the truths delivered to man through His ministers. When a man is confronted with doctrines which involve religious belief and practice, those of Christianity no less than those of other religious bodies, his duty is clear: he must investigate in order to determine their internal probability, which means their coherence with established truths of reason. They may be accepted, for what they are worth, only on this basis.

Deism is opposed to the claims and pretensions, which are regarded as unfounded, of historical religious bodies. For the deist, the evil at the source of the tragic history of religion is the uncritical reliance on authority and the absence of universally valid criteria of true religion. The deist may demand, as a correlative, a purely 'natural religion,' freed from the shackles of dogmatic, ecclesiastical, and institutional Christianity.[27] Deism wants a God and a religion emptied of all but the vaguest and most general attributes, to be acknowledged once and for all and thereafter kept discreetly on the periphery of human thought and existence.

Some differences between paganism, pantheism, deism and atheism can now be summarized. Paganisn seeks its gods, a multitude of them, in the forces of nature and the magnified qualities of human personality, confusing the reality of this world with divine beings. Pantheism carries this inclination to its logical extreme, denying effectively the distinction between finite and infinite, and transferring to the created universe the perfections, now divided and debased, proper to divinity. Deism, lastly, proposes to avoid the exaggerated immanence of monistic pantheism by removing God from all direct contact with His creation, carrying the principle of transcendence to exaggerated lengths and eliminating the possibility of a special divine intervention in the form of revealed religion.

The pagan wants his gods close at hand, but only to serve his own needs and to fulfill a purely useful function. The pantheist goes a step further: he wants the divine to be actually and indissolubly one with the universe so that he is totally and even sensibly submerged in the divine, of which he is but a part. The deist is scandalized at this radical identification of the finite and the infinite, which destroys both the original consistency of the universe, self-moving and self-explanatory, and the pure transcendence of God. He wants a God who will not interfere notably in the operation of natural law in the universe, who is, in effect, absolutely inscrutable beyond the bare fact of His existence as Author of nature.

The unbeliever's claim is to have liberated himself from slavery to any God or any kind of god. He has, he thinks, overcome the stupidity and cowardice which keep men chained to a mythical and wholly dehumanising set of beliefs.

Agnosticism

Agnosticism is the most elaborately reasoned of all the counterparts of unbelief, except possibly that of outright atheism. The reasoning of the skeptic, ending in an admission of ignorance, constructs the doctrine of agnosticism. Agnosticism was highly cherished by men like Huxley in the mid-nineteenth century.[28] To them the cause of scientific discovery was paramount to all else, and whatever even appeared to impede that cause was ruthlessly assailed. Agnostics are inspired chiefly by the conviction that modern science has rendered impossible any kind of knowledge except that based on the hypothetico-deductive method of the positive sciences. One had to admit that 'concerning the origin of things nothing whatever can be known.'

There are two major types of agnosticism, both of which share the common principle that human reason can attain knowledge only of the empirical world and of the laws by which it appears to be governed.[29]

1. Pure agnosticism does not positively deny the existence of God, but does refuse to admit that we can have any certain knowledge of His existence. Pure agnosticism is an agnosticism of unbelief, a basic and deep-rooted skepticism regarding the problem of God. Theoretically it is but a hairsbreadth removed from outright atheism, although in practice the agnostic may vehemently disclaim atheistic pretensions. The atheist is probably a much less common figure in cultural history than the agnostic, whose position may vary from something almost indistinguishable from atheism to one of genuine doubt whether or not there is a God. The pure agnostic is convinced only that, concerning God, we can be sure of absolutely nothing, not even whether He does or does not exist.

There is, in this type of agnosticism, a further refusal to hold to the existence or non-existence of God on any grounds other than that of scientific proof. Since this proof is lacking, the attitude adopted is one of *unbelief*, however attentuated. The pure agnostic will have nothing to do with appeal to reasons of convenience (what Antony Flew calls 'reasons as motives'),[30] to symbolic interpretation of phenomena, or to arguments which purportedly derive from the heart, the depths of human aspiration and affection. Man must adjust to life without God, not rejecting Him but simply accepting one's inability to reach any satisfactory knowledge through the methods established and verified in the positive sciences.

2. Dogmatic agnosticism likewise denies that we can know with objective certitude that God exists, but maintains that we can be subjectively assured of this truth, on grounds of faith, feeling, or moral imperative. Dogmatic agnosticism has as little confidence as pure agnosticism in man's ability to arrive at a certain knowledge of the existence or nature of God through strictly rational processes. The dogmatic agnostic wants to admit that there is a God, not because he is able to discover in objective reality unmistakable evidence leading to this conclusion as a necessary truth, but on alto-

gether other grounds. The concept of God, supreme, wise, and all-good, fulfills a felt need and corresponds to a deep longing in the human heart. Belief in God lends grace and beauty to life and explains man's unquenchable thirst for truth and justice. Dogmatic agnosticism has an affinity for (philosophical) idealism and for a form of pantheism. What is denied on rational grounds is affirmed by 'reasons' that are irrational. This is an agnosticism of *belief*.

Dogmatic agnosticism takes three principal forms; each has in common with the others the denial of the possibility of a reasoned inference to God. Each is distinguished from the others by reason of the basis on which it attempts to restore at least the possibility of a non-rational commitment to the divine and to some form of religion.

The *fideist* despises reason as a broken reed, utterly incapable of supplying man with the arguments whereby the reality of a transcendent Being might be recognized.[31] To compensate for the inability of reason, and because he regards religious conviction as highly estimable, the fideist proposes that man assent on faith, either natural or, in some sense, supernatural, to propositions which affirm the existence and attributes of God.

Romanticist agnosticism appears typically as a reaction to the extremes of arid rationalism; the heart then demands to have its own appetite satisfied, which means the domination of feeling over reasoning in the domain of religion.* The problem of the existence of God is withdrawn from the province of speculative and even of practical reason, and emotion takes over.

Ethico-formal agnosticism, which rests the affirmation of God on the requirements of the moral life, found its most eloquent and systematic development in the philosophy of Kant.[32] This kind of agnosticism received enthusiastic support among intellectuals who were convinced by the Kantian destructive critique of speculative reason but were also intent on bolstering man's adherence to the highest ethical ideals. Idealism sees in the concept of God not a source but the firmest kind of support for the sense of obligation to duty and the dictates of conscience. Kant said that he found it necessary to deny knowledge of God in order to make room for faith. This is not exactly a fideism so much as a declaration of the primacy of ethics over religion. Assent to God is recommended,

---

* This intrusion of emotionalism need not entail the abandonment of religion; Schleiermacher is perhaps the outstanding exponent of a religion of feeling. Yet there are obvious affinities, with respect to the power of reason in religious matters, between a Schleiermachian conception of faith and a romanticist agnosticism.

not because reason has discovered objective grounds in the existential structure of reality but because moral *life* (not moral belief) is thereby strengthened. It is not merely a religious feeling, as with the romanticists, but rather a felt need of reason. Belief in God is a necessary moral corollary, dictated solely by the exigencies of concrete submission to the categorical ethical imperative.

In agnosticism we are very close once again to some of the excesses of pantheism and paganism, from which it might have been expected that non-theistic man had at last been delivered. Only this time the doctrine is highly polished and refined by cultivated minds. The agnostic is not merely in a state of (self-acknowledged) ignorance concerning God; he is certain, or at least very nearly persuaded, that this ignorance is unavoidable in virtue of the inherent limits of human reason. At the same time he is assured that, somehow, out of this recognition of speculative ignorance he can, by his own efforts, come to a position which, if it leaves the mind in the dark, satisfies the heart, and quiets man's fears. Man finds it intolerable to live without God or something to take His place. The agnostic is not an atheist, at least not quite, and so he *makes* a God, according to specifications laid down by himself. The upshot is a mental construct, the finite God, as remote from the living God as are the idols and demons of primitive man.

THE STRUCTURE AND DYNAMICS OF UNBELIEF

In approaching the problems of unbelief, it must be remembered that the various non-theistic and agnostic positions which have been considered will seldom be found realized in a simple, pure form. In any individual, institution, or culture, they will be found mixed in different proportions according to the vagaries of particular circumstances. Yet they embody the elements which constitute the anatomy of unbelief.

A theological study of unbelief that aims to be both incisive and comprehensive will have to recognize unbelief as a human phenomenon, in the first place, but one that must be reckoned with in terms of God's revealed word. There are, then, two extremes to be avoided: one would be to swallow up unbelief as the expression of man's condition and self-understanding in a wholly moralistic and dogmatist diatribe of sin, waywardness, and the refusal of grace. The other would be to settle for a purely descriptive and interpretative analysis of unbelief, without attempting to see it in the light of faith, of salvation history, and of man's eternal vocation.

The purpose of this essay is to explore the several dimensions of unbelief, to examine the subject from every important angle, in order to expose its inner dynamic. Following Hume's useful distinction, the grounds of unbelief are located both in human reason and in human nature, that is, there are arguments for unbelief and reasons for not believing, and there are also, within man, drives and needs and desires which, for some, are released and satisfied only by not believing. Unbelief is both a fact and a problem, a public issue and an all-important given of the self-understanding and self-ideal of some men.

The scope and limits of this study may be summarized, with a brief comment on each, in two propositions:

1. Unbelief as a theological problem stands under the light of revealed truth, and as such must be confronted with faith, the unbeliever with the believer. Ultimately it is unbelieving man, the concrete subject and author and sustainer of unbelief, who requires to be understood. Only then will faith have faced the challenge of its own negation, overcome it, and emerge more clearly and strongly for what it truly is.

2. The only adequate alternative to unbelief is faith and the life which it inspires and to which it gives ultimate meaning. The explicit theoretical critique of unbelief involves a theoretical elaboration of faith and of its life-implications. The differences between an unbeliever's self-critique and a believer's critique of unbelief are many and not insignificant. In any case, it is always to be hoped that honesty and fairness are integral to any serious examination of so vital and grave a subject. Evaluation is inevitable and so, therefore, is the use of evaluative terms: the latter ought not to be interpreted as a kind of sermonizing or moralizing. It is nothing more than the result of applying theological criteria to a phenomenon which is the very antithesis of the principles and personal commitment upon which theology rests.

The theology of unbelief unfolds from a doctrine of faith and a comprehensive analysis of a complex human phenomenon. The faith concept operative throughout this study as a norm and measure against which to appraise the expression of unbelief has already been briefly spelled out. The bearing of this faith doctrine on various aspects of unbelief will be evident in the chapters which follow. God's saving word, His self-revelation, is taken as universal in its appeal and absolutely binding. The race of man stands under the judgment of God, a redeeming and merciful judgment, the only proper response to which is a faith, humble, confident, joyous.

The human condition, subjective and objective, personal and social, in which unbelief is rooted and grounded, is one focus of the present study. Unbelief will be understood only within this compass, as the expression of man's understanding of himself and his world and of his hopes and longings, fears and aversions.

Unbelief may be thoroughly explored in stages, which may be designated as, respectively, the theoretical and the critical. The first chapter has defined the problematic, terms have been settled, working distinctions made, and the subject has been located within a general theological framework. Chapter Two is properly theological and comprises an appraisal of unbelief in the light of God's word in Scripture and the faith of the Church. An attempt is made to assess the theological significance of unbelief as a state, with reference to salvation, and as hidden in the overt faith of the believer. Lastly, in the third chapter, a dialogal approach is taken, irenically concerned with other persons and with presenting the Gospel as unequivocally and persuasively as possible to today's world.

It is the author's most earnest hope that his chosen topic has been developed progressively and consequentially, that it has been logically articulated according to its inner requirements. It is a complex, difficult, and ultimately mysterious subject. The theme which emerges and increasingly dominates the essay is that of unbelief as a condition of fallen man, a state natural and yet unnatural. The senses in which unbelief is each of these will appear as the examination of the question proceeds.

CHAPTER TWO

A Theology of Unbelief: Guidelines

Theology has traditionally proposed to help man reflect on and come to a fruitful understanding of his place and purpose in the ultimate scheme of things as revealed to faith. More recently theologians have felt an urgency, not to say compulsion, to address their thinking also to the immediate setting in which men live and work out that final destiny to which the word of God points. The intent has been, at least in part, to discover to those who will listen, in terms they can grasp and to which they can meaningfully relate, what may be called terrestrial salvation, personal and social. As John Robinson has noted, our generation, so far from being furthest removed from the New Testament outlook, is perhaps closest to it in placing the 'new world' here, on this side of the grave.[1] Secularism, paradoxically, has done its work in detaching us from the idol of defining the purpose of life as 'making a good death.' Theology is expected to explore those dimensions and prospects of human existence which lend it its peculiar quality and tone, positive and negative, so as to bring the illumination of faith to bear on our concrete, everyday condition. Unbelief is, in a sense, outside the pale of religious life, yet it pertains to the problematic set for theology in a sense that exposes dramatically the existential and practical character of this discipline. In this chapter I shall attempt to sketch the course that a fully developed theology of unbelief may follow and to identify the major problems with which theological analysis will have to contend.

The material on which the searchlight of theological penetration is to be played has already been assembled in the preceding chapter. Nor can it be denied that principles of selection and presentation,

28

not to say interpretation and emphasis, derived from a theological outlook and concern, have guided and inspired the lengthy and involved statement of the nature, causes, and expressions of unbelief in thought and action. Faith judges its opposite number by disengaging the impact and consequences of unbelief for man's spiritual well-being as individual and as citizen, by vocation, of the commonwealth of Christ. In this confrontation it is not religion or belief in general, religious belief of any sort, but precisely and specifically Christian faith which is invoked as the point of departure and decisive norm for a theological assessment of unbelief. My own theological acumen or expertise, such as it is, has been acquired within and bears the impress of the Catholic tradition, the community whose faith I share and with which my own experience and test as a believer have been indentified. It is not, however, either my own faith or that of my fellow Catholics as such which furnishes the fundamental criteria by which to carry out a theological investigation of the tortuous phenomenon of unbelief. The word of God, rather, which regulates all faith, nourishes, sustains, and enlightens it, must provide the theologian with his essential and indispensable norm for understanding unbelief, even when the latter seems to lie completely outside the area over which revelation ordinarily presides.*

There is real and not always apparent risk in undertaking a thoroughgoing theological study of unbelief, chiefly because of the intensely personal and idiosyncratic character of unbelief as the choice of life-stance, a decision made with all the complexity and obscurity of one's radical freedom. Another factor complicating a consideration grounded on the word of God is the host of environmental pressures and circumstances, varying indefinitely from age to age and from one milieu to another, under which unbelief arises and flourishes as a historical event. These are not invalidating or

---

* The limits—and limitations—of the present work are glaringly evident in the absence of genuine scholarship in this vital area of scriptural teaching on unbelief. I have had to rely on secondary sources and to accept the suggestions of authors whom I found helpful and trustworthy, without allowing for divergent views or clashing interpretations. Nowhere in this work have I been more painfully conscious of its elementary character or the modesty of its pretensions than in this brief and jejune essay on unbelief in the inspired books. A scriptural study in depth of the mystery of unbelief is a most urgent need; without it the theology of unbelief proceeds only at immense risk and considerably impoverished. A beginning might be made with something like the Kittel's *Theologische Wörterbücher* and eventually we may hope to have a comprehensive guide to the doctrine on unbelief in both Testaments.

insuperable obstacles to sound theological inquiry but they indicate caution and restraint in making value judgments and drawing conclusions. When the ancient writer declared that the man who said there was no God was a fool, he did not, and could not, have Marx or Sartre or Bertrand Russell in mind. When each of these men, in his own words, said the same thing, they did not necessarily intend an identical meaning or rest their denial on the same premise. Still, one naturally looks to the great primary and definitive sources of or witnesses to revelation for God's own judgment on unbelief, expecting from them guidance and instruction, without which no theological progress would be possible. In this area, however, perhaps more than in many others, the theologian will have an immense labor of development and application, of reinterpretation and cooperation with experts in various disciplines. It is, indeed, only in our day that the Church, that is, the body of believers, including those whose office and ministry it is to instruct their brethren, has taken sufficient notice of atheism or unbelief to initiate and encourage an inquiry the principal aim of which is to understand and not merely to condemn.

My first consideration will be with unbelief in Holy Scripture, an exercise that has proved not only difficult and challenging but somewhat disappointing. I had approached the searching of the Scriptures with unrealistic expectations, largely the product of my own enormous ignorance of the sacred books and a naive conception of the role they might play in the construction of a modern theological critique. I hope I have, in the end, allowed the word of God to dominate my own thinking, and that I have not committed the unforgivable blunder of forcing scriptural data to fit preconceived molds or flow into preformed channels. Scriptural experts, theologians as well as Old and New Testament exegetes, vastly more competent and knowledgeable than I can pretend to be, are earnestly invited to elaborate a more authentic and nuanced account of the scriptural doctrine on unbelief. Out of this Biblical matrix and its own recurring and varying experience with unbelief, the Christian Church has formulated a number of positions which express its understanding, in light of God's word, of unbelief as man's persistent rejection of the saving truth and way, which is God's offer of Himself in Christ. From a largely existential and intensely religious mode of discourse in the scriptural books, one passes to a series of dogmatic and otherwise authoritative statements occasioned by defection and deviation from the norm of faith. There is not yet, even after so many centuries of ecclesiastical intervention, a fully articulated dogmatic teaching on this subject, a lack of that suggests a certain unconcern with this problem on the part of the Fathers and Doctors of the Church.

Unbelief is intimately bound up with the choice of a life-style and the resolution of the question of self-identity. The first plane on which theological speculation properly understood encounters unbelief is operative in most, if not all, of those areas in which options are taken on the values which lend quality to our existence. I have singled out four specific problems that I take to be representative of the pastoral dimension of unbelief with which theology must deal most seriously. There is a discernible spectrum across which evidences of unbelief appear, from that of the unevangelized, through that of the indifferent and religiously disinterested, to the frontier region of humanist concern and endeavor shared by believer and unbeliever, and finally to that of the unbelief of the believer, one of the subtlest and most formidable of issues. I should again like to remark that my purpose has been to survey the field and locate the landmarks, describing the terrain briefly and mapping connecting routes. Guidelines to a theology of unbelief should not be taken for the finished or polished product.

UNBELIEF AND THE WORD OF GOD

In the Biblical doctrine on faith, its necessity and the consequences of its rejection, there is concentrated not so much a positive statement of the sacred authors' understanding of unbelief as a gradually crystallized outlook or attitude from which, with due safeguards, a scriptural doctrine on unbelief may be reconstructed.* A prime requisite will be to distinguish peculiar Christian contributions to this artfully assembled body of doctrine from the permanent Biblical structure in which they are embedded and which they serve to enhance and carry forward. The Bible envisages both men in whom

* Speaking to us directly as witnesses of faith, the Bible conveys not only the objective content of revelation but insight into the belief, the faith-life, of the authors of the sacred books and the community of which they are spokesmen. I have considered both what the Bible tells us explicitly about the nature and functioning of faith and the attitudes of those who are described as believing or unbelieving. I have confined myself to certain selected Biblical sources and concentrated on specific aspects of the faith-unfaith opposition. There is no clear-cut concept of unbelief in any single scriptural passage, just as there is no formal Biblical definition of faith. A composite idea of what unbelief stands for will have to be sought from a collation of the texts which provide an understanding of various features of the believing and unbelieving attitudes.

reason predominates and others, more credulous by nature, each resisting or rejecting God's offer of saving truth because the demands of faith are too great. Unbelief is always a possibility because of the voluntary character of faith, which is insisted upon, and because reason can readily withstand the pressure to surrender to transcendence. From this perspective the object of faith may be seen as nothing but darkness and emptiness and the exercise of faith caricatured as a blind leap or a reckless wager.

The Biblical writers dismiss this incredulous attitude as childish, as not coming to grips realistically with man's actual condition.[2] In any case, the object of Biblical faith is not a more or less precise number of truths to which assent is to be given, but a personal and subsistent Truth, from whom all credal propositions derive their meaning and value. The unbeliever, then, declines to enter this meaningful interpersonal relationship because he doubts or denies the reality of the other partner or because he rejects its potential advantage and regards it as a threat to his autonomy. Unbelief has a certain analogy to faith in that both are not original intiatives promoted by human curiosity or desires or whatever but man's responses to God's perpetual initiative. Just as faith is a leap not into emptiness or a void but one that comes to rest on the true and living God, so unbelief is a standing fast in human self-centeredness and self-reliance, excluding the good which God holds out to the man of faith. There is, to be sure, the grave difference that unbelief is all of man's doing, whereas faith arises only from and in virtue of the pure gift of grace, with which, however, man must concur and acquiesce.

To those who seem to be, by character or temperament, more eager and submissive believers, who adhere to the truth of faith with their whole being, the Bible compares the stubborn and strong-willed unbeliever, the man who withholds his mind and heart from such total commitment. Faith must not be doubted, as this would express mistrust of God, a lack of confidence in His power or goodness or wisdom, which would be the death of that religious relationship on which all of life and its prospects are grounded. As for questioning, it would not be entirely accurate to say that the Biblical mentality is uniformly and invariably uncritical, even with respect to the most vital and crucial issues of belief and conduct: examples abound of honored Biblical figures expressing puzzlement or even stronger sentiments concerning the alleged or apparent ways of God.[3] Never, however, does this questioning degenerate into a skeptical calling-into-question or withdrawal of trust; a clear line of demarcation is preserved between religious unrest and turmoil and the turning away from God which is characteristic of unbelief. Faith must, in fact, be continually purified and deepened and is thus subject to endless trials and tests; the life of faith, which brings a peace and serenity beyond all imagining, is by no means one of somnolence or indolence: the challenges to perseverance are likely to be extremely severe, but the grace of God is sufficient to confirm the man of good will in his attachment to the God of mystery. Faith is vulnerable at any moment or period in the individual's lifetime because it has a real history, a capacity for growth or decline. Even when an adult is converted from unbelief to faith, his ultimate surrender is more like a spiritual revolution than the conclusion of a process of reasoning. Both faith and its negation, unbelief, change the meaning and value of everything; in Biblical accounts it is hardly ever the case that what theology calls apologetics plays a preparatory role in conversion to God. By the same token, no intellectual dodges or excuses are allowed the man who falls away from God or hardens his heart against the incursions of His word.[4]

As faith progresses, it takes on heightened certitude and a wider range of applicability to life's most pressing problems; so, in contrast, unbelief approaches total darkness and strips a man of the resources he must have to face up to responsibility. The unbeliever is likened dramatically to the no-sayer, in direct contradiction to Nietzsche's notorious accusation, for the unbeliever is unprepared to make the oft-renewed departure, to suffer the painful separations to which faith exposes the man who does not permit himself the luxury of attachments apart from God. Abraham, the perfect believer, says yes to the God who promises, and by this amen makes an affirmation of utter trust, an attitude utterly absent in the unbeliever. The latter is bound up, enslaved even, by the possessions and concerns which he substitutes for God, whereas there is always a separation imposed on the man of faith, who may bind himself definitively and unreservedly to God alone. Unbelief is disobedience, and this is not the fulfillment but the perversion and ultimate annihilation of true freedom, however much the infidel may deceive himself with delusions and pretensions to absolute autonomy.[5]

The history of Israel is filled with a record of the grossest and most shocking infidelities, the greatest of which, a paradigm for the unbelief of all believers, is the murmuring (a euphemism) in the desert. The account of this rebellion is a classic of man's shutting himself up in his own world to dwell with idols, while excluding the presence of the living God. The sin of unbelief, for such it was, in the strongest sense, seems to have consisted, materially, in the twofold wish to come to terms with the idolatrous pagan peoples the Israelites encountered and to depend exclusively on their own human resources. The precariousness of faith is thus strikingly revealed, as well as the jealousy of God, His intolerance of rivals which would negate or minimize His absolute sovereignty. Later, in Isaiah, faith is posed as the only way of existence possible for the upright man, and belief is an absolute choice, the simple and un-qualified adhering of the whole person to the transcendent God. Life without this absolute faith is inconceivable, that is, it is not life but a form of death, of utter deprivation and pointlessness. These passages in Isaiah represent the summit of Old Testament revelation on faith, a sustained and at times impassioned affirmation of the necessity for man to reach up and beyond himself to the God who saves as He has created.[6] It is a fair estimate of the Old Testament judgment that unbelief is very nearly incomprehensible, a form of insanity or the most radical foolishness, so permeated are the sacred authors, as well as the men and women who make up the long history of the chosen people, with a sense of the active and determining presence of God and of the condition which this creates for man.

In the Synoptic Gospels Jesus asks for no other faith than that which constitutes the heart of man's religious existence in the Old Testament. But faith now has a new object, a new and, to the devout Jew of vigorous monotheistic orthodoxy, severely trying quality, for it must be in Jesus Himself, exactly as it had always been, and will continue to be, in the all-holy God. The man without faith lives in anxiety and fear; no one can find peace or security unless he reposes confidence in God in His Christ. Christ's death is the greatest trial for this faith, but it is also the purifying fire from which faith emerges impregnable to all the powers of earth and beneath the earth and in the heavens. Without our faith, in fact, Jesus is powerless as Savior, His life and work useless, because it is by faith that man consents to what God has done in His Son.[7] St. Paul's special contribution to a theology of unbelief is the ominous portrait he paints of the fate of those who do not share by faith in the fruits of the resurrection of Christ. The worst effect of unbelief, the rejection of grace, on the unconverted is their deluded reliance on their own merits. St. Paul is neither unaware nor unappreciative of the capabilities, the ingenuity and energy, of the natural man, but all of these are nullified by a spiritual blindness which only the acceptance of faith can relieve. Above all it is the scandal, the folly of the Cross, which looms over the world of unbelief and confronts men with a decision the consequences of which extend to his eternal destiny.[8] For St. John, lastly, faith embraces a dramatic option between light and darkness; the unbeliever is submerged in the hopelessness of his own condition, bereft of those aids without which he cannot cope with the problems and challenges of life. To refuse the Truth, i.e., to turn one's back on God's invitation to communion with man in Christ, is to embrace a lie, a condition of culpable falsehood, and this is linked to murder, the killing of the spirit.[9]

Throughout the New Testament the demand for faith is closely connected with that call to repentance, that *metanoia,* which is the heart of conversion.[10] The unbeliever stands revealed as the unconverted in the most radical sense and is always accused of refusing the act of faith because of the demands of conversion. Thus the obduracy of the scribes and Pharisees is identical in terms of the twofold sin of lack of faith and unreadiness to repent. Unbelief in this context is practically coextensive with that man-centered and God-defying posture which the New Testament writers, particularly St. John, designate quite simply as sin, or remaining in sin. Unbelief is the negative side of the failure to be converted, the cold uncommitment to the Gospel, an attitude as total as that of faith itself. From the Old Testament the authors of the Gospels and other Christian Scriptures retain the doctrine of the God of the Covenant, which leads them to see in unbelief a fundamental defect of trust in the promises to which God has pledged Himself. With no Lord, no Savior, the unbeliever has nothing to which he can hold fast, no love in which to take refuge, no help on which he can count in direst need.

Apart from certain passages in the Gospel according to St. John, there are not, in the Gospels, any explicit demands made by Jesus that man should direct their faith toward Him. Yet this exigency is everywhere present and determining throughout the whole of the New Testament and, although not spelled out expressly, is taken for granted by all that Christ did. He does complain more than once of the defect or absence of faith in His followers and others whom He meets and makes it perfectly clear that no response other than that of faith would satisfy Him. Christ is especially concerned to encourage a pure and sincere faith, to expose that pseudofaith, which He rejects, that demands signs and wonders, that seeks self-interest and not closer union with the Father. This form of unbelief, as pernicious as it is covert, highlights the connection between genuine faith and conversion: without humility and sincere repentance no one will believe in Jesus Christ as Lord and Savior.[11]

The unbeliever who refuses God's offer of salvation in His Son must be under diabolical influence: nothing less could account for his self-destructive insanity. The rejection of grace entails a corresponding failure to grow, spiritually, to the full stature of manhood: the unbeliever is childish, stunted, and fails to meet the requirements of spiritual adulthood. Unbelief precludes prayer, of course, and that favorable hearing which is guaranteed to the devout supplicant; without faith, a man is simply cut off from the wellspring of life, so that his existence may be likened to that of the dead. Nothing good or profitable unto salvation can be accomplished by one devoid of faith in God. St. John indicates that the unbeliever cannot begin to measure up to the responsibility or privilege of human existence as called by God to intimate communion with Himself. Faith is the great single Johannine expression covering everything that Jesus asks and expects of men. Unbelief excludes not merely the recognition of who and what Jesus is (and, therefore, of the Father who sent Him), and assent to Him as the Truth, but also that trust and submission that flow from a heart filled with God's presence. The moral significance of unbelief lies in its resistance to Jesus' call to repentance and its evil disobedience to the will of the Father in His Son. St. John frequently explains the disbelief of the Jews by their moral failures; they have not faith because they are wicked and persist in their evil inclinations and attachments. The evangelist describes this unbelief as thoroughly malicious, prompted by the overweening pride of the Jewish leaders and their violent hatred of Jesus, who exposes them for what they are. There can be no faith without conversion; the unbeliever is the unconverted man.[12]

Reconstructing the character of the unbeliever from Biblical sources, one discerns three features which essentially characterize the concrete situation of the man without faith. The unbeliever is hopeless, ignorant, and fatally disobedient, all by his own choice, or rather, as the inevitable outcome of the bad decision he has made, to live without reference to God. It is clear that the scriptural authors have very little, if anything, to say about an unbeliever not responsible for his condition or one who is, secretly and unknowingly, an 'anonymous' believer. Scriptural reasoning and language are more forthright and unequivocal: one believes willingly, one willingly refuses belief. When the latter is discussed, the guilt of the unbeliever and the sorry plight to which he thereby commits himself as a matter of sheer logic are never left out of account. Neither faith nor unbelief are considered in Biblical categories as neutral matters of mere choice or preference, as brute facts, or as morally undetermined.

Unbelief expresses always a definite and deliberate exclusion of oneself from the ambit of divine grace and the vocation which grace alone enables one to pursue effectively. A vast abyss separates the believer from the unbeliever, and it is moral and religious as well as intellectual, so real that no evasion can conceal it. Two fundamental conceptions of life confront each other, but as clashing, as stridently incompatible, so that peaceful coexistence is unthinkable and dialogue out of the question. But the believer has this additional advantage, that he is in a position to understand unbelief, in virtue of the true interior light from above, a supernatural reality superior to man.[13]

The unbeliever lacks confidence; he will not ask for or acknowledge help or confess that Another can and will help. This fills the believer with pity as well as dread, a shudder of concern for his fellow man, caught in the same trap but unable to extricate himself. Geddes MacGregor has described in powerful terms the grasping of man for something by which to liberate himself from his miserable condition, from that tangle of circumstances which oppresses and crushes him, a struggle doomed to fail unless divine assistance is received. The unbeliever often exults in his self-endowed freedom, his independence from external authority and constraint and capacity to pursue his own goals, on his own terms and in his own fashion. The Scriptures evidence nothing but alarm and fear for the ultimate future of the man who thus deceives himself, as if by his own efforts and in his own right he could overcome the forces which weigh him down and imprison him in the confines of his own impotence. It is taken for granted that unbelievers have not actually experienced the presence or goodness of a God deserving of confidence. Theirs is, to this extent, an excusable ignorance, but they will be held responsible if they shut themselves up in a world from which the God of promise is excluded. It is a question of God's benevolence and concern for His creatures reaching down to touch the lives of men, to awaken them to the potential that God puts at their disposal. Unbelief is horrible because it entails helplessness and leads to despair, for the same reason that hope and the assurance of victory are bound up with the obedience of faith. In the Gospels Jesus is extraordinarily concerned to point the way to this necessary experience of the nearness and benevolent power of God, an experience to which all men have ready access in and through Jesus Himself.[14]

The unbeliever plans his entire life and moves toward his future with no concern for the trustworthiness of God. His chief defect is that of confidence, the all-important concomitant of faith, or it may be said that the one is complementary to the other: without faith, St. Paul asks, what is there to hope for? None of the New Testament authors reflects at length on the miserable condition of the faithless individual, but there is enough material scattered throughout their writings from which to piece together the somber and chilling portrait of this foolish man and of the 'nations' who make his option a public one.* The unbeliever ventures upon life unconverted and unrenewed in spirit; St. Paul, above all, stresses

---

* I do not wish to leave the impression, which would be seriously misleading, that the scriptural material is such, either in quantity or in variety and scope, to provide a broad base for a comprehensive theology of unbelief. One must choose words here with circumspection; I have not the command of the sacred books requisite to making any flat or definitive statements; I can only offer an opinion prompted entirely by the results of my research for the purpose of this chapter. The Scriptures are concerned, almost without interruption, with faith, its demands, consequences, and the pitfalls which beset it; inevitably, then, the problem of unfaith inserts itself with expected urgency, so that the phenomenon of man refusing or rejecting faith, abusing and prostituting it, is a reality with which the sacred authors are quite familiar. The point is, quite simply, that these authors were definitely concerned with unbelief, and with the moral and spiritual implications of this radical resistance to God's universal call, but their experience of actual unbelief was limited both in extent and in depth of penetration. There is little or no development, across the centuries, in the scriptural concept of unbelief, so that St. Paul's remarks in Romans, chapter I could have been made by a writer in the Biblical tradition long before the advent of Christ. If this is an exaggeration, it is not a wild one, and it raises the question of the reason for this relative narrowness and shallowness of vision, if these terms are not inappropriate. Positively, I would suggest a central and undeviating prepossession with man's personal responsibility for his eternal destiny: Biblical anthropology is thoroughly realist: God is; man and the world are His; man is answerable to Him, directly, for the conduct of his life. The unbeliever lives in a world which is God's yet perversely declines to acknowledge his creatureliness and the sovereignty of the Creator. This failure is often ascribed to the nations as such, because the false worship which is equivalent to unbelief is the choice of whole peoples. Negatively, the Biblical writers, and the people whose experiences and convictions they record, have no contact with, and apparently no conception of, any other form or cause of unbelief. Without pursuing this as a promising lead, my further suggestion is that the possibilities of unbelief have expanded and become more diverse and complex along with man's progressive discovery of richer and more sophisticated ways of getting along, in thought and in practice, without reference to God. Another factor contributing to this vastly changed situation is the record of scandal and perversity made by generations upon generations of men who were both professing Christians and unrepentant predators on their fellow human beings. A theology of unbelief will found itself, originally and permanently, on the inspired word of God; but it will be developed in line with the whole experience of mankind in the conditions and circumstances which the Bible neither foresees nor explains in advance.

the laggard, retrogressive mentality of one who imcomprehensibly remains attached to an order stripped of positive meaning and value, a reactionary stance in face of God's gracious act of throwing open the door to a new life here on earth, bathed in a light that makes intelligible what is otherwise the absurdity and desperation of earthbound existence.[15] Unbelief is also a tragedy, for it reduces to nought—and worse—what might have been a fruitful and productive life, making of the time allotted to man a travesty and a rebuke to God's willingness to show mercy.

The vagueness and emptiness of the unbeliever's life derive from his failure to make a decision for Christ and his attempt to conduct himself under standards to which God is irrelevant. The unbeliever makes a grave error of calculation, a mistake for which he must bear the awful responsibility and pay the terrible consequences: in his judgment the tangible rewards of self-assertion and self-confidence are of infinite value. Weighed against this experience of immediate satisfaction, the promise of supernatural gifts or heavenly rewards is not esteemed of sufficient value to warrant the commitment of freedom to an invisible order. So the unbeliever lives without encountering Christ, perhaps the greatest and most poignant of tragedies, for he is bereft of all the light and strength, the inspiration and power which communion with Christ brings. He persists in clinging to his old securities, which are nothing without God, and refuses submission, ignorant of the new dimension which faith brings to life. Without the knowledge of Jesus Christ the unbeliever is incapable of deep inner growth or of ingestion into a common life with the Lord as his own.[16] The course of life of the unbeliever lacks the qualities named in connection with faith: endurance, patience, forbearance, and a serene joy. Believer and unbeliever alike are subject to life's trials and vicissitudes; the New Testament does not suggest any exception or immunity from ill for the man of faith, but it does deplore the unpreparedness and powerlessness of the infidel to meet evil and frustration and declares the ability, God-given, of the believer to stand courageously in face of any opposition.

The unbeliever is, above all, disobedient: unbelief rejects the testimony of authority and withdraws into independently obtained insight. More than any other expression, this view represents the New Testament judgment on unbelief, a total response away from God, paralleling and reproducing the original fall from grace of the first man and woman. The unbeliever's aim is disclosed in his will to be, himself and not in subordination, the first and last arbiter of good and evil; he rejects God not only as Supreme Truth but also as source and guarantor of all value. He sets up, or would aspire to, a kingdom which declares its absolute sovereignty and will not recognize another and superior Lord.[17] Unbelievers as a group have no peaceful commerce with God's people; between the two there are enmity and warfare. Laxness and a spirit of compromise on the part of Christians is dangerous and leads to corruption and the pollution of spiritual outlook. The New Testament does not envisage a humane and appreciative intercourse between the spheres of faith and the world because the latter is defined in terms of a knowing, deliberate turning away from God. The unbeliever holds back consent to the future dictated by God, and his nay-saying, his disobedience, makes victory unattainable. With this source of defeat and despair the children of light are to have no truck.

If it is safe to say that in the Bible one does not encounter that kind of theoretical or metaphysical atheism or unbelief which features so prominently in contemporary culture, it is nevertheless possible to reconstruct the Biblical portrait of the godless man with an eye on today's unbeliever. For the writers of the Jewish Scriptures, as for those of the New Testament, the problem of atheism is not primarily theoretical but intensely practical. Atheism is an existential rather than a speculative problem, the free choice of a mode of being.[18] Even when there appears to be a reference to the formal denial of the existence of God, the context indicates that it is a practical atheism which is implied, not a theoretical one. The Old Testament writers do not recognize such a thing as absolute non-faith or doubt, except among the most remote and abandoned Gentiles, who have never heard the word of God and so may not be said to have rejected it. One could not, of course, deny God without affirming something else, which is why the Biblical consideration of unbelief is often tied in with that of idolatry, the inevitable concomitant of the denial of God. In the prophetic tradition Israel is not so much accused of the denial of Yahweh as it is of 'going after other gods,' the affirmation of false gods. As often as not, this 'going after other gods' also carries with it a kind of behavior which is not acceptable to the prophet and which he condemns equally with the false worship. This is the reason that the message of the Prophets to Israel is to repent, i.e., to turn back from following after false gods to following after the one, true, living God. It is against this background that we must understand the preaching of Jesus, who comes on the scene announcing His message of conversion, but now in the light of the imminent advent of the Kingdom of

God. Both Jesus and John the Baptist before Him stand in the prophetic tradition with their admonition for Israel to repent. It is probably fair to say, however, that by the time of Jesus the situation with regard to Israel is somewhat more complicated than it had been in the times of the last of the Prophets.[19]

In a brilliant and incisive reconstruction of scriptural themes, with reference to today's problem of God, John Courtney Murray has discerned three major types or prototypes of the godless man of the Bible.[20] There is, in the first place, unbelief among believers, the insidious corruption of the faith of God's own people. He is the 'fool' of the psalmist, whose denial bears not on God's objective existence (a concept metaphysical in nature, not likely to appeal to the Hebrew mentality) but on His concerned and intervening presence to men. The fool lives as if God were not judge and savior, as if he could prosper without grace and sin without responsibility. Unbelief thus defined embraces not only wickedness but stupidity; by it those who cling stubbornly to evil are exposed to the gravest peril and indeed can expect ultimate disaster. The folly here is blameworthy: practical unbelief feeds on unrestrained self-will and leads to moral outrages of the worst sort. The New Testament knows nothing of the upright pagan who has both heard the Gospel preached and, deliberately turning a deaf ear, retains his integrity and a pure conscience. Unbelief entails a will to libertinage which signals a serious failure in the moral order. As Murray observes, the unbelieving fool is the Biblical archetype of the unbelieving believer, whose fault is located not in the realm of theory but in the active ignoring of God's saving presence and inexorable judgment.[21]

Both Testaments rail frequently against the godlessness of whole peoples: outside the people of God a defect of faith is the inevitable condition of those who remain untouched by grace. The favored position of the chosen people, however, is not due to any superior racial quality, to clever political manipulation, or to ritual importunity. It is a purely religious category and binds the people to God in faith and obedience, a public and social establishment of religion diametrically opposite to that political atheism professed in contemporary life. The two cities of St. Augustine find an analogue in the political unbelief of the Bible's two peoples. The scriptural witness is uncompromising and regards a people without God as practically non-existent. The religious knowledge of God is so vitally important to corporate indentity and welfare that people deprived of it have no principle of spiritual existence; theirs is a state of radical absurdity. Faith is bound up with every aspect of the people's temporal destiny, in a way which brands the culpable ignorance of God an absurdity, 'darkness and the shadow of death.' Agnosticism is as foreign to this outlook as that implicit belief which somehow manages to arouse a measure of sympathy for the sincerely held convictions of the unbelieving. The passionately religious affectivity of the Biblical writers and figures expands to a deeply concerned attitude toward a public philosophy or social consensus from which belief in God is systematically excluded. Between idolatry and a knowledge of the true God there is no defensible middle ground; the Christian is not to indulge either a pseudo-sophisticated agnosticism or a polite skepticism.

The Prophets reduce the idols of pagan nations to nothingness because they are utterly devoid of the power to save; they are sheer emptiness, and it is absurd to trust in them.[22] For the Prophets, be it remembered, idolatry is the only recognized form of a-theism. Because idols are impotent, their cult only harms their worshipers and drains them of moral fiber and spiritual substance. In the well-known passage from the first chapter of Romans, St. Paul declares that the godless peoples are not to be excused because the evidence of God, which they choose to ignore, is completely overwhelming. Only impiety and wicked attachments could support an ignorance so perverse and self-seeking. Idolatry is neither a natural nor an intellectually respectable practice; immorality prompts it and an enormous pride sustains it. Their choice is of a lie, intentional and not excusable. Spiritual insensitivity, bolstered by the basest kind of self-indulgence, fastens one's affection on tangible, created satisfactions and leaves one careless of higher, nobler values. The mystery of evil is here involved, the fatal attractiveness of goods which turn one away from the all-good God, betraying the source of their own being and value.[23] The Scriptures always regard unbelief as engaging human freedom; one's fundamental life-orientation is not the casual product of accident or inadvertence. Present-day thinking tends, by contrast, to minimize the role of active, conscious decision in the direction of one's life toward its ultimate goal.

The third type of unbeliever portrayed in the Bible is the godless philosopher or, as we should say, intellectual, a type encountered late in Israel's history, largely by way of contact with Hellenic culture. The Book of Wisdom speaks of the very learned man, the profound scholar, whose labors uncover the secrets of the physical universe, yet fail, strangely, to disclose the Creator Himself. This godless sage then becomes obsessed with his own worldly wisdom and deifies it, compounding the blunder and leaving him abysmally anchorless and rudderless in a perilous sea. Yet the author of Wisdom is not entirely lacking in understanding, and even a certain sympathy, for those whose fault is not idolatry, in the literal sense, but a waywardness and perversity which has led them astray. 'It may be,' the sacred writer muses (Wis 13.6–7), 'that they but lose the way in the course of a search for God, with a will to find Him. Absorbed in His works they strive to fathom them; but they let themselves be caught in outward appearances, so beautiful are the things that come beneath their eyes.'[24] This striking passage identifies a long line of scientists caught by the endless fascination of the secrets of nature and unable or unwilling—it is not clearly distinguished in the text—to read these as evidence of the existence of their Maker. Their earnestness in the pursuit of truth is not in question, and indeed this lessens somewhat the gravity of their guilt. God is hidden, it is true, but not so impenetrably that His traces cannot be found, for He is 'not far from any one of us.' In any case, an honest examination both of the universe itself and of man the inquirer should make one aware that the divinity is not identical with the world of our experience. Whether or not the ancient scientists succeeded in reaching a knowledge of God the transcendent Creator, they had no reasonable ground for attributing godlike qualities to creation. The root failure is the blindness to the evidence that the cosmos is not divine but that, as the work of God, it reveals its Artisan.

The Biblical position is that unbelief is bad faith, a mode of inauthentic existence, its ultimate cause located in an act of choice, made in the name of a freedom which is, in reality, an illusion. The Scriptures stress God's pressing will to be known by men: He does not merely permit men to find Him, He commands them to seek Him with all their strength. When, despite the capacity for discovering Him that God has placed in their minds and hearts, men do not in fact come to acknowledge Him, the real reason lies not in any intellectual shortcoming but in a moral and spiritual perversion. The godless 'lose themselves in vanities,' and the Bible describes them as chasing after nothingness and so themselves falling victim to it. Murray contends that this Biblical view of unbelief reappears in certain post-modern philosophies the basis of which is postulatory atheism.[25] Men make it their intention, explicit or not, that God be absent from the world, that it be, for all practical purposes, a godless universe, so that they may lose themselves in a rebellion which can only bring them to disaster. On the Biblical view the problem is to discern the variant modalities of the will to unbelief that lie at the basis of its variant historical forms. In the individual case, of course, the root of unbelief is ultimately ineffable; it is buried in the mystery of the self rejecting its own authentic existence in the refusal of God. The will to unbelief is the choice of what is, objectively, absurd, since God belongs to, although He is not identical with or reducible to, the structure of all reality.

The Biblical word on unbelief, as thus understood, finds moving expression in this passage from St. Paul which asserts God's wrath on those who remain aloof from the grace of faith:

> For the wrath of God is revealed from heaven against all ungodliness and wickedness of those men who in wickedness hold back the truth of God, seeing that what may be known about God is manifest to them. For since the creation of the world His invisible attributes are clearly seen, His everlasting power and divinity being understood through the things that are made. And so they are without excuse, seeing that although they knew God they did not glorify Him as God or give thanks but became vain in their reasonings, and their senseless minds have been darkened. For while professing to be wise, they have become fools, and they have changed the glory of the incorruptible God for an image made like to corruptible man and to birds and four-footed beasts and creeping things. Therefore God has given them up in the lustful desires of their heart to uncleanness, so that they dishonor their own body among themselves—they who exchanged the truth of God for a lie and worshipped and served the creature rather than the Creator who is blessed forever, amen. (Rom 1.18-25).[26]

And the Apostle goes on to detail the shameful and unnatural vices to which God has delivered up these reprobates who 'have resolved against possessing the knowledge of God.' What fearsome words, what an enormous indictment!

UNBELIEF IN THE TEACHING OF THE CHURCH

If faith in the full scriptural sense defines the life of the pilgrim people of God, the new Israel which seeks ever more intimate and loving union with its Lord and Savior, then the historical existence of this people will consist, very importantly, in the progressive appropriation of the meaning of faith. Faith's relation to the world, its relevance to the changing conditions in which the Church, the called and gathered community of believers, lives, is unfolded and recognized in and through the successive confrontations with that world which the Church experiences as it moves across time. From the beginning Christians realized clearly that theirs was to be a life founded on and inspired by faith, but only the thrust into temporal existence and exposure to the winds of secular culture would afford the opportunity to learn the import of St. Paul's dictum about using the things of the world as though one used them not. The Church, through its ministers and those appointed to safeguard and interpret the deposit of revealed truth handed down from the Apostles, never ceases to examine the word of God, to meditate on it, and, from this reverent and grace-filled reflection, to deepen both its grasp of what God has done for man in Christ and its own self-understanding.[27] It is against this background, and in the light of its own appreciation of faith as man's most precious gift, that church leaders turned to the phenomenon of unbelief and passed judgment on it, a judgment perhaps more conspicuous by the pastoral zeal which prompted it than by the adequacy with which it encompassed a complex and mysterious human propensity. The first point to be noted in a cursory sketch of the Church's handling of the problem of unbelief is that it has had an actual history, a career marked by stages of growth and decline paralleling the Church's understanding of what faith itself is all about.[28]

When the author of the Epistle to the Hebrews, in the classical opening verses and subsequently, sets himself to find faith throughout the history of the Old Testament, he discovers, in the course of his inquiry, that faith has opposition in many guises, the most insidious of which is that overweening reliance on human resources which cloaks itself in the external profession of belief in God. The Church thereafter became increasingly aware that purity of faith alone marked it with the sign of divine election, so that the rejection of faith is more reprehensible, more fraught with the most dire consequences for the individual and for society, than anything else. In pagan religions the ideal of trusting the gods is not lacking, but there is nothing in paganism comparable to the detestation of Christians for the sin of infidelity and its counterparts. The concept of faith, as Hatch informs us, has, outside of the history of the Christian Church, nothing approaching the vital significance, the supreme importance, it enjoys at the center of that history.[29] Because the object or content of faith was, in the relatively short space of a few centuries, articulated in a series of confessions or dogmas, and because faith was professed within a structured group, it had a public, social identity which made it relatively easy to detect falling away from the norm of religious belief. Unbelief is

C

possible, in some sense, to those who seem to be Christians, just as
it is obviously the condition of those who do not accept the Gospel.
The mind of the Church, embodied in declarations and statements
received as official and binding, bears on unbelief largely, if not
entirely, by way of pronouncements on the necessity and quality
of faith. These statements reveal the Church's preoccupation with
the reasonableness of faith as well as its religious or salvific character,
a concern which fairly plots the course and direction of ecclesiastical
teaching on the varieties of unbelief.

During the sixteenth century, largely in answer to Protestant
positions taken at the Reformation, a series of dogmatic definitions
were promulgated on the necessity and supernatural character of
faith.[30] Yet faith is not lost except by a sin directly contrary to it, that
is, by sins of what is technically called infidelity or unbelief. Even after
this period, direct and explicit statements by the Church's supreme
teaching authority are very few and sketchy at best. The official
teaching centers almost entirely on sins against, or defects of, faith
and falls into four principal categories.

The first contention is that the certitude of faith is beyond
question, and faith, far from being subject to reason's arbitrary
judgment, itself defines the power, offices, and limits of reason with
respect to God and the things of God. The Church believes in the
primacy of faith in man's intellectual existence, but only in relation
to his religious life, the orientation of his entire being toward his
ultimate end. At the outset, then, the Christian affirms unequivocally
the privileged status of God's gift and refuses to admit the right of
reason, unenlightened by grace, to bring the word of God and man's
appropriate response to it down to the level of destructive criticism.[31]
To deny the perfect integrity of faith in its own domain is to lapse
into or at least to skirt unbelief. The chief thrust of unbelief, under
this rubric, is to overwhelm the act of faith with the overweening
demands and extravagant claims of unregenerate human reason,
man's endless capacity to find escape-holes from the assent which
God invites to His revealed word. At the time of the Reformation,
however, and under pressure from the anti-rationalist emphases
of later Protestantism, Catholic teaching tended to seek out the
ways in which faith and reason harmonize, grace building on and
perfecting nature. As a result the rise and growth of rationalism,
which eventually attacked Christian doctrine at every point and in
both Catholic and Protestant versions, impinged earlier and with
temporarily greater force on those Protestant groups which professed
a faith admittedly antithetical to reason.[32]

The admission, or rather insistence, that reason cannot provide arguments to make revealed truths evident had the unintended effect of furnishing ammunition to those who defined reasonableness precisely in terms of empirical verifiability. Without the grace of faith man cannot discover his supernatural end or lay hold of the means to pursue and attain it; it is outright unbelief to postulate an actual, purely natural end or purpose to life and to reject the necessity of grace. Further, the inherent limits of reason, even when elevated by grace, preclude a comprehensive penetration of revealed truth, thus making the need for faith and grace absolute but leaving man ineluctably set in the economy of salvation through faith. Faith liberates and strengthens reason for the task of apprehending what it can of the first Truth; it also brings with it a powerful motive to investigate all of reality insofar as everything reflects and leads to a knowledge of the God whose imprint it bears.[33] Unbelief is not a purifying of reason or a release of its highest potential but a closing-in and sealing-off of man from the vocation which is his, to share in God's own self-revelation. The doctrine that faith constitutes a negative norm of rational inquiry has been much discussed by theologians, although interest in the controversy has considerably waned in recent years.[34] In any case it is a point of grievance for all of modern unbelief, which rejects religion's interference and dictation in the resolution of secular matters even more bitterly than religious posturing in its own proper domain. Against this rejection the Church reiterates the defensive position that theology, when it is based on the solid sources of revelation, is impervious to the destructive attacks of unbelief and of anti-religious skepticism. Whether theology can hope to retain or win intellectual respectability by dogmatic fiat is a question which churchmen have begun seriously to ponder.[35]

The second category of authoritative statement bearing on the challenge of unbelief includes a number of propositions which affirm that faith has a genuine and authentic intellectual character. The opposition here includes both those concepts of faith within Christianity, Catholic and non-Catholic, and the contentions of secular rationalism, each of which, for vastly different reasons, would deny to faith the qualities of a truly intellectual assent and enlightenment. The concept of faith as a kind of religious sense or sensitivity, largely imaginative and emotional, is excluded by the anti-Modernist decrees, which characterize faith as a true (supernatural) source of knowledge.[36] This principle, cognitive in effect, is yet distinct and radically different from any kind of merely natural knowledge. The believer's assent, however, although it is not compelled by intrinsic evidence of the truths adhered to, is not blind or contrary to reason. It is above reason's proper reach and is not produced by the necessity of rational argument but by man's free choice, his voluntary submission to God revealing Himself. The act of faith is intensely personal and responsible, even though it cannot be elicited as a sheer response to empirical evidence or apodictic logic. Unbelief, it goes without saying, seizes upon every one of these nuances and erects arguments for rejecting faith in the name of the integrity and autonomy of reason. Those concepts of religious faith, also excluded by these Catholic definitions, which play down or in fact eliminate the authentically intellectual nature of faith are able, in some instances, to come to terms with modern rationalist unbelief.[37] The compromise is achieved by a radical re-interpretation of faith, leaving only a subjective and affective shell from which objectivity and realism have been excised.

The principal sin against faith, in the Church's traditional perspective of pastoral concern, is heresy, although this perspective is bound to shift and a change is already discernible in the Church's recognition that not heresy but simple unbelief is now the great and threatening fact. Heresy is not to be confused with unbelief and Catholics are warned not to accuse dissenting Christians of outright loss of faith or to lump them with unbelievers.[38] There are several other sins against faith which are not identical with unbelief, so that care and discrimination are imperative in sizing up the actual positions of those who do not share one's understanding of what Christian commitment entails. The point is that only a direct act of infidelity can literally destroy faith, and not all unbelief is to be summarily identified with infidelity.[39] Here one encounters the developing and not yet settled ecclesial conception of the spiritual state of various types of unbelievers, a problem I shall consider in its own right later in this chapter.

The Church does hold, and this comprises the third category of authoritative statements, that unbelief excludes man from the way of salvation, for without faith no one can be saved. In the context, as many times as the *extra ecclesiam nulla salus* has been reiterated, it is clearly a question of the conscious and willful rejection of faith by those to whom the Gospel has been sufficiently preached.[40] Yet by itself, without the perfection of charity, faith is not enough for salvation, nor is unbelief necessarily incompatible with morally good dispositions and an upright conscience. Unbelief cannot claim solid support from the facts and evidence of experience; the word of God can withstand the assaults of doubt and denial. To bolster this claim, the Church's theologians have for centuries, and with increasing earnestness since the Reformation jolt and the infinitely more shocking experience of modern rationalism, engaged in the apologetic enterprise, the defense of the reasonableness of faith.[41] During the century of Enlightenment, churchmen remained incredibly slow to appreciate the virulence of the atheistic campaign mounted by the *philosophes*. Even in France, seedbed of anti-religious thinking, it was not until the sixth or seventh decade that serious notice was taken by the episcopate of contemporary irreligion and unbelief. After 1770, condemnations and warnings multiplied as the Advocate General, the Parlement of Paris, and the body of French bishops issued document after document, rich in expletives and dire predictions, but failing, on the whole, to meet the unbeliever on his own ground or to uncover the basic reasons for wholesale defection from religion. Fabro writes: 'Catholic apologetics sallied forth at once against irreligion and atheism, especially in France which was the chief battlefield, but it is not difficult to discern in all this heady writing a jarring note; not always, indeed, is it improvised and excessively oratorical; but almost always there is a drastic want of insight into the deep-seated principles of the whole Enlightenment movement. Instead of going to the root of the matter, as speculative analysis demands, it tended to highlight the "consequences" in the practical and moral order, often going so far as to disregard Bayle's famous polemic.'[42]

It was only in the nineteenth century that explicit condemnations of atheism, indifferentism, and agnosticism were made. At the First Vatican Council these declarations were repeated and concentrated in the most solemn fashion possible. The Fathers of the Council defined that 'God, the beginning and end of all things, may be known for certain by the natural light of human reason, by means of created things, "for the invisible things of Him from the creation of the world are clearly seen, being understood from the things that are made" (Rom 1.20); but that it pleased His wisdom and goodness to reveal Himself and the eternal decrees of His will to mankind by another, namely, the supernatural way.'[43] Hence it is heretical to maintain, as do the atheists and the Positivists, that there is no way by which man can arrive at the knowledge of God, or to assert, with the most extreme Traditionalists and Fideists, that God can be known only through revelation or by some positive teaching received by tradition. Faith, being a supernatural gift, presupposes revelation, and hence cannot be consistently invoked to prove the existence of

God against an atheist. In the report which he presented to the council in the name of the commission on faith, Bishop Gasser addressed the Fathers thus: 'You know, very Reverend Fathers, what opinion has become prevalent in the minds of many through the teaching of the French encyclopedists and the former defenders of the critical philosophy in Germany; this widely spread opinion is none other than that the existence of God cannot be proved with full certainty, and that the arguments which have at all times been so highly regarded are still open to discussion. As a result, religion has been despised as if it had no foundation. Moreover, in these latter days attempts have been made in various places to separate morality from all religion; this is said to be necessary because of the fear that when a man has reached a certain age and perceives that there is nothing certain in religion, not even the existence of God, he may become a moral pervert. . . .'[44] I cite this remarkable passage both because it summarizes neatly the mentality prevailing in the Catholic Church in the late nineteenth and well into the twentieth century and because it may serve as a point against which to measure the transformation achieved at the time of the Second Vatican Council.

In the Modernist crisis, even more specifically, there are ecclesiastical statements on agnosticism, but like almost all the previous statements, these are wholly negative and prohibitive. The Church professed its faith that God, the beginning and end of all things, can be known with certainty to exist, and His existence even proved by the natural light of reason, through the medium of created things, just as a cause is known and proved by its effects. The characteristic mark of the new age, the epoch into which the Western world has been moving perceptibly for the past three centuries, is here openly displayed. As Jean Guitton has put it, there is not enough religious enthusiasm left to give rise to an explicitly religious heresy; the First Vatican Council could find none that called for condemnation, but only philosophies that were a danger for right reason.[45] The papal and curial pronouncements at the time of the Modernist crisis represented the official thinking within Catholicism on the obviously growing problem of unbelief. After the rise of Communism, later Church statements concentrated on denouncing the atheistic teachings of the Soviets and their world-wide supporters and the paganism and secularism of various political and social movements which encroached upon the freedom of religion. By the end of the reign of Pope Pius XII the world was sufficiently aware that Catholics disapproved, officially and without reservation, of every contemporary form of atheism and religious indifferentism. Those who expected anything other or more than condemnation were destined to be disappointed.

The Catholic Church's stand in face of the massive fact of atheism was adopted in Council by the Fathers assembled at the Vatican in the Pastoral Constitution on the Church in the Modern World (*Gaudium et Spes*). I should like first to reproduce those paragraphs from this remarkable document which express the view of the Council and fill in some of the details surrounding the final working out and adoption of the text. After this I shall report the discussions and interventions of the Fathers and experts charged with defining the mind of the Church and shall attempt briefly to assess the significance and import of this statement as the authoritative background for theological inquiry.[46]

The Council's remarks on atheism (the term usually employed, in place of unbelief, which I have preferred in the present work) are inserted in a lengthy discourse in which the Church deliberately initiates a dialogue with the modern world. The tone and clear intent of this document are positive, encouraging, open, and pastoral in the best and most authentic sense. The world is given to understand that churchmen, and all Catholics, are interested as much in this fraternal conversation as in their own internal reform and renewal. Mankind today, 'though . . . struck with wonder at its own discoveries and power, . . . often raises anxious questions about the current trend of the world, about the place and role of man in the universe, about the meaning of his individual and collective strivings, and about the ultimate destiny of reality and of humanity.'[47] In an address on the closing day of the council, Pope Paul VI affirmed that the Church's desire 'has been to be heard and understood by everyone; it has not merely concentrated on intellectual understanding but has also sought to express itself in simple, up-to-date conversational style, derived from actual experience and a cordial approach which make it more vital, attractive and persuasive.'[48] And in a comment on the text proposed for discussion on the enormous topic of the Church in the world today, the same Holy Father states that 'The Council considers the world in all its realities with loving attention, capable of discovering everywhere traces of God and therefore of goodness, beauty, and truth.'[49] With this serene and confident optimism, not oblivious to the gravity of the question or the range of its practical consequences, the Fathers produced the text on

atheism. These paragraphs are inserted, I think with profound insight
and far-reaching implications, in the first major section of the
Constitution, after the rather extended introductory sections on
'The Dignity of the Human Person.' The text reads as follows:

19. An outstanding cause of human dignity lies in man's call to
communion with God. From the very circumstance of his origin,
man is already invited to converse with God. For man would not
exist were he not created by God's love and constantly preserved
by it. And he cannot live fully according to truth unless he
freely acknowledges that love and devotes himself to his Creator.

Still, many of our contemporaries have never recognized this
intimate and vital link with God, or have explicitly rejected it.
Thus atheism must be accounted among the most serious problems
of this age, and is deserving of closer examination.

The word atheism is applied to phenomena which are quite
distinct from one another. For while God is expressly denied
by some, others believe that man can assert absolutely nothing
about Him. Still others use such a method so to scrutinize
the question of God as to make it seem devoid of meaning. Many,
unduly transgressing the limits of the positive sciences, contend
that everything can be explained by this kind of scientific reasoning alone, or, by contrast, they altogether disallow that there is
any absolute truth.

Some laud men so extravagantly that their faith in God
lapses into a kind of anemia, though they seem more inclined to
affirm man than to deny God. Again some form for themselves
such a fallacious idea of God that when they repudiate this
figment they are by no means rejecting the God of the Gospel.
Some never get to the point of raising questions about God, since
they seem to experience no religious stirrings nor do they see
why they should trouble themselves about religion.

Moreover, atheism results not rarely from a violent protest
against the evil in this world, or from the absolute character
with which certain values are unduly invested, and which thereby
already accords them the stature of God. Modern civilization
itself often complicates the approach to God, not for any essential
reason, but because it is excessively engrossed in earthly affairs.

Undeniably, those who willfully shut out God from their
hearts and try to dodge religious questions are not following
the dictates of their consciences. Hence they are not free of blame.

Yet believers themselves frequently bear some responsibility
for this situation. For, taken as a whole, atheism is not a spontaneous development but stems from a variety of causes, including
a critical reaction against religious beliefs, and in some places

against the Christian religion in particular. Hence believers can have more than a little to do with the birth of atheism. To the extent that they neglect their own training in the faith, or teach erroneous doctrine, or are deficient in their religious, moral, or social life, they must be said to conceal rather than reveal the authentic face of God and religion.

20. Modern atheism often takes on a systematic expression, which, in addition to other arguments against God, stretches the desire for human independence to such a point that it finds difficulties with any kind of dependence on God. Those who profess atheism of this sort maintain that it gives man freedom to be an end unto himself, the sole artisan and creator of his own history. They claim that this freedom cannot be reconciled with the affirmation of a Lord who is author and purpose of all things, or at least that this freedom makes such an affirmation altogether superfluous. The sense of power which modern technical progress generates in man can give color to such a doctrine.

Not to be overlooked among the forms of modern atheism is that which anticipates the liberation of man, especially his economic and social emancipation. This form argues that by its nature religion thwarts such liberation by arousing man's hope for a deceptive future life, thereby diverting him from the constructing of the earthly city. Consequently, when the proponents of this doctrine gain governmental power they vigorously fight against religion. They promote atheism by using those means of pressure which public power has at its disposal. Such is especially the case in the work of educating the young.

21. In her loyal devotion to God and men, the Church has already repudiated and cannot cease repudiating, sorrowfully but as firmly as possible, those poisonous doctrines and actions which contradict reason and the common experience of humanity, and dethrone man from his native excellence.

Still, she strives to detect in the atheistic mind the hidden causes for the denial of God. Conscious of how weighty are the questions which atheism raises, and motivated by love for all men, she believes these questions ought to be examined seriously and more profoundly.

The Church holds that the recognition of God is in no way hostile to man's dignity, since this dignity is rooted and perfected in God. For man was made an intelligent and free member of society by the God who created him. Even more importantly, man is called as a son to commune with God and to share in His happiness. She further teaches that a hope related to the end of time does not diminish the importance of intervening duties, but rather undergirds the acquittal of them with fresh incentives. By contrast, when a divine substructure and the hope of life eternal are wanting, man's dignity is most grievously lacerated, as current events often attest. The riddles of life and death, of guilt and of grief go unsolved, with the frequent result that men succumb to despair.

Meanwhile, every man remains to himself an unsolved puzzle, however obscurely he may perceive it. For on certain occasions no one can entirely escape the kind of self-questioning mentioned earlier, especially when life's major events take place. To this questioning only God fully and most certainly provides an answer as He summons man to higher knowledge and humbler probing.

The remedy which must be applied to atheism, however, is to be sought in a proper presentation of the Church's teaching as well as in the integral life of the Church and her members. For it is the function of the Church, led by the Holy Spirit who renews and purifies her ceaselessly, to make God the Father and His Incarnate Son present and in a sense visible.

This result is achieved chiefly by the witness of a living and mature faith, namely, one trained to see difficulties clearly and to master them. Very many martyrs have given luminous witness to this faith and continue to do so. This faith needs to prove its fruitfulness by penetrating the believer's entire life, including its worldly dimensions, and by activating him toward justice and love, especially regarding the needy. What does the most to reveal God's presence, however, is the brotherly charity of the faithful who are united in spirit as they work together for the faith of the Gospel and who prove themselves a sign of unity.

While rejecting atheism, root and branch, the Church sincerely professes that all men, believers and unbelievers alike, ought to work for the rightful betterment of this world in which all alike live. Such an ideal cannot be realized, however, apart from sincere and prudent dialogue. Hence the Church protests against the distinction which some state authorities unjustly make between believers and unbelievers, thereby ignoring fundamental rights of the human person. The Church calls for the active liberty of believers to build up in this world God's temple too. She courteously invites atheists to examine the Gospel of Christ with an open mind.

Above all the Church knows that her message is in harmony with the most secret desires of the human heart when she champions the dignity of the human vocation, restoring hope to those who have already despaired of anything higher than their present lot. Far from diminishing man, her message brings to his development light, life, and freedom. Apart from this message nothing will avail to fill up the heart of man: 'Thou hast made us for Thyself,' O Lord, 'and our hearts are restless until they rest in Thee.'[50]

The definitive statement, comprising the three paragraphs numbered 19, 20, and 21, was adopted during the Fourth Session of the Council, after intense discussion of a text submitted to the Fathers in September, 1965. The reception of this proposed schema was followed by study and several public interventions, or series of remarks, by those entitled to address the Council.[51] The text distributed at the beginning of the Fourth and final session (sometimes referred to as the Arricia text) aroused the most intense and vigorous interest on the part of a number of very capable and well-informed conciliar members and experts, an interest which very shortly narrowed precisely on the draft paragraph devoted to the question of atheism. The interventions of three cardinals, an Eastern patriarch, several bishops, and the superior general of a major religious order exposed important outlooks and attitudes, pointed out alleged weaknesses in the proposed text and indicated in general a spectrum of difference and disagreement which would have to be resolved, as usual, by compromise.

The first intervention, on September 24, 1965, was offered by the Yugoslav Cardinal Seper of Zagreb, whose complaint was that a problem as serious as that of atheism had received what he regarded as inadequate treatment. In the eyes of our contemporaries, Seper stated, atheism is a mark of true progress and the bulwark of a genuine and promising humanism. It would never do simply to produce a condemnation of atheism or to reproduce another alleged demonstration of the existence of God. The Church must display a real and profound understanding of atheism as an intellectual system and of the tremendous confidence which men place in it as an instrument of the progress and welfare of mankind. It was Seper who insisted that those Christians who defended an unjust and irrational social order, investing oppression and degradation with divine sanction, must be held at least partially responsible for unbelief. God teaches and demands that we pursue justice and charity with all our strength, to make the world ever increasingly a witness to Himself. From true religion a proper humanism derives its firmest support, although atheists, too, can work for the promotion of human dignity.

On September 27, four interventions of the utmost value and importance were entered. Maximos IV Saigh, a Cardinal and the Patriarch of Antioch, praised the entire document's centering on Christ in a spirit of love but disapproved of the section on atheism as too negative in emphasis. Humanity would not be saved from atheism merely by a rigid condemnation (however well deserved) of atheistic Communism. The patriarch announced the search for the causes of atheism as a new and constructive element and proposed a dynamic mystique and vigorous social morality that would reveal Christ as the source of the workers' liberation. The helpful, positive attitude displayed by Pope John's *Pacem in terris* and Pope Paul's *Ecclesiam suam* was preferred by Patriarch Maximos to a futile 'deploring and regretting.' The Church should recognize, he said, that not all atheists are hostile to religion; they are motivated primarily by a desire, however unrecognized as such, for a truer presentation of God, a religion in harmony with the present state of the evolution of the human race, and above all a Church in solidarity with the poor. Some are calling for a denunciation of the sins of the world, but the most glaring and awful of sins is egotism, the exploitation of man by man. The wretched working people of the world bear the heaviest cross and seek to emerge from their miserable condition, unfortunately, through a system that is not only socialist (which the patriarch does not object to) but atheist. Modern socioeconomic systems need not condemnation but the leaven of the Gospel. The poor are driven to embrace atheism, not for its own sake, but because they are scandalized by a mediocre, selfish Christianity which relies on force and wealth, defending its own interests instead of living and preaching brotherhood.

The learned and distinguished Cardinal König, Archbishop of Vienna, expressed agreement with Seper's point, that the schema failed to distinguish adequately the various forms of atheism, of which militant Communism was only a single type. König proposed that four points should be developed: (1) the different types and essential nature of atheism, (2) the causes of atheism, (3) the remedies to be sought, and (4) the Church's mode of dealing with the phenomenon. The cardinal then spelled out briefly his thoughts on each of these points and called above all for a thoroughgoing theological study of the spread of atheism in the world. Ignorance about atheism is a great disservice to the Church to the extent that it hampers the apostolic labors of priests and missionaries. The roots of atheism are traced to the false conception of God which all too many Christians entertain and to the perverse and unnecessary antipathy posited between the worship of God and the full flowering of man's free potential. The Church should be a stanch supporter of fraternal cooperation and social justice and should encourage experts to explore the origins of atheism and the arguments advanced in its support. König's final recommendation was that Catholics should condemn no one but should try to live at peace with all men, including atheistic regimes, which are invited to implement the principle of true liberty of conscience for all men.

The Archbishop of Florence, Cardinal Florit, spoke of materialistic atheism, the practical atheism which so many Western people adopt in our day. He deplored the misguided attempt to accept Marxist political economy as if it could be separated from its atheistic and materialistic basis. Florit then identified the principle of immanence, the decline of morality, and an anti-metaphysical scientism as the chief sources of contemporary atheism, and the overwhelming fact of evil as the most pervasive and enduring source of the rejection of God. Believers, he concluded, should devote serious attention to the mystery of evil and not take lightly the scandal which it constitutes for the unbeliever.

Father Pedro Arrupe, recently elected General of the Society of Jesus, delivered his first speech on this same day, a lengthy intervention which evoked an immediate and somewhat sensational response in the world press. Arrupe's opening remark was to the effect that the schema overly intellectualized the problem of atheism and, secondly, relied in a naive and unrealistic fashion on resources already commonly possessed. In highly colored language the Jesuit deplored the infiltration of atheism even within the City of God, where it insidiously influenced the minds of believers, including priests and religious, producing the poisonous fruits of naturalism, distrust, and rebellion. Citing statistics to prove his point, Arrupe argued that the Church was failing to evangelize the world, to share her spiritual treasure with the men of our time, because she did not know effectively how to relate theory to action. The godless society, in contrast, operated with maximum efficiency and had gained almost complete control of international life, finance, and the mass communications media. Arrupe's remarks along these lines became nearly hysterical and took shape in stridently militant and combative tones, as he called for a coordinated plan of action. His terminology, in particular, disturbed and offended those sensitive to the new spirit which infused the schema itself. Father Arrupe later tried to answer objections in a press interview, but it cannot be said that he aroused confidence in the line his order would take in carrying out its papal mission to tackle the problem of atheism.

On the next day, September 28, three more noteworthy interventions were made. The first by the Ruthenian bishop of Pittsburgh, Nicholas Elko, dealt exclusively with dialectical materialism, which was excoriated as the plague of present-day civilization and likened to the beast of the Apocalypse. Bishop Elko called for a simple, clear, strong and explicit condemnation, nothing more or less. The Ukrainian-rite Auxiliary Bishop Michele Rusnack of Toronto insisted that the Council speak out on the dangers of that atheism which he associated with the inhuman totalitarian regimes behind the Iron Curtain. Archbishop Wojtyla struck a moderate note, pointing to the complexity of the question of atheism, which made it extremely difficult to deal with.

Archbishop Marty, of Paris, shared a widely felt view that the proposed text's treatment of atheism was too abstract and negative. He thought Christians should recognize the humanism which motivated those atheists who saw faith in God as an obstacle to building a better world. The atheist is not the man who systematically denies God but one who refuses faith as an illusion which diminishes man; positively, the atheist proposes his own message of salvation, an ethic and a spirituality designed to liberate man from the slavery of traditional religious ethics. Dialogue between believers and unbelievers is imperative, a work which Marty hoped would be undertaken by the Vatican Secretariat for Non-Believers as well as by those who work as missionaries among unbelievers. In conclusion Marty suggested that the rewriting of Schema 13 be entrusted to the Secretariat for Non-Believers.

The Councils of the Church had never before addressed the problem of atheism in this explicit and forthright fashion, so that even the choice of this topic as a subject of discussion was a first for the Second Vatican Council and marked a significant step forward in world-consciousness. The First Vatican Council spoke of the knowability of God by reason, largely with the fideists and traditionalists in mind and in view of the atheistic conclusions of Enlightenment, Rationalism and Positivism. The Second Vatican Council took its lead and inspiration, actually, from Popes Paul VI and, less immediately, John XXIII. Pope John summoned a Council that was to extend its pastoral concern to all men, to the entire world of which Christ is the light. Pope Paul had pointed to a completely new and disconcerting fact: the existence of militant atheism which is active on a world level. The conciliar Fathers took this point to heart and, through the particular efforts of some of their number, saw to it that the Council undertook a clarification of the position of the Church vis-à-vis the modern world, a world in which unbelief was a widespread fact not to be ignored. This clarification, which occupied much of the Fourth Session (September–December, 1965), was made possible and was called for by the Church's self-scrutiny in the Second Session, which produced the Constitution on the

Church. Of this document Archbishop Garrone later said frankly that 'The Church is tidying herself up for dialogue with the world.' As conciliar background to the subsequent discussion on atheism, the proceedings of the Second, Third and Fourth Sessions should be reviewed along with two relevant papal pronouncements, namely, Pope John's *Pacem in terris* and Pope Paul's *Ecclesiam suam*.

In a sense *Pacem in terris*, dated Holy Thursday, 1963, is Pope John's last legacy, for he died some weeks later, on Pentecost Sunday. The significance of this encyclical for the Church's attitude toward unbelief lies in its form of address, in the questions touched upon, and, above all, in the spirit in which it is conceived and delivered. In the first place, John makes it clear that he is speaking to all men of good will, something never before undertaken in this form of papal pronouncement, undoubtedly inspiring the members of the Council to take seriously the Church's responsibility to engage in, or at least indicate a willingness to initiate, a dialogue with the world. The question of atheism is touched upon, at a point of utmost delicacy, when the Pope reaffirmed the distinction between the person who errs, retaining his full dignity and rights as a person, and his error. An even more apposite and instructive distinction was employed in Pope John's assertion that false philosophical teachings with respect to the nature, origin, and destiny of the universe and of man are not to be confused with historical movements, whose ends are cultural or political, social or economic. The Pontiff's confidence that 'false doctrines and viewpoints . . . are all so obviously opposed to every principle of honor and are producing such baneful results that today men are condemning them of their own accord' lent support to those in the Council who were opposed to the issuing of reiterated condemnations.[52] In an even more startling phrase Pope John reminds us that 'those movements, insofar as they conform to the dictates of right reason and are interpreters of the lawful aspirations of the human person, contain elements that are positive and deserving of approval.'

Pope John's successor issued his first encyclical on August 6, 1964, in the form of a simple 'conversational letter.' Paul treated a number of fiercely controverted subjects calling for the utmost skill and perspicacity in their formulation. After pondering the mystery of the Church's inner nature and divine constitution and searching out the best conditions for its thorough renewal, the Pope set forth a truly remarkable papal estimate of the purposes and circumstances of dialogue. I shall examine this third part of the encyclical, on dialogue, in the next chapter and here note only the air of diplomatic and cautious firmness, balanced beautifully by a frank and open humaneness, which served well those in the Council who wanted to respect the complexity of the problem of atheism while evidencing a sense of respect for the unbeliever and a positive appreciation of his honest and genuine values.

During the Third Session the Fathers had to be made more keenly aware of the dimensions of the question of unbelief and the urgency of a free and uninhibited examination of its many aspects. Cardinal Silva Henriquez of Santiago, Chile, admonished his confrères, on the first day of debate (October 20, 1964), that they must go beyond mere condemnation and seek out the hidden causes which lead to the denial of God, to find the truths which nourish the atheist error and to live up to those truths. The Cardinal's plea was eloquent: '. . . the answer which the Church must give to modern humanism is a new man in whose personality the earthly and eschatological dimensions of his vocation are harmoniously balanced; we need a true Christian anthropology.'[53] Cardinal Suenens, of Belgium, declared that Catholics should examine their way of speaking of God and living the faith and ask whether they do not sometimes darken the sun of the living God.

Some of the Council Fathers, particularly those from countries with oppressive Communist regimes, urged that more or less strong condemnations of atheistic Communism be included in that part of the statement which would deal with unbelief. These same spokesmen expressed doubt as to the wisdom or prospects of initiating dialogue with the unbeliever, who was envisaged almost exclusively as a doctrinaire Marxist who would only exploit such a rapprochement for nefarious political ends. The Polish bishops, however, although they described in graphic terms the terrible conditions under which religion suffered in their country, refrained from joining in the call for a hard line denunciation. The important point to note is that there was in fact no such condemnation, and this left room, indeed it called, for a new and more tolerant understanding, not of atheism as an abstract or objective theoretical system, but of the unbeliever as a human being and a potential partner in dialogue. The Constitution on the Church had declared: 'Nor does divine Providence deny the help necessary for salvation to those who, without blame on their part, have not yet arrived at an explicit knowledge of God, but who strive to live a good life, thanks to His grace. Whatever goodness or truth is found among them is looked upon by the Church as a preparation for the Gospel.'[54]

The general attitude which prevailed at the Third Session, although it cannot be said to have been universal, was to meet the unbeliever in a spirit of sincere good will. The brief description of the various ideals and aspirations which characterize the modern world was inserted as a preface to the schema in order to emphasize the Church's desire to respect and respond to contemporary man's deepest striving and most determined purposes. The intervention of the Auxiliary Bishop of Madrid, Guerra Campos, one of the most extraordinary discourses at this session, must have had an enormous influence on the rewriting of the original schema. The bishop evidenced a subtle and realistic appreciation of the prevailing situation and the kind of statement called for in the light thereof. The bishops had to recognize, he said, that, to alienated man, religion appeared to be but one of the 'ideologies' by which man is kept in bondage to the forces of enslavement. Guerra Campos invited his confrères to dwell on the possibility that the eschatology of Marxist atheism might be not simply a wild utopia but a thrust to realize by man's own effort what he has been seeking in religion, and secondly, on the nature of transcendence in the projected perfect society of the future. The atheist must be brought to see in the drive to God not an alienation but the dynamic perfection of man. More positively, he added: 'The Christian fact throws light on all things, insofar as it points to a definitive meaning and generates faith in Christ with us; we should make it clear that we do not deduce the whole of reality from a set of given principles, as though it were some sort of mechanistic rationalism.'[55]

The Dutch Cardinal Alfrink entered the last intervention of the session on the subject, reminding his listeners that Communism had been condemned repeatedly in the past and that condemnation, in any case, served only to harden atheists in their position. 'Let us avoid any aggressive declaration,' Alfrink concluded; 'what we can do with regard to communism is to declare the true religious liberty of all men everywhere. What we have to do is to realize social justice and create the conditions of a dialogue in which we shall have to bear witness to our faith.'[56] Between the Third and Fourth Sessions a mixed commission set to work preparing a revised version of the definitive text which the Fathers would be asked to approve and make their own. It was during this inter-session period, in April, 1965, that the Holy Father established the Vatican Secretariat for Non-Believers, a momentous act, which will be examined in the following chapter. In May of that year the Jesuits were asked by the Pope to devote themselves to the problem of atheism in a special manner.* It was in the Fourth Session, as we have seen, that the discussion and comments of the Fathers and experts led to the adoption of the Pastoral Constitution with the paragraphs on atheism reproduced above.

In a perceptive essay on the significance of the Council's teaching on atheism, Karl Rahner discerns two new and surprising developments, which he characterizes as the thesis that it is possible for a normal adult to accept explicit atheism, even for a lifetime, without moral guilt, and that atheism need not exclude one from salvation, on condition that it does not lead one to act contrary to conscience.[57] The first thesis is not propounded in so many words but is implicit in the refusal to condemn all atheists in the contemporary world. The question of guilt is touched upon only once, in paragraph 3 of number 19, and there only in the brief mention of the obvious fact that when a man shuts out God from his heart, or deliberately and against the dictate of conscience, evades facing the question of religion, he cannot be held blameless. It is nowhere asserted that only the conscious and willful exclusion of God or avoidance of the problem constitutes atheism. After the Council it is impossible for a theologian to go on regarding the atheist as such as a fool or a villain; his present and most urgent task is to seek out the many and diverse causes of atheism, which can no longer be reduced merely to stupidity or moral perversity. The conciliar text enumerates several of the more obvious factors responsible for present-day atheism, but there is clearly a mission for theologians to carry out, to make a thoroughgoing analysis of these causes.

An even more surprising development is the declaration that all men of good will may share in Christ's resurrection, with the reference to n.16 of the Constitution on the Church, where we read that 'those also can attain to everlasting salvation who through no fault of their own do not know the Gospel of Christ or His Church, yet sincerely seek God and, moved by grace, strive by their deeds to do His will as it is known to them through the dictates of conscience.' Nowhere is it simply presumed that this good will and moral uprightness is unfailingly realized in every atheist; the point is that the Council likewise rejects the presumption to the contrary: the

---

* The Pope's directive was issued on the occasion of the General Congregation or chapter of the Society meeting in Rome to elect a new superior and prepare for the updating and renewal of the Society in the spirit of conciliar *aggiornamento*. In response to the papal request, the Jesuits undertook to organize a study in depth of the atheistic phenomenon, a search for causes before remedies were recommended, in a spirit of apostolic zeal, without political preoccupation.

possibility is affirmed, but no more. As Rahner puts it, it would be arbitrary to maintain that a polytheistic pagan who, according to Paul (Eph 2.12), is also 'godless,' has in principle an essentially greater chance of being saved than a modern atheist whose 'personal' atheism is, after all, mainly the product of his social situation. The Council thus sets two related and extremely important theological problems on a new plane and opens a new perspective from which to pursue more adequate solutions. The history of official doctrine in this matter is instructive, from the line taken by Pius IX and the declaration of the Holy Office in 1849, to the startling 'optimism about salvation' which explicitly includes atheists in the clearest terms.

Besides these two principal developments Rahner finds eleven other points, relatively new and important for a deeper understanding of the religious status of the unbeliever: (1) the emphasis on the fact that, as the gravest phenomenon of our time, atheism requires careful examination (19, par. 1; 21, par. 2); (2) the statement that the notion of atheism covers very different phenomena, the causes and motives of which show an extraordinary variety among themselves (19, par. 2 and 3); (3) the emphasis on the influence of sociological factors (20, par. 2); (4) the reference to an existentialist atheism (20, par. 1); (5) the reference to a positivist atheism which declares that the question of God is already meaningless as such (19, par. 2); (6) the reference to a postulated atheism that sees in the absurdity of existence and the evil of the world a proof of the non-existence of God (19, par. 2); (7) the insistence that atheism is often the denial of a God who in fact does not exist and has nothing to do with the God of the Gospel (19, par. 2); (8) the inclusion of atheists in the obligatory freedom of conscience (21, par. 6); (9) the emphasis on the possibility of a dialogue and cooperation in the world between theists and atheists; (10) the recognition that Christians are to some extent responsible for modern atheism (19, par. 3); and (11) all the allusions to a 'mystical introduction' into the religious experience of God that go far beyond the classical proofs of God's existence in the rational manner of scholastic philosophy, and which are spread throughout these three sections of the Pastoral Constitution.

While fully appreciating the soundness of the Council's approach to the reality of unbelief, as well as the genuine advance it marked in the Church's understanding of this challenge, one may note certain limitations in the doctrine propounded in the conciliar text. It is not only through culpable neglect of the faith or the teaching of downright erroneous doctrine that Christians have scandalized the unbeliever: as long as even orthodox Christian doctrine is left undeveloped, underdeveloped, or un-redeveloped, it may become obsolete to the needs of contemporary man. One will then have to be willing and able to divorce himself from his time and live in the past in order to assimilate a doctrine clothed in conceptual forms derived from an outmoded cultural milieu.[58] The effects of this cultural lag in religious categories may include a diminution of the sense of the presence of God. Article 20 of the Pastoral Constitution, alluding to modern philosophical systems which supported atheism, opens the question of the truth contained in these positions, which can be incorporated into a theism rendered more intelligible to the contemporary mind.

The Council was not concerned merely to multiply classifications of the forms of unbelief, an effort that has become a perennial theological pastime since the beginning of the modern age. What marks the conciliar effort as most serious and promising is the accompanying invitation to believers to take a hard, concerned look at the world and to confess their own deep involvement in the human problem of atheism. Religious chauvinism and self-interested political preoccupations are unwarranted elements in what has been a prevailing conception of unbelief. The conventional image of the unbeliever has been that of a stiff-necked antagonist resisting grace; the accusation would perhaps be only less odious if it were not, often, associated with political intolerance. The unbeliever must be able to read the conciliar text and feel that he was being truly understood and unreservedly loved. At last the Christian resolves to study atheism carefully, not lumping together separate phenomena, blurring shades of meaning, freezing life in static formulas, or relegating to the historical shades forms of thought that are by no means defunct. The mentality expressed in the Council's pronouncement on atheism is that of a dynamic, evolving, and even self-transfiguring body and ground. The Church wants to acknowledge that today the human race is engaged in a turning-point of history and that unbelief is somehow, in many ways not entirely clear, bound up with this evolutionary process. While speaking in the name of Christ to the whole of this humanity, the Church deemed it imperative to cling to an image of Christ which allowed little if any room for that dynamic and evolving element. It is objected that the Constitution's language remains curiously archaic even while its pastoral and practical concern is genuinely modern. When the text says that in our world the basic source of human dignity lies in man's call to communion with God, it speaks in static terms of an unchanging human nature eternally dependent upon God. It is significant that the name of God is so frequently invoked whenever the Church wishes to call attention to man's weakness and dependence. It seems inevitable, then, that an intense quest for human independence should veer in the direction of a new and comprehensive atheism, when the name of God is, rightly or wrongly, associated historically with an arbitrary and unbending Sovereign who demands total and unquestioning submission.[59]

In its teachings on atheism the Council may indeed have exposed the Church to uncertainty and risk, at least until what is new has been appropriated and well understood by the faithful. Uncertainty and risk, as Cardinal König has remarked, are words inscribed above the gate through which the Church at the Council went out into the world, not in order to assimilate itself to the world but in order to enter into contact with all men. Unbelief is not only a worldwide fact, it is a pastoral problem, the dimensions of which have been underscored by the attention devoted to it at an Ecumenical Council of the Church. It remains for those who are competent to continue to explore the various aspects of this problem, to understand the fact of unbelief in the light of faith under the direction and guidance of the Holy Spirit.

UNBELIEF AS A THEOLOGICAL PROBLEM

Before analyzing the theoretical credentials or arguments by which the unbeliever defends and justifies the option he has made, it will be wise to recognize the specific utility his atheism possesses, as a social and psychological factor determining his historical engagement. Atheism's primary and most radical thrust is against faith or religious belief not as a set of reflective doctrines or dogmatic formulas but as a way of life, as the principal component in the choice of a self-identity and life-style. The first task is the examination of what unbelief has, or claims to have, as stimulus and inspiration to a fuller, richer, more humanly satisfying existence; this means, in practice, an honest and close-hand look at the kind of life the atheist proposes to man, liberated, as he thinks, from religious commitment. The burden of study here is on the believer, but the unbeliever, too, has a responsibility, to wit, that of providing a realistic program, or at least an attainable ideal, of a world that is at once godless and livable. There will be a confrontation not only of theism and atheism, of Christian theology and atheology, but of conflicting humanisms.[60] Insofar as atheism, as a would-be humanism, is more concerned

with sweeping away the false absolutes that block human development, it may be more an ally of faith than an adversary.

Atheism as agent or at least catalyst of reform, of that continuing
self-criticism by which men seek to improve both their self-understanding and the quality of their existence, personal and social,
finds its most articulate and in some ways most representative
contemporary expression in Marxism, particularly in the recent
concern of Marxists to construct a solid and attractive humanism.[61]
One may question the willingness or readiness of Communist regimes
to implement such a humanism; this does not appreciably diminish
the plausibility of a way of life conceived in terms of atheism and
the exclusion of religion. Marxist atheism illustrates the highly
pragmatic and functional quality prized by our contemporaries;
the emphasis is on the reform and improvement of the conditions
and circumstances of existence. This emphasis constitutes the most
telling critique of religion, striking as it does at the latter's impotence
and ineffectiveness as a working principle, a source of norms and
standards by which to define and enhance the life of the individual
and of mankind. In a penetrating essay in which he projects a future
Marxist culture, Jaroslav Krejci outlines four points which he sees
as establishing the psychosocial function of Marxist atheism, its
potential contribution towards the creation and maintenance of
'the fullest measure of human development, happiness, and freedom
for the greatest number of human beings.' [62] I suggest that the Christian, the theological critic, reflect soberly on the kind or quality of
human existence implicit in this outline, with a view to evaluation
and response.

Atheism is conceived in the first place as the indispensable tool
of radical anthropological criticism, the instrument for undertaking
the revision of man's self-understanding. The supposition is that,
in spite of centuries of religious thinking, man does not yet know
himself, as a whole within the cosmos and not a mere part, a subject
who determines his own destiny and is not totally determined. It
will, undoubtedly, surprise those who see in Marxism nothing but
the ideological substrate of Communist tyranny to be told that
Marxist atheism, where it forms the official social doctrine of a
state, serves as a restraining force on dogmatic and reactionary
tendencies in the system. The state cannot be consecrated, influential
persons cannot be apotheosized, the status quo cannot be glorified,
as long as the 'detheologizing' function of atheism is intact and
operative. Atheism spurs man on to the merciless critique against
stifling conformity, to seek out uncompromisingly all the dead

weight which fetters the human mind. The atheist can leave no idols overthrown; he can permit none to be fabricated. Because he cares so deeply about man's earthly lot, he must combat that political indifference which prevents the individual's self-realization, which is attained in and through social relationships. Atheism has also an ethical function, which it discharges by liberating conscience from pseudo-values and illusory norms. The touchstone of atheistic morality is man's autonomy, his ability to struggle manfully against the restrictions and limitations which block the exercise of complete freedom. The atheist destroys fatalism, the subject's resignation before the object, and every kind of harmful passivity.

Only atheism, according to Krejci, is in harmony with the age's philosophical and anthropological avant-garde. In his opinion man today wants above all to transcend the antagonisms and grievances that in the past have eaten at the core of those interpersonal relationships and social institutions which form the web of human existence. This heightened philosophical awareness is atheistic, necessarily, in order to escape the deceptive fabrications of a pseudo-future. The atheist's perspective of humanity and of the vistas of development and change provides a bridge to the real future, of what lies ahead, in a never-ending initiative. Religion over-determines man's lot, which is decided for him by the will of God. Atheism, by contrast, assures man that he belongs to none but himself. Religion excuses man's weakness, imperfection, quietism, relieving him of the burden of his own life. Atheism teaches man that, in a godless universe, he is his own legislator, his fate is in his own hands, and he alone can create value. The process of history, never absolutely achieved, opens out perpetually anew. It is claimed that atheism has already definite accomplishments to its credit in those societies in which it has been accorded public status and widespread cultural influence. In the first place, it seems appropriate to credit atheism with a large share in undermining the religious fanaticism that sets men against each other in harsh aggression. The abandonment of religious illusion has made men realize increasingly that they must, by their own resources, shape their world and create humanity. Perhaps the most far-reaching impact of dynamic atheism has been felt in breaking down the strongly religious conception of universal and eternal moral values. Despite its shortcomings, atheism has been the pilot in the direction of a healthy, realistic anthropocentric world. Krejci's final word, however, is to admit the onesidedness and simplistic character of the 'traditional type of atheism,' and he identifies eight 'elements and features of stagnation' which are worth recording here. The older type of atheism, not yet sufficiently developed along humanist lines: (1) had no conception of dialogue, attributing to the ideological opponent a satanic character and pursuing aims more destructive than constructive; (2) did not struggle against the forms of alienation in socialism itself, the idols and fetishes by which reality is evacuated; (3) did not take into account the tragic side of life, the fears and misfortunes of mankind; (4) was unable to communicate with religious believers because it was unable to evaluate, on a non-religious basis, most of the ultimate questions, such as death transcendence, finitude, which to some extent find a solution in religion; (5) lost depth and intensity by trying for total victory, a maximum spread; (6) was not supported by a sociological and psychological description of actual group ideology, whether religious or atheistic; (7) had no conception of a non-religious type of belief; and (8) did not realize the possibility of joining forces with religion against common enemies, such as militarism, totalitarianism, etc.

An atheist manifesto that is self-searching and sophisticated, as Krejci's must be taken to be, is the most serious challenge yet faced by Christian faith in its claim to be an integral part of any choice of a way of life. It will be the religionist's immediate task to re-examine this statement, to determine in the first place in what respects and to what extent its propositions are inextricably bound up with the profession of atheism. It may be that on several important issues the theist may find himself able to agree with what is proposed as a new humanism because the latter, while it may be thoroughly secularist and even anti-religious in intent, is not essentially linked to atheism in the proper sense. In any case it is imperative that theologians, and more generally church people, discern in this bold model an unbelief emerging out of and supported by specific features of a definite cultural context. Atheism now is experienced and understood by its proponents as part of a way of life, one which they think alone likely to survive and carry mankind forward at this juncture of history. By the same token, the unbeliever sees religion, especially supernatural theism, as a relic of a past dead and deadly, not only theoretically bankrupt but practically discredited. This means, effectively, that traditional apologetics has lost its power to capture the attention or interest of the unbeliever; it had better be recognized for what it has always been, the logically adroit and aggressive self-justification of the faith of believers, convincing to themselves because based entirely on principles and an interpretation of experience which they alone shared.[63]

It would be misleading to proceed as if ours were, at last, a godless age, in the sense that religion counted for nothing with most men or that the dynamism of collective life were supplied largely, if not exclusively, by an atheistic ideology. It is my contention, precisely, that contemporary man's life-style, his self-determination, may be brought under the aegis either of faith or unbelief; that this, too, is a matter of human choice and decision. Men will continue to opt for one way or the other; it is the responsibility and opportunity of believers, according to the Vatican Council, to understand, appreciatively and from within, the full force of atheism, in its various current manifestations, as responding to the needs and aspirations most deeply felt by our contemporaries. It is not at all certain, in the judgment of a number of well-placed observers, that those charged with high office in the Church accurately assess the most important of the ideals and values by which men today strive to work out the problems which confront them and to realize a measure of happiness and fulfillment. The likelihood, or at least the risk, is that believers, theologians included, will persist in addressing themselves overwhelmingly, if not exclusively, to the speculative counter-arguments for theism, ignoring or underestimating the massive force of atheism as a major inspiration of contemporary humanism.[64]

In coming to terms with this phenomenon the theologian must take another hard look at the prevailing image of religion, on the level of human striving and concern. A religious culture has been identified almost completely, and quite one-sidedly, with modes of thinking and acting colored variously by interests and convictions irrelevant to those which dominate modern civilization. In face of this enormous cultural irrelevance, justifiably or not, men find in unbelief a life-style admirably suited to their needs and aspirations, without bothering to examine closely, much less to refute, the claims proper to religious faith. One cannot any longer reasonably speak of a crisis of faith at this stage, with two or three centuries behind us of increasing secularization and the gradual exclusion of religion from broader and broader areas of public life. Great masses of people, among them some of our age's most intelligent, best educated, and most ardently concerned, no longer raise specific objections to Christian doctrine; they simply find the religious posture as such unintelligible, without meaning or significance to the concerns of the times. It may very well be that the theological apparatus elaborated over a very long period, since the high Middle Ages at least, is today seriously deficient and incapable of being employed to deal with this sort of challenge. The emphasis on authority, even on reasonableness, is now largely futile and misplaced when the burning concern is with meaning and significance. The former questions have not disappeared, nor have they lost their intrinsic validity, but they have become secondary. Daniel Callahan speaks for both believer and unbeliever when he writes that: 'Today men want to know what it is to live the Christian life; what it means to be committed to Christ and the Church; what it means to be a morally reponsible person. Questions of this kind cannot be answered in any summary fashion; even less can one reduce the answers to tight systems capable of being encapsulated in manuals and textbooks. They are all questions which encompass mystery, questions posed by the self, seeking not specific directions for this or that decision in life but some sense of what it means for a man to engage himself with God in the first place.'[65]

In psychological, personalist terms, the commitment to unbelief is dictated by, and in turn contributes to, the decision to be and to think of oneself as a certain individual-in-the-world. Unless religion finds a fresh language to express insights still seen to be valuable, and a rich language for compelling new insights, it will not appeal to the restlessness of contemporary man. Man does not live in the past era with which so much about the Church—religion incarnate and institutionalized—is still palpably identified, an era which is strange and alien, not venerable or sacred. The Church's renewal, then, is seen as a matter not only of being true to its own essential nature and vocation but of carrying out its mission to the world of today, a mission as temporal as the men entrusted with it. It may be that, as men move into a future less and less impregnated with the felt and operative presence of religion, however this fact be interpreted, the isolation and the agony will be experienced, painfully, not by the unbeliever but by the man of faith. Despite the steps which have already been taken within the Church, particularly at and as a result of the Council, there are unmistakable indications that a far-reaching malaise is preventing us from summoning the courage and energy to tackle the immensely complex problem of unbelief. Theology is ever and in all its parts a pastoral and ecclesial enterprise; as such it suffers from the bewilderment and obscurantism which becloud the minds of believers in a given age. Renewal as a realistic, ongoing process is difficult and slow and may be honored at the highest levels in ways which have little or no effect on the dialogue with unbelievers to which, in part and by the Church's own declared intent, renewal is ordered.[66]

When it is viewed theologically, in light of the doctrine of God's universal salvific will, unbelief is rooted in resistance to the offer of the grace of faith, an offer which is always mysterious and sometimes, humanly speaking, ambiguous. Yet the believer does not *feel* or *sense* or, in any ordinary sense of the term, *experience* the reality of God, the presence of grace, any more than the unbeliever, who denies the reality and dismisses the alleged presence. The believer must speak of God in the only language available, not always solicitous to correct or refine a vocabulary which has lost its communicative ability, its power to convey intelligible meaning not contrary to or contradicted by the best prevailing criteria, gnosiological and onomastic. Language about God is felt to be an insuperable stumbling block, for reasons which are well-known to the diligent and sufficiently well-educated unbeliever but, curiously, not evident to otherwise concerned and conscientious churchmen.[67] The mystery of human freedom is fully engaged in the decision not to believe or to remain indifferent, a decision which affects the meaningfulness of the whole of reality in both its affirmation and its negation. The unbeliever's lived-world is one in which the irrational and evil take on an especially distinctive character, and mystery is not so much dispelled as exchanged for a large measure of absurdity. The humanism of unbelief must pit man against any intrusion of or concern for the numinously transcendent as well as support him in face of the difficulties of creating a viable community. Unbelief as a theological problem is fraught with all the complexity and dynamism of life itself, the life of the individual, responsible and free, set in a world to which a variety of responses must be made at different levels, and which holds out threat and promise alike. The theology of unbelief will take as its most promising point of departure not a rehearsal of time-worn rationalist arguments on behalf of a theism foreign to Biblical faith, but a confrontation of humanisms.

A Conflict of Humanisms: Believing and Unbelieving

The agony of Christian faith in the present age is cultural, which means that it is as social as it is personal and that unbelief finds its greatest opportunity in an incapacity for God as well as a disavowal of God supported by a radical immanentism, which has pervaded every corner of contemporary life. Christianity, in its popular and sometimes semi-official image, is taken to have promised the realization, in a future life beyond this one, of mankind's age-old dream of peace and security, tranquillity and prosperity, both bodily

and spiritual. The present cultural climate, however, gravitates
around the progressive realization of these ideals here and now and,
to paraphrase what Baudelaire said of beauty, whether happiness
comes from heaven or hell does not much matter, so long as it
comes, quickly and surely. Gabriel Vahanian analyzes this new,
post-religious temper in its perspective on faith and unbelief: if
faith does not work, in measurable pragmatic terms, then unbelief
is preferable.[68] For the recent 'temper of religiosity' neither purity
of faith nor purity of heart matters so much as the efficacy of some
belief system or other, a clear substitution of idolatrous concern
about secular matters for Biblical faith. The new secularist
humanism has a faith, i.e., a will to belief and even a set of beliefs,
with a certain degree of coherence and stability, but open to the
main chance of life, to history's expanding opportunities for worldly
satisfaction and achievement. It is a belief peculiar to a self-reliant
universe, radically precarious, it may be, but nonetheless powerful
and appealing and partially the offspring of Christianity's own
accommodation to cultural relativities and misalliances. In this
climate a non- and anti-Christian humanism flourishes in several
varieties or versions, confronting religious faith with a challenge
that promises to test its secular viability as well as its essential
and alleged divine origin and strength.

It is a question, in other words, of faith's capacity to enter
directly into man's being and concern in the world of his own
making, what is being called the humanized world.[69] Christianity
does not now face a void, as though in this age men had discarded
faith and been left with empty hands, in Eliot's phrase. I should
like first to describe the actual situation, as it might be appraised
by a thoughtful secular humanist, and then bring his vision (not in
the lame sense of visionary but of outlook on the future) into contrast with that of Christian faith. At this point of confrontation I
believe the theologian will find a formidable task, that of reappraising
the Christian concept, not to conform it to the world, which would
be its death and against which the word of God issues stern warning,
but to gauge more nearly its contemporary relevance and chances
of survival.

The secular humanist does his share of whistling in the dark;
it is in the interest of his program for a godless world order to minimize the darker, unrelieved facets of human existence, those about
which man seems powerless to accomplish anything in the way of
correction or deliverance. Surveying the arguments on both sides
for a future with or without faith, Charles Davis composed a state-

ment of optimistic, confident purpose which deserves to be quoted in full. The statement expresses a fairly widespread attitude, often unformulated and more practical than theoretical:

It is not that science has disproved religion; it has simply made it irrelevant. There is no cause for excited talk about this; let the inevitable take its time. The conviction grows that the age of religion is past, that faith is an incongruous feature in our modern mental landscape—a Gothic Church embedded in a new town; some still cling to it, most ignore it, and eventually the far-seeing will be able to have it quietly removed. The pitched battles are past; the real conquest is being achieved by the general change in mental climate. The unimaginable immensity of the universe reduces the God conceived in function of the cozy universe of the past to an unimportant figure projected by man's mind. If man had so little idea of the real universe, he is hardly likely to have achieved much accuracy in conceiving the Power that governs it.

Man himself formerly held the center of the stage. He was lord of the material creation; his God looked down on him in love or in anger and became incarnate in his nature, anxious to save him from his folly; the destiny of the entire universe was correlative to his own. This now looks as out-of-date as an ancient myth. Man, though a wonderfully interesting organism, is but a fragile and insignificant unit in the cosmos as a whole. His origin and his future are bound up with remote cosmic forces of which he is a lesser by-product. He might eliminate himself or be eliminated without repercussions of any magnitude. Why inflate man's understandable concern with himself to cosmic proportions? Why, too, hold on to the postulates of his past ignorance?

The ever-increasing knowledge of matter in its complexity and potentialities is making it more and more unnecessary to demand a fiat of a Creator to explain the origin of man or of life or of the cosmic process. In the cosmological field religion has nothing to offer and, despite the ingenuity of theologians, it still bears all the marks of an outlook long since surpassed. Nor need it claim our attention in the moral order. Christians are not notably better than others in their personal lives and relationships, and if technical progress has not immediately brought a more civilized behavior—well, religion has no cause to boast. What is clear and what is seeping into the consciousness of ordinary people from every side is that it is applied science and not religion that is determining man's way of life. It is to science that we must look to draw mankind from its poverty and misery, and many research workers and technicians have in the contrast between their own lives and those of their parents a private support to their confidence in what their knowledge and skill can do for the human race.

That does not mean a facile optimism. There are fools who may destroy all in a senseless war. But risk often accompanies human enterprise. A climber on a dangerous ascent recognizes the risk that all may end in disaster; but he feels within him the strength of his limbs, experiences the thrill of the climb, and is spurred on by the thought of the summit. And there is no easier way. Religion is not going to stop a war, and the Christian moral code was never intended for this technical age. It will be even more out of place when man not only changes his environment but also, by his knowledge of genetics, begins to change himself. No wonder, then, that any news of a notable advance in science, from whatever quarter it comes, is received with a firm satisfaction. Political issues are secondary. What matters is the continual reassurance that science retains its power to transform human existence and that this power is gathering in momentum. Religion? Why mention it? It is no longer relevant! And if there is much talk of a religious revival, it is because eddies always make more disturbance when the current is strong.[70]

To this extended humanist manifesto I think a preliminary response ought to be one of critical evaluation, after careful examination and reflection. A number of exceptions may reasonably be taken to the affirmations and negations of secular humanism, and an effort should be made to correct certain distortions and errors of fact in the image of Christian faith against which the entire statement is aimed. One may note in particular the tendentious character, the indulgence in exaggeration and overgeneralization, of much of the statement. The lines along which a sober and calm criticism might be constructed may be indicated in the following four basic points: (1) There is a running confusion of alleged sociological fact with hard, theoretical, objective invalidation: it is asserted gratuitously that a theistic religious world-view has been discarded by those who actively pursue and promote the modern scientific-technological disciplines, but there is no shred of proof that the truths and values of this contemporary mentality and purpose cancel out religion. (2) It is simply not the case that the dignity attributed to man within a religious perspective is essentially relative to or dependent upon the position assigned him within the spatio-temporal cosmos. Neither evolutionary descent nor the indefinite expansion of the physical universe's dimensions substantially affect man's status as created and redeemed by God, the true source of his ultimate value and reason for his self-esteem. (3) There is a curious but not untypical shift from the realm of moral probity to that of material well-being and improvement. It is fallacious to take this tack while pretending to uphold ethical standards on secular human- ist grounds, but one should allow in this connection, that this fallacy is not characteristic of the best or most representative humanist thinking. It is not among the best-informed and most enlightened humanists that one finds the strongest support for that facile optimis- tic materialism which is as much at home with a superficial and debased religiosity as it is with a shallow and opportunist atheism which has actually substituted a wholly immanent idol for the God of faith. (4) The statement emphasizes the element of risk and adventure in unbelief, compensating for the smugness apparent in the preceding paragraph, but it implies that the faith option, the religious attitude, allows man to escape risk and adventure, which is contrary to fact. St. Thomas Aquinas stresses repeatedly the paradoxical coexistence of certainty and uncertainty which constitutes the psychological condition of the believer. Today the soil of belief, the cultural ambience in which it must be professed and lived, lacks almost completely a common theological language or religious community.[71] Faith always entails risk, a leap beyond oneself to respond to God's grace when the grace is perceived, if that word be allowed, as only the faintest glimmer.

It is important to get straight what distinguishes the religious from the non-religious, secular humanist mentality, to avoid a confusion which reduces the religious to a species of humanist and the humanist to a kind of religious outlook. It seems unhelpful to call religious a sense of awe at what a man feels is greater or better than himself, together with a horror at the desecration of nature and humanity. The humanist may, however, regard Christianity as a historical transition between the theism of pagan antiquity and the new, post-religious ethos. His complaint centers on the a priori and arbitrary nature of the Christian ideal for human aspiration, a blueprint imposed once for all and *ab extra*, pre-empting man's need and right to lay down his own ideals. The theme of humani- zation, of the process whereby man makes himself and his world, has begun to receive serious attention from theologians. A point of fundamental controversy is the traditional Christian insistence that the ideal of humanity is given, revealed by the Bible and Church tradition, to which absolute primacy must be accorded. The theolo- gian is justified, as this point, in demurring at the contrast of the alleged monolithic and exclusive ideals set up by faith and the tolerant and experimental approach inculcated by an enlightened humanism. If one draws the line, however, between religion and irreligion on the basis of love of and reverence for human life, then humanism would come down on the side of religion, while some Christians, whose God seems little more than a projection of their fear of and repressive attitude toward themselves and their fellows, are veritable idolaters.

The humanist believes that holy things should not be treated without feeling, but he does not find anything objectively holier than man himself, holy both in what he is and for what he is capable of becoming. Religion, he believes, has been all too ready to ask man to sacrifice himself to an abstraction. Humanism, it is admitted, is exposed to the danger of sacrificing present men for the sake of the future; man as such, all men, therefore, are precious. The humanist still presses the charge that transcendent theism can support only a heteronomous morality and man's subservience to something distinct from himself. Karl Barth has exposed the liberal theology which so identified divinity with humanity at its highest power that nothing but the traditional language of religion remained, clothing a crypto-humanism which makes man at his best the proper object of devotion. The humanist, of course, welcomes the support of muddle-headed theologians and preachers whose motto seems to be accommodation at any price. Humanists have, in recent years, celebrated, sometimes ironically and even cynically, what one of their number has called the 'return of Moses the Raven': '. . . reversing that proverb about rats deserting sinking ships: if you saw a body of wise old rats, experienced in the ways of ships of state, swimming *towards* one of them instead of away from it, you would be entitled to judge that ship A–1 at Lloyds. Well, brothers, they are coming our way; humanists and anti-clerical though some of us may be, let us hasten to pipe them aboard. For their instinct for joining the side which is shortly going to be the dispenser of good things, the tenant of the throne, is infallible; and the history of the last 50 years has shown clearly that although some of the people can dispense with opium, many cannot.'[72]

Thomas Merton makes the wise observation: 'whether or not "the world" is a problem, *a confused idea of what the world might possibly be* is quite definitely a problem.' He adds that the confusion is on the way to being dispelled when one distinguishes the world as an object of choice, and the world as something about which there is and can be no choice.[73] The world is a problem only in the sense that everyone in it is a problem to himself, which adds up to a collective of self-doubting and clashing freedoms. Nothing has been more of a barrier to the realization of an authentic concept of Christian humanism than the hovering image of a sacred and hierarchical cosmos in which everything is decided beforehand and in which the only choice is to accept gladly what is imposed as part of an immobile and established structure, social as well as natural. Theologians reject this antiquated view but have thus far not made much headway in replacing it with one that is applicable and realistic. As part of the task of meeting the challenge of unbelief, the theologian must examine in all candor and without recourse to irrelevant abstractions the key contention of secular humanism, that man can live an honorable and satisfying life and achieve a reasonable measure of happiness without reference to God. The conventional religious claim that without divine revelation and grace men do not understand their own happiness well enough to be capable of laying down principles for its achievement is dismissed as the silliest and most maddening of all the usual religious objections to humanism. It is at least doubtful that intelligent, sensitive men are going to admit the necessity or desirability of religious faith on the ground that the latter provides an exact specification of the material states which conduce to the greatest happiness, is capable of enumerating happy states and contrasting them with unhappy ones, and is not appreciably enlightened or helped by the kind of massive, complex analyses *de fine ultimo*, *de beatitudine*, etc., which transport the bewildered mortal into a realm worlds removed from that in which life is lived. Whatever the objective validity of questions about what happiness in itself may be, further theological excursions into the depths of analytical subtlety and obscurity are unlikely to contribute positively to a Christian understanding of the world and man's destiny.

Concentrating on the task of living can persuade one that, whether He exists or not, God is irrelevant to man's purpose, that he can dispense with the question of ultimate end and make do with prospects and resources at hand or within his grasp. Christian theology, it is asserted, has perpetuated the believer's naive assumption that unbelief strips a man of hope and comfort. In *Flight*, John Updike rejects this attitude. '. . . how touchingly gauche our assumption was that an atheist is a lonely rebel; for mobs of men are united in atheism, and oblivion—the dense lead-like sea that would occasionally sweep over me—is to them a weight as negligible as the faint pressure of their wallets in their hip pockets.'[74] If the traditional structures of faith—church, worship, prayer, Christ—neither frighten nor fascinate great masses of people any longer, still it cannot be easily assumed that they are therefore without the motive or strength

D

to try to live meaningfully. The humanist declines, sometimes indignantly, the suggestion that men will perish in despair, unless faith helps them to smooth life out, to alleviate the terror, remove the shame, resolve the confusion. Job may be as much a hero to the courageous secularist as he is supposed to be to the believer, because he was sickened by the silly comfort men tried to make out of fake answers and rejected a divine protector of privilege and prejudice. The prospects for a viable and convincing Christian humanism hinge largely on the believer's ability and willingness to bring into resonance with this world a faith that is humane and humanizing. The alternatives are an inhumane religion or an irreligious humanism.

It has been noted that secular humanists find man lovable in purely human categories, without recourse to divine creation or redemption. The question is put: does Christian faith offer as profound a notion of love as secular humanism? And it may be taken as a crucial test of the worthwhileness of putting together the elements of a Christian humanism. The charge has to be met that the Christian ideal of love is purely formalist, extrinsicist, life-denying, protective in the sense of smothering initiative and free experimentation, passionless and other-worldly. As I have said before, the new humanist does not reject Christian moral standards in order to follow a line of least resistance and heedless self-indulgence, but precisely because he believes that humanism offers more by which men can effectively be true to themselves than does religion. Is it the case, as has been claimed, that of late the secular humanist, rather than the theologian or religious writer, has explored most tellingly and sensitively the depths of human existence and concern, life and death, love and hope?[75] Surveying the past two centuries of Western culture, one discerns a decrease of specifically Christian contribution to man's progressive understanding and mastery of himself and his world. Religious thought has constantly been characterized by an openness in which all things are held in an infinite transcendence and nothing is self-sufficient. The transcendent element, it is claimed, intrudes into the newly realized relationships of man and the world, one of free inquiry and a practical concern for the betterment of mankind. The making of excuses for past failures on the part of the Church is unimpressive to those who deplore the lack of initiative or support for the major cultural developments of the past two hundred years. The quarrel is not merely with believers, who, after all, are fallible and limited human beings, not alone in their obscurantism or reaction, but with the essence of Christianity, which is other-worldly and world-despising. Any future humanism will insist on values and structures totally immanent in the human condition, rejecting out of hand the 'If God is dead, everything is permitted' of Dostoevsky's atheist.

Human values have been promoted by the Church, it is admitted, but only by appealing to supernatural motivation, the lure of eternal reward or the threat of eternal punishment. This appeal is under threefold attack, as linguistically meaningless, morally degrading, and psychologically or pragmatically irrelevant and ineffective. Adult maturity and integrity are defined in terms of an individual's capacity to operate increasingly in virtue of motives intrinsically value-laden and self-justifying, meaningful in their own right and not merely or primarily by reason of extrinsic denomination or approval from above. It is a question of recognizing and safeguarding the pursuit of truth for its own sake, in response to genuine questions to which answers fabricated and 'authorized' beforehand are not, however surreptitiously, already available and beyond criticism. Does faith or the theological mentality encourage a man to work productively, to love his work, because it expresses his own personality and affords him immediate, palpable satisfaction? Psychologists hold that the degree to which an adult is capable of living realistically and happily in the present, even under trying or frustrating circumstances, is an important index of mental and emotional health. That religious faith or its distorted substitute may present as an alternative a future that is humanly alienating and motivationally abstract, something suited to those not emotionally secure enough to live realistically, is not a recommendation.[76]

A far-reaching theological re-examination is called for, to determine if, and to what extent, Christian faith has the power to guide mature men and women in the direction of those values and structures productive of the future. The issue is seen to be as practical as it is speculative; it is a pragmatic question in a perfectly legitimate sense, one that raises the prospects for living by faith in the world that has come into being and is being progressively appropriated by those who are also responsible for its construction. It may well be disclosed both that religious faith is relevant only minimally and remotely, if at all, to some of the major tasks involved in world-building and that, in ways not previously suspected, or only partially and imperfectly understood, faith may deliver spiritual and moral resources without which the most prosperous and successful life is an empty and hollow existence. Pragmatic tests are foreign, even repulsive, only to a theological mind which castigates them peremptorily as superficial, and sees theology's chief concern in theoretical nicety and dogmatic orthodoxy rather than effective religious value. There has been not too much concern over theoretical exactness, for that in itself is not bad, but an appalling unconcern for the relevance to actual Christian life, in the world of the twentieth century, of doctrinal constructs into which everything seems to have been infused but a comprehensive grasp of that life which, according to St. Thomas Aquinas, doctrine ought to serve. There is no other verification in this world of the faith men profess than the quality and meaningfulness of the kind of life that faith inspires or ought to. If I have belabored this point, it is not only because I am convinced that it is absolutely essential to the development of a sound Christian humanism, but also because theologians in the past have not sufficiently recognized that statements without reference to experience of any kind are meaningless.[77]

Indispensable to a theology of temporal values is an indication of where God or Christ enters man's life and demands the commitment to ultimate values which marks a line of distinction between simple belief and living faith. Theology must be more than transcendental, personalist, and existential, although it must be all of these; too great stress on the present moment limits faith and loses sight of the sweeping temporal dimension in which personal decision is touched by the past and moves toward the future. The modern mentality is primarily operative, not contemplative, that is to say, fundamentally oriented toward the future. Theology cannot sustain an image of the world as an imposed fate or a sacred order given from above; there will be no Christian world-understanding save of our experience of raw material with which we can build our own new world. Nor can the Christian humanist distinguish himself from the secularist solely by reason of a different theory of the nature and destiny of man and reality in general; he must know what it means, concretely and in practice, to say that Christ lives in him. An answer to this question may be worked out in terms of what it means to be personally present to one another.[78] Those who have never significantly achieved this presence, who have been alone, even in a crowd or in what should be the most intimate and endearing interrelationships, hardly know what the experience of genuine community, of love and friendship, which are at the heart of God's seizing man and revealing Himself, consists of. In very simple and not fanciful terms, a premise of Christian humanism will be the power of the Gospel, of faith in the word of God, to lead men out of a vague shallowness and the loneliness which leads to so much desperate action in the world. Even those who are able to communicate on a deeply personal level remain disturbed by further questions concerning the meaning of the human condition, in which communication is so difficult, even for the most fortunate, and in which some men find a reasonable happiness while others are left miserably troubled and lonely.

The humanist rejects religion as unnecessary, however useful or satisfying to those unable to find life worthwhile in its own right. But one's own life may know sufficient fulfillment, a happiness which makes it emotionally acceptable, and still fail to find ultimate meaning in the face of suffering and death. If, as we believe, it is precisely to this kind of question that God speaks to us in Christ, uniquely and in power, then it is in these terms that we must demonstrate the relevance and viability today of Christian humanism. Let those who believe in Christ understand that proclaiming Him as living in them involves a presence that is ineradicable, that they are not and never will be completely alone. One may find it impossible to put unqualified trust in any man; this does not make such trust unrealistic, for one can place it in God, encountered in prayer, confident that He wants man's friendship and will never abandon him. A humanism that ministers thus to the profound need for certain and complete interpersonal communication effects an experience of redemption that reveals unfathomable depths. Mercy and faithfulness enter man's existence when he accepts God's invitation to turn to Him, lets down his defenses, and opens himself to the divine presence. Humanism is Christian only if its roots are in prayer and interpersonal communion, inspired by faith as a free response to God's own initiative. This faith is then experienced as being saved from radical loneliness and for personal communication and a fulfillment that is already under way.[79]

In this light the world, its values and its history, is taken with utmost seriousness by a faith in a transcendence that redeems us for, and not from, commitment to the enrichment of present experience. It is a faith within history, not fearful or anxious but hopeful about the present, and one which points up the importance of witness. A Christian communicates his faith primarily through the way he lives and only secondarily through what he professes to believe, not only because theory never exhausts reality but because man must act before he can adequately develop a theory. The world is well advised to pray only if those who do pray communicate a joy and a strength which nothing else can give. The trust and force of Christian humanism are utterly voided, however grandiose the doctrinal scheme invoked in its support, if the lives of professed believers are dishonest, emotionally attached to convictions which cannot withstand scrutiny, and apparently no better than those who deny the reality of God. Our contemporaries are perhaps more sensitive than ever to the emptiness of inauthentic and humanly inoperative motives, which makes credible witness all the more imperative, even if all the Christian is asking for is a hearing. Gary Schouberg concludes his essay on faith and humanism by noting that: 'Unfortunately, many Christians have abused the hearing given them and wasted the time of people who trusted them enough to listen to what they had to say. For that reason, it is quite understandable that many people today listen to Christians with only the slightest patience and greatest skepticism. The Christian's life must be humanly believable so that he will be given the hearing necessary for him to communicate what he really believes. Only until such communication is achieved can Christ through human history confront the non-Christian in his most radical selfhood and invite him to follow him.'[80]

This witness will operate in a historical situation in which man has all but contemplated the transition from a divinized, or sacral, to a humanized, or secular, world. Man's orientation to the future and his understanding of the world as history marks a shift from a cosmocentric to an anthropocentric viewpoint and finds an echo in the Biblical belief in the promises of God. Pre-modern experience largely locked man within a world permeated with strong religious overtones, in which God's presence and power are felt everywhere and at every level of existence. Today nature is no longer rigidly categorized or arranged in a so-called hierarchical order of objective values; the unity and significance of the world are imposed by man, not *ex nihilo* of course, but along with the humanization built into his surroundings by man himself. If the pre-modern world was numinized, as Johannes Metz says, then the recently continuingly humanized world looks 'de-numinized,' which means both that God seems absent and the world seems closed in upon itself.[81] When God is not seen, readily and meaningfully, in nature or in the events of history, has man become atheistic, as some think? Faith is undoubtedly challenged by the important forms of theoretical unbelief which claim to express most accurately the important dimensions of this new experience. It is by no means clear, however, that theocentrism, as man's recognition of the primacy of God, is irreconcilable with an anthropocentrism which consists in the recognition of the world as an arising and not a static reality and of man as freely committed to its alteration and innovation in his own interest.

There are insights of faith which serve a Christian humanism by suggesting and promoting the humanism of the world, that external and social aspect which complements the experience of community, of security in the friendship of God, which is its subjective aspect. Faith in the absolutely transcendent God is precisely what liberates man from any sort of bondage to the world and inspires a certain and militant eschatology.[82] The Christian's responsibility for the world stems from its initial secularization, and the latter is simply man's coming to the awareness of the non-divine nature of things, that they are there for man to know and understand and use. Christian detachment, and even renunciation, are legitimate and valuable, not as an expression of contempt or a failure to appreciate the world, but to the extent that they emphasize man's hope in the world's future as proclaimed in God's promises. Without this faith and hope it is easy to apotheosize the world, whereas it must be re-created and purified to prepare it for the final advent of the Kingdom of God. Each man in faith stands assured of the incomparable individuality of his personal existence and freedom, and for the first time, no matter what his talents or opportunity, limitations or defects. The Incarnation not only revealed God to man in definitive and historical terms; it also revealed man to himself and delivered the commission to undertake the humanization of a world already redeemed. As such, then, the process of secularization presents the kind of challenge that imposes or illumines a task rather than poses a threat, although there is, as always, considerable risk and no results guaranteed beforehand.

In virtue of the very real progress theology has made recently, in an effort to come to terms with the world-historical demands of faith and the religious life, the most pressing present danger is to canonize the concrete process of humanization, to bow before the world, in Jacques Maritain's scornful phrase. Even worse would be the complacency in an order or an ongoing and complex endeavor as though it were the definitive achievement of civilization. A balance can be maintained, in principle at least, if it is kept in mind that a world on the way to being humanized is not structurally less Christian than earlier world configurations or situations. It should not still be necessary to expose the myth that a theocratic arrangement, in which even secular life is closely bound up with the fortunes of religion, represents an order closer to that living realization of the meaning of God in the world toward which faith is ever striving. One of the principal accomplishments of a Christian

humanism will be to show the connection between the spirit of
faith and the humanization of the world. Above all it must be seen
that the place of faith is not the non-world; it is, rather, that part of
the world in which man strives to live from the promised future of God
and to call that other part of the world to question which seeks to
live within its own limited possibilities, closed to transcendence.
That is why believers form a pilgrim or exodus community, celebrating Christ's death and resurrection until He comes. Faith, or
rather religion, is not the goal of its own activity: this goal is the
Kingdom of God, even now coming into existence, of which the
faith-life is the unique sign and instrument.[83]

As man turns increasingly from what has proved to be largely
fruitless speculation to intense concern with practical and constructive work, so theology seeks to be both personalist and existential and, in the sense explicated by Metz, political and social.
A Christian hope, directed essentially to the world of brothers and
fulfilling itself in love for the least of these, means that humanization
need not be claimed as a future for unbelief, although the prospect,
or perhaps only the fear, thereof may force the believer to reflect
and to reform. Nor does humanization, as man's persevering effort
to discover his own identity and to actualize his potential by making
his world more livable and responsive to his needs, receive an accurate or adequate interpretation in the Marxist doctrine of man's own
self-creation in history, a confused and grossly unsophisticated
concept. Through its de-idolization of the world, it is Christianity
which has occasioned a death of god, of the false and empty god
Pan on the world horizon. The believer is not thereby automatically
and totally relieved of all perplexity or of all passion and suffering.
Perplexity there will be, in part at least because the classic molds
in which self-understanding has long been frozen have not yet been
broken by theology, and a new way is not yet marked out. Theologians
are even less at ease than other men in the presence of perplexity,
but they must assist in setting up the signposts and constructing
the language for a new Christian humanism.

Faith brings courage and the conviction that the experience
of the new world will disclose not a future of unbelief but one to
which belief in God may be supremely relevant. If the world situation
drives home to an enlightened faith that all of life is limited and
limiting, it will be a lesson well learned. Certain features of a humanized world stand out as particularly important for the possibility
of deepening and broadening the experience of faith. A world that
is unprecedentedly pluralistic, in man's understanding as well as

socially, can never be reduced to a perfectly manageable unity, controlled and appreciated, a priori, by dogmatic or theological categories.[84] The obscurity of faith extends to creation as such, to the world and man redeemed by grace, no less than to the Creator and Redeemer Himself. The patient acceptance of faith, intimately bound up with the impossibility of comprehending everything, will prevent religion from becoming an agnosticism of overweening pride and pretentiousness. The secularist professes confidence in the brave new world of a future without God, but the pathetic sense of oppressiveness and confusion, of abandonment to forces aroused by man's own folly and perversity, can leave man open to God, the invincible, free, and sovereign future of man, as He is called. When this world is stripped of wonder and mystery, the secularization can condition man for a more just estimate of the event of absolute revelation in its singular and eschatological definitiveness. Under the aegis of faith and hope, humanization does not threaten but opens man to his brother and reveals that this brother, rather than brute nature, is the true center of his experience of the numinous. Not only is his eternal salvation affected by his concept of and attitude toward the world, but what he believes or does not believe determines whether humanization situates him before God or shuts him off from the transcendent mystery of unity and fullness.

One may say a great deal, in fact, about the worldly character of faith and the humanizing potential of grace, but there is another side to the coin with which a Christian humanism must be purchased. The unnatural concentration of religion into one place and one set of special words, ideas, and feelings has created an artificial situation in which, as it were, the believer finds himself posing and gesturing before a mirror. The point has been made, I trust, that the proper milieu of religion is the world, because it is God's world. Thus Buber: 'Only he who believes in the world is given power to enter into dealings with it, and if he gives himself to this he cannot remain godless. If only we love the real world, that will not let itself be extinguished, really in its horror, if only we venture to surround it with the arms of our spirit, our hands will meet hands that grip them. I know nothing of a "world" and a "life in the world" that might separate a man from God. What is thus described is actually life with an alienated world.'[85] But the really hard thing for a world-affirming man to swallow is expressed in the words of Rudolf Bultmann: '... The grace of God is not visible like worldly entities. His treasures are hidden in earthly vessels (2 Cor 4.7). The resurrection life is manifested in the world in the guise of death (2 Cor 12.9).

Only in human weakness is the power of God made known.'[86] Of course one is quick to see the absurdity of a faith which is so invisible that it makes no difference, and is simply conformed in every respect to the ordinary world. But the manifestation of faith is dialectical not simple: the expectation of a series of miracles, whose origin is the direct effect of faith and whose consequence is the empirical establishment of the truth of faith, is a desire for a mythological and undialectical substitute for faith and its works. The thoroughly paradoxical nature of the existence of the man of faith is disclosed when this question of the manifestation of faith, its empirical or phenomenal indices, is asked. The answer has a crucial bearing on the concept of a Christian humanism and its viability in face of the challenge of unbelief.

It is impossible to reduce the manifestation of faith to a formula, an impossibility notoriously ignored by those who speak so blithely and exclusively of 'being for others' and the like. Even the self-giving of Christ Himself, the model of our life in faith, remains ambiguous in the sense at least that at no point does His life *impose* its truth upon others. In this restraint the paradoxical nature of the end of all human life in Christ is disclosed, the eschatological reality of Christ as the Word made flesh. When we ask for or about the manifestation of faith, we are not entitled to look for a simple, directly observable state of being or affairs; we cannot make a catalogue of possible manifestations by means of which the humanist relevance of faith might be judged. Faith is active primarily in the perpetual tension of man's relation with God, and in this tension it is renewed, against all appearances. The solidity of faith is established in the midst of the temptations and tribulations which are integral to life and in the face also of the doubt which is the permanent other side of faith, as an ever provisional, makeshift, uncertain and struggling certainty. From the standpoint of the believer, the issue or fruit of faith is love in hope, but from the standpoint of the grace of God which constitutes faith and makes it possible, you can neither prove nor disprove faith. This is true not only of the individual's faith but also of the expressions or deposits of faith as they may be found in history.

Christian humanism is a partial but extremely important answer to the contention that the world of the future belongs to unbelief and to the spirit which rejects God and the transcendent as inhuman and alienating. The life of faith is situated squarely in this world and is for the sake of the world, or it is nothing but pharisaical, smug complacency. A final word of caution is in order, however, to keep the project of Christian humanism from floundering on a mistaken notion of what the world is, to which our good intentions are to be directed. We may have allowed ourselves to be mesmerized by the world's own self-advertisement, which is designed to boost its morale, as all boastfulness is. We have taken at their face value the claims of self-sufficiency, self-confidence, optimism, and Nietzschean superiority that the world (as articulated by its intellectuals and propagandists) has put forward. The world has, in spite of all its vaunted self-congratulation, been visited by the Spirit who moves where He will, so that many who have no allegiance to, or even conscious awareness of, the Christian message have at least become very clearly aware of the futility and pathos of the secular city's boastful self-justification. They are saying that this bland, confident society that has no need of God is sick, rotting, and desperate. It is to this cry that the would-be Christian humanist should pay attention and not waste his time trying to make his faith over to please the secular world. The young people in a godforsaking world may have something to teach us because they have been most acutely and tragically aware of the evil in that world.[87] So much of what is called Christianity is mixed up with what they recognize as despicable worldliness, cynicism, and selfishness; yet to this known situation they strenuously bring a generous love that can endure rejection and suspicion. The world proclaims that it does not need the Gospel, to which the real answer is: 'Behold, I am with you always.'

Religious Indifference

Indifference to religious matters is the single most formidable challenge to the effective witness of faith and the theological understanding of the mystery of unbelief. It is clear, as St. Paul indicates, that one cannot believe unless he hears the Gospel preached, but it is no less evident that the good news of salvation cannot be communicated to those who will not listen. It is extraordinarily difficult to assemble all the materials for a theology of indifference to religion, partly because this is a personal and social phenomenon not yet sufficiently analyzed and partly because, of its nature, indifference is negative, inarticulate, amorphous, and diffusely vague. The temptation will be to characterize it, wrongly, but for the purpose of more precise analysis, as explicit and self-assertive, whereas for the most part it represents a lack, an absence, a lacuna in the lives of people, not the turning against but the turning away from something or, more accurately, the turning toward something else instead. I should like to suggest guidelines for serious theological inquiry into this problem, first by situating it in the general context of man's search for meaning and then by identifying specific factors in contemporary life which define this search in such a way that God seems to be simply out of the picture, not so much deliberately and positively excluded as left out in fact. A reorientation will be called for, in thinking about unbelief, a shift from the concept of atheism as the denial of God, and of anti-theism as opposition to God, and of infidelity as the rejection or renunciation of faith to that of non-belief as the failure to consider seriously the question of belief or unbelief.[88]

Man is the animal who asks questions, but he does not always realistically expect an answer to every question and, indeed, he can hardly expect one in every instance. At the outset one very important distinction must be made, one which will be clarified and illustrated in the course of our inquiry. It is a distinction which, however necessary, at first complicates and obscures as much as it throws light on realities which ought not to be confused. Religion and God must never be simply identified or made equivalent to each other; there are two questions here actually, not unrelated but not the same: indifference to religion and indifference to God. I include both, indiscriminately, but the more fundamental, vastly more significant, is the latter. God is God; religion is man's relationship with Him, a relationship entered into more or less consciously and deliberately, even when the concept of God is almost totally distorted and inadequate. My primary concern is with the question of indifference to God, recognizing that this will involve, at certain points, attitudes toward and estimates of the value and importance of religion.

No definitive answer is possible to the question whether people are in fact seeking God, thinking about Him, concerned with Him, for this touches that inner region of the heart which essentially, although not completely, escapes scrutiny. No one fully understands even himself in this regard, and what he claims to know, he cannot fully verify: he stands judged by Another. Still less can anyone pass judgment on whether other people are, or are not, earnestly searching for that union with God which is the soul of religion. Our problem is a real one, a fact of the concrete lives of men and women, yet we can deal with it best in terms which leave its living reality still largely buried in the secret of the inner self, which only God penetrates. Later I shall address myself to that aspect of the problem which is immeasurably more open to observation and critical evaluation, and that is indifference to religion. One is a most elusive and intimate phenomenon (strictly speaking, not a phenomenon at all), the other has ostensible public and social overtones, it is patently behavioral.

Statistics and sociological estimates and impressions fall abysmally short of answering the question whether God is still an active force in the lives of individuals, if only in the sense that man is breaking through involvement with self as the beginning and end of existence. The staggering growth of atheism on a world scale still does not reveal the extent to which unbelief has captured the hearts of our contemporaries, or whether what has been latent and insufficiently observed for centuries has only become more visible and assertive. Ideas which were once the principles of bold non-conformists, held clandestinely by an elite, have now succeeded in informing actively the lives and decisions of large masses. We are more keenly aware, moreover, of the innumerably greater masses, with whom we live in one world, who have never come within the ambit of Christianity or heard the Gospel preached in a meaningful way. The pagan is among us, as well, and to him the question of making a choice for or against faith is of no real importance. To many people the alleged power of God appears to be a perverse and contradictory name for powerlessness, as the world goes on, pursuing its inexorable course. Politics, social life in general, is deaf in a new way to the question of God; the influence of Christian ethics has waned, and religious considerations are simply irrelevant. It is not at all certain, I repeat, that it was quite otherwise in former times, when Christianity occupied a position of external influence and domination. Historical comparison suggests, in fact, that the problem of determining the shape or extent of religious indifference in this age may be more complex and difficult than one may have imagined.

The history of thought is more readily traced when it is available in written works, fictional and non-fictional, and this history suggests that the search for God has had a larger place than some Christian critics have been willing to allow. Here, especially, statistics are of little help, when so many people, and not only those living under a dictatorship where atheism is the state ideology, conceal their true attitude toward the question of God. Beneath an uninterrupted silence about this matter, there may be very strong feelings, pro and con, feelings which remain impervious to the diagnoses of spiritual-cultural historians, such as Spengler and Toynbee, Jung and Jaspers. It is far from proved that mounting technical and industrial progress inevitably diminishes man's contact with his inner self and destroys that sensitivity without which the inner life withers and dies. It is entirely possible that men are already turning more intently toward an intimate contact with their inner selves and the realm of the spirit. Man can refuse to submit to collectivization and persist in thinking for himself, in questioning his beginning and his end and extending his questioning even beyond. However reduced his field of action, man can still inquire after meaning and exert his freedom of choice. He can, by the same token, live for the day—or possibly for tomorrow—and limit his curiosity, content to take life as it comes and death when it comes. To many of our contemporaries the better part of wisdom is to avoid final questions; their pursuit is burdensome and discomfiting and does not seem to terminate in clear and positive understanding. Theologians have perhaps underestimated the influence gained steadily over a period of at least two centuries by the empiricist restrictions on the scope and depth of knowledge.[89] This as well as the other factors I have mentioned can provide support to a will to indifference, and religious indifference, where it does flourish, constitutes an acute and particularly insidious form of present-day unbelief.

By definition, indifference is neither articulate at the level of doctrinal formulation nor aggressive at the level of practical action. Those who ignore religion and rarely think or do anything about God, His existence, or the possibility of knowing Him, are neither militant nor intrusive, so that theologians hardly know how to deal with them in terms of analysis and understanding, and those with the care of souls are at a loss to deal with them in terms of preaching and pastoral concern. For the indifferent the problem of God is drained of urgency and consistency: it does not demand serious attention because its implications are so remote to the business of getting on in this world as to be of no consequence. God's absence is even more total and uncompromised than in the case of the most violently self-assertive atheism. We are here very close to that accidie, or lack of taste for spiritual things, which usually includes an unconcern for any high ethical ideals or values. I can think of nothing more impervious to dialogue with religious interests or less accessible to the reach of religious propaganda and efforts at evangelization. The very language of religion, about God and the categories in which men attempt to describe their relationship with Him, are lost on the man whose sights are fixed rigidly on a world from which all reference to God is effectively blotted out. The outright atheist returns answers diametrically opposed to those of the believer, but at least they share a common problematic and respond to the same basic questions.

Religious indifference today is a phenomenon of world civilization, significant for its wide extent as well as for its connection with certain outstanding features of modern life and thought.[90] The Vatican Council declared, it will be recalled, that the denial of God and religion or the ignoring of them is no longer unusual or remarkable but often taken for granted as bound up with the demands of the new humanism and of scientific enlightenment. This negative posture affects not only the speculations of philosophers but has infiltrated the arts and literature, the interpretation of history, and the field of jurisprudence. The degree to which so many minds are attracted by a way of life which dispenses altogether with the search for God is a clue to the depth to which this situation is rooted in major trends and tendencies of our culture. Giulio Girardi adds the observation that the phenomenon of indifference and the problems it raises cannot be confined to the psychological and sociological order, that 'it is related to a certain philosophical and theological image of religion, to which by that very fact it is a challenge.'[91] There is an obvious link between this problem and what is usually called practical atheism, a reminder that indifference ranges across a spectrum of possibilities, from the complete absence of all concern to the low-keyed assent to the idea of religion that entails nothing in the way of spiritual substance or moral commitment. The immediate task of religious leaders is to understand the various manifestations of indifference, distinguishing it from cognate but divergent attitudes and tracing it to its principal causes. On this foundation the renewal of religious faith and the life of the believing community may be directed toward an active search for the attention and respect of those whose expectations have thus far not been met by what the churches have had to offer. At the least we may discover why it is that some men 'never even raise questions about God, since they never seem to feel any religious disquiet or see why they should bother about religion.' So much religious discourse is wasted on those who 'make so much of man that all vitality is taken out of faith in God.' The autonomy of man inspires in the systematic atheist a contempt for faith in the Lordship of a transcendent God or at least renders that faith superfluous.

In the first century before Christ, Lucretius wrote six books in an attempt to convince men that they were free of the power of gods and could live unconcerned with them. Lucretius contended that the gods haven't the slightest contact with the world and with men; hence men should forget about them and concentrate on the world of natural causes and events. One should not be afraid to take this stand toward religion, he advised, for religion itself has done far more harm than good, and as long as it interferes in human thinking and decision-making, man cannot live in peace and reason and freedom. This advice, repeated and re-enforced by generations and generations of Western secularists and naturalists, has become the way of life assumed without question by people in every stratum of contemporary society. The religious dimension makes no impact, has no point of entry, in the experience of persons for whom God, whether He exists or not, is not a value and does not count, one way or the other. The kind of argument, of reasoning, apologists use to defend and promote the claims of faith fails to breach a mentality and feeling-complex the essential affirmation of which is that the question of God is simply not interesting, When religious indifference is not only a matter of personal experience but an element of the social situation, everything transpires and is interpreted as if God mattered not in the least. The difference between practical atheism and religious indifferences lies in the theoretical affirmation of God by the former and the failure of the latter to adopt any position on the objective question. In the religious sphere, where man makes those profound decisions which give spiritual and moral quality and direction to his life, this difference is meaningless and insignificant.

I have noted that indifference to God is not wholly reducible to indifference to religion; the two may be compared. The problem may be not that God is uninteresting or without importance but that those through whom He speaks, or rather who claim to speak for Him, are unattractive and unconvincing as human beings. The responsibility of Christians for the prevalence of unbelief has been noted by the Second Vatican Council. The complacency of the unbeliever, his indifference to religious values, is an appropriate, or at least an understandable, reaction to the uninspiring and even disedifying example of those who claim supreme importance for these values. The pretensions of Christians are lofty, but their lives are not conspicuously free of ambition and ruthlessness, selfishness, smugness, self-justification, and dishonesty. The unbeliever need not insist that the faithful are worse than others; it is enough that he finds them no better. He may go further and claim to find more of the virtue so highly prized by Christians in unbelievers, the most militant atheists, than in those who believe their lives are supernaturally energized by grace. It may be faulty logic to infer the absence of God from the weakness of those who believe He is near, but it is psychologically almost inevitable: what sense can be made of a God whom men declare to be close and infinitely concerned, but who is nowhere to be found in a world turned upside down? Anthropomorphism springs from the original concoction of a God made to man's own image; once this has been done, those who still find meaning or satisfaction in the God they have confected shed the responsibility of full humanity and take refuge in the idol. Once the projection of ideals and aspirations of an age or culture becomes a substitute for reality, it is only to be expected that a later age, and another culture with different ideals, will reject this projection. Religious indifference today is, almost certainly, partially a reaction to what is judged to be an antiquated and highly anthropomorphic image of God, as difficult to believe in as the image of human nature, which has long been discarded.[92]

At this level the problem of unbelief comes down to the question whether the God men are asked to believe in is believable, that is, whether belief in such a God would be a significant or rewarding human attitude. When the answer is in the negative, it is not difficult to see that indifference might be adopted as morally superior and intellectually imperative—Ludwig Feuerbach remarked that today's atheism is tomorrow's religion. The most drastic error religionists could make in this connection would be to read disinterest in religion as ethical callousness or an aversion to all spiritual values. It is wise to keep track of the positive motivation which is not entirely lacking even in the most capricious disinclination to consider the question of God, for this negative posture cannot fully explain the phenomenon. Except in the case of perfect accidie or anomie, no one is completely devoid of value-appropriation, so that religious indifference must be explained also by the values to which the individual is sensitive. The situation is almost invariably bi-polar; secular, anthropocentric values move in where there is a vacuum and absorb the indifferent man in various degrees. The values of greatest interest may be purely selfish, eudaemonist in a pejorative sense, a mere thirst for immediate satisfaction or the enjoyment of experiences without serious purpose. It may be that indifference to religion is a by-product of general value-insensitivity, but one may not presume that this is ordinarily the case. More usual is the absence of interest in religion due to a more or less passionate involvement with interests of an entirely different order. There is an enormous psychological and moral distance between religious faith and absolute indifference, much greater than that between faith in God and faith in secular values. The last-named may be concerned with theoretical principles or world-outlooks or may be relatively independent of ideological presuppositions.[93]

It has been a favorite tack of theological apologetics to seize
upon the 'immense longing' of the human heart to escape the great
sorrows and sufferings of life as a universal basis for the desire for
God. The argument has proceeded on the assumption that man will
not accept as a meaningless jest the whole of human history, with
its pain and anxiety, frustration and failure. A further assumption
is that men experience life as a question which outruns any answer
they ever find, a hope pitched higher than any concrete realization.
If the heart remains set on total security, it is asserted that religious
indifference snuffs out a fundamental natural urge, for a love that
endures, an unclouded happiness. A new and closer look ought to
be taken at the claim that religion corresponds to a longing that is
never fulfilled but stays with man whatever he may do and sets the
tone for every day of his life.[94] Nothing can satisfy him totally; there
is never a moment when he is fully content, and this is called the
marvelous tragedy of dissatisfaction. Indifference can only be shat-
tered if this, together with the experience of the joy of mutual fulfillment, is made to open on to wider perspectives. Both happiness and
sorrow should afford a hint of something beyond our finite bounds,
and one should not let the deep simplicity of the hope for something
better be argued away by superficial explanations that support
indifference by avoiding the level of this essential question. A shallow
and careless existence ignores the insistence of conscience that our
partial goodness calls for the reaching out of perfect good, our
feeble strength for the omnipotent. St. Paul makes it clear that reason
speaks out of the fullness of life, and that it is clouded not only by
personal sin but by environment, education, and psychological
structure. I doubt very much that men will feel any interest in
rational evidence before they have become familiar with the concrete
effects of faith in the lives of believers. The most profound questions
of existence are too great to be comprised within fixed formulas;
faith itself is betrayed and the infinity of God mocked when excessive
reliance is placed on the doctrinal elaborations by which orthodoxy is
preserved, while the transformation of life by grace is dimmed and
obscured.

The origins of religious indifference may be sought in those
situations whereby secular values acquire so great a power of at-
traction that the question of God ceases to be of concern. Man is
both diverted by the many immediate attractions of life in this world
of beauty and abundance, of intriguing mystery and beckoning
opportunity, and sorely distressed by the multiple dimensions of
evil, and from both sources he is fortified with sufficient reason to

concentrate his attention and energy on the demands of worldly existence. The worldwide objective character of this attitude is linked to several forces operative in our culture: the critical spirit, ideological pluralism, world unification, the existential impotence of religion, a sense of sober reality, and the historicity of truth. In short, the world is too much with us, while religion is powerless to enlighten, inspire, or move to action.

It remains to be seen whether, in the long run, or for how long, men can fill, more surely and efficiently, the role formerly played by God. Science more intelligibly explains natural phenomena than the occult causes of a debased pseudo-metaphysics or the deus ex machina of religious superstition. Technology, spurred on by a developed social conscience, is in a position to minister to man's need for security, liberating him increasingly from dependence on the providence of God. The coming of age of the world involves an emergence from tutelage to priests and self-appointed sages and the admission that secular institutions, resting only on man's intrinsic dignity, are palpably capable of undertaking the tasks traditionally entrusted to the ministers and works of religion. Religion's own claim to transcendence and other-worldliness apparently authorizes men to exclude it from the sphere of the secular. As Girardi puts it, on a deeper level, if God is habitually silent in history, is it surprising that man does not listen to Him?[95] Theologians will go a long way toward understanding religious indifference if they will re-examine closely the patterns and claims of unbelief. Consider, in sum, the eventual impact on religious sensibility of years and years in which the following working assumptions, pseudo-myths Adolfs calls them, attain the status of a prevailing ideology:

'With the help of work, science, and technology, mankind makes progress; progress is greater welfare; welfare is the consequence of satisfying our material needs; man's spiritual needs (culture and religion) must be looked after in the private sector of society; everything that cannot be looked after in the private sector and therefore threatens the smooth running of affairs in the public sector must be taken out of the hands of private initiative; time is money; money is power; success (financial, political or in one's career) means happiness; the best paid job is the best job; you must succeed in life, it doesn't matter how; all uncertainties must be eliminated; only useful things are good; too much speculation can be dangerous; *our* social system is good, etc.'[96]

Not all of these statements are problem-free or expressive of a crude and mindless optimism, but through all there breathes a

firm spirit of confidence in the resources of secular man to get
on with the business of living. Against this, and as a correlative
principle of contemporary religious indifference, there is the impotence or inefficacy, real and imagined, of Christianity, about which
much has been said, and there seems no end to the story. Disaffection from existing ecclesial structures and movements is the point at
which a major part of unbelief finds concrete expression; there is
perhaps no other single stumbling block to faith as large or as resis-
tant as that which is referred to as 'organized religion.' Faith breaks
down initially, in many cases, over the all too obvious flaws in the
fabric of the Church and in the Church's popular self-image. The
basic charge is that the Church is saddled with outworn, dehumanizing elements and is failing to change—that it is hopelessly irrelevant
and cannot change, except to become more itself, that is, worse.
Theologians may dutifully echo popes and bishops in proclaiming
the living presence of God in the Church and insist, rightly, that
only faith can reveal the divine character of this Church, beneath
the all too human elements which obtrude themselves. There is a
logical misstep here, however, as if one were being told that he must
believe that what is patently human, in the limiting and even dero-
gatory sense, was in reality more than human. One replies that
theologians are trying to play the game with loaded dice, forgetting
Christ's own words, that men would know His followers by their
fruits. It seems appropriate to reflect briefly on what one author
dubs 'the end of conventional Christianity,' searching for additional
insight into one of the chief causes of religious indifference.[97]

In one of his short stories John Updike tells of a group of high
school students celebrating after a football game. They are drinking
beer and gazing down from a hilltop on the city below. A single
light glows in the darkness, so they head towards it, hoping at this
very late hour to find excitement—'action.' The light is discovered
coming from a church, through a stained-glass window on which the
figure of Christ is depicted. Christ is represented on the window
facing in toward the church, not out to them, and as they drive
by, He seems to give them a sinister wave—good-bye; on your
way.[98] No contact is made; church and young people do not speak
to each other. Yet traditionally the Church has accepted responsibility for caring for man in his deepest desires and uncertainties, face
to face with anxieties and suffering, misery and death, joy and hope.
In view of the undoubted Christ-Church identification of Biblical
faith, belief in one is inseparably bound up with belief in the other.
If, or when, the image of Christ our Savior does not shine strongly

and beautifully in and through the visible visage of the Church, what credibility has the latter, what loyalty or support can it expect? On the other hand, there is a way of rejecting the Church, and Christ, of course, on account of its foibles and failures, that is as dishonest as the self-seeking credulity that masks as faith. There are people whose difficulties concerning the divine reality and power of the Church arise chiefly because they are reluctant to face honestly the claim which membership in the Church might have upon their lives. They are too proud or think too highly of themselves, as enlightened and emancipated, to associate with the meek and lowly masses who shelter in the safety of a heavenly Father.[99]

Grace, it has been said, makes all the difference and makes no difference. Faith is grace, of course, so it is superfluous to add that it makes a difference only to and for faith. But this way of speaking brings out the active and pragmatic character of faith, an acceptance of the real presence of God under the urgency of the question as to how a man shall live. I suspect that a great deal of the religious indifference of contemporary intellectuals is vitiated or colored by a blind refusal to see the inextricable involvement of the question of ethics and of the ultimate meaning and purpose of life. It is confidently assumed that the moral life can continue to stand in its own right even when the throne of the universe has been shown to be vacant. In any case it has already been indicated that man must be sustained in and by the spirit of love; if not a love directed positively toward the God whose existence is ignored, love toward the truth and therefore, necessarily, love toward one's neighbor in the truth. This may seem to beg the whole question, for the whole point of religious indifference—so far as it has a point—is to call into question the radical and existential quality of religious values such as love. My answer is that we are here up against something in the human situation which ought not to be evaded and cannot be transcended: indifference is dishonest unless it is disinterested, and unselfishness cannot be achieved without love of the truth. Further, without love of neighbor, love of truth is false to itself, is a form of self-love which leads inevitably to that distortion of the truth in the interests of one's pride which is of the essence of spiritual dishonesty.

Religious indifference is understood as a specimen of a present restlessness and dissatisfaction in ways of adjusting to the demands of reality. Underlying and implicit in contemporary man's negative reaction to the demands of traditional religion is the interpretation of experience as creative interaction, a process of generating ever new and richer life-meanings open to endless enhancement. Religion is felt to impede the full flowering of this process, by integrating man too one-sidedly and in an over-determined fashion in a world-order already fixed and permanently established. Christian faith has managed to recognize man's freedom and selfhood but has never allowed sufficient outlet for the critical, creative, and transforming role of human intelligence or sufficient awareness of the importance of temporal process and development. The doctrine of salvation is one that especially displeases those who believe that the primary function of intelligence is creativity and not conformity. One is not favorably impressed by a faith which is not impelled to invite man to intervene enthusiastically with the full range of his inventive powers. Man today is painfully conscious of a wide spectrum of problems and anxieties, but along with this he feels he has come of age as a responsible agent with a task proportionate to the whole scope of his personal and collective capacities. Harvey Cox's thesis for the viability of the secular city is also an analysis of religious indifference: being in the world makes sense without God. Patterns and structures are no longer revered as unalterably given but beckon to be over-turned and rebuilt, to make greater sense and conform more nearly, not to an alleged divine economy, but to palpable human needs and desires. Theologians and metaphysicians may find employment in invoking a Creator to account for the existence of man and the world and a Savior to give man hope against despair. Men are more energetic than ever in pursuing realistic temporal goals, in struggling for social justice and a better life, and yet many profess no religion at all. God and religion are irrelevant because they do not relate signifi-cantly to what Robert Johann calls the prevailing quality of life.[100]

The most dramatic aspect of the contemporary situation is not the decline of the old solutions—a neuralgic situation of which the most enlightened theologians had been aware for some years—but of the problems themselves. I have referred to the pastoral element in this situation; its correct understanding will enlist the contribu-tions of behavioral scientists and a more intensive examination of the already much discussed relationship of religion and life in the modern world. Religionists have been able to deal more confidently, almost to take in stride, those assertions of unbelief entailing militant denials and commitments to an anti-theism; they are considerably less competent in coming to grips with a tranquil and untroubled indifference.[101] In the following chapter I shall pose an alternative of the order of practical action: shall the Church engage in a dialogue with those who champion a secularized culture or stick to her mission but lose contact with large masses? Nothing reveals the stark and unsettling nature of the meaning of our age more than the fact of religious indifference.

The Salvation of the Unbeliever

A lively and continuing theological discussion, over a period of several decades, has thrown a remarkable light on a problem that was still very poorly defined as late as the end of the nineteenth century. This development was brought to a culmination and transcended in unexpected ways in the Pastoral Constitution on The Church in the Modern World, at the Second Vatican Council. My survey of the problem, the salvation of the unbeliever, will be based on this conciliar teaching and will comprise three parts: a brief definition of the essential elements of salvation as a category of Christian faith, together with a proposal for solving the problem of the salvation of the unbeliever, in part on terms worked out for a cognate problem; second, a summary of the most authoritative and comprehensive theological doctrine on the question; third, a proposed new framework for formulating a solution to outstanding difficulties.

If men do not feel the least need for salvation, it may be because the Christian message has never been heard as a convincing promise of joy and liberation.[102] Salvation is closely associated with liberation in all religious preaching and writing, a release from all kinds of slavery and loneliness, guilt and powerlessness, the alienation which burdens man and blocks his self-realization and creativity, his striving for truth, justice, peace, and love. Man thirsts for salvation in the degree to which he seeks final answers to ultimate questions and release from the claims which bind him and prevent his attainment of happiness. Technology and civilization are born of man's urge to dominate the world and make it a fit place in which to live. At a deeper level, man searches for a right use of his power over nature and a way of behaving worthy of his humanity, out of which are born his ethics and the law which fosters justice. Lastly, man returns again and again to that peace and happiness which he craves but ever fails to obtain, to the victory over his own perversity, a blind fate, and death, the merciless leveller. Salvation centers on hope, which gives meaning to everything and makes life worth living.[103]

What the higher religions promise to the faithful, secular humanism holds out as a possibility within the grasp of man's own best efforts, provided he will learn to actualize his own resources. Whatever differences separate them, all men share in common an unquenchable longing for deliverance and fulfillment, the negative and positive initial and consummate moments of unlimited life. This amounts to a spiritual kinship which can and should provide a background against which the Gospel is proclaimed. The theologian must speak of salvation by way of a conversation that is animated by a sympathetic understanding of human nature. The proclamation of the good news speaks to a need and an aspiration of which all honest and reflective men are sensible, or it speaks a language unintelligible and repugnant to the mind and the heart. The Catholic conception of salvation has traditionally been linked to membership in the Church, which calls for an excursus on the history of this doctrine before examining directly the condition of the unbeliever as it is currently understood.[104]

In the patristic era the Church was thought of as *oikumene,* the *ecclesia catholica,* which was assumed spontaneously to be coextensive with the known world. In the limited and imperfect geographical perspectives of those centuries, it could be taken for granted easily that every person would, or could, come to hear the Gospel preached and thus be given the option of accepting Christ and salvation in His Church. Unbelievers, including adherents of other religions on the fringes of Christendom, must be convicted of being in bad faith; both the power of free choice and the indispensability of faith for salvation were taken with maximum seriousness, while the fact of countless human beings beyond the range of effective evangelization and the presence among unbelievers of positive religious or ethico-spiritual values were glossed over or minimized. The axiom *extra ecclesiam nulla salus* came to be interpreted literally and with severe juridical consequentiality. Hans Küng suggests that a wiser and more prudent course would have been to read this formula in a positive and inclusive sense as 'salvation inside the Church,' but his observation seems pointless in view of the mentality prevailing during the early period.[105] The close indentification of the Church with Christ, the only Savior, made the actual interpretation all but inevitable. It was not, in fact, new or changed understanding of the article of faith that God wills the salvation of all men in Christ which led to a shift in emphasis, because this change never took place, either among Catholics or Reformed. The great age of exploration, from the sixteenth century on, and increasingly, opened up a hitherto unknown world that revealed both the minority status of true believers (and the 'Christian' heretics and schismatics with whom they had to contend) and the existence of huge masses of humanity untouched by the revealed word of God or the presence of His ministers. By the nineteenth century theologians saw clearly the need to take another look at the principles by which they had been trying to account for the relationship of people under various conditions to God's saving grace. Pope Pius IX declared that those who live in ignorance of the true religion incur no guilt in the eyes of the Lord if their ignorance is invincible, and, perhaps even more significantly, the Pope thought it rash, if not impossible, to try to fix the limits of this ignorance 'according to the type and variety of peoples, regions, natural dispositions and so many other things.'[106] The proposition about no salvation outside the Church can no longer be taken in a strict and harsh sense, since even the Holy Office has protested this interpretation and declared excommunicated anyone who rejects flatly the possibility of salvation for those not visibly members of the Church. At the Second Vatican Council, finally, it is declared that divine Providence does not 'deny the help necessary for salvation to those who, without blame on their part, have not yet arrived at an explicit knowledge of God, but who strive to live a good life, thanks to His grace.'[107]

The axiom 'no salvation outside' may be retained, as an expression of authentic Catholic tradition, but it is obviously hampered by limitations and misconceptions and has lost most of its serviceability and is more of a hindrance than a help in the Church's mission today. Küng writes: 'The words are interpreted more often as either intolerance or duplicity: as intolerance when they are understood literally and exclusively in accordance with the old tradition; as duplicity when it means on the one hand that no one will be saved outside the Catholic Church and on the other hand does not exclude the fact that people outside the Catholic Church are saved, in fact millions and billions of them, the greater part of mankind.'[108] Attempts to shore up a creaking and shaky position with clever expedients have proved futile, from a dubious extension of the concept of the Church to an arbitrary and offensive re-definition of explicit and conscious unbelievers as secret and implicit Catholics. All men are equally in the hands of God, who wills their salvation and makes His grace available to all. What is needed is a theological synthesis in which all the pertinent dogmatic principles are understood realistically in terms of the state of mankind as it actually prevails in the world.

A declaration to the effect that invincible ignorance excuses from guilt is not an unequivocal affirmation that the invincibly ignorant person is blameless on all counts and not merely with respect to the precept of which he is unwittingly ignorant. As St. Thomas puts it, an infidel may be innocent of a sin against faith but go to hell for other acts against his conscience, for murder or rape or suchlike.[109] The positive question centers on the unbeliever's capacity for grace: granted that not all atheism is personally blameworthy, how is it possible for the atheist to be justified and attain salvation? The Vatican Council's Decree on the Missionary Activity of the Church affirms that all men, including unbelievers, can be saved, but adds that, for them as for everyone else, it is through faith that salvation is achieved, although in their case only God knows how faith works.[110] The principles for the solution of this problem are inherited from a rich and laboriously constructed dogmatic and theological tradition, principles set in a new context of meaning and understood with fresh insight and broadened application. Three such principles dominate and illumine this entire question: the universal salvific will of God, the necessity of faith, and the possibility of such faith as is necessary and sufficient to fulfill God's will. These principles are taken into consideration in the light of what is the truly new teaching of Vatican II by Karl Rahner's magnificently argued thesis of atheism and anonymous, or implicit, Christianity. Rahner represents not a radical departure from previous theological opinion but rather a more daring and far-seeing interpretation of what was authoritatively sanctioned at the Council. I shall here simply set forth the highlights of Rahner's thinking, pointing out those few places where the reasoning is less clear or convincing or conclusive than it might be and those aspects which require further elucidation. I do not intend to confine myself rigidly to Rahner's terminology or to his sometimes tortuous and needlessly prolix way of stating questions.[111]

The man with whom theology is here wrestling is one who is *simul iustus et peccator* in a strikingly paradoxical sense, for he is not a believer; he may never even have heard of the Holy Spirit, let alone been invited to accept Him, and yet he may be living in a state of grace, justified and actually capable of being saved. Leaving aside the question as to whether in fact such a man exists, or how he could be identified in practice, if at all, one may proceed to discuss his alleged condition as a real possibility. Rahner speaks in this connection of 'implicit Christianity,' because the essence of Christianity is present, namely, justifying grace by which man is reconciled to God and united with Him in love, but this presence remains unrecognized and unacknowledged and may even be openly and vehemently repudiated or scoffed at. It must be noted, at once and at the very outset, that God wills all men to be saved, with a will that antecedes and is sovereignly independent of whatever any man, at whatever age, actually and freely wills or decides or desires or pursues or loves. This is a first crucial principle: in whatever condition he may find himself, or be, objectively or in his own eyes, every man stands in an order willed by God, which is one of supernatural existence, redeemed by God's gracious and utterly gratuitous mercy. No man is or can be, no matter what his will or efforts in respect to this order, in another mode of existence, to which the universal salvific will of God is inapplicable or ineffectively relevant. It must be emphasized that we are describing a possibility, but one that is real, objective, universal, and not dependent upon or in any way conditioned by anything any man may do or not do, be or not be. God has created all men, without exception, to receive at least the offer of salvation in and through His Incarnate Son, Jesus Christ. It is the contention of Rahner, and those who agree with him, that positive atheism, in and of itself and invariably, even when it has been deliberately maintained by a responsible and mature person and possibly even for a lifetime, does not automatically exclude an individual from the possibility of salvation. It is further asserted that such a person can live such a life that in fact, and not as a mere possibility, he is saved.

The problematic character of this twofold thesis derives first from the theological view, of respectable stature and longevity, that personal guilt is inseparable from such a condition, and secondly from the historico-sociological assumption which underlay this view, to the effect that theism, or some kind of belief in the living God, was within reach of every man—it was part of the socio-cultural landscape, in the air one breathed, so that one had to place himself radically beyond the pale to embrace atheism. The inhabitants of the 'civilized Christian world' could barely conceive of anything so utterly removed from their experience as a well-established, self-assured secularism within which unbelief flourishes as a matter of course. Because religious belief was looked upon as intrinsic to and inseparable from human nature itself, it could not be allowed that atheism might be free of moral guilt. The teaching of the Second Vatican Council may be invoked here in support of a new and different estimate of atheism, not only its declaration on this subject but also what was said about paganism and missionary efforts in lands which have not been evangelized.

Nowhere does the Council uphold the theological view that explicit long-term atheism must be morally culpable, and indeed what it teaches is flatly incompatible with that position. The mind of the Council on this point is expressed, not with explicit reference to the academic argument against the possibility of a guiltless unbelief, but with reference first, to an explicit and socially diffused atheism that is treated as a matter of simple fact, and second, to the general principle that no one has a right to pass judgment on the guilt-before-God of those who profess such atheism. The Constitution on the Church in the Modern World, in the text I have reproduced earlier in this chapter, barely touches on the question of guilt, and only to say that willfully shutting one's mind or heart to the reality of God or religion is sinful. From this self-evident truth nothing at all can be deduced concerning the moral condition of one who has embraced atheism in fact for a fairly long period. The Council does, indeed, insist that conscience must be respected when the religious question is confronted, but that one may not without blame shunt this aside and refuse to face up to its exigencies. Atheism as an objective doctrine is branded poisonous and reprehensible, nor does the Council hesitate to deplore its evil consequences and the harm it wreaks on individual and society. But the atheist himself may be an intelligent and upright man, neither vicious nor stupid, so that the real causes of unbelief will have to be sought elsewhere as well as in the depths of human wickedness and perversity, a search which theology has only just begun to take seriously.

More positively, the Council allows that atheism need not bar a man from the way of salvation, provided he has not acted contrary to the dictate of his conscience. The atheist must, then, be capable of receiving justifying grace and of cooperating with it, while yet remaining an atheist, and this defines precisely the terms of the problem as presently understood. It is important that the conciliar teaching not be misconstrued as implying first a conversion to theism, which would take all the force and impact out of the statement and reduce it to an uninteresting platitude. There is no way of excluding all atheists from the universal salvific will of God, which means concretely a share in the grace of Christ, albeit in a manner which theology has not yet succeeded in identifying, in spite of a great deal of conjecture, some of it hardly plausible.[112] The pagans in missionary countries may not be reckoned better off in this respect than unbelievers who feel compelled to reject God and religion in order to remain true to their moral ideals honestly held.

The Council is here certainly leading theological thought away from paths traditionally trod, into a perspective in which optimism over the possible salvation of atheists mounts toward an unprecedented pitch. There is no question here of allowances being made for some sort of happiness or reward different in kind and inferior to the supernatural destiny in terms of which Biblical faith has always understood salvation. The conciliar decrees always envisage only one salvation, that effected by the grace of God in Christ, to which all men without exception or distinction are called.[113] We are still left in the dark, however, as to what this means in the actual life of the unbeliever, who does not assent to the sharing in the paschal mystery of Christ. This aspect of the problem will have to be examined largely without help from the conciliar documents; the latter are limited to affirming the possibility for an unbeliever to live in the state of grace, without penetrating in detail the obscure area of how this grace operates to effect his salvation. There is no suggestion that either grace or justification is easy, or that the unevangelized or persistent unbeliever evades the challenge and responsibility of grace by the expedient of a death-bed confrontation with an alleged natural moral goodness. Previous historical ages, during the course of which the mainstream theological conclusions were drawn, did not experience the comparatively recent phenomenon of a worldwide and growing atheism, intellectually well-supported and sophisticated and sociologically established securely in major institutions and movements. It is not surprising, then, that theologians formerly saw little or no cause except that of personal choice by which to account for the appearance of unbelief. What has been considered thus far in the development of Christian thinking involved in the conciliar statements raises a problem to which the closest attention must now be given. The most urgent question is, in what terms may one reasonably understand the ways by which the atheist is in a position to attain grace and work out his salvation? Any progress toward a solution to this problem will be a major contribution to the theology of unbelief.

There is no salvation, understood as man's liberation and elevation by divine grace, apart from faith, and it is this precisely which constitutes the thorniest aspect of the problem.[114] I do not see any license for reinterpreting salvation to encompass something as vague and remote as good will or the equivalent, or to settle for a minimum content of faith, based on Heb 11.6, for this includes belief in God as rewarder and punisher, which of course is completely ruled out by atheism. The atheist must believe in order to be saved, but what? Not divine revelation, as such, which the atheist in question either rejects outright or has not so much as heard of, or those truths about God which natural reason is able to attain and which are equally objectionable to radical unbelief. A clue is almost certainly provided in the repeated reference of the conciliar texts to the fidelity

to conscience, the honest seeking for truth, and the vigorous sensitivity
to the demands of moral awareness, all of which characterize the
upright atheist who cannot be excluded from the path of salvation.
One must take this reference seriously and ask bluntly whether, or
in what sense, moral integrity can supply for explicit belief in God
or serve as its surrogate. If the answer proves to be affirmative, it
will mean a recasting of theological thought, the implications of
which have not yet begun to strike our minds with their potential
and far-reaching force. Perhaps no other single point is of such
importance for the thoroughgoing confrontation of faith and unbelief as this; hence we must proceed with great care and concern,
not making a false step or overlooking a vital fact or principle.

One may affirm as implicitly an act of faith the sincere adherence
to the demands of moral conscience only if the latter is understood
and consented to as absolutely binding, as enlisting the individual's
deepest and most courageous commitment to what is of supreme
value in life, the orientation toward the good, unselfishly and with
a willingness to sacrifice all, suffer all, and attempt all, in its single-
minded and unswerving pursuit.[115] We must see, first, what is
involved in an act, or rather a sustained attitude based on conviction
and passion, which binds a man freely to a moral absolute, and, in
the second place, how this relates man to God in a way that effects
his justification unto salvation. It is important to keep in mind that
the stance of submission to moral imperative as absolute need not be
maintained with full reflection on its logical or ontological presuppositions, subjective or objective. Man's action is sensible and logical in
itself; what he is doing, and is choosing to do, is objectively right and
establishes him in a realm of goodness of which he may not, and
need not, grasp completely the implications or principles of an abstract
nature.[116] It is always possible that a person direct himself toward a
goal, or objective, which he believes to be morally binding but not
clearly and explicitly understand as such or in its consequences for
himself. He pursues the good as he sees it, with upright conscience
and firm resolution, and in this good, even if he explicitly deny and
reject it, is the God whom believers acknowledge and trust in faith.
Essential to this affirmation is the much controverted thesis that
God is known unreflexively but really in every experience of the
transcendent, every unlimited openness of the spirit to being as such,
even though this knowledge is not objectified, conceptualized, or
propositionalized.

Man's basic relationship to God is chartered by Rahner in four
graded modes, in each of which his free response may be one of

acceptance or rejection.[117] The first possibility is that God is grasped by man in his understanding of his own capacity for transcendence, and this recognition is translated by the individual himself into a theism which may be freely accepted in a moral assent of faith, i.e., in the actions of daily life. This theism is, presumably, conceptually adequate, correct both in its transcendent grounding and its categorical expression, the relationship of a justified believer to God in Christ. The second possibility is identical to the first, except that the person who knows God, correctly and reflectively, chooses freely to disbelieve. It was taken for granted in earlier ages that this was the condition of the typical atheist, who rejected God, either as a sinner, or theoretically, or in practice. It is possible, in the third instance, for man to experience God transcendentally and to accept this experience, freely and positively, but to interpret it incorrectly and substitute some other value or concept for that of the living God. On the level of conceptualization the individual remains an atheist, in that he has not reflectively recognized the God of pure theism or Biblical faith, but on the transcendental level he is morally oriented toward God and is blameless. He makes the decision to open himself to his God, especially by binding himself in conscience to a moral absolute, even though he may reject a concept of God formally objectified, which leaves him in a state of categorical unbelief. The last possibility is that of profound and real atheism, in terms of grave infidelity to the dictate of conscience or a culpably false attitude toward existence, but covered over and perhaps totally concealed by a categorical affirmation of the reality of God— although this affirmation may be absent. This atheism is undoubtedly blameworthy, and responsibility for it, the extreme bad faith it involves, excludes one from the way of salvation, no matter what or how fervent the faith he professes.[118]

Two considerations emerge from this classification of possibilities, which is neither exhaustive nor completely nuanced, and they are that atheism is not necessarily an insuperable barrier to salvation nor does it necessarily preclude a real, although hidden and unacknowledged, positive relationship toward God, in which salvation consists. When atheism does constitute a bar to salvation, it is because the person has freely closed his openness to a moral absolute binding his conscience, a radical rejection of transcendence which cannot co-exist with a meaningful and salutary relationship to God. Men can and do try to have it otherwise, to have it both ways, to play false to their innermost consciences and still apply for salvation by categorically affirming the reality of God—and even of His supreme law. Unbelief in this case consists of a profound disorder at the transcendental level of unique personal freedom and is accompanied by what may be an elaborate attempt at deception and self-deception and cannot be without more or less serious guilt. The Vatican Council's concern was simply to indicate the twofold possibility, of a blameless and blameworthy unbelief, without explaining in what manner or terms salvation is within reach of that atheist who lives honorably in accord with the light of his conscience. A clue and guideline is provided in this last reference, which I have followed Rahner in exploiting, employing the useful and apposite distinction of categorical and transcendental affirmation and negation. The central working principle in this account is that in the dimension of man's most fundamental moral option, the level on which he chooses to be true to his best self as he knows it, or to betray his conscience and debase himself, the presence of God is real and intimate, whether He be recognized and chosen at the level of explicit thematic understanding and decision or not. He is thus not far from any of us; He may be God unknown, but every man moves and has being in Him.

In this sense there is no man utterly devoid of any sort of experience of God, even though one may never have encountered Him in the categories of explicit and conscious awareness and choice. When an individual is mature enough to discern the exigencies of moral conscience, he has the opportunity, and responsibility, to meet these demands by free decision or to neglect or reject them by a similar act. The merit or blame he thereby incurs relates him to God in the deepest reaches of his being, existentially, although not necessarily in virtue of his own self-understanding and acceptance. Categorical atheism does not compare, in significance or ultimate import, to transcendental atheism, and even when the former is avoided, or rooted out by overt conversion, the latter may remain and do grave harm. By argument, for example, one may be brought to the point where he can find no further reasonable ground on which to continue to deny the existence of God as conceptualized and intended in the proffered 'proofs.' Yet this assent may be meaningless and inoperative at the radical level at which one's life is basically oriented, toward or away from the absolute moral good, however dimly discerned. By the same token, one may embrace and pursue this good, selflessly and lovingly, and still find the concept of God, as presented to him, impossible or repugnant and so reject it as of no value or interest, unworthy of the adherence of a free and honorable man. This leads us to a discussion of the correct pastoral treatment of atheism, which will be left for the following chapter. There remains only the question of the relationship of the justified atheist to the Church, a relationship which must be investigated along the same lines by which his salvation has been discovered.

I have not overlooked, much less denied, the necessity of faith for salvation; the Council has emboldened, and indeed authorized, us to find an equivalent of faith in the firm and freely undertaken engagement with moral value seen to be absolutely binding.[119] This moral commitment is itself a grace, and one which of itself tends to unite a person to all that is good and all those who share in it, which means the creating, at least in objective intent, of a human community, a brotherhood of love and justice in which men support and edify each other. The Church is, in fact and by God's dispensation, the place on earth where He calls men together to acknowledge His mercy and the power of His name in and through their renewed life together. It is in this congregation, for the purposes of worship and enriched fellowship, that men receive the benefits of Christ's redemptive death and resurrection. In the Church faith hears the word of God and commemorates His wondrous deeds in the reception of the sacraments. The important thing is the building up of a community of trust and service, inspired by love, to which the entire apparatus of the institutional Church is ordered and subordinated. The power and authority of the Church, prophetical and priestly, far from being ends in themselves, are means placed at mankind's disposal to put them in touch with God's self-revelation and to energize them spiritually with the example of real brotherhood in His name. The atheist who is justified without his ceasing to be an atheist is somehow joined to this body of the faithful; his faithfulness is, categorically although not exclusively, to the dictate of conscience, but this binds him to a transcendent order of which God is author and ultimate foundation. It must be admitted that, up to the present, theologians have not devoted sufficient attention to this problem to produce formulas with which to describe more in detail the relationship between Church and justified infidel. I cannot see any reason to work out this problem on terms other than those employed by the conciliar Fathers, which link closely the salvation of the atheist and his fidelity to moral absolutes imposed by conscience. This connection should not be overlooked or cast aside once this further question of the unbeliever and the Church is broached. The implications of this approach are intriguing enough to give promise of results that may prove illuminating for the entire theology of unbelief.

E

The elements of a solution to the problem of the salvation of the unbeliever emphasize the supreme importance of unconditional loyalty, absolute truthfulness, unselfish commitment to the welfare of others, and similar basic moral values. One thinks spontaneously of the insistence in the Gospels and other New Testament writings on the one thing necessary, on charity above all and in all, on the necessity of purity of heart and single-mindedness, on the emulation of the Lord Jesus as the holy One of God, the humble and sinless Savior, and on the bonds of friendship which unite those who walk in the way of justice and truth. It should not be forgotten that God is no more evident to the theist than to the self-styled atheist or that the latter may appeal to a noble and authentic ideal of human integrity in support of his rejection of the idea of God. Resentment of evil, scandal at the supposed crimes perpetrated in the name of religion, the vagueness and arbitrariness of much that is labelled religious experience, the threat presented to human freedom and inititative by distorted and intimidating concepts of God—none of these convicts a man of that moral infidelity which makes atheism culpable and cuts the atheist off from the grace of God. The confusion of God with His universe or reduction of Him to any of the forces or elements in that universe is idolatry, whether the fault be attributable to a believer or an unbeliever. The justified atheist escapes this idolatry by keeping himself free and open to that transcendent good which infuses the pure moral value to which he binds himself absolutely in conscience. Does this suggestion in effect make salvation easier for the unbeliever, who apparently has only to remain loyal to his conscience, than for the faithful Christian who, in addition, must perform various acts of religion, keep a number of observances, obey precepts, and believe so much which the atheist is exempt from accepting? Not at all, in my judgment, except for those who foolishly think that salvation is merited by—or even consists in—all those rites and observances and orthodoxies, rather than by the charity which springs, under grace, from a pure and upright heart. The works of religion are, in fact, an aid and support to the practice of charity, in which respect the Christian has an obvious and immense advantage over the atheist who must carry on the same struggle without benefit of revealed word, sacrament, or community of the faithful.

The Unbelief of Believers

We have singled out three special theological problems, each of which illustrates one aspect of the continuing mystery of human existence and all of which clearly call for intensified and expanded reflection and analysis. Unbelief is a problem for the theologian primarily because it is a problem of faith; the problem will be understood and dealt with effectively, insofar as this may be possible, only as and to the extent that the believer understands his own situation and sees it as subject to the same threats and pressures which make of the human condition as such a test of courage and a risk that must be undergone. I shall try to relate this question of the unbelief of believers in three stages, considering first the theological status of this question, second, three degrees of belief-unbelief, and third, what unbelief, properly understood, can reveal of the nature and function of faith.

In spite of the formidable number of publications on the subject of unbelief, particularly within the past decade and in the aftermath of the Council, unbelief has not yet been accorded a clear and well-defined place within the total theological framework. Johannes Metz sees this problem undergoing a shift in significance in current theological thinking, a transposition from the periphery, where theology conducts its apologetical defense or comes to grips with other world-outlooks, to the very heart of this science of faith, where the thinking believer lays hold of the essence of man's free commitment to God in Christ and meditates, systematically, on its prerequisites, its variations, and its consequences.[120] When unbelief is thus viewed as an integral part of the question of faith itself, it assumes at last its proper theological identity and its importance for the spiritual life of all men, believer and unbeliever alike. The recognition of this central theological relevance has been stimulated, in part, by the realization that faith and its opposite were given short shrift in conventional apologetics, which for too long tended to envisage its task in terms of an unbelief of more or less unreal, overly abstract proportions, motivated almost exclusively by bad will and supported by rational considerations which have long since ceased to attract or be of interest. For one thing, it is no longer only a small elite band of sophisticated intellectuals who find it impossible to believe the Gospel. Jean Lacroix speaks of contemporary unbelief as, overwhelmingly and increasingly, a function of man's self-concept, more a humanism than an atheism or anti-theism. The firm thrust of this serenely godless humanism is to sweep away the false absolutes standing athwart man's self-development and in this respect one must look upon it as more an ally of sound religion than its enemy.[121] Man is summoned peremptorily by an inconoclastic humanism, even one with God-denying overtones, to persevere in the difficult vocation to unceasing reform.

In the past men have found in religion impressive sanction for nailing down the shape and course of experience, for prescribing beforehand, according to fixed and traditional patterns, a way into the future. A thoroughly critical atheism has the salutary effect of keeping man open to the inexhaustible possibilities of the real and of preventing him from ever settling for the world as given, instead of as intelligent love can make it.

A lesson of immense value has been learned in the dismal failure over the past two centuries of conventional apologetics to pierce the armor of well-fortified and entrenched unbelief. There is no real gain to be expected from a frontal assault on the atheist option, largely because the opposed views operate from premises which are not so much antithetical as irrelevant to each other. Unbelief is supported not by a string of syllogisms, the terms and propositions of which can be exposed to logical and real critique, but by a style and way of life that is chosen and maintained because it is found humanly rewarding, while the alternatives of religious belief are found seriously wanting. The theologian has at last come to realize that it is the positive values and ideals which he embraces, rather than the rejection of God, which most strongly motivate the unbeliever and define his world-outlook. I have been reluctant to call this commitment a faith, but it is that, of course; so that belief determines the life-stance of the atheist (except, perhaps, for the sheer nihilist, but inconsistency renders even this exception dubious) no less than that of the Christian or other religious person. The recognition of atheism's dialectical character locates the problem of unbelief closer to that of the theology of faith and establishes its pertinence to theology as a whole, as touching on the very foundations of man's existence in faith. Out of this insight a new and more fruitful apologetic may be constructed, which may be described as an understanding rather than a polemic, but one which is critical and draws heavily on the infinite riches of God's word. Theological concern is focusing more and more, as I see it, on that mysterious point of conjunction of faith and unbelief, bringing both into a single complex perspective and refusing to analyze either apart from the other.

In all of the analyses of faith, from myriad points of view, the unbelief of believers has not yet been taken into account because it has not yet been located properly within the theology of faith. Defective faith, as a sin, has been identified and discussed, but very cursorily and in an almost wholly abstract and impersonal fashion, in terms of the immoral risks of doubt and questioning, acceptance of the immoral risks of doubt and questioning, acceptance of the definitions of the magisterium and the Church's alleged rights in public life over against the lack thereof of those unpersuaded by the Gospel. Unbelief is part of the mystery of sin, as I have noted, but it is more than a particular sin, opposed to the specific theological virtue of faith as defined in scholastic theology; as faith in the broadest sense is the root and ground of all justification, so its counterpart, taken in the same breadth, extends to the full capacity of man for resisting grace and closing himself off from God's giving of Himself in Christ. It is a grave mistake to approach unbelief either as a particular vice or as the status exclusively of those visibly and voluntarily separated from religion. The error here includes the excessive narrowing of the basis of belief, compounded by a blindness to the presence of unbelief in believers, with the effect of situating the problem too far from the heart of the theology of faith as ever precarious and ever beyond our comprehension or absolute possession. In the explicitly avowed unbelief of the other, the believer encounters, starkly and without disguise and concealment, more than a possibility which intrudes on his own life and accompanies him in every twist and turn in the road he follows after God, who beckons but never shows Himself face to face.[122] The faith described meticulously in all its certitude and directness, plotted out as object, act, and habit, and skillfully dissected in its psychological complexity as a will-intellect engagement of the individual, is inadequate as a pole of comparison. This is not the place to criticize other outstanding shortcomings in this academic concept of faith, but it is impossible not to take notice of its inadequacy as a framework within which to explore the unbelief of believers. The intersubjective dimension of faith, also badly neglected, is a key factor in fitting into place the overhang of belief, as Metz calls it, toward unbelief. This weakness, not accidental or exceptional, but affecting the experience of faith inescapably and from within, derives both from the freedom which the believer retains and from the wound which afflicts this freedom as a result of the universal human condition.[123]

The freedom that surrounds and penetrates faith arises from the nature that God Himself has bestowed on man and which He respects in inviting him to respond to the offer of grace. But more fundamentally, there is the infinite and absolutely unconditioned freedom of God whose gift this grace is and never ceases to be: God gives Himself to man for no reason other than His own impenetrable and superabundant mercy, and His grace remains always that, the gratuitous donation of a Father, sovereign and omnipotent in His love. It is this gratuitousness that envelops faith in a radically precarious condition and forbids its being solidified as a thing-like possession over which a man might come to have control or which he might dispose of or not, completely according to his fancy. I think the notion of fidelity is extremely useful in seizing the uniqueness of the relationship between God and man entered into in faith: fidelity involving a mutual indwelling, which calls for constant and perpetual renewal and leaves both God and His creature free.[124] The precariousness of faith must be attached not to God, whose fidelity is as unshakable as it is unconditioned, but to the waywardness of man and his utter powerlessness to guarantee infallibly a right response to the offer of divine friendship.

The psychology of faith does not fully reveal this precariousness, as St. Paul admits: 'For I have nothing on my conscience, yet I am not thereby justified; but He who judges me is the Lord. Therefore, pass no judgment before the time, until the Lord comes, who will both bring to light the things hidden in darkness and make manifest the counsel of hearts; and then everyone will have his praise from God' (1 Cor 4.4–5). What, then, will convince the believer of his proneness to unbelief, or persuade him that it is always necessary to pray humbly that God may confirm and increase his faith and spare him the terrible temptation of apostasy? Reassurance as to conscious intention is here insufficient and may be worse than fear and insecurity—that fear and trembling without which we cannot work out our salvation. Even more futile and irrelevant would be a test of orthodoxy, a self-examination on the correctness or depth of understanding of one's assent to the prescribed articles of belief. The criterion prominently emphasized in the New Testament is that of living, doing the truth in charity, proving faith by fidelity, above all by compassion and concern for the needy brother. One may say that nothing done, sincerely, for the relief of misery will go unnoticed by the Lord, and equally, that a genuine faith in Him will bear such fruits as the individual, sustained by community, is capable of. It is in action that man's freedom is ultimately engaged and only thereby that anyone's real faith can be determined and judged, action being understood as a man's life-thrust, directed and inspired by his intention, wavering or firm. As long as faith is conceived largely, if not entirely, in terms of intellectual assent to defined propositions, this dimension of action, immeasurably more important, is lost sight of and the possibilities of unbelief are crowded into a context of withholding or withdrawing assent. The condition of believer is precarious with the risk of life, the ambiguity of existing intelligent and free yet never so translucent to oneself, or so totally self-possessed, that he can endow his faith with both infallibility of assent and indefectibility of practice.

An enormous gaffe was committed in perpetuating, uncritically and even enthusiastically, a theology which counted faith too easily as an element in the personality structure, although divinely 'infused,' of course, and failed to take seriously its utterly mysterious character. Faith, man's original bond with God revealing Himself in Christ, is truly human; it belongs to the condition only of man and of no other creature, but the understanding it gives is insight more than trust, and is incomparable to any of the ways of knowing acquired by man's own effort, save by an analogy in which the more that is said, the less is really affirmed. This must surely be one of the two or three spiritual lessons the Scriptures repeat most insistently, and divine instruction tries most urgently to inculcate: that man is to allow himself to be taken up by God to an order of thinking and willing, of feeling and striving, which means a new life, surpassing anything he might on his own dream of, or imagine, or aspire to, transforming him and leading him thence into unfathomable depths of intimacy and familiarity with God. Yet it all may seem the same, so that grace, which makes all the difference, is experienced as making no difference at all, or rather, as inviting and invigorating man to make a difference, but not laying out clearly a map of the new life that is his or leading him literally into a new country. Believer and unbeliever alike find themselves confronted with the same existential challenge, danger, and opportunity; faith in no wise spares a man the rough and tearing edges of life or exempts him from the effort needed to establish for himself, and thus for mankind, a humanized world.

Unbelief lurks in the obscurity of faith, not only with respect to the infinite transcendence of the object, or, better, the Person believed and believed in, but also with respect to the believer's own self-understanding in faith. Negative theology carefully and adoringly stressed the transcendence of God, but the result was partially to leave men with the impression that between this and the realm of experience, between the supernatural and the natural, there is a qualitative difference which immerses the former member in darkness and impenetrability and leaves the latter open to progressive analysis and comprehension. This is a first foundation for unbelief and consists in a simultaneous mythologizing of the divine and rationalizing or naturalizing of the human. One effect is to handle carelessly the mental images and categories derived from experience but used, after discovering a certain appropriateness in their employment, in interpreting the truths of faith. Faith lays hold of the truth about man, as well as God, of man in God, and the mystery of the One envelops the other, as he strives to understand what God's word means when it speaks not only to but about him. Theologians need periodically a forceful and effective reminder of the inadequacy of all conceptual schemes and doctrinal formulas, so as to avoid that gnosticism which turns faith into human wisdom, violating St. Paul's disjunction and dispensing with belief in an area where it is demanded.[125] A second effect is that of separating faith from the experience of faith and thus regarding the precariousness of faith and its concealment of unbelief as a merely logical or psychological problem, affecting our experience of faith but not our essential status before God as faithful. On this point Metz observes: 'Here the question may arise how this description of the radical threat to existence in faith is compatible with the teaching of theology on faith, i.e., that the act of faith is an act of the *total* man. Where is there room for unbelief? Our answer is that this existential totality of the act of faith cannot be comprehended with fullness and clarity. Because the *whole* of man is involved, the possibility of objective certainty about this engagement vanishes. It is exactly on the plane of reflective consciousness and theological discourse that the act of faith becomes endangered and uncertain. This does not exclude "firmness" and "certainty" which are contained and experienced in the act, as long as these qualities are not understood apart from the very act itself.'[126] The believer must confess that he has no more (indeed, he has less) control over the understanding of himself in faith than he has over the possession itself of faith. To substitute for this humble and sober self-estimate an illuminist assertiveness is to infect faith with a particularly virulent and subtle form of unbelief.

A great deal of stress is laid by Metz on the actual unbelief involved in the temptation described by theologians as concupiscence or the 'negative existential' expressed as part of the inheritance of original sin. Without subscribing fully to the thesis Metz attempts to substantiate, or seeing the cogency of every point he makes in the course of his argument, I think Metz has hit upon another possibility of the simultaneous co-presence of belief and unbelief, at the deepest level of human existence.[127] Temptation is first of all a feature of the universal condition done and left undone, to bequeath a world in which falsehood and weakness, selfishness and violence have the run of the place and beckon and entice from countless entrenched positions, some of them camouflaged with consummate artistry. Into this world the individual believer is born and, as he grows and matures, increasingly assimilated; and no grace, no gift of God's mercy, is more desperately needed by him than the wisdom to discern temptation for what it is, and where it is, and the strength to resist, to will steadfastness in the Lord, not relying on one's own resources or making excuses or losing heart should one stumble and fall. We are concerned here with the temptation to sin rather than with what might be identified literally as specific temptations against faith, but, again, the latter are comprised in a mysterious but potent way under the former and are involved, if vaguely and only generically, in man's whole captivity to concupiscence. Theology, following the explicit teaching of the Council of Trent, distinguishes scrupulously sin from mere temptation, but this distinction, unquestionably valid in the order of abstract essences and applicable in the concrete, is not always verified in actual experience. It is not only the Lutheran who recognizes man as *simul iustus et peccator*: my faith, in my living experience, is not so pure and beyond reproach that I am authorized to exclude it entirely from the area of my existence for which I must reproach myself before God, confess my infidelity, and throw myself on His mercy.[128]

This ambivalence—it is not, objectively, a confusion of opposites or an ambiguity, for faith is not un-faith and is irreducible to it— is conditioned by the gap in every man between the power offered in grace and his actual exercise of that power for his own spiritual edification. The traditional theological doctrine of the gifts of the Holy Spirit was elaborated precisely on the premise that, even when justified and believing in love, man needed divine assistance to make right and full use of grace. How painfully conscious St. Paul was of this existential burden of faith; his references to precious treasure in earthen vessels; his dismay at man's ignorance of his own spiritual best interests, to the extent that he does not even know how to pray; his constant and agonizing awareness of his own proneness to slip back, to fall short of what the Lord expects of him in view of the ineffable gifts and mission which were his! At this point the communal character of faith is recognized in its most essential and dynamic relevance to the precariousness and inner instability of its exercise. Unbelief inserts itself here in the ostensible believer's withdrawal of love and trust and participation in the faith-judgment, for it emphasizes the necessity in the believing community for integrity and growth in faith, and it exposes the replacement of genuine faith by its counterfeit when the professed believer does not open himself to his brother. We are again back to the unique and indispensable test of the authenticity of faith, that purity of life which overcomes the alienation that closes man in upon himself and isolates him from both God the Father and the brotherhood of his fellows.[129] To the extent that a believer fails, i.e., refuses, to translate the ideals of charity and self-giving into the stuff of earnest endeavor, he makes a mockery of those ideals and scandalizes those who see in his duplicity proof of the inhumanity of religion.[130]

Unbelief has its counterpart in the unbeliever's creeping sclerosis of the spirit, the confusing of limited truths with *the* truth; and all men, in their unbounded passion for security, build for themselves a well-fortified place in which to settle down, to enjoy themselves and shut out the intrusions and demands of others. As the full significance for faith of personalist intersubjectivity is explored, it is becoming clearly evident that the believer's specific relationship to God is as one with all men and not as an individual in exclusive singularity, in brotherly love and not in private monadic subjectivity. Our salvation is attained in and with our brothers in faith; God resolves the elusive pluralism and ambivalence of our condition, uniting us with Him, and with all who are His, in a gift that calls for our response. If the response is not made, or only halfheartedly and ungenerously, the gift withers in our heart and our belief is clouded over by that most dangerous lie, as Emmanuel Mounier called it, invoking the name of God with our lips only. The frank and honest confession of this capacity for unbelief in the believer should teach him his closeness, his solidarity even, with those who openly and gladly profess their unbelief. Theologians have suggested the relevance here of a distinction between actual faith resting on inadequate theoretical arguments or a gap between orthodoxy and orthopraxis, a discrepancy between the actual lived position and the reflectively articulated statement of one's belief.[131]

The philosopher-psychiatrist Paul Matussek has analyzed the possibility that the believer's unbelief may be repressed, i.e., more or less consciously rejected or excluded from the level of full awareness.[132] This process is better called suppression, reserving repression for the unconscious mechanism in which neither process nor content is present in awareness. Belief may, of course, be banished from self-awareness in this other, more radical, and usually pathological sense. Matussek is not interested in the inherent capacity for belief, loss of which occurs only in rare and extremely severe cases, but in that uubelief which rejects certain commitments of faith or the ressponsibility to translate belief into commitment. It is a question of consciously clinging to religion, of professing one's assent to the teachings of the Church and one's loyalty to the Church as institution and society, but interiorly withholding consent to certain demands of faith. This holding back may or may not induce guilt feelings, which disturb one in the possession of faith and may arise from the unwillingness of the believer to make a free decision that will comply with the imperatives of faith when these run counter to his personal desires and attachments. When this phenomenon presents itself, the individual continues to hold on to the profession and practice of faith, but it is vitiated at its core by a defection that is not less damaging for being completely insidious and unrecognized. In these brief remarks I shall confine myself to that form of repressed or suppressed unbelief in which neurosis or severe mental-emotional disturbance is not involved and technical therapeutic measures are not necessarily indicated.

The outward behavior of the believers in question may be religiously correct in every respect, in terms of church attendance, observance of church precepts, and adherence to the system of dogmas prescribed by official authority. Of them it may be said, not unfairly I trust, that their belief in the Church, in the importance of clinging to it externally and respecting its institutions, is in inverse proportion to their belief in the living God and their readiness to comply with His demand of unselfish concern for others. Not that their conscience greatly troubles them; on the contrary, they seem to be oblivious of the profound inconsistency between their way of life and the religious ideals to which they subscribe, or which, at least, they have not explicitly repudiated. Somewhat after the style of the Pharisees of the Gospels, they are able to combine a pious self-righteousness with a latent unbelief, unrecognized precisely because they are careful to observe dutifully all of the rules and regulations of religion. Religion is made an end in itself and not the means of closer intimacy with God and a freer self-donation to one's brethren; thus, the very instrumentalities designed to mediate God's call become an obstacle to hearing it. Faith is ideologized and used as a self-justifying idol, and this distortion is sometimes supported by the prevailing image of religious adherence. There is undoubtedly, in most such cases, a false identification of moral uprightness with that justice which, according to the word of God, is rather the merciful gift of a loving and forgiving Father, and then a reduction of the whole of the religious relationship to the level of ethical correctness. What has probably happened, Mastussek suggests, is that the unbelieving believer has formed a bad conscience which has never been seriously challenged; compounding this, exaggerated emphasis is placed on that conventional way of life which Paul Furfey stigmatizes as 'respectability,' and the latent unbeliever comes to regard his condition as not only defensible but normal.[133] He is left undisturbed and never feels the responsibility of making a radical decision or undertaking a major reform in the light of his faith. Matussek explains: '... in the actual activities of our daily lives the failure to make real moral decisions gives an inner motivating force to latent unbelief in the theological sense. This is especially the case today because faith and belief in modern society are not supported by a public and general conviction, with the result that a decision or attitude in questions of morality develops much more easily and quickly than in earlier ages into actual unbelief. This unbelief is of course nonetheless powerful for being suppressed or repressed.'[134]

The self-deluded believer in this connection is, I am afraid, reproducing in his own personal life a failure practiced at large by the Church as a whole, and particularly by those who assume the office of authoritative spokesmen but tend rather to behave like self-interested publicists and apologists, more concerned to preserve a spotless reputation than to stand naked before God and the world. No pope or council has yet expressed with anything but perfunctory and routine conviction a consciousness of the sinfulness of the Church, not merely of individuals but of the People of God as such, whose election is a vocation and not a confirmation in grace or an immunity to temptation. Christians long accustomed to the inflated and outrageously presumptuous language of self-laudation, a vocabulary overloaded with references of blessedness, sacredness, holiness, reverence, solemnity, eminence, excellency, etc., and a panoply of structures and functions, offices and institutions, rites and ceremonies surrounded and propped up with an artificial protocol of deference and awe are all too easily confused as to the objective priority of values and the depths to which all of humanity is affected by the consequences of sin and involved in the world which is the natural habitat of sin because men have so made it. It is a problem of psychological conditioning, at least in part, whereby the lax and unauthentic believer, impregnated with an especially subtle form of unbelief, never confronts his own enslavement to sin because, in ways of which he is keenly aware, he remains a Church-member in good standing.

Because bishops and other preachers rarely if ever acknowledge in a thoroughly convincing and specific fashion the proneness of the Church to sin or the sins actually committed under the cover of pursuing ecclesiastical aims and satisfying clerical ambition, the rest are quite understandably impressed with the idea that not charity—which the Scriptures indicate—but religiosity, that is, religious propriety, covers over an array of sins. Some Christians do, in fact, have a sense of uneasiness about their lack of authentic faith, but fear and anxiety prevent them from facing squarely what might be a shattering experience to their entire ego-image. It is in the avoidance of a violent challenge to one's faith-system that a deep and complex unbelief can insinuate itself, very often as a rigid and immature form of belief which remains fixated at a level on which the individual can enjoy the luxury of a favorable self-image while sparing himself the pain and effort, the risk and burden, of shouldering the responsibility of an adult faith. The evangelical dictum about dying in order to live lays the believer under a lifelong injunction to keep moving on a progressive journey along which new needs and demands open up and a new point of departure must be made from time to time. No one can carry intact and unchanged to his dying day the form or shape of belief received in childhood or adhere to notions meaningful at one stage in one's life-history but incapable of bearing the weight of an experience enriched and deepened in the course of normal growth. The unbelief, that is, the element of un-faith which feeds like a parasite on what is left of the good seed planted by grace but fallen on barren ground, is hidden by the outward forms of religion. The problem is not that of sin in general, because sin acknowledged and repented of does not afflict faith with its counterfeit, or that of doubt, for there is room in the community of believers for a certain kind of doubt, a doubt which is not to be confused with genuine unbelief, as I propose now to show.

The faith which introduces one to God's gifts and begins that friendship which blossoms into a mutual self-giving and the intimacy of eternal life together is a germinal act of the Spirit and not the fruit of logical reasoning or the pure product of experience. This is why a firm adherence in faith, which deserves the name of fidelity, is not incompatible with what may rightly be called doubt. I am speaking of a doubt in one who thinks of himself as, and wants to continue to be, a believer, but the thesis I am proposing has a certain element of novelty and has not yet found widespread support among theologians who have studied the legitimacy of doubt in the life of faith. The problem is not new, but heretofore doubt has been defined in terms which would exclude it from the realm of faith and would, were it present, constitute another instance of unbelief in the believer. Our faith is in God but through the Church, the community of those gathered by Him to transmit His truth and introduce the believer into the new life of grace. The Church is rejected and even hated by 'the world' because it preaches God's word, which is upsetting and contrary to the deliverances of the senses and the desires of the flesh, and this rejection is a pure unbelief. We may not allow appearances or the comfortable canons of naturalism to dictate the response to what God reveals to us of Himself and of our relation to Him. The condition of faith is always unsettled and unfinished, that of a pilgrim on his way and not yet arrived at his final destination; the word of God comes to us in affirmations which are not always clear and sometimes are fragmentary and disconcerting, and this is far from congenial to the rationalist taste for neatness and didactic precision. Yet, once accepted in faith, this truth brings unparalleled light and joy and penetrates to our innermost selves, to carry us forward in fulfillment of our destiny.

But is it so evident that a given word is in fact revealed by God? The obscurity of the content of faith extends also to its divine origin and guarantee and is exacerbated by some of the language and thought patterns out of which dogmatic definitions are formulated. Faith strains to grasp the essence of God's truth, but to accomplish this—never definitely, in any event—it must penetrate the husk of human interpretation. There is nothing wrong, either, in demanding that those who claim to teach in Christ's name justify their contention that what they say is, in fact, faithful to God's word, that they have kept the deposit intact. Not every believer will ask these questions, or with equal intensity of purpose, but they are not illegitimate in themselves nor is it reprehensible to seek sufficient reason for so momentous a decision. It is not a priori forbidden to examine the historical beginnings of Christianity or the alleged documents of divine revelation, but there cannot be any serious objection, either, to the hypothesis or sheer possibility that, if God exists, He may have spoken to man, somehow, but certainly in human ideas and words. There are those who experience very keenly the need for truth, for sober and realistic assessment of what they are told by others, so that renouncing the obligation to verify would be the most serious violation of conscience. One who has never felt the urge to make a mature personal decision about a matter of faith cannot properly appreciate the resolve to withhold assent as long as one is not honestly convinced. This is applicable in particular to a certain clericalist mentality for which ecclesiastical statements as such are automatically endowed with an acceptability that makes questioning superfluous. Doubt can, nevertheless, be an expression of a vigorous concern for one s spiritual integrity, whereas both denial and blind conformity are an easy way, the substitution of an extreme absolute for the difficult task of refining and deepening one's conviction through personal inquiry. For those whose fidelity is incomplete without this open and searching doubt, the certitude of an unexamined faith, such as it is, is impossible. This kind of doubt does not destroy faith; it strengthens it and removes bitterness and disaffection; when one has paid dearly for religious certainties, they are clung to and lived by, and one knows clearly the difference between the living truth and conventional opinion.

Theologians have not seen the possibility that doubt may actually relate one more directly and meaningfully to God than an assent that neither doubts nor questions, neither thinks nor understands. Churchmen in general too readily identify God and His word as the object of doubt, whereas in reality it is very often they who are unbelievable, not mediators of truth but impediments to it.[135] When this is the case, an honest and perceptive man is not afraid to dispense with the fixed demands of a mental system: the thoughts of churchmen and theologians are not God's, and they may be a luxury and a trap which pure faith cannot afford and need not tolerate. The vast difference between a perfunctory adherence to religion and the passionate search for God Himself is not all that evident to those whose habit it is to shut their eyes to the latter and gild the former until it shines brightly enough to satisfy their self-image. It is not the Christian Pharisee who opts for total purification, without shrinking from inner desolation and the desert of the soul, who is prepared to offer God his obedience and adore Him while begging for greater light. We cannot leave out of consideration, while assembling the materials and identifying the specific key problems for a theology of unbelief, that imperious demand, not of the intellect alone, but of man the truth-seeker, for as much light as he needs and for not less than is obtainable. An attitude of sincere and profound reverence for this sensitivity to intellectual values is a prerequisite to bridging the gap between the official interpretation of what faith requires and what the enlightened and honestly searching mind of man can accept.[136] Thus far theologians have not known how to deal with the problem of doubt in faith, in all its implications, except in an almost wholly negative and unsympathetic manner or on the highly abstract and largely irrelevant level of logical and psychological gymnastics. Once the problem is recognized in its complexity, a period of perhaps troubled and unsettling exploration will be needed.

The point is best put by Rabut in his statement that human doubt must be redeemed, that man must inevitably exercise without undue restraint his critical intelligence, even within the province of faith.[137] There is risk of the sin of unbelief, but, as long as good will inspires all and the proper bounds are observed, what might be a tormenting experience may be the highest fidelity to conscience and a holy endeavor. It is very likely that the crux of the problem is located somewhere in the need for verification on a critical level, a need which has simply not been taken sufficiently into account or allowed its legitimate role in the faith-life of at least some believers— and these not the least admirable, as may be. As a start, a step in the right direction and a proof of readiness to understand, religionists must be prepared to respect the probity and religious generosity of those who ask for a reasonable defense and exposition of what their faith prompts them to accept only if it is, indeed, the word of God and not any merely human wisdom. A sound method for incorporating doubt into the theology of faith, and not under the rubric of unbelief, at least not exclusively and without qualification, is needed right now. Doubt must not torture people into thinking that there is no room for them among the community of the faithful or that those who do not experience this persistent critical questioning have a right to reject them as traitors to the vocation they have received. I do not for the present see clearly the way in which theology may work out a solution to this question, but it is plain enough that new and reformed modes of thinking are called for, and along lines which I shall try briefly to suggest. My intention in these remarks, as frequently throughout this work, is to point to pressing problems which require theological elucidation, and not to propose definitive answers of my own.

(1) Because it is assent with thinking (*assensus cum cogitatione*, in the formula of St. Augustine adopted by St. Thomas Aquinas), faith does not suppress or prohibit a lively and continuing reflection upon what is to be believed, seeking a greater understanding.[138] This active questioning may assume the features of doubt, i.e., suspension of judgment, but need not cancel the commitment to God revealing Himself, which is the heart of faith, or the solidarity with others in the community of believers, which is not broken by the intent to doubt.

(2) When this doubt bears on the authenticity of a specific doctrine, i.e., whether it be truly from God and express His word and not the words of men, or on its intelligibility, including its coherence with the elementary canons of realistic thinking and

with experience, it demands the highest devotion to the dictates of conscience and the exigencies of intellectual honesty. This reference extends to anyone who with due prudence and diligence poses hard questions concerning doctrines which have had even the highest and broadest official sanction, and a fortiori to the corps of professional theologians whose task it is to probe the significance of such doctrine and the adequacy of the categories and terminology in which it is couched.[139]

(3) A much more difficult question, with practical and public ramifications, is that of the status of these doubters within or in relation to the Church. It has been held traditionally that bona fide Church membership excludes dissent on matters of faith and morals which have been settled by the highest authority, but relatively little has been done to update this simplistic position or to incorporate new insights into the function and value of creative doubt. The emphasis has been retarded in its development by the confusion and misapprehension which still prevail over the problem of the doubting believer.[140]

(4) What is needed at bottom is a fundamental transformation of the concept of faith which has succeeded in prevailing not so much in the actual grace-filled lives of sincere believers as in the highly formalized and rigidly schematized doctrine of faith constructed over the centuries. Faith has for its object God, and He alone is man's supreme Good; therefore it is understandable if one hesitates, for reasons which seem sufficient and compelling to an enlightened conscience, to extend this unreserved trust and confidence to those, men like ourselves, who claim to speak in God's name, but whose statements cannot be adequately and convincingly related to God and His word as one cannot help but expect Him.

(5) No question or doubt should be ruled out of court or dismissed as impermissible and spiritually destructive, and it goes without saying that the questioner himself should never be held in contempt. Through searching questions the doubting believer can lead all of us to a more significant understanding of our basic faith-certainties. This leads naturally to the need of dialogue to replace the brusque and arbitrary imposition of an indefinite number of doctrines, the essential connection of which to the central tenets of Christian faith is far from self-evident.

Very similar in many respects to this phenomenon of doubt in the life of faith is another which has been described as indirect believing. The indirectness removes it from the category of faith, which constitutes the subject of the official pronouncements and the great theological synthesis which believers have developed to express their reflective, systematic understanding of what faith is. I have already alluded to this indirect belief—so disguised as to have all the appearances of unbelief—in my discussion of the salvation of the unbeliever; I should like here to spell out in somewhat fuller detail the characteristics of this phenomenon and to reveal it as a species not of unbelief but of belief. The question may be analyzed fruitfully within the context of the interrelationship of faith and good works, in the vocabulary of one of the classical controversies surrounding the Reformation upheaval. The just man, St. Paul says, lives by faith; knowingly or not, intentionally or not, he does something that, in its immanent existential quality, is dynamically ordered to God and puts him in a vital interrelationship with God. According to the Gospels (e.g., Mt 15.34–46; Mk 12.28–34; and cf. Rom 13.8–10), it is faith which is embodied, actually realized, in the loving concern for one's neighbor, and authorizes us to identify with justifying faith what is not *ex professo* faith but rather the relief of the needy. This orientation is simultaneously toward the neighbor and toward God; the requirements of Christian faith are fulfilled even when explicit Christian motivation is absent. Even more than the profession of faith, unselfish love is the supreme realization of what is intended in and by faith, which is to transform man increasingly into the image of an all-merciful and loving Father. Experiences of loving concern already put him into touch with the *reality* of faith because Christ Himself assures us that whatever we do for the needy in itself turns us toward Him.

Luther rightly rejected works as a substitution for faith, in the sense of justifying oneself on the basis of one's work rather than in the legitimate sense of faith overflowing and realizing itself in a good life. There is the difficulty, not yet faced up to frankly, of Luther's aversion to the celebrated passage in St. James' Epistle, which relates faith and works in a manner calculated to illuminate the immediately preceding statement that 'judgment is without mercy to him who has not shown mercy; but mercy triumphs over judgment' (2.13).[141] I think the relationship in question provides an indispensable clue to the mystery of the faith-unfaith tension in all of mankind, a clash that is also a co-existence, the boundaries of which, St. Augustine estimates, are far from clear. St. Paul's insistence on the subordination of all, even good, works to grace points to a condition these have in common with faith: 'For by grace you have been saved through faith; and that not from yourselves, for it is the gift of God; not as the outcome of works, lest anyone may boast. For his workmanship we are, created in Christ Jesus in good works, which God has made ready beforehand that we may walk in them' (Eph 2.8–10). Love is inseparable from a living faith and is the work in which faith is fully realized and made perfect (Jas 2.17; 22.26). The difference between Christian faith and merely religious piety is sharp and striking: according to St. James, pure and undefiled religion consists less in cultic service than in active loving concern for those in need (1.27). Quite obviously, then, the salvation God effects applies to the whole man in his total physical and spiritual existence. The Christian may not limit his concept of Christian faith-response to matters of doctrine; he is enjoined to enter into concrete fellowship with the other, lending a helping hand.

This insight of the New Testament has a bearing on the belief of unbelievers and the unbelief of believers.[142] To be interested in and concerned about the needs of the whole man, without ulterior motive, is the carrying out of the greatest commandment and the beginning here of eternal life. What then of faith when honesty and sympathy, willing service, generosity, all the aspects of love which St. Paul mentions in First Corinthians are lacking? These qualities are not a dispensable supplement to authentic Christianity but its very proof and confirmation, the actual realization of God's salvific will. What God wills is that His creature experience the loving concern of others and reciprocate in kind, not in an infinitely far-off future but here and now, so far as possible. Where this love is, there is God the Savior, present in the authentic humanity of the neighbor rather than in the man who, caring nothing except for himself, piously shouts 'Lord, Lord.' The latter is a pseudo-belief, a belief without commitment, which fails by the New Testament standard of faith, and by which no one can be saved. The hypothesis ought to be seriously explored that, if one does not affirm what faith necessarily entails, it is at the same time an unbelief. Affirmation here means involvement, personal commitment, without which the profession of faith—all too easy, because really undemanding, and indeed comfortably gratifying, cheap grace, as Søren Kierkegaard and Dietrich Bonhoeffer declare—is a mere empty formalism. The commitment is, at once and indivisibly, to God and to one's fellows and, let it be reiterated with the greatest emphasis, it is dictated by faith and not supererogatory in any sense. If this means anything, Quentin Lauer writes: '. . . it means loving man, precisely because he is man, not because love is a divine command or a moral law, not because in loving man we are loving God, but because we have eyes to see that man is lovable and that we are less than human if we do not love him.'[143]

One keeps alternating between what faith is and what it is not, for it is in this contrast that the theology of unbelief must be worked out. Faith is none of the following, and when it assumes any of the following guises it is not faith but crypto-unbelief: ideology, metaphysical world-view, mythological world-picture, moralistic justification. With a rapid review of each of these possibilities, by way of rejecting all, I shall bring to a close these thoughts on the unbelief of the believer.

(1) Faith is not ideology, but unbelief characteristically assumes this form. By this I mean that faith is not a pseudo-scientific interpretation of reality in the service of some socio-political end, which in turn is invoked to render the interpretation sacrosanct. Men have used religion in just this fashion, and the Christian religion itself has been prostituted in the interests of a status quo or a revolutionary enterprise, but these abuses have dealt a death-blow to Biblical faith and replaced it with its counterfeit. The message of faith does not comprise concrete imperatives and programs, archetypal patterns for the shaping or interpreting of history. Hence belief in no wise relieves one of the existential burden of hazardous decisions and their possible frustration or protects one from blind alleys by the ready application of transcendent norms to the alternatives of history. Above all, it is not incumbent on the believer to pose as champion of God's interests: for one thing, God is perfectly able to look after Himself, and for another, it is no easy matter to define precisely what His interests are, especially in the long run. The rights of men must be respected in any case, even against the imperious encroachments of an overzealous legalistic Church, which men have fashioned out of fear and mistrust and a gnawing self-hatred. The principle of authority is perfectly legitimate, of course, but those who exercise authority are not above wielding it in the service of an ideology, of apotheosizing human self-will under cover of an unexceptionable principle.[144] It is not unbelief to resist this abuse but a part of the commitment to pure truth of which ideology is the worst betrayal. It is, on the other hand, nothing but ideological cowardice which unfailingly justifies ecclesiastical decisions and avoids the hard questioning which constantly measures claims against norms, performance against ideals. Only the ideologist insists upon antecedent assurance that no question will return an unpleasant or unexpected answer, that inquiry be made only into matters of secondary importance or into questions that are already answered. The ideologist is quick to charge with suspicion and disloyalty anyone who breaks through absolutized formulation, weighted down with

a dead past. Because faith is historical, it keeps pace with experience without losing its essential nature.[145] Grace is always the grace of preserving us from ideology, from betraying faith into the absolutizing of man in the name of religion.

(2) Faith embraces no metaphysical world-view arrived at independently of God's revelation and the history of salvation; the attempt to freeze God's word in humanly achieved metaphysical categories has been repeated over and over since the earliest period of Christianity. It is an attempt inspired by a belief so weak and impure that it seeks avidly the company and support of philosophical systems. The seriousness of the problem which faces the inquiring believer is exemplified in one of the earliest and nearly the most disastrous of confrontations of Christian faith and a non-scriptural world-view. Hans Jonas' monumental studies of Gnosticism have established this world-view as primarily a cosmology asserting a radical difference between human existence and the nature of the world outside man. Contrary to the Christian doctrine of creation and redemption, the Gnostic reads the evil in the world as a cosmic misfortune which removes the world from God's providence. The assimilation of Gnostic dualism would have spelled disaster for Biblical faith, yet the Gnostic-Christians would undoubtedly have gone on to further dilute the faith professed until belief became out-and-out unbelief.[146] Faith can never be reduced to a view of the world because it relates primarily to a historical experience which carried its own distinctive understanding of God and man, one inspired by God Himself. Today believers are asking intently whether they ought not dispense altogether with any dominant metaphysic and rely on the historicity of faith itself for its own form and style of expression. I do not wish to involve myself in this question, so hotly disputed in recent decades, or to deny that creative and fruitful tension may be maintained between belief and metaphysical views.

(3) Mythology in the sense in which I am using it purports to talk about the transcendent, the other-worldly, in terms constructed out of objects in the world of experience. The objection to mythologizing faith, or the understanding of faith, is that it tends to evaporate the realism and historicity of faith in a mist of artificial thought-patterns and images which are extensions of ourselves. The paradox of the Gospel, the junction of sheer otherness with sheer grace, is dissolved in a confusion of the other-worldly, which mythology seeks to grasp, and the this-worldly, which it seeks to link with the other-worldly. In the elision of historical reality with would-be 'objective' formulations, transcendence is lost, and God is drawn into the scope of

human understanding in a way similar to that in which ordinary objects may be used and exploited. At a popular level mythology accomplishes a debasing and nullifying of faith comparable to that effected by metaphysical confusion at a more sophisticated intellectual level.[147]

(4) It is a great mistake to circumscribe faith, essentially and pre-eminently historical and transcendent as it is, by a moralistic demand. Yet at times the uniqueness of faith, and especially its utter gratuitousness, has been overwhelmed, or at least obscured, by the moralistic view of man in the world. At first Christians had to contend with the heritage of a Law which had been revered and exalted, by God's own direction, but from which they believed they had been delivered by the grace of Christ. In subsequent periods the moralistic interpretation of Christian life assumed formidable power and influence over minds, perpetually supported by the deep-rooted drive in men to earn their own justification and not depend for it on another. There is, further, a truth in the desire for a good will and the reality of an upright heart, which remains intact, although profoundly transformed, under the impact of divine grace. For Biblical faith the overriding truth is that man's moral integrity has no control over the mercy of God; indeed, the will of man, which is to say, man himself, is redeemed by that mercy while yet remaining subject to the grip of evil. It is not a straightforward movement of a good will leading to moral betterment but deliverance through God's forgiveness.[148] The free decision of faith is always a response to the call to accept the forgiving and liberating word of God—a free response, yet set free by God's grace. It would be un-faith, unbelief in the guise of belief, to diminish this basic paradox so as to leave man's will-power dominant and impose a Pelagian or semi-Palagian construction on the condition of man under the new law of grace. Grace is not an extra, certainly not an unnecessary extra, imported into the moral situation, which is otherwise fully and satisfactorily determined by man's voluntary decision. Unless faith acknowledges the justified man's total dependence on God, as the giver of total existence, the moral situation is falsified and belief abandoned. The moral condition of man is seen to be a relation that thoroughly constitutes him in a righteousness which liberates him for service.

Unbelief bears a witness to the reality of God and the authenticity of faith which is as striking and as powerful as it is strange and unexpected. In turning its attention to each of the specific problems I have touched upon in this chapter, contemporary theology is both drawing upon and contributing to a deepened and purified understanding of faith. I have, I hope, pinpointed a limited number of these key problems, the exposition of which has disclosed the interconnection of basic aspects of the theology of unbelief with other crucial points of Christian teaching. We have had a brisk reminder that the self-critical function of theology is always indicated, not only to answer the charges and objections put to belief by the world of unbelief but to correct and refine the believer's self-understanding in faith. The task of apologetics may not be as near to that loving contemplation of divine truth to which dogmatic theology aspires, but its purpose is no less obvious if the theologian is to take full responsibility before his contemporaries for the meaningfulness and truth of his assertions. Unbelief as a theological problem will be situated in both a dogmatic and an apologetic framework, speaking appropriately to the witness of Scripture and understandably to the men of today. I have never advocated conforming the claims of faith to the secular thought of any situation, although there is advantage to be hoped for, without impermissible compromise, in establishing the validity of these claims by the same general standards of experience and reason to which the best and most reliable thought is subject. The Scriptures imply that the truth Christ represents is somehow of a piece with whatever men know anywhere —surpassing it but not contradicting it. The theologian has both the right and the duty to question the validity of other men's claims to truth in a dialogue with the exponents of secular experience and wisdom.[149] It is to this practical task of dialogue, the confrontation of believer and unbeliever, that the analysis of belief and unbelief is ultimately ordered and to which I turn in the chapter which follows.

CHAPTER THREE

Toward a Dialogue

The grace of faith enables man to come alive, to be born a second time and grow in the spirit. From God, the believer receives a mission and a mandate, in a relationship which is doubly open-ended: faith is not possessed unchallenged nor can it safely be taken for granted, for it is not an adjunct or perfection of human nature, such as a skill or art or laboriously acquired virtue. The believer is tested and questioned in the very depths of his being and summoned to a destiny, which he must consciously and freely embrace. He knows his capacity for failing, that is, for rejecting himself in faith and deciding to live by another light and another law. The law of faith is bound up with the mandate to discover oneself, to become what one can and must be, in freedom and without guile. Unbelief reveals the alternative to this decision and confirms that faith cannot be arbitrary or a matter of mere whim; neither option is devoid of law and its own proper order. The force of unbelief is demonstrated in the earnestness and enthusiasm with which it may be chosen and influence a man's way of life. Thus the free project of realizing one's humanity exposes one to this most fateful of choices, a prospect with its own risks and dangers. Eventually, faith must confront its contrary, not only in the separate lives of believer and unbeliever, but within the heart of every man.

In this final chapter I propose to outline the conditions and suggest briefly the elements of a dialogue of believer and unbeliever, the goal towards which the analyses and interpretations of the present work have been directed. It is by no means evident that believers are as yet properly prepared to enter into dialogue, although some churchmen and theologians have expressed an interest and a desire

132

to undertake precisely this. The contact will be personal, an encounter of individuals; there are no official spokesmen for unbelief, of course, and in any case the believer will have to make his own terms with the challenge to faith as he experiences it. I propose to address myself to my brethren in the household of faith, to explore with them, as I see it, the path to a dialogue that promises to be fruitful. Because Christian faith is in and of a community, the action of believers vis-à-vis those who do not share their faith, or any faith at all in God, dialogue must be a concern of the Church as such, as the body of those who, together and in unity, profess a faith that is not the esoteric vision of private souls but the shared heritage of a congregation, a community of those who have heard a common message and made a common commitment. The Church is still very much absorbed—perhaps rather less, and less vigorously, than some might have hoped—in the enormous and quite taxing business of renewal. The dialogue will emerge from that moment at which this effort of self-criticism and self-reform rises to a pitch of genuine seriousness and intensity, so that nothing like a realistic and responsible dialogue will get under way if the resolution and impetus to renew are blunted and stifled. This must be so, if it is true, as I hold it to be, that the confrontation with unbelief is a variable function of the purity and authenticity of faith, as it is, indeed, one of the most urgent demands placed upon the believer in this world. Renewal is, to be sure, an end in its own right, but for the purpose of my study it is situated squarely on the path which must be pursued on the way to dialogue. The first step is to recognize unbelief in its contemporary dimensions, as a concrete fact of immense historical significance and the perennial threat to the peace and security of believing. In the light of this awareness of the phenomenon (although not, to repeat, primarily or exclusively in this connection or for this purpose), the Church will continue to seek the renovation of both doctrine and life, together and by concerted means. The action of the Church with respect to unbelief is twofold, not only dialogue, which has hardly begun, but proclamation of the word of God, the announcement to all peoples of the Gospel, with the summons to conversion and faith.

UNBELIEF AS A SUMMONS TO CHRISTIAN WITNESS AND CONCERN

When it is a believer, within the perspective of faith and on the basis of religious understanding and concern, who looks at unbelief, the latter is more than a concrete fact and more than a mere speculative question. It is a problem with many sides, rendered acute by certain historical data; above all it is a problem of understanding and unity, or, rather, of the lack of these which produces division. The atheist is not as easy to identify as it was once thought, yet the pressures of unbelief are felt, more or less intensely, from many directions, so that it is hardly possible to ignore this massive presence, although it is unfortunately quite possible to miss its essential features and misinterpret its total significance. The temptation to unbelief is a real one, for the sensitive and troubled believer, one which he is obliged to resist at any cost, with God's grace. There is, further, the need to protect, in a reasonable manner, the young and unformed from influences of various kinds as well as to answer objections and charges made against the claims of religion by a sober and honest apologetical defense. In a sense, lastly, believers have always had to contend with the challenge of atheism, particularly in the form of succumbing to the allurements of the world in a way which effectively shuts out God from everyday life and concern. When all has been conceded and admitted that may lawfully be, another and newer direction remains to be taken by the man of faith facing unbelief. This new stance comprises neither 'Christian atheism' nor a retreat before secularism, in any of the versions that have recently been proposed, as these are not an assertion of faith but its dissolution and betrayal.

One is dealing with a post-Christian unbelief, in large part, at least wherever the Gospel has been heard and faith has at one time been accepted. Unbelief in the Western world is not a primitive or original datum so much as the critique, the negative response, to a centuries-old religious fact. For many people, especially the better educated, atheism represents a preferred function of modern emancipation of profound human significance.[1] The question posed for the believer is how most effectively to confront man's denial of God with lived faith, which means the believer himself, as witnessing to the God whom others declare to be non-existent, unknowable, or insupportable. It is not, in the long run, a matter of philosophical discussion, certainly not of moral denunciation, although exhortation and civilized debate are perfectly in order. Faith, however, is not an abstract of definite formulas, nor is it a superior ethical system; it is the whole of existence for one who believes, in which all is included in an ineffable experience of the mercy of God in Christ. The unbeliever meets authentic faith in another when the other has surrendered himself, in the midst of his faltering existence, to God; he may not admit the objective value or meaningfulness of this faith-attitude, but it will be a challenge to him because it is the expression of that humanity common to all. The fact of unbelief, on the other hand, constitutes only one threat to faith; the courage to believe is constantly subject to the test of doubt and the affront of denial. It is only in this situation of risk and danger that the pilgrim's faith stands exposed as at once a saving act given by God and the affirmation of weak and fallible man, because as such it constitutes the ultimate basis of man's existence at the deepest level.[2]

The climate of spiritual unity and homogeneity of belief may have contributed to a certainty of faith that was perhaps too glib, too comfortable, but which has ceased to be viable. What of the arguments for the credibility of faith, the ideal proof which was supposed to be positive, direct, universal, and scientifically objective? May one still expect to bring to a confrontation with the unbeliever the well-developed defense produced by traditional apologetics? It is highly improbable that anyone, professional or layman, can master the many diverse areas of knowledge involved or the method by which a satisfactory scientific basis for faith (supposing there is such) may be made convincing to the modern mind. I should think that part of the awareness of the challenge of unbelief must include a reflective consciousness of the need for a radical change in the concept of fundamental theology and its role in relation to the reasonableness of faith. There is a twofold risk, or rather danger, in maintaining faith in the midst of a world which encourages unbelief; one is that of not really believing inwardly, and the other is that of not translating what we profess into the way we live. As long as a self-serving pretense and hypocrisy is kept up, we will manage to avoid acknowledging the flimsiness and weakness of faith. That is why I insist, at the outset, that only an honestly examined faith is fit to confront unbelief, and this entails a confession that the strength of faith derives not from human resolve or ingenuity or uprightness but from the same merciful grace by which it is given us originally to believe. St. Paul was convinced, from his own experience, that it was out of the recognition of his own frailty, his helplessness, that the grace of salvation worked in him powerfully. The unbeliever is not alone in contending with a universe that seems drained of meaning and purpose; as men, we who yet trust in God are equally menaced by 'the apparently irreversible process of inner decay, the helplessness of the spirit against the powers of the flesh, violence, and death, the apparently senseless cruelty of history, the progressive crushing of defenseless truth by the brutality of so-called realism, the way we are engulfed by the petty concerns of everyday life . . .'[3]

This is not excessive anxiety or a false and destructive self-depreca-
tion; the believer is admitting to neither a worse nor a more frighten-
ing condition than any other man, only that he lives, fully a man, in
the same world as his fellows.

The goal towards which encounter rightly tends becomes clearly
not the refutation of unbelief, for the latter is a lived option, which
can no more be 'refuted' than the decision to live by faith, but rather
the comprehension and surpassing of unbelief. Speaking henceforth
in the name of those who believe, whose faith is in God in Christ, I
assert that we must firstly identify accurately who those are who do
not believe, wherever they are. That is to say, we must engage to look
at them, to get to know them and see them for what they are, so
far as men reveal their inner selves. Neither domestic concerns,
including intramural squabbling, nor the dead weight of an old
legacy of polemic and suspicion may be allowed to prevent this
indispensable preliminary task, one of which I have been aware
throughout the present work. A first task, then, is a complete and
accurate phenomenology or typology of unbelief, so far as this is
feasible—and here I feel I have only just scratched the surface. One
must not confuse abstract schemes, however attractive, with the
real knowledge of persons in their concreteness, or settle for the former when one must bend every effort to attain the latter. What is
met with in life are impure and mixed forms of unbelief, ranging
across a spectrum of explicit articulateness and personal intensity.
The most aggressive, the most self-confident and clearly formulated
lend a structure and force to others and should be sought out,
almost as a point of honor.[4] It is significant, surely, that so many
unbelievers today occupy positions of cultural and political leadership, or aspire to them, as if the predominant shape and impetus
of social life had to be dictated on terms which excluded religious
conviction. Yet for such men and women unbelief is itself a matter
of deep, conscientious conviction. If the believer is adamant, that
is, firmly and even passionately attached to his faith, he should not
be offended or disconcerted to find extremes of stubbornness and
recalcitrance in the unbeliever. Again, one witnesses to one's own
faith but God is never revealed unambiguously in any of us; the
spiritual honesty and integrity of conscience of the other must be
respected. At the same time the terrible depths of unbelief, which I
think can be penetrated only by the most discerning and understanding faith, harbor a conflict of light and darkness which renders
unbelief, ultimately, a part of the mystery of our universal human
condition.

Dialogue will be achieved gradually in a series of steps, no one of which may be slighted or bypassed, and all of which depend for their success on the continued recognition of the true dimensions of unbelief as a lived option. This recognition will be impossible unless the unbeliever is permitted, indeed encouraged, to state his position, so that its human significance may be appreciated, and he may be aware of receiving a courteous and sympathetic hearing. The religionist overly concerned about cherished rights and preroga- tives, about what he takes to be the special privileges and innate superiority of his role as God's spokesman and champion, may be commended for what used to be called the zeal for God's house that consumes him, but he is obviously not prepared, intellectually or emotionally, to enter into dialogue with those 'less well favored' by divine providence than himself. When one reflects on the fact that all men, without exception, live in a world in which God is not visible, but in which the freaks and foibles of religion are all too evident, one becomes excruciatingly sensitive to the need for that poverty of spirit which is simply the confession of one's indigence before God. In this same spirit one may, without compunctions and gladly, search out the fullest possible agreement not of belief and unbelief, for this seems highly problematic, but of believer and unbeliever, and on this basis push on to find in the other whatever may be discoverable of the presence of grace and of a common humanity. This attitude is one of the hallmarks of the post-conciliar Church and deserves further development.

This world, an already (if only partially and very imperfectly) humanized world, is, always and in every aspect, God's world, with- out in the least ceasing to be wholly *world*, i.e., not-God. For many years now, reaching back at least to the turn of the century and the current of thought labeled as 'immanence,' Christians have insisted, hesitantly, gropingly at first, that the natural and the supernatural form a unity in the concrete.[5] This harmony, in spite of the resistance and rebellion of what Scripture calls 'the flesh,' is expressed in concepts such as the openness of nature to grace, the existential exigency of man for the gift of grace, and the radical orientation of all men to the vision of God. Immanence, however, threatened in some measure the inherent autonomy and consistency of nature and grace alike, a danger corrected and counterbalanced, in my judgment, by the somewhat more recent movement of Christian secularity. I do not propose here to offer an adequate definition of this concept because I think a few more decades of lived experience of it are needed before its full ramifications are disclosed. As I use the term in the

present context, secularity means the recognition and respect by man
of the inner intelligibility and value of the *saeculum,* the world
and time, not a perfect or perfectly clear and accessible intelligibility
or a flawless and limitless value, but one that is identical with thy
reality of the world—including man, of course—and not merely
attributed to it extrinsically, in virtue of the eminent and superabundant reality of its Creator. These theological considerations are
tedious to rehearse, it may be, but without them one is, logically at
least, exposed to the vagaries of an arbitrary benevolence, assumed
magnanimously by a conciliatory supernaturalist, but not compelled
by the world's own inalienable structure and density. The relevance
of this point to our immediate subject is not slight: in St. Augustine's
brilliant and touching phrase, the Church is the world reconciled.
It is not only the sign of Christ but the sign of the world, recognized,
endorsed, and borne on its way to fulfillment. In other words, the
believer is at once citizen both of Church and of world and in both
finds the being, truth, goodness, and beauty which image God and
point to Him, without ceasing to be—the world. The believer is
not at all surprised to find in the unbeliever, precisely because and
to the extent that he is a knowing and loving and serving man in
the world, the qualities he cherishes and admires. The world today
is not blind to these values and is not likely to respond to any attempt
to belittle or overlook their importance. I should like to dwell on
this point because it is integral to the Church's self-examination
in preparation for dialogue. The point is that believers stand to
profit a great deal by a generous and unconcealed recognition of
the positive value to be found in the thinking and in the spiritual
ethos of some of our unbelieving contemporaries.

   It is not only within the ambit of religious faith that genuine
moral and humane values are sought; an ecclesial outlet is not
required for the release of energies in pursuit of personal integrity,
brotherhood, justice, and peace. Community is highly prized even
under secular auspices, and there are available secular symbols
and agencies for social and political reform. Atheists are among the
most serious and imaginative leaders in the effort to realize fundamental moral imperatives. Since faith inspires the quest for these same
values, although it transcends them and enhances their status,
God and man are reconciled, and it remains to carry out, with confidence in the outcome, the project of purifying religion of every
inhuman and anti-human element. If examination at length indicates
that certain insights are somehow peculiar to the atheistic approach,
then the believer must admit that he has something to learn from

this approach. By the same token, it is the believer's prerogative and duty to put unbelief to the test, to question it and make it give an account of itself; the unbeliever should not be spared the healthy exercise of reflecting and meeting objections. A man like Bertrand Russell, for example, has spent most of a very long lifetime polemicizing against religion generally, and Christianity in particular, without ever taking a long, hard look at Christian faith. Dialogue with such persons is out of the question, and Newman's dictum, uttered almost a century ago, is still apropos, that we must make the others look at us.

There is risk in this, in opening ourselves, exposing our weakness and shortcomings, in all the free and unfettered interchange that moves us toward dialogue. We must be able to count on our awareness of our responsibility as believers, whether or not we expect to succeed in helping the other to surpass himself, to come to realize his own responsibility as a human being. Awareness of the risk inseparable from the activity of dialogue in no wise diminishes the urgency of the task or excuses from undertaking it. Renewal and reform begin with recognition of the mass of practicing believers who are too easily and too complacently Christian; to bring them to genuine encounter with God will require a purification of faith that will engage every work of renewal and reform. The desired result will be a more authentic and meaningful witness to the truth of God and a more realistic identification of the essence of Christianity as lived out in a world which is trying to exclude the presence of God. One of the first illusions to be discarded, I would think, is that as Christians we go out or forth into a paganized world—a curious geographical mistake, involving the fantastic image of a foray from a fortress into a spiritual jungle. Nowhere has this concept served to mold an attitude and sustain a mentality more thoroughly or systematically than in the philosophy of education, of Christian formation, which prevailed in our universities and colleges, and especially in our seminaries. I should like to offer here some thoughts on the preparation of priests and future priests for dialogues with unbelievers, a subject obviously not of immediate interest to everyone but of far-reaching importance for the future of dialogue.[6]

The priestly ministry incorporates a man into the clergy, an ecclesiastical state of a determined historical character and background, a point that demands consideration in view of the marked individualist attitude, especially of young persons. It is not a question of an individual, as such, preparing and equipping himself, as a believer, to fulfill his personal obligation of witnessing to Christ. Imprecision and confusion of priesthood and clerical state can adversely affect the appreciation of the priest-witness's role in this dialogue. Adaptation and reform raise the issue of the demands of local conditions, the variations in tone and emphasis which dialogue will necessarily assume in different regions and under divergent circumstances. The seminarian is a citizen of a world in which revolution and the prospects of revolution are real concerns, and he is exposed to the currents of thought and the aspirations and occupations of the men of this time. The future priest's training must be, integrally and totally, doctrinal and pastoral, just as theology is completely and of its very nature ecclesial, an organic reflection of the Church in its nature and in its dynamic presence in the world. Because pastoral preparation must take account of the specific environment, it is unwise to attempt a detailed program of preparation of seminarians for dialogue. In any case, the seminary is not a lumber mill or a smelter, organized and geared to turn out identical products, given whatever raw materials. Seminary moderators and professors will be incapable of effecting the integration of the doctrinal and pastoral aspects and purposes of formation unless they are themselves cultured men, which means liberally educated and alive to the forces and movements of our civilization.

The seminary cannot make a man of open mind and heart out of nothing. All the people of God are involved in creating a matrix in which suitable priestly vocations will be cradled, nourished, and promoted. Candidates are apt to profit by a deliberate formation, for dialogue must come out of an atmosphere in which the positive values of dialogue are widely recognized and duly prized. Seminarians will respond more readily and comprehendingly to their training for dialogue if they have been raised in the bosom of Catholic people conscious of the Church's call to dialogue. It is doubtful that we have this atmosphere as yet, and to complicate matters, we have, very nearly, a caricature of the real thing. I mean that we have a situation in which young Catholics are misled into mistaking open-hearted and generous concern for all men for a well-informed grasp of what makes our world modern and what in it is responsive or not to the announcement of the Gospel.

It has become as clear to today's seminarians as it has to many of the laity that there has been a terrible lack of seriousness in the entire clerico-ecclesiastical system. Illusions have been generated from particular historical situations which have persisted for generations. Historical living, if it is to be genuinely and intelligently creative, must struggle with the systematized ideas of the past, analyzed and criticized out of the recognition of a new situation.

The pattern of Catholic living has been described countless times and with variations in recent years, and its weaknesses and defects have received perhaps as much attention as they could bear. It is a question at this point of higher Church officials, including those in the very top echelon, catching up with the more perceptive members and of implementing valid insights in a program of far-reaching reform. Too many prelates have become rigid and conformed to an unhistorical, paternalist view of living, and taken a particular view of truth as a logical, abstractly coherent notion by which final truth has been formulated and fallen into our grasp, once and for all, built into an airtight system. This has been said and repeated, but some have not heard it, or it has meant nothing to them, for they continue to speak and act as if it were not to be taken seriously. They use the language of 'search for truth,' but merely as an observation of and within the system; basically, truth is not something one wrestles with in history, but something handed down to be learned, analyzed, commented on, and translated without remainder into a predictable way of life. Such a mentality is able to neglect, to be ignorant of, extremely important aspects of one's historical present, to withdraw and operate inside the safe and familiar formulations of the past rather than to re-examine these, critically and forthrightly.* One often

* Truthfulness (Küng) or honesty (Novak) is a prime imperative in the life of the Church today; for want of it, possibly more than any other single defect, real or imagined, Catholics, clergy, religious, lay people, have for the past few years been dissociating themselves, in varying degrees, from the ecclesial institution. As we experience this current period of transition, we are disturbed, more or less, by what appears to be a curious mixture of survivals from the preceding age with the new attitudes and kinds of behavior which the present demands. This happens in such a way, sometimes, that it is difficult, morally, to interpret an event or situation, and some define it as the collapse of faith, which it need not be. Truthfulness will be satisfied; it is an exigency which will not be compromised or caricatured, as it has been in the past, yet this new and more Christian attitude, as well as other motives, may operate in structures which are moribund or corrupt—or utterly useless, even though not corrupt. The essential wrongness of these structures may then be partially obscured, because they appear, misleadingly, to have adjusted to the moral and spiritual renewal, but this only demonstrates the oddity of a Church in a state of turmoil. There is indeed not a little moral ambiguity about much of what has been happening in the Church recently, as old ways continue to succeed in smothering new attempts at understanding and action. Some churchmen, with a stolid endurance learned not from the Gospel but from centuries of clericalist political maneuvering, are presently digging in for a long wait, prepared to sit out the storm of renewal, which they expect will, must, eventually blow over. When the winds die, they opine, the old cherished structures and ways of doing things will have weathered the tempest and the old familiar certainties and attachments will be found intact.

F

calls for docility to the paternalist structure, fidelity to the old truth-pattern.

Formulations as such are necessary and useful; they minister to illusion only when they harden into handed-on rather than lived-out tradition and become an end in themselves, a kind of fetish, unrelatable to the historicity of contemporary existence. The moral and spiritual seriousness of society is refuted or minimized in the name of eternal truths and the alleged superiority of an encrusted dogmatism. The world must not see the Church as emerging from Jerusalem and passing by on the way to Jericho on the other side. We live in a clearly de-christianized society but even more clearly and emphatically in a culture in which ecclesiastical personages and structures and ambitions neither dominate nor capture allegiance. Our ecumenical outreach has been of some consequence, it would appear, in opening windows onto the non-Catholic world, but it might be that those who profess belief in God will be left holding hands as the world moves out and away from them. I am trying, because I still believe 'in the holy Catholic Church,' to keep dialogue within an ecclesial framework, but certain matters need to be aired, and there must be no self-deception in this connection. Some Catholics, bound emotionally or in conscience to the paternalist-dogmatist illusion, are hurt and bewildered by change, or the cry for reform. Some others feel that modern seriousness has become so convincingly and obviously right that it is neither desirable nor possible any longer to live apart from it. Dialogue for these latter is seen as much more than a sincere show of fraternal concern for the other; it is a means of survival: the need to communicate, to share spiritual insight and value, with the other, in a common cooperative effort.

The believer will have to face up to the responsibility and opportunity of dialogue, with or without official ecclesiastical leadership and guidance, for the Church's own sake, that it may fulfill its commission of witness and presence in and for the world. What is new in this is the recognition, at last, that witness includes and demands dialogue, a recognition that presupposes awareness of where we stand in the light of our own most vital and authentic ideals. There is danger, otherwise, of confronting unbelief—which we may have mistakenly erected into a monolithic system—with just another such system, unrenewed and largely unprepared for the meeting. Atheism today is, in great part, quite simply one way in which some people live, try to solve problems, write novels, make films. Instead of seeing it in this perspective, our preoccupation with ourselves as militant, besieged, has prompted us to erect unbelief into a monstrous force with which we could and ought to do battle. Unbelief is by this time a thoroughly historical, and therefore relative, term in that it serves people well, liberating them from a pattern of living which they find intolerably suffocating. As Schnier says, in Heinrich Böll's novel, *Ansichten eines Clowns*, atheists bore us, they are always talking about God—Schnier is not an atheist; he is, as he boasts, simply a non-believer. The professional atheists are much more interesting to the professional Christians—those with a heightened concern for the future of faith.

Because faith is social, incorporating the believer into a community of witness and concern, the dialogue in question will have an ecclesial dimension, as we shall see, not only when it engages public spokesmen or Church officials but always, and inescapably, as long as full faith is involved. Thus far I have been speaking of recognition, awareness on the part of believers both of the shape and thrust of unbelief and of the need for the purification of faith and the life of the Church, to meet the challenge and to witness more effectively. Renewal, to which I shall turn in a moment, may be experienced partially as a kind of godforsakenness, which will mean only that the breaking of idols is painful, a crucifixion of attitudes and values that have been our life for so long. The pain is nothing, however, if it will contribute to the resurrection from the graveyard of illusion and the lifting of a strain that has driven some noble souls to the brink of despair.

RENEWAL AND PREPARATION FOR DIALOGUE

Theology is, or should be, a fairly accurate reflection of the life of the faithful, allowing for the tidying of loose ends and the speculative projections to which one man is addicted and which another cannot manage. It may very well be the case, nevertheless, that theological work outstrips or is outstripped by the conditions of actual Christian living in the community of believers. It is still true that thought should mirror existence or at least that the single undivided life of man, internal and external, intellectual, affective and operative, should form a coherent and consistent whole. St. Thomas Aquinas is fond of quoting St. Augustine's *prius vita quam doctrina* because he is a profound realist and would abhor a situation in which a theology of renewal or the renewal of theology found neither support nor confirmation in the life of the Church, its devotion to the task of witness, the sincerity of its continual conversion, its prayer and

concern for men's needs. This excursion into the sticky thickets of
theological renewal takes into account the total renewal of Christian
existence of which it is a part and to the general aims of which it
must conform, but my ulterior purpose is still that of the preparation
for action, the proclamation and dialogue which constitute the
points of contact of faith as such with the world of unbelief. After
a survey of the main features of general renewal in theology, as this
is conceived by the most highly respected proponents of reform,
I shall turn directly to the theology of unbelief and of the preaching of
the Gospel in today's world.

In spite of a massive complacency in the years immediately
preceding the Second Vatican Council, a relatively small band of
theologians of superior talent and perspicuity saw the defects which
plagued their discipline, and were bold enough to point them out,
when they could get a hearing. Yves Congar, one of these courageous
critics, describes the then incumbent conception of theology as one
in which everything has been defined in a way which leaves no
aspect unfixed.[7] This theology subjects the whole of reality, in
principle at least, to a process of standard formulation by which an
established and fixed doctrine is elicited from a number of theses
or propositions. The finished product can be learned and taught
in a fairly mechanical or rote fashion, and development consists in
making further deductions and affirmations as soon as a word (a
concept) is supported by enough evidence from tradition or the
Church's teaching authority. This concept of theology has proved
inadequate on three counts: (1) it ignores the solid results of the
work carried on for almost half a century (much longer, by Protestants) in the areas of *ressourcement*, Biblical and patristic, research
and dialogue; (2) it ignores the questions and needs of the men of
the present time and is content to exist independently of the conditions in which men experience and reflect upon the problems which
life poses; (3) it supposes that 'doctrine' is an object to be trans-
mitted and not also a subject of research, failing to see that truth
can be better seen and formulated through 'resourcing' and dialogue.
It is not a question of discarding what is definitively true but of
nourishing and enriching the knowledge of truth from within, less
by refining and elaborating concepts and words than by re-reading
the sources, Holy Scripture in particular, in a context of contemporary questioning and in the light of our experience of the *reality*
in question.

A renewed theology avoids the negative approach of imposing
strictures and censures, most of which in the past have been con-

spicuously fatuous and irrelevant, but which suit very well, unfortunately, the practice of an overly conceptualized defensive-polemical theology. The truth as understood in the context of faith must be re-affirmed but not without development and presentation for men and in commerce with others. The real, substantial advance in theology evidenced at the Council and in the past several years has been promoted overwhelmingly not by men in Rome or in seminaries closely following the traditional line but by men working in freedom and responsibility in touch with others, Christians and non-believers, and with currents of thought and life in the non-ecclesial world. The guardians of the incumbent system had hardly any contact with those who led the creative research and most lively inquiry which characterize the contemporary scene. There was no incentive or motive to make such contact as long as the work of theology was confined to making a solid front *against* what was interpreted as the hostile and corrosive influences of modern thought. Since the Council of Trent, roughly, and more especially since the French Revolution, the emphasis in Catholic thinking, carefully cultivated by clerical censors and supervisors, has been on operating cautiously and dutifully within efficiently regulated ecclesiastical structures. The system's doctrine was zealously protected by security measures paralleling those in the Soviet Union and by a continuing apologetic enterprise undertaken by safe, reliable men recruited entirely from within the system itself.

Despite overwhelmingly adverse conditions, however, a number of thinkers of remarkable ability and acumen succeeded in laying the groundwork for a renewal of theology and persevered under the most outrageuous persecution and misunderstanding for more than twenty years. There were unmistakable fresh and invigorating currents blowing through the Church at the Council, the 'informing' and the 'teaching' Church, according to a happy phrase. A truly inspired and inspiring pope, John XXIII, broke down the image of the Church set up as a bastion to resist the modern world. One likes to think that an irreversible process has been initiated in which nothing is finished beyond question and in which dialogue replaces monologue. It is extremely important, in order to appreciate precisely the significance of this development, to situate what has taken place in its actual historical framework. It may be indicated briefly by noting that the reform thus far realized—and it is by no means ended —has been accomplished by men whose personal integrity, spiritual depth, loyalty to the Gospel and to the faith of the Church, not to speak of their professional expertise, are firmly established. They include cardinals and bishops as well as priests and laymen, and they operate collegially, in a broad sense, as the people of God reflecting, lovingly, seriously, with the utmost concern for the good of souls, and not as disaffected rebels or subversives. They need not be apotheosized or prematurely canonized; they are not infallible, nor are they immune to criticism or disagreement. It strikes me as a curious but revealing instance of the psychological mechanism known as projection to find those most vociferously opposed to this band of theological renewers and reformers objecting most strongly to claims and prerogatives that the latter have never made or assumed. Those who have regarded themselves as the watchdogs of an immobile deposit of frozen formulas need have no fear for their jobs; they have no rivals and no successors; nobody wants to replace them, least of all the men toward whom they are most hostile. Nobody wants to do their thinking for them either. All that is desired is the freedom to think for oneself and to be true to conscience as a member of the believing community. This means fidelity to the facts of life of that community, which understands itself increasingly as a pilgrim, on the move in a complex changing world. A theology with the ambition to proceed in a purely analytical, deductive, and defining mode does not have to be rejected; it has been transcended and replaced, even though remnants and relics still clutter the scene.

A renewed theology, serviceable to a Church assuming the attitude of partner in a dialogue with the world of unbelief, will be open to and in constant interchange with lived experience and by careful attention to the language and logic of proclamation and witness will be concerned to keep channels of communication unclogged. The theologian's appeal must be to human experience in its widest scope and not exclusively to that of the Christian; not that faith is simply a component of or conclusion from common experience but because the exposition of the Christian belief should not absolutely leave that experience out of account. The truth of God, to which the believer claims to bear witness, must be seen to be also and at the same time the truth of the meaning of human existence.[8] No witness will convince or impress the other which does not in some way relate to the fulfillment of man's destiny, entailing a clearly discernible reference to transcendence, to man's surpassing all that he is and can be. The faith of some men in this connection must appeal to the need and desire of all men for liberation and wholeness and this connection must be explored and clearly presented in theological reflection. Theology stands in need, at this point, of a sophisticated logic of human existence, a comprehensive doctrine of man that will establish the deep-rooted harmony of the grace offered man with the exigencies of his time-bound nature. Christianity is more than a remedy for failure (in one sense, it is not that), a stopgap, a consolation for the pains of sin, suffering, and death. A renewed doctrine of man is at the very heart of a theology sensitive to the anxiety and mistrust which haunt modern man but pulsating also with the thirst for fuller and more abundant life, which inspires him and motivates his best efforts. The Gospel must be preached, as Moeller observes, to man in flesh and bones, greatness and weakness, enthusiasm and whim, and for this purpose, too, a theology of the whole man, concrete and existential, is a prime desideratum. Charles Moeller has outlined the principal features of such a theology, which I find admirably suited to the requirements of dialogue with unbelievers.[9]

When we contemplate the depths of man's interior life, which modern psychology has only just begun to penetrate, we are made aware of the primitiveness of our scientific self-understanding. A new vision of man is emerging, still in the first stages but making progress and pointing the way to an essential link with theology. Theology is not reducible without remainder to anthropology, contrary to Feuerbach's dictum, but it is true that all talk of God in some fashion involves talk of man himself. God in Christ is our salvation, which enables us to define ourselves in terms of a possible dimension other than our own, not an alienation but the realization of what we are and ought to be. Theological elucidation must begin with the recognition of the human condition, not a humanism of cultural amelioration for a favored few but of the salvation of all men from the misery, the trap, they have dug for themselves or been caught in. The Word Incarnate has taken on this very same condition, the frailty and risk, the contingency which leads to death, the bounds of intersubjectivity in freedom and responsibility. Theologians have yet to look into the possibilities and significance for their discipline of the new structuralism, which has exercised a fascination and influence on European intellectuals comparable to that of existentialism in past decades.[10] Man is, in fact, captive to numerous interacting structures, and the salvation promised in Christ consists neither in flight nor in deliverance from the conditions of space and time but in the meaningful participation in true events, true happenings. in which time is ransomed, and despair is transformed into hope, The hope of salvation is not divorced from or irrelevant to man's subjugation of the natural world or the creation of human community in solidarity with all men. I shall return again to the theme of the linking of theology and anthropology, under the heading of norms for Christian presence in the proclamation of the Gospel. The theology of hope, one of the brightest and most promising of recent developments, aims not to reduce the life of grace to a mere humanism but to open grace to the strivings and expectations of the historical world.[11]

While theology must continue to learn to speak more lucidly and appropriately of man and his ongoing search for meaning and value under various conditions, it must do so always in reference to God, who remains the formal subject of this science, as St. Thomas Aquinas has decisively shown.[12] The unbeliever should not be deceived or misled when he is invited to dialogue with us; we may very well not speak with him, directly or immediately, about God, but what differentiates us from each other is a conviction about the possibility, the validity, and the appropriateness of just this talk. Yet the mystery of God has been not the most carefully and seriously studied under the old regime in theology, especially in the training of seminarians—with what regrettable consequences one can perhaps imagine—so that we cannot be certain that we can speak about God in a way that is both meaningful and relevant. The renewal of theology on this score is basic to the entire intellectual posture of belief and is not merely indicated as useful to the development of a particular tract. Communication with unbelievers is severely hampered unless we on our part make the effort to establish our own lives in God more firmly and with more personal commitment. In speaking of God the believer should at least be intelligible and not give the impression that he has had recourse to myth or nonsense. The ground of mutual understanding here is the phenomenon of man—in Teilhard de Chardin's phrase, the human person who interests all of us. All strive for an answer to the question of the basic meaning and value of life in the face of overwhelming irony and defeat. The believer is one who hears the message of salvation effected by the passion, death, and resurrection of Jesus and who begins a new life in Christ. His God breaks into human history; his religion is a response to God's offer and demands.

There are many ways, and not just a single one, of speaking of God meaningfully in today's world. Theology should engage in the thorough analysis and critique of these several modes of speech and cease concentrating almost exclusively on one way. Three major types of discourse offer particular advantages for communicating under different conditions and for different purposes. These have been described as the ways of witness, understanding, and discussion, and these categories are applicable, as we shall see, to the tasks of renewal and to the functions of dialogue.[13] We witness to the Gospel that God saves us in Christ, and this is our first and last duty, which I shall consider under the rubric of proclamation. For this task the themes and thought-patterns of God's inspired work are indispensable and irreplaceable, although they call for exegesis and may be translated into an idiom more readily suited to the capacity of modern intelligence and sensibility. Let the twentieth-century mind be jolted and shaken by the absolute transcendence yet immanence of the God of Biblical faith. This fundamental thought-pattern plays upon oppositions that prevent either anthropomorphism or myth from hardening: God is nothing of earth or of earthly experience, neither here nor there, etc. Biblical language is admirably adaptable to the aims of religious understanding and response by reason of its rich imagery and strong emotional tone. God and His saving action are synthesized into a concrete historical pattern and a true Christian wisdom, providing an insight into our own personal and historical existence.

Theological renewal has already made remarkable progress through the broader and more intensive appropriation of the wealth of scriptural material, but in another area, at a level of discourse which has come to dominate theology since the Middle Ages, the way to renewal appears to be rather less certain and more difficult. Biblical language is heavy with symbol and metaphor, but the disciplined mind, in the tradition of Western culture at least, seeks for an understanding controlled by the formal operation of definition and reasoning and expressed in a terminology carefully worked out for this purpose. John Courtney Murray has traced the stages by which the problem of God was transposed from the level of religious experience to that of philosophical explication.[14] This second mode has advantages as well as built-in limitations; above all, it is self-critical and self-correcting unless it degenerates or is debased, and it can account for the imperfection of faith-knowledge, quiet doubts, and answer objections. Metaphysics is unappreciated and out of favor today, in the arid and unconvincing form it had assumed during centuries of scholastic and modern rationalism; yet without a solid, realist metaphysic theology has nothing with which to elaborate a systematic knowledge of God's existence, nature, and attributes. The achievement of St. Thomas Aquinas, at its best, reached a peak of existential bite and seriousness which not many, today, are able to grasp, simply because a sense of metaphysics has suffered eclipse. Conversion, the very heart of religious experience, is foreign to this manner of speaking, which remains almost wholly in the realm of theoretical understanding without engaging directly the affectivity. This is not to say, however, that the kind of understanding of God cultivated and refined by this function of theology does not figure, and importantly, in the religious experience of the community of believers as well as in that of the individual. What has not been clearly seen is that rational understanding, the drive toward it and its systematic elaboration, is not literally and totally identical with the Aristotelian ideal of demonstration, although this is one of its legitimate expressions. Natural theology involves the exploitation of a specific metaphysic for the thematic movement of reason from creatures to the existence of a Creator. This movement is regulative of the discussion of God's nature and perfections as well as of our knowledge of God and the language we are able to use in speaking of Him. Not that conversion can be effected or sustained by a dexterous application of well-constructed demonstrative argument, as those who are already believers know very well. Demonstration can be properly grasped by a very small minority, and even by these it is not experienced, i.e., appreciated, primarily or essentially as a vehicle of religious conversion or nourishment. It may be safely allowed that an atheist will find it morally impossible to accept theistic arguments and that, in any case, it is not any major defect in this area that is preventing him from embracing faith.

One may speak of God, in the third place, on the plane of apologetics, the defensive function of the believer answering the difficulties, objections, and charges of unbelieving adversaries. This mode of discourse preoccupied theologians heavily at one time, in face of militant rationalists and anti-clerical humanists, but it is highly doubtful whether the apologetics constructed succeeded notably in achieving either the conversion of the others or the positive edification of the bases of Christian belief. Van Roo is probably right in calling for a moratorium on the adversary emphasis, such as it has been, in order to rebuild and reunify theology through discussion conducted in a spirit of mutual love and respect. On this score the renewal of theology in general shades off into that of a theology of dialogue and proclamation. The division of believer and unbeliever will not be healed by mere discussion, of any sort, for the split involves wounds and scars inflicted more by mistrust and persecution, even hatred, than by differences of a theoretical or ideological nature. If theology is to contribute, as it should, to disposing us to dialogue, it will wisely begin by putting in order its own house, to correspond more

nearly to the attitudes of openness and understanding which characterize the post-conciliar Church, true to its own best, grace-inspired
instincts. Renewal in this line will revitalize the formulas of traditional
apologetical thinking to produce a language fresher, more direct,
more pungent, more exactly in accord with our experience in its
fullest range. This task is indispensable equally for those who already
believe, who otherwise run the risk of remaining desiccated in a
dogma devoid of life, and for those who do not believe, if these are
to approach the believer hopeful of finding in the other partner to
dialogue a sensitivity to the demands of realism and honesty.[15]

In what direction will a renewed theology proceed to construct
a working hypothesis on which the Church may enter upon dialogue
with unbelievers? Theology has validity, i.e., truth-value, for the
believer who assents to the principles upon which theology draws
because they are bound up with the content of faith itself. A theology
of unbelief will have interest, by the same token, only for the believer;
I have no illusions about the impression even a radically and intelligently renewed theology may have on the others, but then renewal
is an internal necessity for the life of the responsible and engaged
Christian. Our world, the cultural ambience we share with our
contemporaries, accepts without protest the lengthening of the
distance between its most urgent and important concerns and those
of organized religion. A theology aware of this state of the world
cannot continue to define unbelief as though it were an unfortunate
accident and not an attitude accepted now as perfectly normal and
understandable. There have always been unbelievers but, because
they constituted an eccentric and little respected minority, in the
past they were treated by theologians as insane, perverse, willfully
guilty of pride and infidelity. The sin of unbelief has not disappeared,
one may presume; the massive fact of unbelief, however, is not in
itself a sin-phenomenon but a social, worldwide condition recognizable more clearly and accurately with the help of modern diagnostic
techniques and, indeed, of a distinction of sacred and secular.
Theologians may not regard the fact of unbelief solely *ad extra*, since
it penetrates the ranks of those who claim to believe, a claim belied by
the idolatry and faithlessness denounced by prophets and still latent
beneath external professions of faith.

The tremendous impact of our awakening to the problem of
unbelief is felt very importantly in a heightened awareness of the
hiddenness and inaccessibility of the God whom we had perhaps
tended to idolize, to domesticate. The theology of unbelief should
not let this opportunity pass to weigh seriously and with due respect

the proposals for renovating our thinking about God, measured by the legitimate demands of a Christian humanism and the needs of a world which senses the absence of God in the inhumanity of those who claim to speak for Him. Only an exhaustive inquiry into the whole of experience, and not a quickly dispatched exercise in metaphysical theology, can prepare and dispose men alienated from religion to comprehend the potential value of faith-commitment, even though it will not motivate them, of itself, to make that commitment. The restraint and modesty incumbent on those who do speak of a God, in whom they do believe, should indicate a spirit of continuing search and dispel the unbeliever's anxiety about the intellectual integrity of a man of faith.[16] Faith, it will be seen, is not a protection from the chasm of doubt, the abyss of questioning; the committed believer can be an authentic intellectual precisely because the very nature of faith entails a restless co-existence of belief and wonder. Theology will follow up this insight that faith partakes of the tenuousness, uneasiness, and lack of security which is man's inescapable lot. I shall suggest lines along which this theme might be developed when I come to the problem of making faith credible, later in this chapter.

The differences between forms of unbelief, on which I think emphasis has been laid throughout the present work, are pastorally relevant, especially those between lived and systematized unbelief. This is reason enough for further theological analysis, with a view to reducing the distortions and impoverishment which systematic abstraction may have produced in our previous concept of unbelief. Theoretical distinctions are useful, to be sure, and their usefulness is enhanced by a solid phenomenological underpinning and the recognition of their limited scope and possible inapplicability. These distinctions are valid, within the limits indicated, but they are crossed by the common and increasingly apparent fact that most modern unbelievers are not so much unwilling as unable to make the act of faith. Unbelief is tinged, variously, with agnosticism and nostalgia, with a mixture of despair, mistrust, and resentment. I would submit for further discussion and interpretation the several varieties of unbelief identified in the first chapter, not to achieve systematic neatness for its own sake but to understand the other and not impose upon him generalizations which ignore his uniqueness. Moeller's opinion is that the sociological, psychological, and cultural study of the different forms of unbelief has hardly begun, and that mixed varieties are far more common than pure types.[17] Of particular importance today are practical atheism, religious indifference, and a culturally induced and supported unbelief, the product of social pressures rather than explicit reflection.

The theology of unbelief is provided with a hermeneutic in which the entire phenomenon may be envisaged from three possible and complementary approaches, each according to its own criterion. Explicit unbelief is the most readily recognizable and yields most easily to analysis; faith in God is rejected as a contradiction, and atheism is embraced with full consciousness and a sense of satisfaction. Another approach focuses on underlying motivations, the basic feeling about life, whether it be exile or threat, loss or resentment, exhilaration or ambition, to relate this to the particular form taken by unbelief. Certain experiences, events, incidents may reveal the deepest levels of a person's life and give rise to an expressly avowed unbelief; emotional reaction to trauma is closely bound up with convictions realized at a more intellectual level. Underlying affective structures strongly condition mental attitudes and should not be overlooked while the theologian concentrates exclusively on theoretical propositions and arguments. The presence or absence of certain key symbols indicate a religious or a religious interpretation of existence. A. Vergote has traced this revelatory power in interpersonal relations, Moeller in works of art, literature, drama, and films, and Paul Ricoeur in philosophy.[18] A hermeneutic, or in-depth reading, of those symbols may convince us that the unbelievers are perhaps not always those whom we think, or that along with their professed unbelief there is a positive religious feeling straining to find an outlet and a means of survival. Moeller cites Sartre as extremely revealing in this respect: through the caricature of 'the words' in which the family lives, we catch a glimpse of what the true word, which creates, re-creates, saves, and judges, would be.[19] The unbeliever can be approached in this way, one reading complementing another, not in a spirit of making value-judgment (although this is not entirely ruled out and is indeed unavoidable), but penetrating what may be only superficial layers, to reach the core. An original experience and a basic feeling about life can be far more illuminating than arguments and defensive positions taken up in order to endow the choice of unbelief with manifest rationality and justification. One should exercise a certain prudential restraint in accepting at face-value protests of either religious zeal or anti-religious bias.

Whatever the reasons offered for unbelief, it is always useful to explore possible motives lying beneath the surface, four of which seem to have a peculiar force and influence at the present time.

Each of these calls for a full-scale theological inquiry, based on reliable evidence and conducted in a sober and judicial spirit, without the sensationalism and floundering that have characterized popular expositions in recent years. Unbelief is, in the first place and as I have remarked more than once, profoundly humanist and anti-dualist. In the excellent symposium conducted in France some years ago, G. Morel noted a whole pessimistic and withdrawn puritanism which had penetrated the depths of Western man's consciousness, a dualism for which Christian faith, or even its distortion and degeneration, cannot be held entirely or originally responsible, but which has undoubtedly been supported by the invoking, however unwarranted, of principles of Christian supernaturalism. Freud's complaint about precious psychic energy being drained off by religious dualism is echoed in these remarkable lines from Sean O'Casey: 'How much time has been lost since the origin of man in striving to know what the other world will be like! The more earnest the effort expended in this direction, the less man knew about the present world in which he lived. . . . But when we say that this must be our home, there is nothing sad about this. Even if it could only afford us a simple shelter and our barest needs in clothing and food, but adding to this the lily and the rose, the apple and the pear, it would still be a home for man, whether he is mortal or immortal.'[20] Even a socialist-humanist such as Herbert Marcuse complains that the worst effect of mass conversion to Christianity has been the impoverishing and alienating of men's feel for the value of experienced reality.

There are a few very recent signs of a counter-trend, but in general, over a period of some decades now, the approach to God through the cosmos, the attempt to provide faith with support from the sciences of nature, has suffered eclipse and fallen quite out of favor. What Hans Urs von Balthasar called the centuries of Christian stoicism have retreated before a new, non-religious humanism which naturalizes man so thoroughly that the transcendence of faith is undercut. It has been seriously questioned, however, whether cosmological theism really does justice to man's actual condition. The discovery of man's solitude and responsibility for and in face of a world essentially indifferent to his needs and aspirations is complicated by the shocking suspicion that science and technology, instead of reconciling man to an increasingly humanized world, may in fact only be de-naturing him. I incline to reject this last suggestion, but in any case man does cease to feel spontaneously at one with a pristine nature or in touch with the benign and gracious divinity whom the cosmos was thought to disclose. Harvey Cox's musings on secularization recall the process, now in its advanced and possibly declining stage, by which a once sacralized society has been stripped of its religious aura, defatalizing, and subjected to criticism and the thrust of reform to which no a priori limits are granted. We are in this as in every other respect firmly convinced empiricists and pragmatists, or at least we profess to be, and we use this conviction in order to rule out of court the claims of special mystical or esoterically religious experience. Emotional reverie, a nostalgia for a blissful state perhaps dreamed of in youth, is construed as fear in the face of reality and shunned as a combination of infantile omnipotence fantasies, a regression toward the archaic and prelogical. This psychoanalytic interpretation sees religious belief as a projection of the father figure and a means of escaping the responsibility of difficult and threatening free decisions. Lastly, religion has meant the God of explanation and relief from disaster, but faith has not succeeded notably either in accounting for the structures of reality or in warding off the distress and misery that beset humankind. As Cardinal Suhard observed, God has been cut down to the size of a children's nurse and found to carry out very badly His assigned duties. Theology must purge effectively from the popular understanding of faith every trace of what Bonhoeffer calls the God of the gaps.[21]

Dialogue does not preclude or replace the essential task of proclamation, the believing community's announcement of the good news it has heard and to which faith is the only appropriate response. Updating the content of this proclamation, its manner of presentation and the spirit in which the task is undertaken, is part of the current renewal to which theology must be exposed. I shall outline briefly the possibilities for reducing the Gospel message to its essentials, eliminating what is mere image, especially if it be outworn, confusing, misleading, or repugnant to good sense. As Rahner puts it, modern man should be able to hear the Gospel as something that touches profoundly his innermost being and summons him to live up to his own best aspirations, to surpass them indeed and to set aside whatever is trivial and fantastic. For this purpose the same author proposes a short 'formula' which he has devised to meet the legitimate needs and actual capacity of the man of today, living in a pluralist society, forced to make his own personal choices and grown quite unfamiliar with the terminology, and even the conceptualization, of traditional Christian confessions.[22] The construction of newer, more serviceable formulas should, ideally, be the work of the entire believing community, but it will fall to theologians, sensitive both to the faith of the Church and the various exigencies of contemporary life and thought, to distill the essence of this faith and clothe it in language scrupulously expressive of what is believed and intelligible to most well-informed and educated, thinking people. No single formula will be equally suited to every kind and condition of person, and in our age of rapid and far-reaching cultural change none will retain its maximum value for very long. The following are requirements which a new formula of faith ought reasonably to meet: (1) immediate assimilability and existential self-explicability, dispensing with lengthy and involved preliminary explanation; (2) immediate intelligibility in terms of modern man's own experience and sphere of thought, using a contemporary vocabulary and exploiting those presuppositions which are especially self-evident to modern man; and (3) refusal to take for granted anything that is not evident in such a way that it can be experienced and basically understood as such without special pleading.[23]

I am interested here in those aspects of the formula which promise to be most useful for proclaiming the Gospel in a pluralistic age and in a society where, for the first time since the conversion of the West, unbelief plays a notable role. Subsequent history has witnessed repeated attempts to reformulate the early confessions of faith in symbols or creeds that spoke more meaningfully to self-understanding and the interpretation of the Gospel in one age after another. In our time, in the light of twentieth-century man's predominant self-understanding and of the emphasis in Christian life and experience, the creed will follow the most insistent recommendations of catechists and religious education and take on a clearly anthropological (not anthropocentric, although in our faith God and man are not rivals; competition is introduced by sin) and humanist cast and bent. The new formulas will not represent a new faith but rather the fruit of concerned and loving reflection on the one faith of which St. Paul speaks so often, like its Lord, the same yesterday, today, and for all time. The distinction between what is of the heart and core of God's self-revelation and what is only accidental, secondary, derivative, time-bound, and outmoded should determine both what is included as content and the order and emphasis with which this is arranged. I have followed Rahner substantially, altering some of his expressions and making more explicit the self-consciousness of the believer bearing witness to and before a world of unbelief. To articulate more clearly the total creed, I have numbered the essential propositions and added a brief comment designed to point up the importance of the proposition to a possible dialogue with the unbeliever.

1. When man reflects sufficiently on his own existence he comes, eventually, face to face with the mystery of being itself, i.e., the sheer gratuitousness of all that is, himself included. This insight may be more or less clear and sharp once achieved, and as it develops it describes the felt circumference of our knowing and wanting, our doing and suffering. By this mystery, which is so intimate to us yet is not ourselves or any part of the world or the whole of it —for all of this lies within its orbit—I am and move and grope for meaning and value. This is every man's lot, not the peculiar experience of the man who has or who comes to religious faith; the believer takes it for the presence, the reality of God. All our action, our striving and seeking, has a ground, whether or not the latter is recognized or adverted to, and the ultimate ground is most deeply within us and yet so far beyond us that we are inspired to reverence and worship. Whether he calls it God or by some other name, any man who accepts full responsibility for his existence, embracing life and the charges it lays upon him trustingly and conscientiously, has found what, i.e., the One whom, the believer calls God.

2. In spite of his uncertainty and vacillation, man feels that he not only may but ought to approach this mystery, to draw closer and ever closer to it, though it reveals to him both his inescapable finitude and the moral faults of which he must be held guilty. The believer interprets his efforts to make contact with God, to enter into the mystery, as an act of trust, of confidence in his ultimate well-being, as long as he allows the possibilities of love to be wider than the confines of his own creatureliness and guilt. God gives Himself, love endless and unbounded, and this self-giving transforms our very being, bringing light and the promise of everlasting life. In this hope the believer lives; all men live in the reality of which the promise is the explicit and compelling affirmation and guarantee, so long as they freely and perseveringly embrace courage and concern for the other, fidelity to conscience and long-suffering for the sake of justice.

3. Man's salvation, i.e., God's transcendent self-donation, is progressively manifest in history, however thwarted and obscured by man's resistance and refusal. The offer of salvation is not an imposition forced upon man but an opportunity for him, if he chooses, to break out of his self-centeredness by living in and by the grace of Jesus Christ. Every man who lives in obedience to the absolute dictate of conscience approaches this one Man in whom the issue of salvation and God's resolution of that issue have become

one and definitively validated. The believer looks for liberation and fulfillment, the realization of his humanity and its transcendence, which is not really so different from any man's fondest desire, but he has the courage to confess that what he seeks, God has promised, in Christ.

4. Because of Christ he accepts both life and death, and in this obedience he encounters Christ and again experiences God's forgiveness. Wherever he is in life, under whatever circumstances, God is there, and the believer confesses that all of mankind finds fulfillment in sharing in the excellence of Christ's life, death, and resurrection. In yielding its own ground to that of Christ, mankind is the victor and not the loser, entering more confidently and purposefully into history and not fleeing its demands. We call God Father, communicating Himself without loss; Son, appearing in the true reality of our manhood; and Spirit, more intimately present to us than we are to ourselves.

5. The Church is the community of those who share a common faith and hope, a community over which preside those who continue to exercise the authority first entrusted to the college of apostles. The Church continues as witness to God's self-communication, His victorious will to save. In the Church the world's salvation is made manifest and effective, so that the Church is a sacrament of grace and proclaims the word of God's mercy and love for all. There are seven such words of grace, above all the Eucharist, where the community commemorates its salvation and renews its union with the Lord.

6. The believer knows that he must share with Christ the fate of death, surrendering his life to God after loving and hoping and remaining faithful to the end. He expects, when the history of mankind draws to an end, that he, together with all who have persevered, will see in unveiled fullness what God has already given in faith, namely, Himself. Each and all of these articles demand to be further explained and one may expect difficulties to mount in that very enterprise, expect and not fear or shrink from them. The believer lives encompassed by a *sense* of mystery, not in Gnostic illumination but in a darkness which the grace of faith only partially dispels. What he professes is the reality of God and salvation, but it is a transcendent God, not an idol, not a master-puppeteer but a hidden God whose presence is experienced in silence and paradox. Faith looks to the future, resolute and geared to the effort to realize it, not nostalgically or regressively to a primitive bliss to which return is sought. Hope, as Ricoeur says, is the same as remembering,

not an isolating and withdrawn looking backward but a recollection which is, in fact, open to the future. The believer lives according to a supreme reality principle, confronting reality, seeking and searching, and not languishing in a state of passive self-indulgence. At the heart of the anthropology of faith, man is endowed with autonomy and responsibility so that he may transform his world. His vocation to subdue the elements is one with a summons to accept all the labors of life, suffering, even death, in the service of his brethren. Central, therefore, to the believer's self-understanding stands Jesus Christ, the Man for others, servant of God and men. There is no one form or model of 'Christian civilization,' which, if found, would constitute the world-historical ideal for all of mankind. God puts only one question to man: will you choose life? Will you put away the nostalgic memories of childhood and grow up to the full measure of loving, trusting responsibility and concern, and in that find your God? I have no desire to eliminate the unexpected and unforeseen, the transcendent, what St. Paul called the scandal and foolishness of the Cross. God does not stand before me, the believer, visible, verifiable, definable, any more than He does for the unbeliever. Theology has undoubtedly leaned too far in the direction of a 'sweet reasonableness,' for obvious apologetic purposes, whereas faith produces a shaking of the foundations, an uprooting, dissolution, and makes hard demands. All the natural forces, the 'flesh' in Paul's sense, mobilize to persuade us not to make the choice, not to be faithful to it, to settle down, rather, in one's own country, with one's own substance. Conversion is the fruit of grace and of man's free response, not a determinism or the conclusion of a chain of reasoning.

Life itself seems to move in a perpetual dialectic of sense and nonsense, so that faith is not remote or foreign in this respect. In his contribution to the 1965 *Semaine des intellectuels catholiques*, Paul Ricoeur explains why the Church can never be simply identified with the world but must always witness to God transcending and transfiguring this world: 'The modern world can be viewed under the twofold sign of a growing rationality along with a growing absurdity. We discover that men certainly lack justice and, most assuredly, love, but even more they lack meaning; the meaninglessness of work, leisure and sexuality—these are the problems that we encounter today. Faced with these problems, our task is not one of recrimination or regret: the function of the believing community is to be a witness and representative of some fundamental meaning. ... You might ask: why are Christians needed for this responsibility?

I do not say that others could not bear this burden; but I do say that the Christian has his own reasons for doing so; the proclamation of the death and resurrection of Christ helps him to see the surplus of sense over nonsense in history. . . . Being a Christian means detecting the signs of this superabundance in the very order that the human race expresses its own designs. The Christian stands as the adversary of the absurd and the prophet of the meaning of things. Not through some despairing act of the will, but through a recognition of the fact that meaning has been made clear in the events proclaimed by Scripture. He will never finish the task of spelling out and forming a complete picture of this inner meaning.'[24] Ricoeur goes on to say that the Church cannot lose itself without a trace in the world because it must preserve a place where the true meaning and sense of reality are preserved and a dialectic with the world may be carried on. The specific action of the Church is to worship and to preach, to proclaim God in its worship, its inner life; renewal stretches to this life and is not limited only to theology.

Renewal properly understood is motivated primarily by a desire to be more faithful, truer to what custom and the debility of age have worn away, distorted, and internally weakened. The *ressourcement* of which I spoke in connection with the renewal of theology is equally important in the effort to derive from its genuine and primary sources a revitalization, to listen more faithfully to the word of God and speak more effectively to men. Nothing of that word or of what the Lord Himself has ordained to last may be surrendered, changed, or let fall away, but faithfulness will almost unavoidably clash with reform in the task of renewal, or at least there will be a tension which may be painful but must be borne with as part of the price of renewal. The Church's self-renewal, it has been suggested, is a constant of its history, a law of its life, and a condition of its faithfulness; *ecclesia semper reformanda* is the hallowed phrase which accompanies the existence of the people of God until the Lord comes.

The history of the Church discloses changes and reforms carried out in practically every century, in response to the needs and dispositions and conditions characteristic of those who make up the Church and who themselves change. Renewal when it succeeds in no wise follows fashion, gives in to feebleness or makes concessions out of fear and confusion, although to an outsider, to an unbeliever, such may seem to be the very motives behind the protests of courageous concern and self-abnegation. Change for its own sake is worlds removed from, and contrary to, the spirit of authentic renewal, and indeed the most important and far-reaching change is not always the most spectacular or even the most hotly contested. Controversy and recalcitrance are not safe indexes to the scope or depth of renewal, whether it be a question of ways of expressing the Christian mystery, transposing thought into contemporary modes, Church-state relations, attitude toward non-Catholics, those of non-Christian religions, and those of no religion at all, the appreciation of secular values, or whatever else. The Church has a life, the lives of successive generations of believers, and this entails growth, the overcoming of obstacles and the recovery from setbacks and decline, from relapse caused by human stupidity and perversity. Cardinal Leger writes: 'Sin in the Church makes a perpetual renewal necessary. . . . *Aggiornamento* is the natural state of the Church,' and he quotes Newman's famous remark: 'The Church must renew herself in the preservation of her type, and the continuity of her principles, with a power of assimilation, according to a logical sequence, with an anticipation of its future and a conservative action upon its past, in order to maintain its chronic vigour.'[25] In his profound essay on *The Mystery of Time*, Jean Mouroux observes that when the Church takes account only of the present, it does nothing but change, just as, when it looks only to the future, it does nothing but dream; renewal is possible only when the Church is conscious of the whole of time, gives the revelation received from tradition to the men of today and thus remains open to tomorrow. Ignorance of tradition, or contempt for it, endangers rather than promotes renewal; what is asked of us, instead, is a humble and judicious submission to unceasing and unsparing self-criticism. Cardinal Leger's criterion is sound when he says that renewal should make us abandon everything which hurts our brothers uselessly and impedes their progress toward the truth. Renewal is the work of the entire people of God; no one can arrogate to himself exclusive rights in this regard or proceed contrary to that charity and justice which unite and bind the whole people together.[26]

The life of the Church which is to be renewed consists in conversion, a constant turning and turning back to God, and witness, a turning to the world to proclaim and exemplify the merciful love of God in service to and concern for all men. But how free are we, who make up the Church, to plunge earnestly into the task of renewal? The world has long entertained the impression, indeed the conviction, that toleration and freedom are radically foreign to the spirit and tradition of Catholicism; hence they consider impossible a thorough-going renewal, which does not spare structures or practices, institu-

tions or procedures if they require reform and updating, no matter
how hallowed the tradition to which they may be attached or the
sentiment by which they are protected. Supposing that the obligation
of conversion, the most fundamental of all areas to which renewal
is relevant, continues undiminished in importance, three other areas
call for a renewal especially urgent at the present time, these being
witness, prayer, and the purification of motives. The Christian
witnesses more authentically and with greater effectiveness when
he sees in the facts of contemporary life stepping-stones for proclaiming Christ to alienated man. Men today live in several 'worlds,' diff-
erentiated, split off and even clashing with each other. The Christian
witnesses to a world in which an array of new substitute cults is
being set up, values considered mandatory and adequate to take
the place of God. Believers continue to bear witness by clinging to
God and rejecting fantasies and myths, by insisting that it is God's
world and man's and that the realm of the secular is as serious and
valuable to them as it is alleged to be by the most ardent secular
humanists. Witness is ultimately effective (not without grace, it is
needless to add) when it directs men, from within their world and
themselves, to the discovery of the divine gift that founds and
supports them. Part of the renewal of witness will consist in an
allowance of the greater difficulty modern man experiences in seeing
his world as a revelation of God, not a concession but a realistic
appraisal of what has become the perceptive habit of unbelievers.

Nothing has changed in the objective, ontological relationship
of the world to God but in the relationship which man experiences
to the world, which no longer rises to the Absolute through the
contemplation of nature. Hans Urs von Balthasar has sketched the
chief stages in modern intellectual and cultural history by which
men have been brought to this point, the death of the metaphysical
sense.[27] The Church's witness today will not be to a theophanous
world, for indeed Christianity has liberated man from a theological
metaphysics and confronted him, through faith, with the living,
personal God who reveals Himself in Christ. It will require a great
act of courage, one which only a fervent faith may sustain, to set
the Biblical knowledge of God above and in critical opposition to
the metaphysical reflection on the mystery of being. Then perhaps
we shall be able to face honestly a question which we have refused
to acknowledge since the Middle Ages, namely, whence all this
certain knowledge about God, which so few are able to attain and so
many find incomprehensible? The logical culmination of the tradition
of a metaphysical theology turned increasingly rationalist is

Hegel, in whose philosophy cosmos and the Absolute merge and blend so sinuously that faith in the Biblical sense is unnecessary and impossible. The Church must renew its spirit of witness to a world in which men have given up the metaphysical effort precisely because they are infinitely more aware of their own transcendence over nature than of any reality purportedly transcending themselves. Witness must heighten and not dilute the sense of mystery in the unique and gratuitous revelation in Christ of God's love. In its individual and corporate life the community of the faithful bears witness to what God wills to be for man, and what man's dutiful and grateful response ought to be. Always the love of God, which enlivens and sustains all, is manifest in love of and concern for the neighbor, the touchstone of Christian witness and the only test and proof of faith, according to the Gospel.

At this point renewal centers on what is absolutely essential to our faith-witness, the challenge and responsibility we meet when we discover ourselves led, as it was predicted to Peter, where we had not intended or foreseen. Faith has unsettled us, then, by demanding of us a love which we had been unprepared and unwilling to give; recognition of this incapacity and selfishness is the beginning of possible renewal. We cannot go on repeating the most extravagant slogans about a love that is real, accessible by grace, unbounded, transfiguring, supremely altruistic, and the source of true happiness and well-being, the pledge of eternal life, and betray this by the shabbiness and pusillanimity, the meanness and miserliness of our lives. Christian life as such, that of the community as such, must be deeply involved in the need and suffering and no less in the striving and accomplishment, the joy and the triumph of mankind. The point of renewal is made in the disturbing words of one of the most perceptive spiritual writers of our time: 'If so many of our young people grow up without any taste for the Church, it is because they have never really seen it. It has never been revealed to them. It could have been revealed to them only by a group of adults who love one another, and that is something they have never seen. They have seen people who do not even look at one another, who obviously do not love one another, who go through the motions of even the sacrament of unity, the Eucharist, firmly resolved to remain completely separate, who come to Communion but never commune with the distress, the cares, the ill-fortune of their neighbors, their brothers.'[28] Witness is ineffective, it is a mockery and a source of deep disedification, if real charity is not its heart and its most typical expression; it is not trite or superfluous to add that charity must begin at home, among the brethren who share a common faith, an exigency of which I shall have more to say apropos the norms of Christian presence in the world. The Church has been around now for quite a long period of time, and Christians, including those who as a matter of course are in schism or cut off from each other formally, have had ample opportunity to wear on each other's nerves and patience, to grow cold and indifferent, to find in others a bore, a nuisance, perhaps a threat. The honeymoon period of overflowing love and concern, described in The Acts of the Apostles and early Christian writings, has long since faded in the mists of time; witness today calls not for a second honeymoon but for a second resolve, a new determination, in these latter days, to live out the love we profess by giving of ourselves, of affection and understanding, confidence and concern. The believer is compelled by the charity of Christ, as St. Paul was, by the principal commandment, to search for God and to find Him in the neighbor and thereby to recall him to God and reveal God to him. This encounter is the sacrament in which God wills to be among us, the experience in which the Christian witness becomes theophanous.

But thus far I have only described the course which witness must take in any age; in what respects, specifically, is renewal called for, to bring it closer to realization in a world of unbelief? It is a question of being truer to oneself and therefore more relevant to the real needs of our time, not of newer, neater interpretations of what Christianity is all about, not grander theological syntheses but fresh and resolute commitment to the solution of real problems. Witness by the believer will be a way of life and not merely or primarily the expression of a world-view; the religious model cannot function realistically in abstraction from concrete social and political structures, the pressures and ideals which impinge upon men in their actual situation. The new model, obviously, is not going to be the hermit, the enclosed monk, the ascetic withdrawn from and unconcerned about the world's pain and confusion. It is temerarious to discount or underestimate the intrinsic value, in its own right, of the way of self-denying detachment and contemplation; that is not what I am doing; rather it is a positive suggestion that the most convincing and desperately needed witness today will be what Michael Novak calls 'the secular saint.' One is easily persuaded that the notion of setting up specific examples or models of virtue has comparatively little appeal for modern men. The great majority added to the official calendar of saints in the past and even in the present century are not serving as examples of Christian living for many. Not that true religion has become something other than it has always been, in its Biblical understanding, but that closeness to God cannot be divorced from the loving service of the neighbor and enjoyed without this concern for others. In any case, the other's demand on my justice and charity can remind me of God's demand and make it present to me, but it can never be the adequate measure of God's demand on me in Christ. The believer's basic relationship as such is not dialogue with other men but an immediate and loving adoration of God.[29] This is the paradoxical juxtaposition of which the Apostle spoke, in terms of wealth and poverty, living and dying, using the things of this world as if one did not use them, possessing nothing yet having all things.

The Church renews its life in a world coming to unification, a world in which many are convinced that, whatever the upshot of renewal, in the short or the long run, the Church will never be able to inspire or promote this unification, for it (the Church) is past revitalization. Triumphalism is more than ridiculous in this age; it is criminal at a time when masses are drifting from allegiance to the ecclesiastical institution, the ecclesial structure. I must say a word about triumphalism, or what is left of it, not the rather shabby tatters and remnants of comic-opera Renaissance splendor and baroque pageantry that still clutter the Vatican, but the attitude of complacency, of domineering over a fallen and dependent world, the 'let us stay as we are' arrogance which identifies renewal quite simply with sell-out, conformity to the image of the world. Separation from the world is the only guarantee of fidelity; this view may spring from a genuine love of God and the Church, but in it there is also a great deal of anxiety and suspicion and insecurity. At bottom an ancient error reappears, confusing the Church with the transient forms it puts on; as Étienne Gilson once said, the Church's task is not to preserve itself as it has always been but to sanctify a world that is passing away. The Church would not have survived intact without periodic and timely eliminations; at the right moment, and without regret or looking back, it has had to put off all that was merely 'vesture,' for at no time does any structure coincide with the total Church. There is not and has never been in history one single ideal of Christian living or civilization to be taken as a type, nor a uniform model of holiness. There have only been institutions or persons, to a greater or lesser degree penetrated by Christianity and its virtues. The intransigent reactionary Christian commits the same error as the unbeliever who reverses the real relation and sees the Church as inextricable from its external condition and ephemeral attachments. Renewal cannot take any other form than a vigorous and determined purging away of such accidental and extraneous elements, so far as these interfere with the full flowering of the Church's true nature. The Church's effort will be to throw off the dead weight of accumulated traditions, to establish itself in a firmer and more secure grasp of its own authentic mission.

The Church has been following a certain way for fifteen centuries, a way entered upon when the opportunity was presented to assume public status and identity within the social structure of the late Roman Empire. Robert Adolfs describes the course actually followed: 'Faced with the possibility of choosing between the prophetic servant-figure, the form of unpretentious service, and the political king-figure, the form of power and worldly distinction, she chose the second. This was the Constantinian turning-point in the Church's way. This choice may perhaps have been necessary at the time. It may even have been the right choice, since choosing the other road may have led to the Church's becoming an insignificant sect. But it certainly was a choice which determined the whole of the subsequent history of the Church. It resulted in the gradual emergence in the Church of thought and action in terms of power. By this I do not mean that the Church misused power, but that she tended to think from this time onward that the establishment of the Kingdom of God in fact meant the spread of the Church's power over the entire world.'[30] For better or worse, in subsequent centuries the Church developed a powerful presence in Europe by which it was able to exercise enormous influence over major policy decisions as well as over the daily lives of masses of people. After the Reformation, as the Church split and intense rivalry arose among the separated Christian groups and bodies, the Catholic Church found itself increasingly stripped of the power and influence it had formerly exercised, without, however, making the effort clearly to distinguish power and authority or to assess, in an evangelical spirit, the relationship of power to the other values, natural and supernatural, which men admire and pursue. As example, the Catholic hierarchy has assumed as perfectly acceptable, indeed as a matter of course, a feudal pattern in which the Pope is supreme lord and the bishops are his wholly dependent vassals. The feudal mentality towards incumbent power, and the continuing confusion of power and authority (in practice and unless their own position or prerogatives were threatened), prompted bishops to resist and oppose the great social revolutions of the past two centuries, at least until well into the present century.

When a dead end is reached, a choice made in the distant past stands revealed as bankrupt, the Church's future course must follow the alternative to the path that has brought it to the present impasse. Not that a new course is guaranteed in advance against pitfalls, false turns, or overcoming obstacles, or that this effort at renewal of itself is certain to impress the unbeliever with the sincerity or wisdom of Church people. We have no other choice, indeed, but to be converted, for our own sakes, in the first place, and because we want to reach the maturity which only bitter experience and failure have made us appreciate. The new way is distasteful in many respects, because it is severe and demanding, humiliating and quite foreign to the old course. Adolfs uses the Biblical language of *kenosis* and applies to the Church the spirit of service and self-emptying which Jesus took upon Himself. This vocation is not an exaggerated one; it is, indeed, the sole way to recover the Church's pristine freedom and the sense of purpose for which it was founded. The Church suffers now not only an exile in a world which proclaims God's death and repudiates its claims of authority but also the obvious fatuousness of the way of power and glory, magnificence and majesty. Congar has shown that, although the ideal of *kenosis* has been little realized in practice over the centuries, an awareness of this ideal has never entirely disappeared. At the recent Ecumenical Council the theme of the Church's kenotic vocation was heard again and reiterated as especially relevant to the task of renewal upon which the whole people of God were summoned to embark. One after another, the conciliar Fathers rose and declared that the Church's mission was not to rule but to serve; several suggested openly that the members of the hierarchy voluntarily detach themselves from all outward signs of wealth and temporal power.[31] Some individual bishops began in earnest to comply with this suggestion; most have done little or nothing, although the Pope has made a few minor gestures in this direction.

What would a Church seriously engaged in *kenosis*, in imitation of its Lord, look like and be like? It is a question of both structures and spirit, of an interior renewal effected by grace and conforming believers more closely to Christ crucified and risen, and thus motivating them to restructure the institution in ways which show forth this spiritual renovation. There is every good reason, to begin with what is admittedly of lesser importance, to divest the hierarchy, beginning with the Pope and his 'court,' of the visible forms of a non-spiritual royal power with many of the embarrassingly outmoded paraphernalia of Renaissance and seventeenth-century princelings. An unsentimental look ought to be taken at much of the property and other assets of the Vatican and local churches, in particular the palatial residences and vast country estates of bishops and religious orders. The papacy is a spiritual office and has no need or right to invest itself with the marks of a dead empire, marks entirely incompatible with a deep sense of ministry. There is no threat here whatever to the legitimate *authority* with which the officers of the Church are endowed, but it is a sad indication of prevailing confusion and the disregard of priorities that such fears should be entertained. The office of preaching and administering the sacraments, presiding at the Eucharist above all, is undertaken not as a privilege of a few but in obedience to the one Gospel in service to the rest of the brethren. It is through the solicitude of the bishops that the members of the Church are inspired and guided in seeking the unity of mind and heart which is the bond of the spirit of God Himself.

The Church is the sign, the sacrament, of God's presence, hence where the Church is, there must be light and life, liberty and love, not legalism and repression, formalism and extrinsicism. Pluriformity is indispensable and need not be feared as a threat to unanimity, the *communion* of the faithful in one Lord and one faith. A new concept of the priesthood, or rather a return to a more authentically scriptural concept, will expose the distortions and exaggerations of a clericalism that has stressed the exclusivity of a sacramentally ordained priesthood, in a social context of privilege and power that is only faintly, if at all, related to the evangelical calling. The priesthood is essentially an office within and for the sake of the community, not an exalted position set over it as its feudal lordship. A word might be interjected at this point, as fittingly as another, about the right of women in the Church, the right to minister and to hold such offices as authorize them to exercise ministry. *Kenosis* is clearly indicated in the clergy's self-understanding vis-à-vis the laity, for a clericalized institution may have the outward appearance of a Church, composed of active priests and passive laity, but it is conformed to a worldly, feudal social order and not the freedom of the sons of God. Congar observes: 'It seems that the presentation of religion primarily as worship and moral obligations, the classic heritage of the seventeenth century, deprived us in some ways of the realization that Christianity presents a *hope*, a total hope, even for the material world.'[32] There is, lastly, the question of order within the Church; for as a human society offices must be established, rights protected, discipline enforced, claims and counter-claims settled, etc. In the future a considerable decentralization will almost certainly maintain and enhance a due order in the Church.

Nothing is closer to the most pressing needs of renewal than the firm and uncompromising devotion to the truth, all the truth, no matter how unpleasant or unsettling. Serious concern has been expressed about honesty in the Church. Adolfs reports a speech delivered by Josef Pieper, the distinguished philosopher, on 'The Corruption of the Word and Power,' in which the charge is made that churchmen have manipulated language, not to communicate truth but for the purpose of making an impression, obtaining a desired end, defending a vested interest. When this sort of thing is done the 'faithful,' as they are condescendingly called, are addressed as passive material, not as partners in dialogue. There should be a 'zone of truth' in our world, which Pieper suggests should be the university, but which I should think ought, a fortiori, to be the Church. It is doubtful whether this wisely proposed zone of truth can be created or sustained by a hierarchy and Christian layfolk intent on preserving an image of untarnished respectability at all costs, to keep up the pretense or fiction of unbroken continuity in practices and even doctrines, where there has manifestly been change and genuine novelty. The almost paranoid fear of error, of being reproached for *anything* ever said, done, or omitted, has gripped high Church officials, those in the Vatican more than others, and saddled them with the obsession to insist that what seems to be change is, at bottom, precisely the opposite. It is painful to have to report that the unbeliever, not the unscrupulous anti-Christian but the upright man of conscience, has a strong impression that the Church as a whole, and especially its leaders and spokesmen, are not really concerned about plain, unvarnished truthfulness or about confessing error and wrongdoing in any but a perfunctory and inconsequential fashion. Before it can hope to enter into meaningful dialogue with the world, the Church will have to dispel this image, not by the artful creation of a fiction, a mere surface image, but by the courageous, unremitting devotion to honesty and truthfulness at every level.

Renewal takes on increasingly the form of driving out fear, the fear of living simply and to the full by faith, trusting the Lord and grace He will not fail to give. In face of unbelief shall the believer rely on such a weak and irresolute faith or on the worldly resources of power and prestige with which faint-hearted men have misguidedly attempted to shore up such frail defenses? Never having overcome doubt, but covering it up instead with a show of bravado and self-righteousness, some believers manage to convince themselves that the truth of faith is successfully bound up with the traditions and practices they cherish. Faith is rightly experienced as both the constant breaking out of the confine of doubt and the persevering in spite of that which will not be left behind but must be borne. Our faith is not an ideology, not the preserve of a familial or national tradition but the fruit of a personal decision made under grace and requiring repeated confirmation. We do not believe in obedience to any man because no man has the truth to which in faith we adhere. The challenge of unbelief exposes the hollowness and unauthenticity of what many profess to be Christian faith, but which is, in fact, fear of an all-powerful idol, a debased religiosity inferior even to the deism which at least tried to purge religion of superstition and self-seeking. The atheist knows what he is about when he rejects a God of fear or self-interest, a God of oppression, and in this rejection he may be truer to the living God than the idolatrous self-styled believer.

The community of believers renews itself not in order to survive, *tout court*, but in order to live according to the Spirit of truth, pursuing the radical venture of hoping in the transcendent and absolute future. Let the others see us as contemptuous of the will to survive in the merest biological or temporal sense and willing and able to take on our way only the command to hope in the absolute promise. From the premise of faith no one can deduce in the concrete how to exercise this hope in a shedding of worldly attachments, of the illusion that anything temporal has the features of eternal permanence. It should be a reproach to us, and a cause of shame, that others have ever found us so fearful that we would not surrender a sentimental ideology or shed structures that were outworn, empty, and petrified. Unrenewed, in thinking and in life, we are paralyzed, unable to act, to meet the unbeliever and enter into a fraternal dialogue from which, as far at least as our responsibility extends, the obstacle of what is accurately described as inauthenticity, the failure or refusal to assume one's true identity, bars us. It would be the worst error to brand genuine renewal as loss of identity, since it is, quite evidently, precisely the opposite; it is, rather, that what has been allowed by men to degenerate or stagnate may and must be rebuilt and stirred up, that what has been neglected should be attended to. Renewal is not a spiritual cosmetic or anaesthesia; it neither prettifies nor immunizes from pain. What is alive is sensitive and can suffer, but as long as growth is unimpeded, life continues.

MEETING THE CHALLENGE OF UNBELIEF

Fearful of the disastrous consequences of endless controversy and barren discussion, the Russian Marxists of pre-revolutionary days vied with each other in writing inflamed treatises with titles such as 'What Is to be Done?' These passionate appeals for immediate and effective action were, ironically, themselves fuel added to the flames of controversy and discussion, but eventually something was done; it was revolutionary, and it changed the course of history as perhaps nothing else in the present century. Goethe challenged the Prologue to St. John's Gospel by asserting that in the beginning was the deed, but the deed is ever subject, in a human order or where the light of reason plays, to the critical scrutiny of reason, that is, of the word. Unbelief belongs to the total human situation, to the spheres both of word and of deed; hence it calls for both understanding and concrete reaction. It is part of the world and as such a problem for faith, for the life which the believer must live in and for the world. After one has confronted the problem, tried to sort out the component elements and made the various inquiries and analyses, the question remains, what is to be done? How does the believer, the community of believers, act in face of what is a fact and a problem, or rather in the presence of those who do not and will not believe? The answer is twofold, in keeping with the demands of faith and those of the other; the word of God must be announced, in season and out, whether men will listen or not, and the word of man, which is essentially dialogue, must be exchanged. Action here is inspired by faith and by a concern for one's neighbor which is at the same time a concern for the truth and the values which all men of good will are prepared to pursue and defend. Before expanding on the basic and continuing responsibility to proclaim the message of salvation, I shall outline what I take to be the principal aspects of the approach to unbelief as a problem calling for concrete action.[33]

One has to reassure oneself that the unbeliever has been properly identified, that is, that what Martin Marty calls the varieties of unbelief have been carefully distinguished, more basically, that true unbelief has not been confused with species of anti-clericalism, moral and intellectual primitivism, practical religious indifference, total skepticism, or something else. There is no warrant for lumping together every 'ism' one dislikes and making of it some sort of atheism by a strategy that is as dishonest as it is strategically unproductive. The typology employed in earlier chapters of this work has its uses, but different types vary and have properties unique to themselves, not taken into account in broad generalizations. One will approach the unbeliever with a concern to make contact with both the real suffering which may have prompted a rejection of faith and the real value-system which serves as a positive counterpart to faith. Rahner's 'troubled atheist,' however, is perhaps becoming rarer, as the need for salvation is replaced increasingly by felt needs for the resources or opportunity to relieve one's own misery, by one's own effort. Alienation is not less common among people who experience not only the absence of God but a meaninglessness to all existence and the sheer, brutal facticity of everything. Indifference, then, is a mask for and a protection against lurking despair, but there may be instead an aggressive heroism bent on struggling against absurdity. Unbelief today appears to be highly principled and mature; it leads, however, to dead-ends and frustration and has constantly to shift ground or to dissolve in energetic and not always self-consistent activism. The question posed by the mere fact of religion, and with an inescapable urgency by the witness of intelligent and sincere believers, is not stilled or evaporated by proclaiming the death of God. God obviously lives in the faith of those whose religion makes them not less but more human, so that all is not in confusion or obscurity: there are zones of belief and unbelief, even if their frontiers merge and blend at points.[34]

The situation at present is still in flux but not greatly agitated, and definite directions are being taken by both believers and unbelievers, not the great mass, who still co-exist without any mutual intercourse relevant to their respective positions, but small pockets on either side, a few individuals. As long as the other shows only defiance, cold indifference, or an unhelpful silence, nothing can be done; 'approach' is cut off at the start and dialogue is forestalled. Still, both the life-witness of Christians and their theological reflections must embrace the unbeliever, however reluctant the latter may be to look, listen, or cooperate. Theology and preaching must be, from the very beginning and throughout, conscious of this witness for unbelievers, so that this concern will not harden into the special preserve of experts. Let us call the total posture toward unbelief witness and distinguish preaching or proclamation of the word of God, and dialogue or sharing a common word with the other. A methodology worked out for exercising fruitfully our witness to the unbeliever would respect the following three principles: (1) Christian thinking and preaching are sensitive to and share in contemporary man's distress; solidarity is sought, leaving behind the triumphalism which rests on one's spiritual advantage and celebrates past glories and the defensive skirmishes which envisage the other not as brother but as foe. (2) The Christian may and, in all candor, must experience and admit to some extent the doubts and difficulties of unbelief. (3) A reliable basis for a possible dialogue is to be found only in this acceptance of the other and frank acknowledgment of the universal condition of suffering and outraged humanity crying for justice and truth.

If dialogue, and even the willingness to dialogue, is new in the Church today, preaching is as old as the Church itself and the commission to preach as valid and imperative as ever. What is new and different for the preaching Church is the sociological situation of widespread unbelief and its permeation of every sphere of life and thought.[35] Also new, and occasioned by this same situation, is our understanding of the demands of faith and the profound mystery in which our existence is enveloped, a mystery which intellect and will cannot penetrate without grace. Backward-looking lamentation of what are supposed to have been happier and more blessed days of innocence or lively faith is out of place, futile, and almost wholly misinformed. If faith is more difficult today, it is, in part, because men see more clearly the transcendence of faith and the terrible responsibility of it and are uncertain about making the total self-surrender which this demands. The caricature of faith, i.e., superstition, credulity, Gnosticism, wishful thinking, magical thinking, idolizing, none of this is demanding or difficult except for a man of clear intelligence, moral integrity, and spiritual discrimination. Today men are secularized, but this neither dispenses them from hearing the word of God nor us from proclaiming that word in a manner adapted to the prevailing condition. There are no lacunae in the history of salvation, no periods of time when it is unfitting or inopportune to announce to men that God has in Christ redeemed them from sin and death. Or, to put the matter in the clearest possible light, it is always to be expected that men will hear the Gospel indifferently, reluctantly, or with hostility, because the flesh will not easily submit to the discipline of the spirit, because men prefer comfortable and convenient lies and fables to the truth, the two-edged sword of the Spirit. In face of today's pressures—I am speaking of the idols of the times—a skepticism is by no means entirely unhealthy; whether he be disposed to listen, to give credence, or not, the unbeliever may not be excused from hearing the Gospel because God wants all men to know what He has done, and He uses us as His messengers. No one need expect that preaching the word of God will take second place to, much less be superseded by,

G

dialogue or efforts to encounter the world of unbelief in other ways.

The effort to think anew the whole of the Christian message can benefit both preaching and dialogue, enriching our grasp of faith and sharpening our awareness of what needs to be said, and in what order, with what emphasis. This sensitivity to what is essential and central to faith is infinitely more important and valuable than any special virtuosity in detecting varieties or types of unbelief. I think the apologist is coming into his own again in the Church, but his role and function have been considerably revised.[36] Preaching today should be as reasonable, as respectful of the exigencies of sober factual truth and straight thinking, as human limitations permit; an indictment of fanciful, ineffective rationalism is not to be construed as an endorsement of the principle of irrationalism or any of the forms it has taken, romanticist, existentialist, Barthian, or any other. The preacher is not unaware that reasoning, however valid, is convincing only to those who are disposed to be reasonable, but this is as much a source of hope as of caution. Our preaching will not produce God or make Him apparent to the world, any more than St. Paul's (may one say, or Jesus'?), and in any case we have learned the silliness of indulging in verbal sleight-of-hand tactics. The tests an unbelieving world presents make it clear that people cannot be cajoled or deluded into believing. The preacher will ask only that the undecided who are really receptive keep options open and unresolved and not shut themselves off from whatever is truly reasonable and fair. Martin Marty has included every form of involving one's own integrity as witness, with what one has seen and heard, and with a listener to whom one commends this witness, within the scope of preaching in a large sense. This lays on the preacher the burden of standing behind what he says with what he is; the 'do as I say, not as I do' is eliminated. The unbeliever is ready, obviously, to admit that he does not know God because he has not seen Him, or evidence of Him, although he has seen evil. He is not likely to be favorably impressed by the believer's internal conflict of faith and doubt if this is melodramatized and exaggerated. Preaching portrays Christianity as the witness to God's salvation of man; hence it can rightly point to the believing community, the Church, as proof of faith only if this same community shows signs of salvation, if in the actual lives of believers faith makes a difference. The existence of a Church in which the truth is not respected and the canons of honesty and integrity are not observed, in which there is insufficient fraternal love and a concern for the person's freedom and dignity, is not a problem for the unbeliever; to him, it is a reassurance.

We preach salvation by God through Christ, but what does salvation mean in today's world? Shall we promise to relieve life's specific distresses—poverty, disease, pain, hunger, drudgery, and the like—and if not, what then? To see that faith is not in this sort of relief but in something quite different may be a loss, but it is the loss of an illusion and a great gain for insight and courage. Man is agent as well as patient; he can be supplied with much, even all, of what he needs and still be miserable and unfulfilled because he himself must work out his salvation. We preach this precisely: salvation must be won, forged; it cannot be passively taken over. It is still God's gift, but the gift is our transformation, the infusion of a new life, which means a new power to live in a certain way, not to enter a ready-made world but to work to remake one, to counterpose to the world of common sense and technology.

Thinking through the whole of the Christian message aims at making it appear intelligible and credible, so that the unbeliever does not have the feeling that he is being asked to listen to absurdity or what is logically impossible. The world has become godless in its capacity to understand God-talk, so that theological and religious language is not immediately comprehensible. The secularized man with no religious formation or attachment finds most of what the preacher says not only incredible but intellectually impenetrable, a reaction that may shock the churchman out of touch with his contemporaries. Almost without exception, the terms and categories of conventional religious language are flotsam and jetsam out of past ages, overworked for centuries and in contexts which have passed from the scene. Karl Lehmann's point is well taken: 'This is why the simple repetition of important scriptural words and statements is not sufficient. One frequently hears it said that in the dialogue with atheists a simple return to the words of Scripture—far from alienating 'metaphysics' and 'speculation'—would work wonders. One may doubt the 'pastoral' value of this method, even if one is prepared to accept the grain of truth in it and is convinced that Scripture is not to be valued any less highly.'[37] Part of our trouble has been the complacency with which we have, without protest, allowed sacred words to be banalized and trivialized, debased and put to frivolous uses without a feeling for mystery or holiness. Our proclamation has here not kept up with theology when we have forgotten how difficult it is to speak of God at all and have fallen into sloppy and careless modes of speech, under pretext of accommodating our preaching to the limited capacity of our hearers, obscuring the basic significance of what we have been trying to say.

The mysteries of faith remain inexpressible, but we must still make the effort to confess what we believe, and this is complicated by the fact that now the act of faith may have nothing external to hold on to. Constant in-depth training or initiation in the way of religious experience is necessary as never before. Our preaching will then have a solid foundation in the very wellsprings of our existence; however the other may interpret it, as we grow into the ever greater mystery of God so many purely marginal questions are recognized for what they are, and we are spared the trouble of chasing phantoms. A greater caution in appealing to 'the will of God,' as Rahner remarks, and an appreciation of the true significance of frequent reception of the sacraments would emerge from a preaching which took seriously the continuing religious formation of adults. Faith rooted in the living experience of God is not divorced from everyday life or smothered in a false cult of inwardness, fed on pious emotion and subjective feeling. The faith-life is strengthened immensely if we will allow ourselves to be 'taught of God,' eliminating self-advertising fuss and gestures and forgetting self. A careful introduction to the right way of praying is an indispensable step toward the reduction of an over-luxuriant piety and a return to the simplicity enjoined by the Gospel. In the proclamation of our faith, in preaching, we can contribute to renewal without maneuvering ourselves into an esoteric and artificial theology of unbelief. Faith, as lived and in proclamation, will then appear even to unbelievers as fraternal love, not inviting unnecessary controversy because men will be addressed in their humanity, in what is best and most promising in them.

To say that Christian doctrine, comprising, as is claimed, God's revealed and self-revealing word, is credible is felt to be an assault on the emancipation from confining creed and commitment which modern man prizes so highly and for which a hard struggle was fought. We preach this compelling word at our own risk, in view of the almost visceral reaction of some intelligent people to the suggestion that belief is not the suffocation of man's critical sense, his discernment, his concern for the pure truth. This antipathy has been fed in the past by special pleading for a religious establishment carried on under the guise of apostolic preaching in an attempt to impose faith without free inquiry and under a tutelage suited to children and to immature minds. Intellectuals have had enough unhappy experience to make them suspicious of tardy measures, conciliar and post-conciliar, to rehabilitate the intellectual content of the evangelical message. As Robert McAfee Brown notes, however, all the fault has not been on one side, and if preaching has been imperialistic, the disavowal of faith on grounds of intellectual inanity may have been precipitous and premature.[38] The preaching which is too ready to close the gap between faith and reason has an opposite number in the incredulity which enjoys maintaining a gulf between those who believe and those who really know. A mind committed carefully and conscientiously to the truth of the Gospel retains all the integrity, the passion for persevering inquiry, essential to that openness without which even the possession of truth turns into dogmatism and the worst sort of ideologization. McAfee Brown's article sketches the elements of the problem of the relationship of faith and intellectual integrity, elements from which I have assembled a number of points that seem to be especially relevant to the proclamation of the Gospel to a world of unbelief. This alleged relevance is obscured unless the reality of the problem is recognized and its importance admitted, and this means the frank acknowledgment of the alienation from Christian commitment of the intellectual class as a whole. The problem extends not only to those who may be called intellectuals but to all who value the rights and prerogatives of enlightened reason and respect the moral obligation to pursue the truth without let or hindrance.

Faith involves both assent to truth and trust in the truthfulness of God, acceptance of certain propositions (all truth is propositional) and commitment to a way of life indicated by the content of at least some of these propositions. Neither assent on the basis of a witness's competence and reliability nor trust in another's good will and ability to keep his word is impeachable as absolutely incompatible with the canons of sound intellectualism. Every man, even one who claims to disown cosmic presuppositions, lives by and in some sort of belief, and he must do so, whatever the object or quality of his belief or the place it occupies in his scheme of things and his self-understanding. This is a perfectly valid observation, and it ought not to be overlooked in our attempt to show the reasonableness of the service of faith. The option is not between faith and no-faith, not even between faith and knowledge, for all men know something and believe something (all, except the most stupid and abandoned); the competition is between beliefs and between one's belief and what one claims to know. All faith or belief—I am presently using these terms interchangeably—seeks understanding; the full flowering of faith is realized as it assimilates progressively a deeper and more meaningful understanding of what is behind. This thrust drives the believer on to inquire, question, challenge, criticize, analyze, doubt, all of this, whether it be Christian faith or any other faith system. We preach a life of risk, then, when we invite men to listen to God's word and make the response appropriate to it as life-giving truth; at no point is Christian faith an abandonment of critical reason, not in its initial embrace or at any subsequent time when it must be re-appropriated and reaffirmed. Every man who believes and who lives by a faith experiences this as a threat and an adventure; in this respect the Christian is neither better nor worse off than others. It is his faith which gives him the courage and the motive to act: let this action, the kind and quality of life that is lived, be included in any evaluation of the overall human significance of a faith-decision.

The question of the *content* of faith remains, even granted that the act or posture of believing is not necessarily contrary to intellectual integrity. The question turns then on the truth and the relevance of what one believes, for it is not simply in 'faith' that we believe, on analogy with being in love with love. How, briefly, does Christian faith urge us to make use of our rational power, for what purposes, within what limits, and under what conditions? Intellectual life is not and cannot be morally and spiritually neutral; a man is responsible, in conscience, for the effort he makes to inform and enlighten himself and for the uses to which he puts his knowledge. The preacher must hammer away at this aspect of both faith and knowledge: that we are compelled to take a stand by reason of what we think and believe. My final point is that belief is not only not out of place in a sound, healthy intellectual life but that Christian belief can be a powerful liberating force for human understanding. McAfee Brown suggests three ways in which this faith can contribute possibilities of intellectuality in which genuine openness is combined with firm commitment: (1) Christian faith exercises a salutary critique of certain misguided efforts at understanding and of certain false conceptions of intellectuality. There is no knowledge so pure or right that man's perverse will and heart cannot turn it to evil purposes; hence education is not of itself or infallibly a sufficient means to human wholeness. It is at least possible, as Reinhold Niebuhr has frequently reminded us, that one faith may be able to do justice to reality, to the way things actually are, better than another and thus free the believer from error and inaccuracy by which he would otherwise be entrapped. (2) Our faith urges and even enjoins us to persevere in searching out the ways of things, exploring all that is within experience and following every lead in order to understand as much and as deeply as possible. This is God's world, good, orderly, and dependable, just the sort of world that invites exhaustive and untiring scientific investigation and analysis. As for ourselves: 'To believe that man is made in the image of God makes possible a confidence in the creative powers of the human mind and imagination that can unleash bold and venturesome experiments in thinking and living; at the same time, a realistic assessment of the sin of man makes possible a type of investigation which is neither Promethean nor Faustian, and which recognizes that man's built-in biases provide a healthy sagefuard against claiming too much for what he knows.'[39] (3) Faith as trust (*fiducia*) can liberate not only the mind but the whole man, empowering him to act on the basis of what he believes and to live with freedom from fear and anxiety. The man of faith continues to see only dimly, as through a dark glass, and to live in hope, that is, in expectation rather than possession. To the unbeliever he says, candidly and without rancor: my condition is human, I want to be fully human; I challenge you to put your finger on the spot where hearing the word of God makes me inhuman or less than human.

It would be a tragic mistake if, in trying to make our faith more credible and religious experience more accessible through our preaching, we aimed to speak only, or in the first place, to a pragmatic, profane, secularized man. The death-of-God and secular city publicists of the last five or six years have fairly persuaded some religionists that this man is the new arbiter of the truth and value of religion; it must suit him, as it were, or it doesn't cut the mustard. Some Catholic writers have accepted this reading of the current scene but have still tried to hold on to their pet personalist, existentialist, or metaphysical perspectives. The credibility of faith is not manifest in a concept of religion as a hunt for an elusive permanent in face of the fleeting, for ultimate meaning amidst uncertainty— this approach keeps alive an old and dangerous dualism, whatever the good intention of its authors. Credibility must not be identified with or reduced to an egregious type of utilitarianism by trying to show how kindly and benevolently the Church looks upon men's struggle to realize a humane social order, even though its own ultimate interests lie elsewhere. Our preaching may not, at risk of destroying the very foundation from which renewal has been launched, lapse into a covert theologism, merely replacing the old abstractions and flights of fancy with new ones done up in the images and allusion which suggest, in this case deceptively, a latest 'theology of earthly realities' produced, like the Abbé de Sièyes's constitution for the French people, in the studies, libraries, and—above all—convention halls of academic types. If so much of our preaching still seems irrelevant, it is because it is so largely turned in upon itself and nowhere with such painful obviousness than when it tries to talk about faith and the world in the language of theology, even the varieties of new theology. Daniel Callahan's complaint about theology itself may be extended to the preaching which, with other- wise admirable fidelity, is based upon it, namely, that it speaks of a realm that seems to be a delightful place in which to live, except that we who already believe are the only ones who find it inhabitable.[40]

The word of God is proclaimed directly by preaching, in the various forms this takes, but faith is witness to the truth of God indirectly, and perhaps more effectively, in the social and politi- cal presence of Christians in the world. An ecclesial presence is at least as important as the encounter with the Gospel through preaching, in a cultural order in which the unbeliever is capable of avoiding completely those media and occasions on which procla- mation is made. In the past the Church performed a number of social functions and enjoyed certain privileges and an effective power over areas of thought and life; the world of today indicates the renunciation of special consideration in a pluralist society and the concentration of effort on building up a vital community of believers. The world feels threatened, and indeed insulted, when it is approached by a hierarchy which speaks of toleration, freedom of conscience, and fraternal charity but persists in an attitude of supervising the thinking and decision-making of immature people (called 'subjects,' 'children,' 'beloved sons and daughters'). Authority is perfectly intact, and materially strengthened, when it is exercised as service, in humility, and not in a spirit of self-seeking and aggran- dizement. While seeking the way to dialogue with unbelievers, we need to pursue the possibilities of dialogue among ourselves, to be led more deeply into the appropriation of the truth that is already ours in principle. Lastly, in terms of the norms which ought to govern the Christian presence or opening to the unbeliever, I must mention the test of the deed, real action in face of need, violence, and injustice. Let there be anathemas, by all means, but of poverty, war, racism, the oppression of defenseless peoples and the exploitation of classes.

Fraternal charity is not enough, to alter Bruno Bettelheim slightly, but without it nothing else matters much in the long run, not the truth or being in the right or even being devoted to the elimination of concrete abuses and injustices. It is impossible to ideologize one's own position, to rationalize motives or prettify untoward maneuvers as long as one is truly operating from love of neighbor. This love has, further, a unique political dimension which turns us toward the problems of society and inspires in us that protest against deprivation and persecution which the world has a right to expect of us. 'The world today requires of Christians that they remain Christians,' is Albert Camus' way of putting it, which I would translate as recommending that we put our house in order, take stock of our own best principles, and strive earnestly to live up to those principles.[41] The unbeliever has no God, by his own admission, but can he transfer to mankind, collectively or individually, that love and adoration which believers direct toward God? The neighbor mirrors oneself, one's essential humanity, and shows one all the variants of human qualities both good and bad, a spectacle which tends to make him bad-tempered with himself and provokes a malaise and nausea at being inescapably locked up with such unlovely and unlovable fellows. Men suffer, then, by being in a world in which there is so little love; some, especially sensitive or faint-hearted or both, reach a pathological extreme that finds life absolutely unbearable and there is no escape—*huis clos*. If there is truly no way out of this tragic situation, and man knows it, he must feel that he has been cheated in the prison of his nature, in an absurd history on an absurd planet. Christian faith, precisely, enters the scene with the conviction that men are not thus helpless and further proposes that there is a way out, and the Gospel's first word to men is that they are loved by God, whether they recognize Him or not, whether they return His love or not. God's love is felt, seen, heard, as St. John says, in those who love their neighbor; the first presence of the Church to the world of unbelief must be as lover, dispensing love as something that is more than itself. Both the word and the action of the Church, then, spring from a love that comes forth but remains, in its source, hidden to the world without faith. Love is not so much a specific norm of the Christian's presence to the unbeliever as the inspiriting heart and soul of that presence, whatever form it may take.[42]

The New Testament, the Epistles of St. Paul and of St. John as well as the Gospels, in particular, announce repeatedly that God's love breaks down barriers between men and abolishes those considerations on the basis of which men stand off and discriminate against each other. Yet brotherhood, so clearly and forcefully affirmed in these sacred writings, is not a blanket category embracing without qualification all men, simply by reason of their common humanity—this emptying of the concept of all meaning is the product of Enlightenment rationalism and sentimentalism. Meaningful brotherhood implies a definite, visible community which excludes an empty romanticizing and places it on the level of concrete realizability. There are frontiers to Christian brotherhood, those of the community of faith, but they are open. The brethren are expected to respond with a total loving service to anyone who approaches them in need of help; they are told to pray for all men, to respect lawful authority, no matter who holds it, to show themselves by their whole conduct true benefactors of all mankind.[43] Respecting the spiritual integrity of 'those outside,' St. Paul declines to sit in judgment on the moral state or eternal destiny of those who are outside the community of believers (1 Cor 5.12–13), and indeed he recommends that Christians maintain a certain independence and reserve in dealing with pagans. This last injunction highlights the difficulty of translating scriptural texts about brotherhood into the idiom of the experience and conditions of the present time.[44] Some of this difficulty is dispelled by the insistence, also and equally scriptural, that all men are called to this brotherhood, so that Christianity remains wholly free of a desire to form a self-sufficient esoteric group like the mystery cults. But why, under what rubric, include this opening in love to the unbeliever in the scope of the proclamation of the word? Because, in defining the day-to-day manner of Christian presence to the unbeliever, one comes up against the dialectic of the Church's commission from Christ Himself to proclaim openly His word, and, on the other hand, to perform this task of preaching with a certain discretion and even reserve. Our preaching, which is a form of witness from which no one may dispense us, must not try to catch men unawares, without their knowing it, to draw the word of God out of a hat, like a conjurer.

Christian love takes two forms, and first in the relations of Christians to each other and in their own characters love should have a force of example and attractiveness, shining as a light in the midst of a crooked and perverse generation (Phil 2.15; Mt 5.14). But that is not enough: 'if you salute only your brothers what more are you doing than others? Do not even the Gentiles do the same?' (Mt 5.47). They must direct their love to those who neither know nor love their Lord or themselves, to all those who need them, without asking for thanks or a response in kind. Christ Himself is truly present wherever a man recognizes and affirms the claim on his love that goes out from a fellow man in need. Going even further, the Christian is called upon to deny himself and to suffer for the non-believer, and in his place, if necessary. The law of Christ's own life is that also of His followers: 'The Son of man also came not to be served but to serve, and to give His love as a ransom for many' (Mk 10.45). Jesus, the One, stands before the whole of mankind; so His disciples stand as the few before the many, not against but for them. Here the entire Church must keep ever in mind the foolishness of pursuing worldly success, power, triumph and the wisdom of vicarious suffering, surrender, meekness. The poor man comes to live next to us and with us; he nags at us, speaks evil of us, and denounces all that we believe in and stand for; he is, in short, the militant unbeliever. What then? The believer, ardent and zealous in defense of his faith, may want to turn away, to preserve his comfort and security, to live undisturbed, in peace, not wishing harm to anyone. To stop communicating is to fail in charity because the greatest enemy of love is that stony silence which allows misunderstanding to fester. That is why the love which never stops hoping for the other eventually seeks dialogue, the opportunity to exchange thoughts and feelings, to tell him our truth and to listen to his. There is risk in this, personal as well as doctrinal, but it is only by taking the risk that belief will make that definitive encounter with unbelief which has been the vision inspiring the present work from its first pages.

Contact: the Secretariat for Non-Believers

Believer and unbeliever must talk to and with each other; they must come together and be with each other, communicate, dialogue. Communication does not necessarily presuppose completed thought nor does it consist entirely in the manifestation and exchange of such thought; the deepest part of our humanity, our being, is permeated by language, which is social and historical as well as individual and personal. If I may state very briefly the concept of communication which I have used in these reflections on dialogue, I should like in the first place to emphasize that language is not simply thought seeking and finding verbal expression of itself, although it is, of course, thought that gives rise to language and makes it possible. When communication is perfect, it involves a total personal exchange, the opening of one person as such to another, and the other's reciprocity; just as I come to full existence through embodiment, so my being, what I am, finds expression in the word. The humanity of language is revealed in its capacity for conveying agreement and disagreement, i.e., for disclosing the preferences and attachments, enjoyments and desires, as well as their opposites, which constitute the dynamics of personal-social existence. When we communicate, we share not only thought but all that drives us forward, shuts out certain aspects of reality from our world, makes us to be what we are, more and other than pure intellects. Believers and unbelievers will dialogue as human beings, in an encounter that will be something far more than the meeting and confrontation of points of view or conflicting philosophies. There is today a growing body of literature on the nature and conditions of dialogue, a sign of the increasing recognition of the importance of communications in human life. I should like to put off for the moment the theoretical discussion of dialogue, to avoid getting involved with abstract categories or bogged down in obscure and controverted points, none of which may be particularly relevant to the actual task of dialogue between believer and unbeliever. The concrete problems of dialogue have already been experienced and out of this experience, partial and imperfect, varying and continuing, rather than out of purely abstract speculation, a working philosophy of dialogue may be developed. Dialogue grows out of contact, and this has already occurred; contact has been both personal and on an institutional or quasi-official level, and I shall consider each form of contact in turn.

If one leaves aside what has already been said about the unbelief of believers and considers only those who profess to be and manifestly are unbelievers, then it is a matter of fact evident to all that unbelievers may be met with everywhere in social life. When contact is made, however, it is something more than casual encounter or the accidental and unplanned juxtaposition of people who happen to be believer and unbeliever but who do not meet as such or whose meeting in no way involves what each represents, faith and its denial. It is necessary to break the ice, to seek out the other and attempt to establish personal contact in a way that will bring belief and unbelief to the surface, to make of this opposition the very point or purpose of contact, with a view to initiating dialogue. What will be avoided and condemned as a ruse, a dodge, will be the devising of points of contact which smack of the artificial and contrived. The believer whose chief purpose is seen to be to draw attention to himself, in a superficial or frivolous fashion, may succeed in realizing just this aim, but his effort can hardly serve as a basis on which to build a most serious or substantial relationship. Yet the other must find a man, another human being, at the other end of the relationship, and it is in and through the believer's authentic and undiminished humanity that he will be encouraged to cement and deepen the contact that has been made. Contact at a personal level is strengthened by the discovery of a mutual openness to all that is of value in the arts and sciences, in technology and exploration, in the field of human rights, and compassion in the presence of suffering. By the same token, the diminution or absence of human feeling and sensibility throws a gulf, a great abyss, between those who might and ought to have become future partners in dialogue.

The believer may rightly be convinced that in facing up to the trials and challenge of life, in bearing with its frustrations and failures, he is sustained and guided by his faith in God. It would be a travesty, however, if God were wholly confined and reduced to the measure of the problem we have to solve, whereas, precisely in His presence to us, He is God only on condition that He transcends all that we have conceived and built, bursts asunder the forms and categories in which we order and construct our finite world. The unbeliever does not encounter deep faith, at its richest and most authentic, unless he sees clearly, in the life of the believer, a certain margin of grandeur and mystery in which he is steeped, however concerned he may be for the cares and aspirations of the others. In all this the believer makes and cements contact by being there where he is needed, to listen to the other intently, at his disposal. There is nothing idyllic about this sort of contact, indeed there will very quickly be differences and painful moments, withdrawal and refusal. But these same difficulties produce at least this, and it is something positive, namely, the perception of the real dimensions of one's belief (and unbelief, naturally). The very obstacles he meets, the setbacks he experiences in trying to contact the other, reveal both his inability to communicate and the underlying ignorance and lack of understanding which account for this inability. The unbeliever should find in the other a man who knows what his faith is about, what it means to believe, that his identity as a Christian is determined not by ability to impress or by erudition but by his faithfulness to a Master. To point out his defects and faults or those of the Church of which he is a member is not to invalidate the believer's humanity or to remove all reason for making contact with him. The believer has a certainty and a confidence, whether he be reproached for this or not, but he reposes them not in himself but in God, in His faithfulness. It is well to expect in advance that the unbeliever's ideas about our faith are vague and confused, distorted and incomplete. Many ideas formerly more or less clear and secure among Christians have been hotly debated among them, so that the confusion and uncertainty are not all on the outside. In any case I hope I have not seemed to imply, in my remarks about renewal, that it is in terms of some sort of modernization that we as believers ought to make the first and fundamental contact with the atheist. I doubt whether the unbeliever, who in any case is largely indifferent to religious *aggiornamento*, will be notably touched by the Church's massive effort at adaptation and reconciliation to the world. Contact will be made not because the believer holds out ready-made answers to questions but because he is found to be a man of honor and compassion, capable also of joy and courage and of being enthralled by all that makes up the human condition.

While contact with a view to dialogue must always take place on the level of interpersonal encounter, this encounter may, and in some instances ought to, engage the Church in an official or quasi-official capacity. The initiative on this score has already been taken in the establishment by Pope Paul VI of the Vatican Secretariat for Non-Believers (*Secretariatus pro Noncredentibus*). The announcement of this act was made in *L'Osservatore Romano* of April 9, 1965, with no accompanying document outlining in detail the structure or purpose of this body, only a brief statement declaring that it would study the question of atheism and unbelief. It is related that the Pope said to the man chosen to head the new Secretariat, when they met to discuss it, '*Usus docebit*' ('You will learn by experience'). This man was Franziscus Cardinal König, Archbishop of Vienna, one of the Church's most scholarly and enlightened prelates. König has studied the period from the First to the Second Vatican Councils and noted a number of significant landmarks which prepared the Church for the bold and decisive step taken by Paul VI as evidence of its seriousness in seeking dialogue with the world of unbelief.[45]

The Council of 1962–65 excited a worldwide interest, indeed a sympathetic attention, which contrasts sharply with the combination of massive indifference and fierce hostility which greeted its predecessor of 1869–70. Journalists were excluded from the work of the earlier Council, so that factual, objective reporting was all but impossible, and the resulting misinformation undoubtedly exacerbated the adverse public attitude and the great skepticism about what the Council had tried to accomplish. The world opinion which came to prevail during the Second Vatican Council was considerably more favorable, in spite of the unrest and even opposition with which a segment of Catholic people greeted the results. The Council made it abundantly clear that the Church wanted to enter into conversation with 'the others,' to engage in a conversation which meant the breaking down of walls of isolation and the abandonment of monologue and soliloquy in favor of dialogue. The world had already responded with manifest gratification and sincere good will to Pope John's fraternal openness and desire to bring together in understanding and mutual respect those who did not share the faith of Catholics. What Pope John undertook in an intensely personal spirit, his successor systematized and organized in a series of acts and official pronouncements that committed the entire Church to this task of mutual exchange. Catholics, it was now possible to assert with confidence and on the highest authority, were eager to converse with others, not only separated Christians but people of other world religions and those who rejected all religion and perhaps even fought against it. Catholics are not simply or essentially anti-everything non-Catholic, so that the siege mentality is no longer appropriate, if it ever was, and the gearing for combat and attack ought to be replaced by a more positive stance, responding to questions and requests for understanding and cooperation. This point has been reached only by way of the fresh recognition that the world has its own autonomy and integrity which the Church must respect, serve, and encourage and which may not be suppressed, exploited, or negated.

The Secretariat for Non-Believers was the third such Vatican organization commissioned to deal with groups of non-Catholics. The Secretariat for the Promotion of Christian Unity, headed until his death by the great Augustine Cardinal Bea, has made enviable progress in promoting ecumenism and bringing together for purposes of discussion and mutual understanding Catholics and other Christians. This secretariat was established before the Council got under way and has exercised an enormous and beneficent influence in the relations, at all levels, between the Church of Rome and other Christian communities and religious bodies. Simply by its existence, with the Pope's blessing and with an official status fortunately somewhat independent of the curial bureaucracy that rules the Vatican operating machinery, the Christian Unity Secretariat has provided a responsible and authoritative partner for dialogue. The parallel with the Secretariat for Non-Believers breaks down to the extent that it is unrealistic to expect to find well-organized groups of atheists as willing to enter into official conversation with Catholics, on the same scale as Protestants, Orthodox, etc. The second Secretariat is that for Non-Christian Religions, entrusted to the presidency of Cardinal Marella and charged with studying approaches to the religious groups of Judaism and Islam and what Paul VI called 'the followers of the great Afro-Asiatic religions,' including Hinduism, Buddhism, Shintoism, etc. With these peoples Catholics share belief in God, or at least in a higher Being, although there is no intention of putting all on the same footing, e.g., the Jews, whose sacred book is our Old Testament, revered by us as the inspired word of God, and Moslems, whose Koran, although monotheistic, positively excludes the messianic hope in the Christ which unites Jews and Christians at a certain point. The third Secretariat embraces in its field of concern all men who have no religious belief whatever, whom the Church wants to know and understand and with whom it wants to enter into dialogue, to be there where they are and to listen as well as speak to them.

The distinguished Archbishop of Vienna, Cardinal König, has had a career as both scholar and pastor and has long been keenly interested in the immense and complex problems of faith in a world of unbelief. König's major published works include a dictionary of comparative religions, *Religionswissenschaftliches Wörterbuch*, of which he was editor; a very learned monograph on the Zoroastrian concept of the afterlife, *Zarathustras Jenseitsvorstellungen und das Alte Testament*; and a three-volume work on comparative religion, *Christus und die Religionen der Erde*. In his native Austria König followed closely the defection, over a period of years, of thousands who drifted away from religion, often silently, without protest. This problem he faced in a broadcast on Pentecost Sunday, 1962: 'The profound alienation between the Church and the people which came about in the West and certainly also in our own country has many causes. One of the most significant of them, however, is the fact that we have forgotten how to convey God's word in a form that is understood by others. . . . To talk the language of others does not only mean to present the liturgy in the mother tongue; above all, it means to speak to man in all his complexity, to take him seriously in all his desires and hopes, in his joys and pains, in his spirit and in his body. It means to seek him out where he lives, in his environment, in his living conditions, in his social milieu. It means to make his sorrows one's own, it means to understand him, it above all means to approach him. This approaching, dealing with him and taking him seriously has sometimes been forgotten and we have to learn that anew.'[46] The Cardinal has served on several diplomatic *ad hoc* missions, sometimes semi-clandestine or only quasi-official, and is well-known and respected by Communists on both sides of the Iron Curtain. During the sessions of the Council König quickly emerged as one of the leaders and spokesmen for the liberal and progressive majority. It is interesting to note that he declined the post of head of the Secretariat for Non-Christian Religions, for which he is ideally suited, because he did not wish to leave his post in Vienna (Cardinal Cushing of Boston, in fact, suggested that this Secretariat be headquartered in Vienna). It would be far from the mark to describe this man as a revolutionary, either in theology or in his conception of needed practical reform; he is, instead, a man of great experience and learning, perceptiveness and openness, stable, cool-headed, prudent in a strong and positive sense.

World reaction, even within the Catholic Church, to the establishment of the Secretariat for Non-Believers has been surprisingly meager and mild, for reasons which to me are still unclear but on which I will chance a rather hesitant conjecture. There was, in the first place, a great deal of competition for news coverage from a number of intensely interesting and more sensational topics, including the debate on religious freedom and the raging controversy over birth control. The actual announcement of this action by the Holy See was made with relatively little fanfare and obviously caught the press and Catholic spokesmen in various parts of the world unprepared. Cardinal König emphasized the need of study and reflection on the phenomenon of contemporary atheism and on the problems it sets of Christian understanding and conscience. In a press interview of April 8, 1965, the Cardinal made a special point of rejecting the idea of a crusade, stating that it was not the intention of the Secretariat 'to organize a struggle against atheism, not even against militant atheism,' but rather, 'to investigate all the possibilities which can assure religion of its place in society . . . to establish contacts in the hope of setting up an intellectual dialogue . . . to urge concerted action of behalf of peace.' The purpose uppermost in the minds of its president, and one with which the author of the present work readily concurs, is that of serious and intensive study and research. Cooperation for the attainment of practical ends, such as that of world peace, is important but not a primary or immediate goal entertained in the setting up of the Secretariat. The common concern about the steps that must be taken to avoid nuclear holocaust and every kind of war may serve as one means to be used in making contact. The cause of peace is manifestly one where Catholics can begin to persuade their hoped-for partners in dialogue of their good will and sincerity.[47]

Cardinal König distinguished varieties of unbelief: 'There is the practical atheism, which is recognizable today in predominantly urban civilizations, and which is given greater effect by the mass media of modern communications. This type of atheism is continued by a doctrinaire atheism, which strives to maintain its position scientifically by the publication of books and periodicals.' The arguments of this doctrinaire atheism are said to be drawn from 'humanist considerations,' but there is a third, very different 'militant atheism,' which depends on the support of the state and develops an orthodoxy, a rigid conformism of its own, in the service of political purposes. Some months after this interview, on October 24, 1965, during the final session of the Council, Cardinal König went even further, in an interview for the Milan newspaper, *Corriere della Sera*. Communism was still a grave problem for Christians, and in any future dialogue, he said, it will not be disguised that 'we have become conscious of this and want to delve into the reasons why God and man seem to be in competition, with preference being given to man. . . . Perhaps even for the Communists themselves proofs are materializing to show that religion isn't a super-structure but a spiritual need of man in any society.' Just two days prior to this statement, in an interview with the German weekly *Die Zeit*, König said: 'If I, as a Catholic bishop, say that the Church has in part lost the young, then this applies to Communism as well. Indeed, in every respect modern atheism confronts us with a pheno-menon which is as much of the West as of the East. It may well turn out to be true that the problem is even more difficult in the West than in the East.' The Cardinal named 'the need for securing living space for religion' as a prime objective of the new Secretariat: 'It is a matter of eliminating hatred.' Hence the Cardinal expected the Secretariat to promote and encourage scientific research in an effort to trace the roots and sources of atheistic movements and to register the repercussions of atheism in scientific and literary fields. It was not an especially exciting program outlined by the Cardinal, from the beginning, but he was firmly convinced that studies in depth pursued all over the world and properly coordinated and interpreted would contribute immensely to the success of future dialogue, once the time for the latter ripened.[48]

The organization of the Secretariat has been kept to a minimum, based on a group of bishops representing the Church in every part of the world. In November, 1965, 22 bishops were named members of the Secretariat, one from each major European country, two each from the critically sensitive areas of Poland and Yugoslavia, with the United States, Canada, Latin America, Africa, and the Far East duly represented.* These prelates, together with the president, constitute the Secretariat's deliberative assembly; this body held its first meetings during the last weeks of the Council. The episcopal members of the Secretariat maintain contact with national conferences of bishops and are responsible for setting up and presiding, personally or through a fellow bishop, over what will in effect be national secretariats or commissions. In Rome the Secretariat maintains a central office, like the headquarters of the other two secretariats, directed by Don Vincenzo Miano, S.D.B., a professor in the philosophical faculty of the Salesian College of Don Bosco in Rome. Miano's reputation in the field has been earned by the program of studies he directs at the Salesian College and the four-volume *Encyclopedia of Contemporary Atheism* on which, as editor, he has been working for a number of years. Don Vincenzo has a number of associates working with him in Rome and forming the staff of the central headquarters. The chief work of this skeleton staff is to maintain relations with the Holy See, to collect and make available to those who require it information of all kinds about the phenomenon of atheism, supplied from every part of the world, and to perform other services for the episcopal members of the Secretariat and the national episcopal conferences. No general publication for open distribution has yet been contemplated but a very useful Bulletin of Information is sent regularly to the bishops and other interested parties. The Roman headquarters serves largely as a center of information and a source of coordinating and stimulating other groups

---

* Twenty-two bishops were appointed members of the Secretariat in mid-November: Joseph Blomjous, S.F., Bishop of Mwanza, Tanzania; John Bokenfohr, O.M.I., Bishop of Kimberley, South Africa; William Brasseur, C.I.C.M., Vicar Apostolic of Mountain Province, Philippines; Thomas Cahill, Bishop of Cairns, Australia; Alexander Carter, Bishop of Sault Ste. Marie, Canada; John Dearden, Archbishop of Detroit; Gerard DeVet, Bishop of Breda, Netherlands; Neophytus Edelby, Archbishop, Melkite patriarchal counsellor, Damascus, Syria; Angelo Fernandes, Coadjutor Archbishop of Delhi, India; John Gran, O.C.R., Bishop of Oslo, Norway; Thomas Holland, Bishop of Salford, England; José Guerra-Campos, Auxiliary Bishop of Madrid; Janex Jenko, Apostolic Administrator of Slovene territory, Gorizia, Italy; Boleslaw Kominek, Archbishop in Wroclaw (Breslau), Poland; Marc Lallier, Archbishop of Marseille, France; Stanislaus Lokuang, Archbishop of Taipei, Formosa; Marcos McGrath, C.S.C., Bishop of Santiago de Veraguas, Panama; Eduardo Pironio, Auxiliary Bishop of LaPlata, Argentina; Oscar de Oliveira, Archbishop of Mariana, Brazil; Laurentius Satoshi Nagae, Bishop of Urawa, Japan; Hyacinthe Thiandouon, Archbishop of Dakar, Senegal; and Helmut Wittler, Bishop of Osnabrück, Germany.

and individuals within the Church. The Secretariat has been much concerned with establishing contact with universities and institutes of higher studies for the purpose of gathering data both on prevailing conditions and on studies done in this area. There has been talk of the establishment in Rome of a center for scholarly work on problems of contemporary atheism, and the Sacred Congregation of Seminaries and Universities has requested the assistance of the Secretariat in renewing programs of priestly formation and theological studies.

The structure of the Secretariat is completed by the appointment of about sixty consultors to collaborate with the bishops and make available their expert and specialized knowledge. Most of the consultors are clerics and theologians, although there are men (no women) from other fields, particularly philosophy and the social sciences, including a few laymen.*

The Nature of Dialogue

At a meeting of the consultors to the Secretariat for Non-Believers in Rome, called to discuss the philosophy of dialogue which this body would officially adopt, one of the most renowned theologians present insisted with great emphasis that dialogue was an entirely new category in the life and thinking of the Church. Several others present at the meeting wholeheartedly concurred, and they urged study and research as the activity most immediately appropriate and necessary at that organizational period. Ultimately, however, it was to the definition of dialogue and a declaration of intent and

---

* The following is the Secretariat's only circulated list of consultors: Orazio Bettini, O.F.M., Rome; Hervé Carrier, S.J., Rome; Dominique Chenu, O.P., Paris; Yves Congar, O.P., Strasbourg; Georges Cottier, O.P., Geneva; Dominique Dubarle, O.P., Paris; Giuseppe de Rosa, S.J., Rome; Giulio Girardi, S.D.B., Rome; Saverio Cik, C.J.G., Vienna; Henri de Lubac, S.J., Lyon; Jean-Yves Calvez, S.J., Vanves, France; Cornelio Fabro, C.PP.S., Rome; André Godin, S.J., Brussels; Jacques Loew, O.P., Toulouse; Johann Lotz, S.J., Pullach-Munich; Karl Rahner, S.J., Munich; François Russo, S.J., Paris; Raimondo Sigmund, O.P., Rome; John Patrick Reid, O.P., Providence, R.I.; Andrea Varga, S.J., Rome; Tomislaw Sagi-Bunic, Zagreb, Yugoslavia; René Voillaume, Marseille; Gustav Wetter, S.J., Rome; Prof. Bontadini, Milan; Jean Guitton, Paris; R. Gugranyes de Franch, Fribourg; Max Charlesworth, Victoria, Australia; Vittorino Vevonese, Rome; Raniero LaValle, Rome; Giuseppe Tagliapietra, Venice; Arthur Gibson, Winnipeg, Canada; J. M. Cameron, Leeds, England; Adolfo Muñoz Alonso, Madrid; Johannes B. Metz, Münster; Richard Butler, O.P., Chicago; Bernard Haering, C.SS.R., Rome; Prof. Ferdinando Ormes, Rome; Alfonso Alvarez-Bolado, Barcelona; and Prof. Pedro Lain-Entralgo, Madrid.

purpose in seeking the opportune conditions for dialogue that the members and consultors devoted themselves at the first several meetings held in Rome over a period of almost two years. It may be useful to suggest a well-worked-out philosophy of dialogue before examining the results of the labor of those years. The concept is inherited from the period of classical thought, when the advantages of civilized conversation for clarifying issues and resolving them were first explicitly recognized. Philosophers as divergent as Plato and Hume employed a dialogal form of discourse in order more effectively to confront clashing views and highlight the source of differences which might otherwise remain more or less concealed, unless ferreted out under pressure of insistent questioning.[49] Dialogue arises out of the confrontation of opposing views and consists in the exchange of those views, not merely their respective airing, in an exchange of monologues in which each view is presented on its own and no true and mutual interchange evolves. Whether it is a matter of searching for *the* definitive answer to a question patient of such inquiry, or of settling on the relative merits of less than definitive answers, which do not and cannot be made to coincide with each other, each side must be open and attentive to the other. Dialogue will naturally tend toward a meeting of minds (at least, not to speak of a total human rapport which may eventuate), but the meeting may fall far short of actual agreement, and indeed such unanimity may be morally impossible.

A first type of dialogue may be employed in the inquiry which leads to scientific truth, that is, a conclusion or inference based on incontrovertible evidence and arrived at by a process of reasoning in which the successive steps are clearly and distinctly identified and controlled.[50] We expect that truth in this strong and comparatively unequivocal sense prevails especially in the sciences in which mathematics is a major methodological tool; dialogue in this vast field, which is constantly expanding and reaching into question-areas from which it was formerly absent, resembles somewhat a growing monologue, in that personal factors on all sides are excluded as irrelevant and what is sought is the extension of a knowledge already held in a vast anonymous fashion by all who are expert in the particular discipline. The contributions of the collaborators in this enterprise assume the form of uncovering evidence upon which agreement can in principle be reached by procedures upon which there is already a high degree of concurrence. Western civilization has been permeated so deeply and thoroughly by the prospects of this sort of rational achievement that it has, for many, become the ideal, and determines a pattern of social life geared to provide optimal conditions for its pursuit. It is, quite simply, the ideal of science, described by Dominique Dubarle as 'capable of compelling the understanding and determining the judgments and reasoning of all, and consequently susceptible of expression in the intellectual monolith of cooperative knowledge.'[51] The solid corpus of knowledge thus constructed is the product of combined efforts, but at least theoretically the end product bears the stamp of pure and simple rationality, divested of all qualities save those of objective certainty and universal, public verifiability. Individuals meet, actually or equivalently, to formulate the problem and work out obscure and difficult points, a joint venture directed toward unanimous agreement on a matter for which science and not opinion is the proper intellectual vehicle. Dialogue in this mode and with this goal in view has been a staple of the intellectual history of the West, if not often (or frequently) in actual practice, then at least as the ideal manner of arriving at knowledge which anyone can assimilate and evaluate critically by criteria which are accessible to all. Pascal surveys the history of civilized men as a succession throughout the course of centuries of continual learning, correcting and refining what had previously been attained and pushing ever further back the boundaries of ignorance.

A grand ideal of absolute Truth has dominated and inspired the central philosophical tradition, in spite of periodic bouts of skepticism and notwithstanding the growing recognition in the present century of the multiformity of truth and the irreducible pluralism of the scientific disciplines. The intersubjective character of truth emerges strikingly in this concept of its appropriation by a cooperative effort, the public and controllable features of which immeasurably enhance the clarity and certitude of the result. This kind of inquiry imposes severe discipline on those taking part or proposing to share in the outcome; standards of intellectual honesty and objectivity are required, proving indispensable in building up the deposit of scientific knowledge, which is one of the permanent and fundamental elements in Western culture. The ideal was sketched, within the limits of his own experience and the still extremely primitive and undifferentiated state of systematic human knowledge, by Aristotle, in his logical works, and his remarkably comprehensive and sophisticated conception became the nucleus of an intellectual program which took first place in the aspirations of Western man. Mortimer Adler complains of the unrealistic aspects of this ideal which made it largely unattainable, and vitiated or hampered the ongoing progress of the overall program, bringing it to its current confusion and breakdown.[52] His point is that certitude beyond doubt and beyond the possibility of revision, concerning necessary truths which are either self-evident principles or conclusions vigorously demonstrated therefrom, is an ideal not realized in any recognized body of knowledge thus far achieved by men. The first kind of dialogue does deal with the prospects of scientific knowledge, but the exalted virtues of Platonic-Aristotelian *episteme* have been dropped, and a more empirical, tentative, and reformable ideal has taken its place. Unanimity is still a goal, and the dialogue which strives toward it retains purely intellectual ambitions, the resolution, as complete and illuminating as possible, of an objective question to which all other factors are essentially irrelevant.

Not all knowledge enjoys a general perspicuity; in fact, the cognitive life of man assumes the perfection of scientific certitude only rarely, in the case of very few people, and within an extremely narrow scope. Most of what we claim to know is not totally immune to all doubt; it is revisable, reformable on more than one score and from more than one direction, and consists of something other, and less secure and clear, than self-evident principles or vigorously demonstrated conclusions. Aristotle covered all this vast area of knowledge under the blanket designation of 'opinion,' but he failed to analyze thoroughly all of the factors not properly cognitive that have a bearing on the origin, interpretation, or subjective appropriation of such knowledge. Belief is one species of such non-didactic, or, better, undemonstrated and indemonstrable, knowledge, and this too may serve as a subject or object of dialogue. Belief has at its source, besides the experiences and evidences and complex maze of past cognitive essays and constructs, a free assent which is willingly made. This voluntarist aspect accounts in part for the highly personal character of belief-knowledge, not an antithesis but a simultaneity and convergence of the objective and the affective in which the decisive factor is the appeal to the reliability of a witness or of evidence that is undetermined, indirect, remote, incomplete, or any or all of these. One has a sense, a conviction, that it is good —in one sense or other—to hold this view, this opinion, this attitude, this access to reality. Because this kind of knowledge so intimately and so compellingly involves the commitment of oneself, free choice, it is a particularly elusive and opaque phenomenon. Yet belief, which I am calling one very common and familiar type of non-demonstrable knowledge, combines a degree of certitude with that inconclusiveness in the order of pure cognition which characterizes such knowledge. When belief is shared by a group and binds them together by reason of the values to which it relates the individuals, agreement engages the freedom of all and includes a personal commitment over and above the intellectual structuring of content.[53]

This brief excursion into some of the principal features of belief-knowledge comes to focus quickly on the intervention of the personal, affective element, a thrust which is individual and self-assertive. When the liberty of different individuals, holding fast to their separate and sometimes incompatible views, clashes, it is on matters organized and of interest on the basis of personal needs and desires, ideals and values. It is then the whole man who resists change and stands by the conviction; when the differences touch on questions of profound human concern, it creates a mounting social problem which may become a threat to peace and good order. It is morally impossible in such matters that controversy or violence or any kind of polemic restore or achieve unanimity; arbitration by disinterested parties may be feasible, but not always, so that disagreement, without prospect of resolution in virtue of a situation which is almost certainly to persist, must be accommodated. Disagreement should be tolerated not merely for the sake of peace, out of respect for conscience, or in admission of the imperfection and relativity which dog so much of what we profess to know and believe, but for the positive and indeed integral purpose of undertaking a dialogue in which understanding is something quite different from that envisaged in the first kind of dialogue. Dubarle uses the expression 'the confrontation of convictions' and states bluntly that men must, wisely but not in despair, postpone hope of achieving perfect unanimity under conditions presently prevailing. He is explicit on this point: 'Humanity on the whole already possesses sufficient insight . . . to build science and its immense modern monologue. But that does not prevent men's minds being divided in many kinds of ways.'[54] The domain of disagreement in this second, temporarily irreducible, fashion is one into which dialogue not only may but must be inserted, but in full realization of what is at stake and what may be expected. I am concerned, before proceeding, to make as clear as can be the point that we are here in an area in which incontrovertible evidence is not attainable; processes of analysis and interpretation are complicated by value-judgments and preferences, and freedom of choice is both possible and indicated. I might add, even at this point when it is dialogue in general and conviction in general that are under discussion, that most of practical life is included in this domain, as are those profound questions of human destiny and the commitment to value, or what Tillich calls matters of ultimate concern.

The second type of dialogue brings spiritual convictions into mutual confrontation and therefore the freedom, the integral human personality, with which such convictions are bound up. Dubarle explains the difference between the two types of dialogue: '. . . while the regime of the first kind of dialogue is that of "reason-insight" tending towards unanimity, a regime of the second kind of dialogue is that of "reason-liberty." The latter of course does not refuse to see unanimity finally achieved between the partners, but it is nevertheless not anxious about this, puts up with the irreconcilable divergence of human standpoints and consequently aims only at a better regime for everyone's liberty.'[55] If this second form of dialogue involves irreconcilable spiritual convictions, what is to be gained from an attempt at dialogue, other than the potential healing of bitter personal feelings and the removal of certain misunderstandings? A first answer is that a moratorium is necessary after the conflict of highly cherished philosophies is first recognized, and during this period the best that can be reasonably hoped for is peaceful co-existence, an effective neutrality, and the effort to diminish the intensity of those passions which cloud judgment. Dubarle sets three chief kinds of objective for dialogue: (1) disposing of serious matters disputed on both sides to create conditions of more harmonious co-existence; (2) defining common interests sufficiently independent of differences of conviction to make joint action possible; and (3) developing such resources as the other may make available to one, as one's own conscience suggests. This last is the noblest purpose which dialogue can set, to open minds of those who are otherwise fixed in divergent convictions and who can profit by the insights and perspectives and even the options of their opposite numbers. To achieve this aim, all concerned must be prepared and disposed, and the terms of effective dialogue firmly grasped and respected. Going into dialogue is a grave responsibility, with so many and such formidable obstacles threatening success, and so many and such precious human values thrown into the balance.

On October 1, 1968, Cardinal König announced the issuance by the Secretariat for Non-Believers, in Rome, of a 'public document,' the stated purpose of which was to explain clearly the Church's understanding of dialogue. This clarification was meant to encourage dialogue between believers and unbelievers and to insure that it would be fruitful. The differences between dialogue and other types of contact are pointed out, and the conditions laid down that are essential for dialogue. Those responsible for this document (which had been referred to as 'the directory' during the months of its preparation) had been concerned particularly with distinguishing the apostolic dialogue of which the Pope had spoken in *Ecclesiam suam*, and the fraternal dialogue which the conciliar Fathers discussed in *Gaudium et spes*. All dialogue, however, in which Christians take part involves their witness to their faith and is related, even though its aim is not necessarily apostolic in the proper sense, to the Church's commission to preach the Gospel. Dialogue with unbelievers ought to deepen the Christian's understanding of what his own faith ought to mean to him as well as lead him to a fuller recognition of non-religious human values. Because the Secretariat document is addressed primarily to Christians, in the sense that it expresses an understanding arising from the doctrine and concern of faith, it makes liberal use of other official documents. An earnest effort has obviously been made to treat each issue in a manner readily intelligible and, it is hoped, acceptable. The document was publicized in the press and excerpts reprinted, with comments; but on the whole the fact of its issuance passed with a minimum of notice and a reaction which indicated that a considerable work of education and the formation of public opinion is in order. I shall paraphrase the document in its entirety, adding such observations as I think may clarify certain points or identify conditions to which these points are meant to be relevant.[56]

Introduction
Dialogue is identified as a phenomenon peculiar to the conditions of contemporary civilization and closely linked with mankind's increasing recognition of the dignity and value of the human person. Sociocultural life has advanced in recent times, despite certain world conditions which give rise to grave misigivings, and this progress has made it possible, for the first time in history, for people in a highly developed society, which at the same time is pluralist to an unprecedented degree, to seek dialogue as a higher and more promising form of mutual exchange. Because men are so intensely and continuously confronting each other, they are fully aware of the fact and the implications of this pluralism. It is an irreversible trend of modern life, a characteristic dimension in the social order men have made for themselves in the present age, but there is in this fact an enormous threat to peace and the common interest which transcends divisions and differences. Unless individuals and communities of different temperaments and cultures engage in dialogue, the posi-

tive values which only genuine pluralism can sustain are in danger of being undermined. This point is emphasized and confirmed by a quotation from *Ecclesiam suam*, which asserts that dialogue is demanded by 'the custom, which has now become widespread, of conceiving the relations between the sacred and the secular in terms of the transforming dynamism of modern society, in terms of the pluralism of its manifestations, likewise in terms of the maturity of man, be he religious or not, enabled through secular education to think, to speak, and to act through the dignity of dialogue.'[57] Dialogue rests on a mutual relationship between those involved, their recognition of each other's dignity and integrity as persons; this primary consideration is an appeal to humanist principles and not to religious doctrine which the unbeliever rejects. The challenge is thus put to him, and his is the burden of finding sufficient reason to ignore or reject this opening without himself exhibiting bad will or bad grace.

Brotherly love, inspired by the recognition of every man's vocation by God in Christ, affords the believer an additional and, as he judges things, a greater reason for affirming the individual's absolute dignity and value. The Incarnation and the economy of salvation willed by God make Christians more sensitive to the importance of humanizing the temporal order, or at least this should be the case. It pertains to the Church's mission to make a specific contribution to this end, as the Vatican Council recognizes in the Pastoral Constitution on the Church in the Modern World. The Christian's vocation is reaffirmed: to promote in every way possible this universal dialogue, with men of every class and every persuasion, as proof and expression of a brotherly love fully respectful of the requirements of a humanity come of age. By virtue of its very mission, as *Gaudium et spes* declares, to share with the entire world the radiant light of the Gospel message and to unify in one spirit all men of whatever nation, race, or culture, the Church must stand forth as a sign of that fraternal concern which makes possible and lends support to sincere dialogue. Besides dialogue, there are other ways in which men may encounter each other and from which dialogue should be carefully distinguished. The simplest and least exacting form of contact is a confrontation which has no further ambition or purpose than that of bringing opposite parties together, just to meet each other in an atmosphere of mutual respect, to get to know each other better, as human beings, perhaps in the process to remove obstacles to understanding. Thus defined, confrontation is the indispensable foundation of dialogue, but only the foundation, for dialogue entails on both sides a movement toward rapprochement and an interpenetration in depth which includes an ulterior purpose. Neither is dialogue reducible to the kind of discussion in which differing views are aired, perhaps for the information of a third party, but without directly challenging opposing views or responding to the objections these may raise. This sort of non-contact is better described as the coincidence of monologues rather than dialogue, with each party having its say while the other happens to be present. Since dialogue essentially involves a certain reciprocity, a give and take, there is parity between the participants; they are equal partners, and each makes the same sort of contribution as the other. In this respect the dialogue in the strict sense differs from the teaching situation, which is ordered intrinsically to the enriching of one of the parties, the pupil, by the other, the master. The two forms of encounter are not mutually exclusive in a total sense, so that elements of each may be intermingled in the other. In any case, dialogue can enrich the understanding and sensibility of the public so that, in relation to the latter, it can constitute a form of instruction. Dialogue is distinct from polemic and controversy since these are designed explicitly for the defense of one's own position and the refutation of another's, a confrontation of monologists. Lastly, although the participants in dialogue need not renounce the legitimate hope or desire that their opposite numbers may be persuaded by the reasonableness of their own position (and in this sense be 'converted,' if only partially), of its very nature dialogue is not ordered to this as an end in view. Thus it is foreign to proselytizing and, a fortiori, to covert or disguised efforts to win converts. Where basic human values and the rights of the person are in question, their defense may enter into the subject matter of dialogue, if only to allow it to proceed in good faith. That attitude of openness and willingness to understand, which is the prerequisite of every positive social relationship, constitutes the foundation of dialogue. This attitude, as Paul VI states, includes a willingness to be courteous, respectful, and kind and springs from a recognition and acceptance of the other for what he is. This last declaration entails a most serious and demanding responsibility toward the other, and those who make it ought to be held to it strictly and without evasion. That it expresses a readiness or willingness on the part of all churchmen, prelates, and theologians may be doubted without qualm.

The document turns, in the second part of the introduction, to the general renewal of the Church, one of whose aspects it declares is willingness to engage in dialogue. One may not unfairly infer that such willingness is weak or absent where and to the extent that the

Church, that is, the believer, is not renewed or earnestly seeking renewal. This inference is supported by the fact. Of prime importance in this renewal (which, if it is literally meaningful, implies its own need, i.e., a state which requires extensive reform, an implication to which ecclesiastical statements devote the least possible time and attention short of its outright—and self-contradictory—denial) is a more positive appreciation of human freedom. The Council's Declaration on Human Freedom (*Dignitatis humanae*) is quoted because it envisages, in effect, the indispensable condition for the practice of dialogue. Thus: '. . . truth is to be sought after in a manner proper to the dignity of the human person and his social nature. The inquiry is to be free, carried on with the aid of teaching and instruction, communication and dialogue. In the course of these, men explain to one another the truth they have discovered, or think they have discovered, in order to assist one another in the quest for truth. Moreover, as the truth is discovered, it is by a personal assent that men are to adhere to it.'[58] The Constitution on the Church in the Modern World declares: 'For our part, the desire for such dialogue, which can lead to truth through love alone, excludes no one, though an appropriate measure of prudence must undoubtedly be exercised.'[59] The Council was thinking in this passage of the real, and by no means purely imaginary, difficulty and danger of attempting to dialogue with Communists, anywhere, but especially in places where a Communist regime is in power or the Communist Party is a predominant political force.

The three concentric circles indicated in *Ecclesiam suam*, each one smaller than the former, describe the three groups of interlocutors: our non-Catholic brethren in the Christian faith, the members of non-Christian religions, and the rest of mankind which professes no religion at all. The obvious parallel is then drawn between these different groups and the three secretariats, for Christian Unity, for Non-Christian Religions, and for Non-Believers. (The document errs, incidentally, in ascribing the establishment of all three bodies to Pope Paul; Pope John authorized the first Secretariat.) The novelty of the problems attached to the essay at dialogue, especially with non-believers, is recognized, and it is allowed that Catholics properly anxious to remain faithful to the truth and to Christian values may meet with difficulties in some of the initiatives and experiments undertaken to bring about this dialogue. One wonders idly if it is here implied that the absence of these as yet unspecified difficulties would indicate the absence of the stipulated anxiety. At this point the introduction makes a very useful and important clarification, distinguishing two senses in which dialogue had been discussed in major Church documents. In his Encyclical, *Ecclesiam suam,* Pope Paul's lengthy disquisition is concerned chiefly with dialogue as part of the Church's apostolic effort, which fulfills the principal mission entrusted to it of proclaiming the Gospel to all men. The Pope uses the term dialogue there to signify the respect and love with which the Church approaches all men, in order to offer them the gift of grace and truth of which Christ constituted it the trustee. The Secretariat document makes no further comment or criticism, but it does seem to be a highly irregular, not to say misleading, extension of the concept of dialogue, since in its formally and properly apostolic role of dispenser of divine mysteries, the Church really does not engage in an activity of give and take, with parity between the parties involved. *Gaudium et spes*, on the other hand, treats primarily of an inter-exchange between Church and world that is dialogue in an undiminished and unequivocal sense, an encounter that does not aim, for the Church's part, directly at proclaiming the Gospel. This Constitution has in view a dialogue which Christians intend to institute with all men of whatever faith, either to join them in the quest for truth in various fields or to collaborate in finding solutions to the great problems facing mankind today. It is dialogue in this latter sense, between believers and unbelievers, to which the document as a whole refers.

1. *Nature and conditions of dialogue*
a. *Dialogue in general*

In a comprehensive sense dialogue covers every form of meeting and communication between individuals, groups, and communities to bring about a greater grasp of the truth and to achieve better human relations, in a spirit of sincerity, respect for persons, and mutual trust. The greater the differences between people, the more deeply opposed their respective positions, the more complex and difficult the dialogue, of course, but all the more imperative, too, if they want to overcome their mutual prejudices and broaden, as far as possible, their areas of mutual agreement. The impact of dialogue may be felt on the plane of simple human relation; that is to say, genuine dialogue may improve these, make them more tolerable and meaningful, without being subordinated to this effect as means to an end. The quest for truth is the proper and adequate concern of dialogue, but ends of a practical nature may also be envisaged. All of these effects or areas of effect are mentioned in the document, without limiting the intent of dialogue to any one or to one more than other. In each of the different forms of dialogue all of these dimensions—human relations, quest for truth, practical cooperation—may be found co-existing. As one or the other plays a central role, three fundamental types of dialogue may be distinguished, as follows: (1) encounter on the plane of simple human relations, with a view to drawing people out of an isolation which has bred ignorance and suspicion, even contempt and hostility, and to creating an atmosphere in which esteem and respect based on mutual understanding can grow; (2) encounter on the plane of the search for truth, regarding questions of the greatest importance to the persons involved, by a common striving to attain a deeper grasp of truth, a fuller knowledge of reality; and (3) encounter on the plane of action, which aims at establishing the conditions for collaboration toward fixed practical objectives, despite the persistence of doctrinal differences.

The simultaneous achievement of dialogue on all three of these levels is desirable; each, insofar as it is an interpersonal encounter, has its own peculiar value. This brief section on dialogue in general concludes with a comparison of dialogues and the other forms of encounter.

b. *Doctrinal dialogue*
1) *Possibility and legitimacy of this type of dialogue*

The most formidable question facing those seeking dialogue with unbelievers at the level of a search for truth is its very possibility, which has been brought into serious doubt. On one side is an insistence that, once the resolution has been made to embark upon dialogue, everything that is to be the subject matter of dialogue must be put in question. But this poses a major difficulty for a Catholic who is rightly unwilling to discard his faith or to entertain a real and not merely methodological doubt about matters in which, in fact, he has no solid reason to cease to believe. Can a proposed dialogue be sincere and meaningful unless the Catholic party be as prepared to set aside all claim to absolute, i.e., completely final, certain, and irreformable truth, as the unbeliever? If dialogue is to be genuinely open, must it not be completely so, with the participants remaining in an unbroken attitude of indefinite inquiry? These questions imply that as long as the concept of absolute truth, in the sense defined, is retained, and its possession already asserted, the very possibility of dialogue is rejected beforehand. In other words, real dialogue is precluded by the conviction that one is already privy to a truth that is absolutely certain and irrefutable. The logic of this argument is impeccable, but one may challenge both the definition of 'absolute truth' and the accuracy of imputing its claim to Catholics. No truth is intrinsically beyond discussion, nor is anyone constrained to hold to any doctrine of faith without admitting that it may pose quite thorny problems and demand re-examination and critical analysis from various angles, that legitimate objections must be answered and a task of reconceptualization and reformulation undertaken. What is needed, and I speak only as a Catholic and to Catholics for the moment, is a fresh look at the truth-value of faith-statements, which means the construction, as a vehicle for this reappraisal, of a more adequate and apposite theological critique or epistemology. In my judgment such a theological revaluation will enable the believer to meet the charge that he is indisposed to dialogue, without sacrificing the assent or commitment of faith.[60]

Catholic thought has been highly systematized, not once or in a single mold but several times and under the influence of different types of theologians, from St. Augustine to St. Thomas Aquinas, to Newman, to Karl Rahner in our day. This poses another problem which demands attention before the possibility of dialogue is definitively assured, or rather two connected problems are presented. As to the first, I can only identify it and indicate the direction in which resolution might be sought: the question is whether each affirmation dictated by our faith acquires its precise meaning and import only within the framework of a coherent system, so that, if it does, it can be explicated and validated only in terms of the system? This is far too complex and intricate a question to attempt to tackle here. Its relevance to the possibility of dialogue constitutes the other problem, which may be stated by asking whether there is place for genuine dialogue when the point of departure for one or both of the participants is a system, the integrity of which as such is as vitally important as the validity of any of its parts? Just by raising this question the document at hand indicates the urgency and legitimacy of the question and suggests the principle on which a solution might be worked out. Catholic faith (I do not mean to speak exclusively, but I would prefer not to speak of or for the faith of other Christians) does lend itself to theological systematization but is never perfectly identical with or reducible to the latter, and this independence is of utmost significance in weighing the prospects of dialogue. I do not wish to be misinterpreted; the language of the document, while jejune, is accurate on this point: the doctrine of faith does have its own internal unity, which is never simply that of any theological system as distinct or differing from all other such systems, and this coherence may not be ignored or violated for any purpose. It is not at all clear, nonetheless, that our faith is an exception to the established canon that every thought-system contains certain truths and values which do not necessarily derive all their sense and relevance from a single system. These non-systematic truths can be detached from the corpus which in fact embraces them, and placed in their proper light they can command agreement sufficient to initiate fruitful discussion, that minimal degree of agreement which is requisite for genuine disagreement.

The notion of truth as immanent in man himself, which has gained impressive adherence in our time as one of the doleful legacies of idealism, so subjects the determination of truth to man's free personal decision that it cuts off effectively the objective sources of human knowledge. Since every man is the original and sufficient source of what is truth for him, dialogue is rendered impossible. Christians, who reject this principle of immanence, have a completely different notion of truth, yet even among men separated by radical differences of opinion, some points on which agreement, and therefore communication, are possible can always be found. Recalling the internal unity of systems which may confront each other in discussion, one may distinguish in a given case the different levels on which discussion can take place, for dialogue may be feasible at one level and not at another. The immanence theory of truth must be evaluated on its own terms, not by theological apologists but by those philosophically competent, and the autonomy of the secular sphere must be respected here, too.[61] Dialogue will be more difficult, it should be admitted, if the participants hold irreconcilable notions of what constitutes the truth. Without some consensus on the very principles and norms of pursuing the truth, dialogue cannot move forward; the dialogants can then concentrate on this very problem, to try to come to a notion of the truth and of reasoning on which some agreement can be found. If this proves impossible, dialogue, that is, the attempt at it, has not necessarily been entirely unprofitable; for it is no small matter to have found the limits beyond which the dialogue cannot proceed. It drives home the sound principle that dialogue is not to be pursued at all costs or with an enthusiasm that is blind and unrealistic.

It may still be doubted that the Catholic community or any sizable, part of it, is prepared for dialogue, and not only because of the inadequacy of its grasp of the apologetic defense of faith. Each partner should have the capacity, as well as the will and the freedom, for dialogue, a knowledge of the issues chiefly at stake, and the

H

ability to think logically and express oneself clearly. The willingness to make an earnest and continuing mental effort, prompted by a love for truth and the courage to make a personal engagement with others, is also essential.

Doctrinal dialogue, as the Secretariat's document calls it, is a form of encounter requiring forthright sincerity in an atmosphere of complete freedom and respect on doctrinal matters in which the participants are in some way personally involved. It may come about that the parties can mutually enrich each other, not by being won over to each other's position but by deepening mutual understanding and discovering and, so far as may be, enlarging specific points of agreement. The participants can enrich one another spiritually by paying tribute, in practice, to the personal character of the acquisition of truth. It will be perhaps untraditional, even revolutionary, but nonetheless gratifying for people who take incompatible views on issues of tremendous import to respect the uniqueness of each individual in his particular situation, along with the limitations under which every man labors in his search for truth. Without this awareness of the limitations of individuals and of historical communities, there can be no readiness to consider fairly and sufficiently the opinions and efforts of others and to embrace the elements of truth contained in both positions. There is a further imperative in connection with the conditions of dialogue, or rather the very nature of doctrinal dialogue, and that is that, as a quest for truth, dialogue is pointless and senseless unless one is persuaded that objective, intersubjective truth is in principle and in fact attainable, at least to some extent, gradually, by the combined effort of many minds. Truth, when grasped, is what it is, even if the person who has appropriated it is also, in other respects, in error; so that the other may well have a contribution to make, even for those who are convinced that, in some respect, he is in error. He should be taken into account not in spite of but because of the very fact that he attains a view of reality which is different from one's own.

In this concept of truth the affirmation that its attainment is a real possibility is not only compatible with dialogue, it enters into the inner rationale of dialogue. Dialogue is not an interplay of vague hypotheses, of positions assumed without conviction or commitment, because one is ultimately skeptical about all positions. The demands of truth may and need never be subordinated to those of dialogue, as a certain confused and unsound irenicism seems to allow; for their demands are intimately related and essentially identical. Dialogue must be built on the acknowledgment of the moral obligation to seek truth in all matters, above all those which touch on man's reason for being, destiny, and ultimate concern. Since the risk involved in a prevailing diversity of views is inseparable from full participation in today's pluralistic society, Catholics ought to be prepared to face this risk. Public dialogue, in particular, can be the stimulus to a notable maturation in the Catholic people's understanding of their faith. It may also afford both sides the opportunity to present their positions to an audience they would not otherwise be able to reach. Dialogue is not only desirable, it is possible; the risks involved are not such that precaution may not be taken and the truth safeguarded. All the areas of concern to man, all subjects accessible to human reason can be brought into dialogue; believers and unbelievers may discuss not only religious matters but questions of politics and ethics, psychology and metaphysics, sociology, economics, the arts, and culture in general. His fidelity to all authentic spiritual and material values obliges the Christian to recognize these values wherever he finds them. There is no reason, finally, why unbelievers may not be invited to consider the alleged human and cultural benefits that can be derived from a life of faith in obedience to God in Christ.

2) *The conditions for doctrinal dialogue*
Truth and freedom are the norms guiding man's encounter with his fellows in dialogue and the values which dialogue must never slight or offend. Because it must seek the greater, the larger truth with single-mindedness, doctrinal dialogue may never be manipulated, openly or covertly, for the promotion of partisan political ends. This renders especially problematic an honest essay at dialogue with those Marxists who will not set aside such political aims because of their peculiar conception of the inseparability of theory and practice. The least objection to this attitude is that it makes extremely difficult the proper distinction of different levels of dialogue and the diverting of doctrinal dialogue to alternative purposes, which are foreign to it and destructive of its realization. Fidelity to the truth, again the condition of doctrinal dialogue emphatically reiterated in the Secretariat's document, demands an effort to present clearly and compare impartially the respective positions. This may discover that the same terms have different meanings for the participants, concealing divergences rather than reconciling them. Concern for the precise sense in which words are used will enable both parties to proceed properly with discussion and avoid ambiguity. Doctrinal dialogue demands the courage not only to expound one's own posi-

tion with complete sincerity but to recognize the truth wherever it is found, even should this oblige one to revise his doctrinal and practical standpoints. Good will is not enough; dialogue will really be profitable only if those who prepare it and those who engage in it are truly competent. Otherwise the benefits obtainable would not sufficiently outweigh the dangers involved. Truth must be allowed to prevail by its own innate force, which entails the clearest juridical recognition and effective safeguarding of the freedom of the interlocutors. That this freedom has always been respected in the past by churchmen in authority, no one would care to affirm; it remains still to be seen whether they have yet come to understand the intrinsic value and pragmatic necessity of a greatly expanded measure of freedom for the believer in a world come of age. I shall return to these considerations in my brief survey of the world reaction to the document.

3) *Dialogue on the plane of action*
Dialogue can also be initiated with a view to establishing collaboration between individuals or between groups or communities with different or even opposed doctrinal positions. This seeking of ways and means of practical cooperation is dialogue only in an improper and derived sense; its primary thrust is toward action, which presupposes or effects nothing in the way of the ample airing of doctrinal differences and for which all that is required is the common recognition of outstanding human needs, physical, cultural, and spiritual, and the will to attack these needs in concert with those who do not cease to disagree with oneself on matters of utmost importance. In this short section concerned with collaboration, the document exhibits what has always been a special preoccupation of European Catholics interested in the overall problem of unbelief, namely, the presence of Communism as both an ideology with considerable popular appeal and a political power with which the rest of the world must reckon. Thus the text has in mind Communist regimes and the Marxism by which they claim to be guided, without explicitly mentioning either by name, but almost as though they were the chief, if not the only, concern in this consideration of dialogue. An impressively conciliatory point is made in the allowance that 'movements which have their origin in doctrines which a Christian may not accept are sometimes capable of evolving toward positions which are no longer essentially those from which they were derived.'[62] Thus cooperation with members of these movements need not involve the risk of compromising principles or promoting the doctrinal positions

diametrically opposed to one's own. A second, connected point is that divergences which render systems, taken in their totality, mutually incompatible do not prevent these same systems from agreeing with one another on certain points. The autonomy of the secular sphere here serves to permit a convergence between those who find themselves in profound disagreement on the plane of religious thinking.

The possibility of reaching mutual agreement concerning specific practical objectives is not ruled out by a failure of doctrinal agreement, but certain conditions must be fulfilled, to insure the legitimacy of collaboration. These are defined as follows: the objective sought must be good in itself or reducible to good (a distinction not clear to me), and what the parties to the dialogue agree upon must not compromise values which are more fundamental than the benefits hoped for, and mentioned as examples are doctrinal integrity and the rights of the human person, such as civil, cultural, and religious liberty. The norms suggested for ascertaining whether, when a particular dialogue is contemplated, these conditions obtain, include an assessment of the program proposed by the participants and a recalling of past experience. Varying circumstances, of time, place, persons engaged, will determine the opportuneness of such co-operation. One may not like the constant intrusion of cautionary reserve, but the note on which this first major part of the document concludes is not unintelligible: although it is primarily the prerogative of laymen to evaluate these circumstances, it is the duty of the hierarchy to be watchful and to intervene when religious and moral values 'need to be safeguarded,' as the text has it, in an unfortunate choice of language. It is curious, as I see it, that the hierarchy should be thought more concerned about the integrity of these values than laymen; the curiosity is diminished, but not the offense, if one infers that the preservation of systematic orthodoxy or the protection of ecclesiastical interests are implicitly equated with safeguarding religious and moral values. Even in so progressive and liberal a statement as this document, the old clericalist mistrust of the competence, maturity, and integrity of lay people, acting on their own, breaks through the explicit admission of the right and the appropriateness of lay action. The latter is appended as one of those familiar qualifiers by which ecclesiastics love to appear to take back in a second breath what they have conceded in the first, without really retracting anything at all.

2. *Practical directives*

The directives included are intended to corroborate the foregoing considerations on the nature and conditions of dialogue. They are necessarily very general in character, allowing for variations in the situation prevailing from country to country and for the prudence of pastors and faithful in applying particular directives to different concrete local conditions. Different norms will be called for in countries which have traditionally had a Christian presence, from those appropriate to countries in which the Gospel has not yet been preached, and again, from those in which atheistic regimes govern populations composed to a considerable extent of people who are or once were Christians. The Secretariat has no wish to anticipate or place restrictions upon what experience can teach about revising or amplifying these directives in the future.

a. *Directives to promote dialogue*

The first observation, preceding an enumeration of general guidelines, is on the desirability of awakening in the Church a public awareness of the urgent need for dialogue. We may have entered the age of dialogue, in the wake of Vatican II, but not all have caught up, nor has dialogue been transposed from the realm of approbation in principle to that of vigorous exercise, both within the Church and in its external relations. There is a far greater expression of views, more articulate dissent, and a clamorous insistence on the right of free speech, but all of this does not add up to dialogue, as long as it takes shape largely as a succession of conflicting voices outspoken in monologue. It is obviously awkward to get dialogue started in an institution where, for centuries, one group has constituted an overwhelmingly privileged party and claimed divine sanction for the attitude it assumed of the active minority over against the passive majority.

1) In the education and formation of the clergy, philosophical and theological instruction should aim at equipping seminarians with a correct understanding of the mentality of their age, so that they might be properly prepared for dialogue with their contemporaries, including the non-believers. There is about this injunction a faint mustiness, a remoteness that suggests it comes as a warm-hearted and benevolent gesture from a serenely detached dweller on another planet. Discounting this irritant, which may be only a personal reaction on my part, one is still gratified by the recommendation that future priests should be led to a profound knowledge of the principal forms of unbelief, especially those prevalent in

their own countries. Also included as desirable is a knowledge of the philosophical and theological foundations of dialogue, pursued in ecclesiastical universities and faculties on a suitably serious academic level.

2) The problems of dialogue with non-believers should be given special attention through courses, seminars, conferences, and more formal congresses of interested parties, as part of the promotion of the pastoral renewal of the clergy. The preceding provision lays appropriate stress on study and research, while here the emphasis is on orientation to the concrete situations in which the clergy exercise their apostolate.

3) The laity need massive and continuing education to the needs and opportunities in this area, but this does not mean a paternalist supervision or tutelage by clerics. The document looks to intensive courses on dialogue with non-believers at the level of higher religious education, and there is mention of specialized studies, workshops, and congresses. The organization of these study and research facilities will require funds and personnel and obviously a greater concern and estimate of its value and necessity than have heretofore been in evidence. Young people are particularly included in the scope of these considerations, with a view to opening new and important vistas of the apostolate.

4) The Church is open to this new dimension and ready for it in a special way, so that preaching and catechetical instruction must also take it into account.

5) Diocesan and national organizations, attached in some way to the Roman Secretariat for Non-Believers and established under the authority of the local hierarchy, will seek ways of carrying out dialogue and the study of atheism. These commissions will seek the collaboration of ecclesiastical and lay experts, men and women, to promote research, studies, courses, and meetings. It may be hoped that eventually bishops will take this work seriously enough to lead in the establishment and support of this kind of organization.

6) Ecumenical collaboration is desirable between Catholics and other Christians, and this on an international, national, and local level. Much could be accomplished through this inter-Christian cooperation, not only in furthering contact with unbelievers but also in deepening and refining the understanding of what Christian faith means.

7) The last of these general directives makes the same point about collaboration in establishing dialogue with non-believers being extended to those who belong to non-Christian religions, especially

Jews and Moslems. This, like several other of these provisions, is a long way from concrete realization on anything like an extensive scale.

b. *Particular directives*

The thoroughly ecclesiastical character of the document is indicated in many places, not least in the strong distinction made between public and private dialogue.

1) *Private* dialogue is defined as spontaneous discussion or organized meetings open exclusively to certain individuals or restricted groups. For such confrontation, particular directives cannot be given, beyond urging the exercise of prudence and understanding, virtues which must regulate all responsibile human and Christian activity. Four very broad points are made, not by way of specific instructions on the conduct of dialogue but in order to encourage a proper spirit in the Catholic participants.

a. Dialogue will be fruitful only if those taking part in it have a sufficient knowledge about the subject under discussion, not only a familiarity with the viewpoint of the unbeliever but, equally, with what is sound Christian teaching on the subject.

b. Whenever a potential Christian participant realizes that his preparation for dialogue has been inadequate, he ought to have recourse to the advice of a competent person or direct prospective dialogants to such a person.

c. The important moral responsibility must be taken into account of not betraying the authentic content of one's faith by surrendering to a false irenicism or a seductively agreeable syncretism and of not imprudently endangering one's personal adherence to the faith. I am afraid I cannot readily understand the reference to loss of faith made in this statement.

d. One should never underestimate the extent to which the witness of an upright life, led in conformity with one's faith, can contribute to the efficacy of human encounter.

2) *Public* dialogue is dialogue between men who are qualified representatives of their communities, even if they do not participate in their official capacity. The first and only general observation made in the document is that greater prudence is required, in view of the repercussions on public opinion of planning such encounters between believers and those who hold different doctrines and belong to movements which differ from and may even be opposed to Christianity. A half-dozen general recommendations are included:

a. Christians, whether priests or laymen, who take an active part in public dialogue, besides the moral qualities enumerated above for private dialogue, must excel both in doctrinal preparation, in which their qualification must be assured, and in the other qualities which public dialogue calls for, such as moral authority, skill in presentation and exchange.

b. When it is a question of public dialogue at an unofficial level, i.e., without the formal authorization of respective representatives, in order to guarantee the freedom necessary for true dialogue, it seems opportune that persons who occupy positions of such importance that they might compromise public authorities, their own office, or the institution which they represent should not take part in the dialogue. This is prompted, obviously, by a desire to avoid confrontations with Marxists in which Communist political interests might receive support through exploitation of the meeting of Marxists and Catholics. On the other hand, one can only agree with the added remark to the effect that participants must remain faithful to the general standpoint of the community in whose name they are speaking.

c. This paragraph, on official dialogue 'formally authorized,' continues in the same vein of caution and fear and does little to encourage bishops or their 'official' delegates to seek out and take part in dialogue. A negative and reluctant note is sounded in the statement that dialogue at this level cannot be excluded a priori but that the conditions favoring such dialogue between Christians and non-believers are found only rarely, either because most non-believers represent only their individual positions and not that of some community or group, or because of the great differences that obtain between the Church or religious community on the one hand, and a political party or cultural organization on the other. The text here refers implicitly to humanists and Marxists and may be interpreted more benignly not as discouraging a search for dialogue with these organized bodies as such but as simply stating that such dialogue is more likely to be conducted privately or in an unofficial capacity, for the reasons advanced. In such cases, it is asserted, it is important to avoid all ambiguity regarding the meaning of dialogue itself, the objectives to be obtained, and the willingness of all parties to work together. Again, the text has in mind possible undesirable consequences of an encounter in which Communists make partisan propaganda out of the positive gestures of Catholics in their direction.

d. There are circumstances of time and place which must be duly observed with a view to guaranteeing the authenticity of dialogue. By way of illustration, it is wise to avoid excessive publicity and the presence of an audience not sufficiently well-informed, for this could disturb the serenity of the debate and cause it to degenerate into an unseemly argument. My reaction to this example includes the realization that Roman churchmen almost always prefer secrecy and shun open, public discussion of important issues, leaving public demonstrations to the area of mass devotional services in which the populace are allowed prayer and song but no other voice. Decisions and conclusions arrived at through such discussion as may take place are then announced as faits accomplis, for the submission of those who had no say whatever in their shaping. As for unseemly argument, this will have quite a different meaning in Latin countries, with a history of political upheaval and radical disorder alternating with iron dictatorship, and in English-language countries, in which the opposition is loyal and debate can be extremely vigorous without endangering peace or good order. Within the Church itself there has been a long tradition, quite without evangelical sanction, of suppressing free and open debate of the kind which emerged at and after Vatican II. This arbitrary exercise of force and power, masquerading under the guise of legitimate authority, still restricts some debate. The text claims that, as a rule, discussions among a few experts on both sides will prove more profitable, on the assumption, I take it, that they will adhere more readily to the canons of prudence and relevance. At times the rules for the conduct of the debate will have to be established beforehand. Finally, when it becomes evident that public dialogue is being manipulated purely as an instrument in the hands of one of the parties, it should be declined.

e. At times, to avoid misunderstanding or scandal, it will be necessary to make a declaration beforehand, clearly stating the meaning, aim, and content of a proposed dialogue.

f. Priests should obtain the consent of their own ordinary and that of the ordinary of the place in which the dialogue is to be held. The directives of ecclesiastical authorities are to be respected by all Catholics, and these authorities, for their part, are to respect carefully the legitimate freedom of the laity in temporal matters, as well as the general conditions in which they live their daily lives.

The document concludes by noting that dialogue of a sort can be pursued through collaboration of believers and non-believers in editing and publishing periodicals, magazines, journals, etc. This form of public dialogue is more exacting because of the greater repercussions and wider diffusion of the written word. It is more demanding, also, because it places greater responsibility and obligation in conscience on the believers who participate in it. The advantage to dialogue through published exchanges is the greater guarantee it offers in the opportunity to avoid awkward improvisation and superficiality. There is, unfortunately, the added 'advice' that, for dialogue of this nature, believers submit their writings before publication to the judgment of competent persons. The last statement in the document urges all the faithful to observe the canonical norms already in force and any new ones that may be passed in this connection. The signatures of Cardinal König and Don Vincenzo Miano are affixed and the date of August 28, 1968, although the document was not publicly presented until October 1, at a press conference held by König in Rome. The document and some of the statements made at the press conference immediately aroused a violent polemic in the Italian press.[63] During the month of October alone, more than fifty articles referring to the document appeared in the Italian press. In no other country did the issuing of the document lead to such violent and persistent polemics, although its appearance was widely, if somewhat routinely, reported by all the principal news services and picked up by most of the important papers throughout the world. The extensive and, at times, heated Italian reaction revealed the general concern among Catholics with the Communist presence and the hysterical fear of right-wing Catholics of the prospect of dialogue with Marxists. The reactionary press attacked König and Miano, denounced the Secretariat, and warned against the dire consequences of the *aperto a sinistro*, in terms of which it interpreted the document. The French press generally approved the document and evinced a remarkable appreciation of the nuances and difficulties of attempting dialogue with various kinds of unbelievers. The point was made that the optimism and open attitude towards secular values and institutions may not represent the mentality actually predominant in Vatican circles. Spanish reaction, likewise, was favorable on the whole, although some politically minded commentators expressed the opinion that the Communists would derive considerable benefit by skilled and unscrupulous use of the Church's statement.

A Dutch newspaper made the observation that, however important the dialogue with non-believers, dialogue within the Church is of even greater and more immediate urgency. Switzerland produced a surprisingly negative reaction, inspired largely by conservative Protestant sentiment unsympathetic to the spirit of the document. One publication simply dismissed it as far from revolutionary, a harmless and uninteresting statement, while another review quotes a Protestant spokesman who found the text lacking in a reverence for Scripture and in spontaneity. It was, he said, too moralistic and routine, oblivious of the dynamism of the Gospel. Not one paper in East Germany printed a single word on the document, and the justification alleged for this silence was that the already existing close, practical collaboration made dialogue superfluous. In Poland the so-called 'Catholic Left' greeted the document as a recognition from Rome of a policy which the Polish episcopate had consistently refused. A Marxist journalist approved of practical collaboration in political and social matters but rejected outright doctrinal dialogue, ironically, for reasons quite similar to those advanced by conservative Catholics opposed to dialogue with Marxists. *Pax* Catholics admitted that, in a socialist country, dialogue should be concerned primarily with social questions, but this should not completely exclude philosophical dialogue. The *Pax* weekly hailed the document as a vindication of the position of the Catholic Left. Czech Marxists favored the proposal of dialogue with Christians, citing the promise of 'open Communism' to collaborate in good faith. In the Americas, North and South, comments were appreciative, with few exceptions, and largely uninteresting.

The Experience of Dialogue

Catholics and non-believers have met for the purposes of dialogue since 1964, or before the Second Vatican Council was concluded, but the experience is still novel and has not yet been extensive or a matter to be taken for granted. The document on dialogue looks very largely to formal conditions, not spelled out in detail and respecting local and varying needs and modes of doing things but envisaging the more or less official commitment of Catholic churchmen to this undertaking. Some of the suggestions made in the Secretariat document have received serious attention, and some notable steps have been taken to implement in concrete fashion the Church's stated intention. Dialogue as defined by the experts presupposes certain conditions, so that not every confrontation of opposite parties deserves the name. Still, some experience has been had over a period of five years, and it is to be expected that out of this experience lessons may be drawn which may serve as guidelines for future efforts. I should like first to record two other events which, it may be hoped, signal well for the course of understanding of unbelief in the contemporary world. These are the founding of a journal devoted explicitly to providing a vehicle for the exchange of views and information by believers and unbelievers and the discussion of atheism at the first Synod of Bishops convened by the Pope at Rome in 1967.

The journal in question appeared first in January, 1968, under the title *Internationale Dialog Zeitschrift*, published at Freiburg im Breisgau under the joint editorship of Karl Rahner and Herbert Vorgrimler. A distinguished roster of collaborating editors from most of the European countries, the United States, and South America, both Christian and atheist, lends an international outlook to the contributions. Each number offers more than a dozen articles on a wide range of subjects, touching on aspects of such problems as faith and unbelief, hope, dialogue, Marxism, values, and humanism. A catalogue of current publications in the field is included in each number, an extremely useful service one would like to see duplicated in other countries. The contributors thus far have been outstanding scholars, keeping the level of discourse far above that of common journalism and worthy of the urgency and exigency of their subject matter. The publisher has issued an English-language version of the *Zeitschrift*, which it calls *Concurrence* and subtitles 'A Review for the Encounter of Commitments.' The review is described as the organic outgrowth of scores of conversations between believers and non-believers, over the past decade. The editors state their intention to suggest the common humanistic heritage that binds together all men of good will, no matter what their political, social, philosophical, or theological convictions. The encounter of commitments is an excellent way to characterize a candid and forthright exchange from across the ideological spectrum in a pluralist world.

At the Roman Synod of bishops from around the world, the theme first proposed to the assembled Fathers centered on 'dangerous current opinions and atheism,' and attention was directed to the dangers to faith from the diffusion of these forces.[64] Much was made of the 'problem' of overevaluating man and the world, an 'excessive humanism and worldliness,' surely not a promising approach to the positive understanding of unbelief. The attitude was pastoral, but preoccupied almost exclusively with remedies for what is regarded entirely as a grave moral and spiritual evil. This attitude was aroused and made almost inevitable by the initial document, a presentation replete with references to threats, dangers, errors, immorality, the pretensions of scientific rationalism and the loss of a sense of absolute truth and ontological reality. Relativist historicism is scored for its rejection of absolute truth, with dire results in the sphere of religious belief. The contemporary image of man, according to this position, is vitiated by a materialistic determinism and a contrary idealist spiritualism which the curial paper links with present-day atheism. Further discussion identified varieties of unbelief and their proximate and remote causes, among which humanisn and naturalism are named and described as 'an exaggerated affirmation of man and of nature,' and, in the past, Kantian subjectivism and its allied rationalist and idealist positions. The fact of religious alienation is noted with alarm and regret as well as the recent critique of religious language and the human meaningfulness of religion. The Synodal Fathers responded with surprising and, to me, disheartening lack of concern for the problem of atheism: of more than eighty interventions only twenty addressed this problem. One European bishop complained that the schema treated atheism in too schematic and simplistic a fashion, superficially and in too academic terms. Some of these interventions are well worth close study, particularly those which attempt to account for concrete conditions prevailing in different countries, to link atheism with socioeconomic factors and the ambience which supports a culture-atheism, which is even more prevalent than explicit and articulate unbelief. Bishops from every continent analyzed in depth the elements in life and thought which make atheism an attractive option. In sum, the Synod was made aware of some of the major dimensions of the fact of atheism, and the assembled bishops had the opportunity to discuss openly the situations prevailing in different parts of the world. The actual exchange of views revealed the need for sociological research as well as doctrinal studies and an understanding of the complexity of what is assuredly one of the foremost pastoral problems of the day. One note that I find glaringly absent in the interventions is a frank recognition of the aspects of Church life, discipline, and teaching which obscure the beauty and spiritual power of the Gospel message and thus contribute to the resistance of unbelief to the attractions of faith.

The experience of dialogue, other than the informed and unreported encounters of individuals on a purely private basis, has centered on two groups, the humanists and the Marxists. Europeans have far outdistanced American Catholics in their willingness to attempt the confrontation which, it is hoped, will make authentic dialogue possible. Voices have been raised in the Catholic camp, even in advance of any experience of dialogue, warning against alleged dangers and minimizing the benefits that might be expected. At a symposium in New York early in 1968, the conservative Catholic journalist Erick von Keuhnelt-Leddihn admitted that dialogue (he uses this term for what is obviously something quite different) might be useful in helping Christians to understand the mind of the non-theist but that, beyond this, there can be no common denominator between them.[65] Others taking part in this symposium disagreed sharply with this negative and pessimistic view, on the grounds that it is time that religious people disabused themselves of the notion that they have all the answers or that they have nothing to learn from others. The defenders of dialogue held their own and, I daresay, spoke for the majority of Catholics and others (there were Protestants and Jews taking part) who are aware of and concerned about the problem of unbelief and the unbeliever.

The prospects for dialogue with humanists seem to be bright, on the basis of the few encounters achieved in the past few years. Among humanists there was, for a very long time, a strong aversion toward everything religious, expressed in the preamble of a draft declaration of a 1952 congress of the International Humanist and Ethical Union: 'This congress is a response to the widespread demand for an alternative to the religions which claim to be based on revelation on the one hand and totalitarian system on the other. The alternative offered as a third way out of the present crisis of civilization is humanism, which is not a sect, but the outcome of a long tradition that has inspired many of the world's thinkers and creative artists, and given rise to science. Ethical humanism unites all those who cannot any longer believe the various creeds and are willing to base their convictions on respect for man as a spiritual and moral being.'[66] Two other congresses of humanists have since been held, the latest in 1966, and how far the group as a whole had moved from the strident anti-religious posture which had become identified with the movement may be inferred from the presence, at the 1966 meeting, of two invited observers from the Secretariat for Non-Believers. The Paris congress was preceded by a gathering, in April, of six humanists and six representatives from the Vatican Secretariat, at Amersfoort, Holland. At a still earlier and informal meeting in Utrecht, it was agreed that the parties would consider (1) the present position of the Catholic Church and of organized humanism; and (2) practical questions in the context of 'the open society.' That such a meeting took place at all is quite remarkable, given the obstacles on both sides, the persistent antagonism which kept them apart. The great fund of good will manifested in Rome during the Council made an impression which found an outlet in the statements of important humanists. Professor A. J. Ayer, of Oxford, as an example, wrote: 'The humanist movement is gradually changing its character. Until quite recently its energies were mainly absorbed in a kind of religious war against the churches. . . . There are various reasons why these aims no longer seem so important.'[67] The Amersfoort meeting brought together twelve spokesmen, six humanists and six Catholics, led respectively by Professor J. P. van Praag, president of the Dutch Humanist League, and Father Johannes Metz, professor of theology at Münster.

At Amersfoort, before the conference concluded, both sides agreed upon a preliminary report. They regarded the discussion as essentially a confrontation between Christians and humanists, concerned to work out sincerely the significance of agreement and differences. The background of the discussions was recognized as the profound transformation of the Church at the Second Vatican Council, implying a more definitely positive attitude toward secular values. This attitude opens up a new possibility of dialogue with humanists, for whom it constitutes a new starting-point for the re-evaluation of religion. Humanists and Christians found themselves in agreement on the possibility of encounter, at least in principle, not only on minor points but also on the general project of human development in the world. They recognize the possibility of giving a moral meaning to life based on an acknowledgment of the value of man as the agent and aim of history. The fulfillment of man can be realized only by and in a community. Love is the central moral imperative. All resources of science and technology must be devoted to human fulfillment. This realization demands a pluralist society, open to institutions common to men of different faiths and convictions, e.g., cultural programs, youth movements, welfare services. It must also assure the unimpeded fulfillment of persons and associations in their own character, but connected by dialogue and collaboration. Humanists and Christians find further agreement in realizing that this general project does not furnish a complete solution to the problems of men, for example, extreme situations such as suffering and death. At such times the humanist stands for a realistic attitude but has also the resources of human fellowship and solidarity and the will to alleviate and improve the human lot. The Christian, on the other hand, thinks that there are radically new perspectives open to human reflection and existence, and finds that the ultimate foundation of reality, the ultimate positive meaning of life and death, can be given only by discovering and experiencing a Love incarnated in Christ. He lives in a community of love that is the Church, which calls man to resurrection and to an eternal friendship. The Christian believes that this discovery profoundly transforms the meaning of existence on earth and, therefore, of humanism itself. Nevertheless he believes, with Vatican II, that the importance of earthly tasks is given new incentive rather than diminished by eschatological hope. Catholics and humanists are aware of deep divergences which divide them; in deep mutual respect, however, they think it possible to discover a vast area of common values, truths, and tasks, which open up perspectives of collaboration in research and in action.

The breakthrough at Amersfoort placed the relationship between the IHEU and the Church on a new footing. At the July, 1966, Congress of Humanists in Paris, the principal theme acknowledged several distinguishable strands in the humanist tradition and raised the question of how they might be indentified, what attributes they have in common, and how they differ from non-humanist ways of thinking and living. Dr. van Praag declared that humanists share many commitments with enlightened Christians, so that a humanist might be called a virtual Christian and a Christian a virtual humanist. But, van Praag added, this does not really make sense, for humanism is meaningful only in terms of man and presupposes that man is not just irreligious but a-religious and eschews the transcendent. Humanism is life-affirming and not merely god-rejecting, whereas Christians as such stand in opposition to the reality of this world. The concept and practice of world-renunciation, in its extreme form, appears to provide the only valid or operational basis on which to support this allegation of ethical humanism. There was no dialogue with believers in Paris, in spite of the presence, as observers, of two Catholics, but there was an explicit challenge by one side to the other. In pre-empting the humanist label, unbelief posed serious problems; no matter what its critics claim, religion cannot, in any absolute sense, transcend or dispose of humanism—it can augment, intensify, ennoble and enrich it, but it cannot abjure it and hope to survive. Its intrinsic atheism does not altogether preclude organized humanism from according validity and meaningfulness to transcendence, even if only in terms of personal aspiration. Some humanists have gone so far as to admit their own conceptual inadequacy with respect to this issue. Humanists and Catholics have only just begun to contemplate meeting with each other to discuss such issues, but the beginning has been promising.[68]

Where the humanists, as an organized body, form a very small group on a world scale, and are totally without significant political or socioeconomic power, the Marxists find support on an enormous scale from Communist regimes and from countless millions, in every part of the world, who subscribe to Marxism freely and with passionate conviction. What has transpired thus far in the Catholic-humanist encounters hardly claims the name of dialogue; there has been a very broad and largely uncontroversial statement of respective positions, emphasizing points of vague agreement and resting almost entirely at the level of superficial exposition. Humanists and Catholics have not really come to grips seriously with each other's viewpoint or with the fundamental differences between them; conversation has remained at a level where the most that can be expected, by way of direct and proportionate result, is a breaking down of old animosities and improvement of relations between the parties involved. The mutual antagonisms between Marxists and Christians are, to be sure, far more bitter and of a much longer standing; these reasons for enmity make imperative a sober estimate of the prospects of dialogue, so that the first consideration must be whether dialogue is possible and opportune. A measure of agreement must be reached on the aims and objectives which a Marxist-Christian encounter might reasonably strive for, the limitations and obstacles built into or likely to develop in the situation, or, rather, situations, for prevailing conditions vary considerably from one country to another. The prospect, such as it may be, of Christian-Marxist dialogue not only is vitally important in its own right but serves as a touchstone of the future of encounter of belief and unbelief. Actual efforts have already been made to bring representatives of both sides together, and this experience offers the best kind of evidence in answer to the question of whether such meetings are likely to be fruitful. There are those, both Christian and Marxist, who oppose all efforts in the direction of dialogue, public or private, and for reasons not altogether dissimilar.

It has been more than a conventional ideological contest; it has been a decades-long war of attrition on a global scale, a war that has touched the lives and fortunes of peoples in at least one-third of the world's nations. It took great courage and resoluteness for the Fathers at the Second Vatican Council to proclaim the Church's readiness and eagerness to engage in dialogue with the modern world. An argument is advanced that the minimum preconditions for possible dialogue between Christians and Marxists are: freedom of thought, recognition of an existing partnership, and the common goal of arriving at an agreement, even though ineradicable differences may remain. The following observations are put forward as ruling out the possibility of dialogue in states governed by Communist regimes.[69] Excluded a priori are official representatives of these regimes or of the Communist Parties. The latter are always servants of a system which, by its very nature, cannot recognize the Church as a partner in dialogue but, at best, tolerate it as a fellow traveller. The individual Communist remains a human being and may temporarily strip himself of his function in a purely private conversation but never when discussing doctrine with the Church's representatives. For the Communist, the topic of discussion is laid down in advance and must conform to official policy; equally predetermined in advance is the eventual result. Objective criticism is circumscribed, for it might acquire a 'political,' i.e., anti-state, character. Nothing can be published which is considered undesirable. Only 'kept' Christians can pretend to dialogue under Communist regimes, since all financial or administrative support comes from the state. It is contended that Christians are under a moral compulsion to keep furnishing proof of their political usefulness. Under this pressure it becomes necessary to employ an arbitrary selection of forcibly distorted Christian principles and fundamental Christian attitudes.

But what of Christians from outside totalitarian states? Have they not the mission to conduct the dialogue which, for the reasons alleged above, the people of Communist states cannot conduct themselves? The complaint is that such contributions from Christians are useless, since they cannot publish them freely in the Communist country. The ideologically dominated regime will simply exploit the participation of Christians as a weapon against the local 'reactionary' ecclesiastical authorities. Communists will point out triumphantly how a genuinely free dialogue can be conducted in their sphere of influence, and how wrong-headed, therefore, the uncooperative attitude of the local Christians and their bishops. To the Church, any atheist who wishes to engage in dialogue is a welcome partner, for it is the believer's task to understand the position of the other, to submit to questioning, and to reappraise positions previously held. To an ideologically oriented state, however, any discussion of even a remotely public nature is a means to a political end, often even for exerting pressure. This will surprise only those who are blind to the fact that, in a totalitarian state, this same perversion affects all spheres and realms of life, work, sports, literature, schools, family, etc. That a detached, academic and scientific study of atheism, by well-meaning philosophers and theologians, will reveal the actual principles by which an atheistically inspired state operates is an illusion and may be one of the main causes behind the sometimes

painfully naive dialogue-mindedness found among enthusiastic
Christians in Western countries.

These are hard thoughts, of a thoroughly practical nature,
based on an estimate of the motives and procedures adopted in
Communist states; they are usually overlooked or ignored by those
who call euphemistically for an end to the Christian-Communist
vendetta. I do not see any useful purpose to be served by pretending
that these political considerations are unimportant or irrelevant,
that Christians who have suffered Communist persecution have
nothing to offer in forming the mind of the Church on the question
of dialogue.[70] A realistic answer to the charges of these Christians
cannot leave out of the picture the possible abuses and resultant
harm that overtures by believers to Communists may unwittingly
promote. If this is the case, as I believe it to be, it is unaffected by
the plea to stop characterizing all Marxists as agents of Satan and
dragons of godlessness, to discard an emotionally supercharged
anti-Communism. It should be instructive to note that there is not a
chance of genuine dialogue between Christians and Marxists in the
Soviet Union, except at the level of individual and private initiative,
and this is true likewise, at one time or other, of several Iron Curtain
countries but not all. An exchange of sorts has taken place, off and
on, for over a decade in Poland, not always free of polemics or
ideological distortion.[71] A more telling objection, more insistent
because it prescinds from political complications, which may in
some instances be removed, is that neither Christian nor Communist
can hold firmly and unequivocally to his basic values and principles
and still expose them to the allowances and compromises which
serious dialogue would demand. A student of Soviet Marxism argues
that eventual cooperation and effective dialogue cannot be based
on what is common to both parties, to the neglect of what essentially
divides them from each other.[72] The question is whether, as long as
each side believes in its position as irreformable in those very respects
in which it is contradicted by the other side, a confrontation can
take place which involves a genuine common search for truth.
This question can be answered best by the actual attempt to engage
in such dialogue, to find, if possible, both parties, while remaining
faithful to their respective commitments, will remain open to the
possibility of change, revision, development, and therefore intellectual cooperation in the interest of truth. One may read the results
of some of the attempts at dialogue which have been made in recent
years in the light of these considerations.

In April and May an association of Catholic and Protestant

intellectuals, the Paulusgesellschaft, organized a conference of Christians and Marxists at Salzburg, on the theme 'Marxists and Christians Today.' The Paulusgesellschaft was founded in West Germany by Dr. Erich Kellner, a Catholic priest, to facilitate a dialogue with the ideological opponents of Christianity, particularly the Marxists. At Salzburg the participants included ten prominent Marxists from five countries (Italy, France, Yugoslavia, Belgium, and Austria) and a larger number of Christian theologians, philosophers, and churchmen from Germany, France, Italy, and Spain.[73] Discussions lasted three days and explored frankly and temperately the relations of Marxism and Christianity, with a freedom and tolerance on both sides that surprised some of those taking part. At Salzburg a new spirit emerged, but at the same time the direction in which the convergence of Church and Party could and must not be pursued was revealed. Two tendencies appeared, the first placing heavy emphasis on ideological differences and in terms of these rapprochement was impossible; the other emphasized participation in a common struggle for human betterment, and on this issue the two sides could draw together. Gustav Wetter, S.J., thought that dialogue had not taken place and could not, so long as it was a question of fundamental philosophical principles; whereas Professor Reding, who had been associated with the priest-workers, declared the desirability of Christians and Marxists cooperating toward the renovation of a corrupt social order. The distinguished French Communist Roger Garaudy asserted that it was Communism's destiny to accomplish in secular terms what Marx had called 'the human foundations of Christianity.' Geraudy acknowledged the transformation occurring within the Church, its recognition of the importance of man's earthly existence and the consequent possibility that religion might, instead of deadening secular sensibility, spur believers into action. Others, however, agreed that ideological co-existence was quite out of the question, whatever unanimity might be achieved in the sphere of practical collaboration. Out of Salzburg, Catholics became convinced of the future possibilities of continued discussion, while Marxists began to declare openly the folly of a monolithic anti-God campaign.

The written dialogue, of which there is mention in the last paragraph of the Secretariat document, is illustrated in an exchange that took place over an eighteen-month period, from March, 1966, to September, 1967, in the British journal, *Marxism Today*.[74] A dozen contributions were printed, nine by Christians and three by Marxists, and during this whole period, encounters were taking place in various forms on the British scene. The Marxist editors received requests for the organization of a spoken dialogue on a national level and, towards the end of 1966, found the International Committee of the British Council of Churches quite receptive to the proposal. A discussion meeting was held, on October 6 to 8, at the Royal Foundation of St. Katherine of Stepney, with fifteen Marxists and a larger number of Christians participating. The general theme was 'What Sort of Revolution?' and debates were conducted at a theoretical level on 'Man and His Place in Society' and more practically on 'Peace,' 'Poverty and Justice,' 'Change in British Society,' and 'The Future of Dialogue,' Those who took part expressed the importance of not cloaking or concealing deep differences, for this is what makes dialogue, rather than a ploy or a search for an impossible synthesis. Common ground in the vision of a world of brotherhood without barriers of class or race or nation leads to several questions, to which underlying philosophical principles are relevant. How does one achieve such a society or world? What is meant by revolution? Can love be combined with hatred? Is violence necessary for social change? Can men be truly human, with or without a belief in God?

Another meeting between Marxists and Christians, sponsored by the Paulusgesellschaft, was held in the Chiemsee, near Munich, in early May, 1966.[75] The subject of this conference, 'Christian Humanity and Marxist Humanism,' was an indication that hard-core dogmatists in both camps had lost ground, if only by the presence of over three hundred Christians and Communists, the great majority teachers in universities, technical institutes, and theological schools. The list of names was daunting; theologians constituted the largest single group, mainly Catholics, from Germany, Austria, Italy, France, Holland, Spain, and Britain. The Marxists came from France, Italy, Austria, Czechoslovakia, Hungary, Rumania, Bulgaria, Yugoslavia, and Spain-in-exile. Poland's party philosopher Adam Schaff, a bold pioneer of Christian-Marxist *détente*, was barred from attending. The East German academicians were the equally inevitable victims of the internal German ideological cold war, and there were no West German Communists, as the Party is outlawed in the Federal Republic. Extremely significant was the fact that both Communists and Christians began with confessions of shame and guilt, an amazing gesture: Communists stressed that they were ashamed of the past and present failures of Communism, where it holds power, to live up to its principles. Christians replied that, if anything, their failure to practice what they preach had been and still is even more blatant. Roger Garaudy, leading ideologist of the Central Committee of the French Communist Party, combined Gallic sharpness and warm humanity with remarkable open-mindedness. Present, too, was the veteran Czech Protestant pioneer of dialogue Prof. Josef Hromádka, author of *On the Threshold of Dialogue*, much maligned by Christians but come to witness the fruition of what he had worked for.

Upon reading the reports of speeches delivered, papers read, and discussions which took place at Chiemsee, one gets the impression that neither side was seeking to uncover in the other the embodiment of irredeemable evil, but rather to discover more of the other's understanding of the meaning and purpose of *man*. There were émigrés from Eastern Europe who were sufficiently bitter, or at any rate skeptical, to call the whole dialogue into question and who were listened to with respect, but it seemed that somehow their voices would be swallowed up. A certain tension arose, perhaps from the realization that those taking part were neither policy makers nor authoritative officials; but their influence, especially over the long run, was formidable. The questions raised were immensely important: What is man? What are his true needs? How can they be met? Karl Rahner stressed that Christians do not have a priori answers to the complex problems posed by the future of man in a rapidly changing world. He challenged the Marxists to make a similar admission, which they did, and then in their turn they challenged Christians to join them in the exciting venture of changing the world and not just analyzing it. All participants discarded cut-and-dried blueprints, fundamentalism, ivory tower speculation; hence dialogue could begin, or at least the major obstacles had been removed. Christians faced the real question of how to deal with those who are its declared enemies. The organizers of the conference were, in fact, probably too eager to prevent emotive political issues from clouding matters of principle. A young West German seminarian broke the politeness barrier by turning to a Czech Communist and challenging him to state whether he was prepared to fight for the release of those unjustly imprisoned in Czechoslovakia. The Chairman interrupted him and reminded him of the Communists and Christians imprisoned in Catholic Spain. The Czech Communist confided later, privately, that he admired the young man's indignation, that he was much more right in expressing that indignation than the glib theologian who had attempted to soft-soap Communists from a position of assumed neutrality. The one address given a mixed reception was that of the Lutheran, Helmut Thielicke, who skated over the issues and conducted a conversation with a wholly fictitious

Karl Marx. Wetter suggested that the most pressing immediate need
was mutual understanding, and to this end Garaudy proposed a
regular journal of Christian-Marxist dialogue.

Marxists are relatively few in number, and the general American
attitude toward Communism is still largely dictated by cold war
apprehensions and an aversion to ideological discussion. When the
Jesuit University of Santa Clara arranged a Christian-Marxist
symposium, in October, 1967, a storm of criticism blew up, from
alumni and others outraged at the very idea.[76] The dialogants at
Santa Clara discussed the topic, 'Could an open dialogue between
Christian and Marxist scholars illumine past obstacles and clear new
avenues toward a more humane society?' Professor Robert Cohen,
a physicist and Marxist at Boston University, asked both sides to
discard their standard rhetorical devices and try to avoid fostering
prejudice. Marxists, he said, should look for signs of a positive
Christian humanism, while Christians might ask themselves whether
Christ would indulge in vicious Red-baiting. Both shared a regard
for the ideals of brotherhood and an aversion to human exploitation.
In the past, inhumanities had been perpetrated by both parties, but
these should stimulate us today to be more open to the critical
exchanges by which such barbarities may be prevented. Louis Dupré,
of Georgetown University, examined the origins of Marx's opposition
to religion, urged practical co-existence and cooperation but found
the Marxist theory of action too narrow to encompass the religious
dimension of human experience. John Somerville, a Marxist philosopher at California Western University, reviewed the exploitative
economic system against which Marx and Engels raised protesting
voices. The Marxists present were not unwilling to criticize the
weaknesses of Communist systems, especially the failure to recognize
personal freedoms and rights. John Somerville commented: 'I
would say that at least half our grave problems, tensions, and fears
arise out of the fact that each side has a great many . . . misimpressions
about what the other side stands for. And out of this lack of understanding proliferate fears, anxieties and the spirit of having one's
finger always on the trigger. The assumption is always present that
the other party is not only a competitor but an enemy. He is not only
inconvenient, he's immoral. He is not only disagreeable, he's
criminal.' Father Eugene Bianchi, S.J., concluded that: 'On the level
of rethinking past ideas and of forming new attitudes, the dialogue
was generally successful. Some of the participants were so enthusiastic about the outcome of the meeting that they wanted to organize
a sequel in an Eastern university. Such an institution could place

special emphasis on the study and development of a great world tradition like the Christian heritage. But in doing this, it cannot be closed or defensive. A Christian university exists for the welfare of the *whole* community. It must, therefore, cultivate honest and critical confrontation with other traditions in its quest to deepen values and serve human development.'[77] At Santa Clara a step forward was taken in the initiation of an American Marxist-Christian dialogue; the actual results were modest, but a precedent was set and the possibility of further confrontation decisively established.

Some months earlier, in December, 1966, Prof. Roger Garaudy, director of the Center for Marxist Study and Research, visited the John LaFarge Institute in New York City.[78] His visit to this Jesuit center was scheduled as a first attempt at dialogue in that country, and from there he went on to other places, for similar purposes. Garaudy convinced those present that he had not come to propagandize or make converts but solely to open up in America the kind of serious and sincere dialogue which had been inaugurated in Europe. When two opposing camps simply condemn each other's doctrines, he said, dialogue is impossible, and purges and inquisitions will be in order. He felt that dialogue between Christians and Communists had become possible for the first time because of two significant historical developments. One was the Soviet condemnation of Stalinism, the other was the Second Vatican Council. He saw the purpose of dialogue not as proselytism but as finding areas of mutual understanding that might serve as common ground for cooperation toward human progress. In a closed session an attempt at dialogue was made in which Garaudy found himself greatly outnumbered by men such as John Courtney Murray, S.J., then director of the Institute, Avery Dulles, S.J., Robert Johann, S.J., Daniel Berrigan, S.J., and several others. The participants discussed frankly areas of disagreement, beginning with the questions of human freedom and man's ultimate destiny. The extent to which fundamental differences might render cooperation impossible, and the extent to which underlying principles in each other's system could be held responsible for 'historical aberration' were explored. Murray expressed a sense of need for a methodology that would permit all to deal with their own histories, without polemics.

In April, 1967, a third meeting, sponsored jointly by the Paulusgesellschaft and by the Czech Academy of Science, was convened at Marienbad, in Czechoslovakia, for the first time within the confines of a Communist state.[79] The theme of the conference was the building of peace, notwithstanding issues which divide; but there was no thought of vigorously excluding theoretical problems from discussion. The Marxists recognized that religion was not about to die a natural death and that it had a certain function in life. Christians were not blameless regarding past recognition of the freedom of others, nor were Communists. Dr. Kellner regretted that the Soviet Academy had not replied to the invitation, and that the Spanish government had not permitted certain Spanish Catholics to attend. Theologians dominated the Christian delegation. Johannes Metz showed that, in the Bible, salvation is neither private nor of the exclusively religious order, and that eschatological hope is a stimulant to historical commitment. As a thirst for justice and liberty for all, Christian charity can become a revolutionary force inspiring men to resist war, oppression, and exploitation. A theopolitical unity is impossible, nor does Christianity determine the social structure but, in a pluralist order, offers creative criticism. The precept of love of neighbor must be translated above all into the construction of a just social order. Religion, Metz insisted, is not a purely speculative personal anthropology, closed to social and historical dimensions. Père Congar pointed out that Christianity, founded and anchored on Christ, consists of Christians, living in history, and this means innovation, not identical repetition. For the Christian, facts are signs of an invisible reality, but ideals need historical structure, and there must be an interpretation of theory and practice. Professor Jürgen Moltmann, the eminent Protestant theologian of Tübingen, noted that the ideal of liberty is not yet fully realized and must be clarified and broken down: Christian liberty, freedom in the liberal sense, and freedom as emancipation. Professor Josef Hromádka of Prague pointed out differing Christian and Marxist views on the meaning of history. Because the community of faith transcends every social structure (state, race, people, social class, culture), it must avoid two dangers: that of the Church's becoming an ordinary social institution and that of entering into systematic opposition to secular society. The principal Christian theses may be reduced to the following:

(1) the human and social significance of salvation; (2) the transcendence of the Christian message over various social structures; (3) the historical dimension of Christianity and its dynamism; (4) neither a confessional state nor a state atheism; (5) the ideal of freedom progressively realized through dialogue; and (6) openness of the Christian to all of reality.

Garaudy recalled two concepts of liberty, the Graeco-Roman 'knowledge of necessity,' and the Judaeo-Christian, in which the concept of creation, absent from the first conception, is essential. According to the Biblical teaching, the radical transcendence of God over man is the basis of man's transcendence over nature. Creation is a gratuitous act which establishes a relationship of love and unity; hence the desacralization of nature and the de-fatalization of history. This doctrine, however, expressed in the language of Greek philosophy, which is foreign to it, gave rise to the platonism of the people, the emanationism of St. Thomas, and hence a conservatism and immobilism. The necessity of the advent of Socialism is internal and not external, according to which man is a being who does not realize himself without knowledge of his situation and efforts to transform the world. Freedom is impossible without this real transformation of the world or the abolition of private ownership of the means of production. In a bourgeois society only the form of liberty exists; only Socialism in our time can overcome economic and cultural barriers. The problem of freedom and of creation should be posed concretely and historically: only in a society in which freedom from need is realized will man's creative impulse thrive. Freedom and creation are identified by Christians and Marxists; the problem is to recognize more fully, and to provide a more efficacious method of dealing with, man's responsibility for history.

The Italian Marxist Dr. Gruppi said that the recent development of Catholic thought, from *Pacem in terris* to *Populorum progressio*, proves Palmiero Togliatti correct and limits Catholic collaboration to only one part of the worker movement. A Catholic minority dialogues with Communists in spite of diverse and irreconcilable concepts of the world. *Populorum progressio* accepts ideas on which Marxists have insisted for a century. Italian Marxists look forward to a society freed of class antagonisms, admitting different parties and democratic institutions, lay state, without privilege for any ideology, and the construction of a socialist state by democratic means. The Marxist theorist Professor Gardavský of Brno asked how collaboration could be possible between Christians and Marxists in a Socialist state, as long as Christians consider Communism as an evil. Communism is concerned with human interests as such, and this may form a common base with Christian universalism. But, as we read in *Populorum progressio*, a Christian cannot accept a system founded on an atheistic and materialistic philosophy. Gardavský posed several questions: Must atheism necessarily be man's downfall? What is the relationship between man's social nature and his mortality? Is the death of the person society's hope? Professor Milan Machovec saw theism and atheism as responses to the problem of the meaning of life. One should admit that religion has inspired reflection on this problem but has extended its answer to many other areas. For his part, the atheist is tempted to attach himself to a surrogate for transcendence, such as history, progress, society, the state, etc. Marxism ought, therefore, to reject the attractive ideas of progress and of a divinized collectivity. To search out the meaning of life, man must keep up a constant dialogue with other points of view; an authentic Marxist atheism should not become a dogmatism. For a Marxist humanist dialogue is not merely a tactic but an existential need, to discover his own deep convictions. Western Marxists insisted on: (1) the necessity of realizing freedom and creativity concretely; (2) history offers man the opportunity to exercise his own responsibility; (3) the necessity of proceeding to a wider collaboration with respect to democratic method.

The Marxists from Communist countries were concerned with theoretical positions: (1) What have Christianity and Marxism in common concerning revolt against oppression? (2) Is Christianity alone responsible for the struggle against religion? (3) Immanentist atheism is able to give a non-illusory significance to social progress. (4) Alienation is never fully overcome, but this fact can assume a positive, creative meaning. (5) The historical and the social character of man do not exhaust his essence: a dialogue on the meaning of existence is possible. (6) Religion has stimulated reflection on the meaning of life; Marxism should appreciate this contribution. (7) In this search and in the struggle against dehumanization and absurdity, Christians and Marxists should join forces.

The Christian-Marxist meetings have continued, in places as far distant as Rio de Janeiro (May, 1968) and Sydney, Australia (February, 1967), and it is an experience that many have found filled with promise for a brighter future. Has belief at last confronted unbelief, in a forthright fashion, without evasion or compromise? One must answer this question with a highly qualified affirmative. To some extent some unbelievers have sat down with Christians and have not altogether avoided questions of ultimate ideological import, but this is the most that can be said in terms of positive results. The great mass of believers still remain out of touch with their unbelieving fellows, and there is the further fact that faith itself is undergoing intensive re-examination so that not all is settled and assured on that side. What has been tried in Europe on an impressive scale, with first-rate representatives from both camps, has yet to be attempted with a comparable seriousness in the United States. At the end of March, 1969, two dozen scholars from eight countries met in Rome, under the joint sponsorship of the Vatican Secretariat for Non-Believers and the University of California at Berkeley, to explore 'The Culture of Unbelief.'[80] American unbelievers took part in the conference, but it was not a dialogue, rather a joint effort to assess the current scene and tease out the neuralgic spots, as yet undetected, on which attempt at dialogue might founder. The meeting was the first sponsored officially by the Vatican Secretariat and drew crowds numbering as many as four thousand, including many prelates holding high office.

Many see old-fashioned atheism as on the wane, but they see unbelief of other sorts on the ascendant and anti-Christ around the corner. But this image, according to sociologist Robert N. Bellah of Berkeley, is all wrong: 'The modern world,' he said, without irony, 'is as alive with religious possibility as any epoch in human history.' It was the consensus, apparently, that the world's supposed unbelievers are more sinned against than sinning—and perhaps, some of them, even more religious than some of those who call themselves believers. Bellah traced the problem in part to traditional and uncritical ideas of faith. From the days of the Church Fathers, Christians have been too eager to identify belief with intellectual assent given to a body of defined dogma. A young person today, however, according to Bellah, tends to regard faith as a commitment, part of a quest for personal authenticity that can lead him to embrace Black Power or the Peace Corps, become a Zen Buddhist or hippie, turn to sex or drugs. Some of these convictions or practices hardly qualify as beliefs, much less faith, by any standard, and it is not clear that any of them are oriented to God. Nevertheless, Bellah is willing to grant that in them 'the operation of the Holy Spirit' may be reflected—in the Peace Corps, for example, which Bellah sees as 'a secular monastic order whose members take a voluntary vow of poverty and go out to work for the alleviation of the sufferings of the world.' The distinguished American social philosopher, Peter Berger, of New York's School for Social Research, argued that children raised in benevolent American homes often turn to unbelief in their move from the unprecedented happiness of modern childhood to the harsh and demanding world of adulthood. When they encounter structures or institutions which are cruel or are not as benevolent as they should be, they are bitterly disappointed, and they revolt. Sociologist Thomas Luckmann of Frankfurt University predicted that eventually the categories of belief and unbelief will disappear. Institutional specialization represents only one particular form of religion and is on the wane, and as it goes, the distinction between believers and non-believers will blur and may fade. When this happens, one type of person will evolve his private set of ultimate values, while another will find that he can express his best through one of the churches that survive. Luckmann warned, however, that the remaining ecclesial bodies must understand their true role, which will be not to compel belief but to help each person to articulate his beliefs from within himself.

Thus far social scientists have had the floor, and one can well imagine the shock their remarks caused among the observers at the public sessions. The blockbuster was dropped by a theologian, Dr. Harvey Cox of the Harvard Divinity School, author of the widely read and controversial *The Secular City*. It may be, he charged, at the opening-day conference, that the major reason for unbelief is not that people find the Gospel incredible but that they find the churches incredible. 'The church of the Prince of Peace,' he said, 'is unable to take decisive action against war, and the church with the ideal of poverty continues to accumulate real estate.' Cox emphasized that his criticisms were directed at the deficiencies of Christians, not of Christianity, and he described his contacts with members of radical youth groups who, he said, are seeking the transcendent but do not believe that Christians live up to their own creed. Cox's most startling contribution was the following: 'A friend who heard I was going to Rome said the best secretariat they could establish would be a secretariat for hypocrisy, since hypocrisy—not unbelief— is the major religious power of our time.' The Vatican might then be able to deal effectively with Catholics who attend Mass and even give the correct answers but who do not really have a living belief which motivates their life. There are unbelievers, Cox added, but there are more people today who claim to believe in God but who do not live according to their faith, which is why one should speak not of a culture of unbelief but of a civilization of hypocrisy. Cox's final criticism was of the distinction between believers and non-believers, since there are non-believers inside and believers outside the Church. Against hypocritical believers, Cox argued that we cannot really use the label 'unbeliever' for people whose search for the transcendent is sometimes more serious and more ardent. They may think of themselves as Marxists or scientific humanists or behaviorists, but ' "non-believers" 'is not the name bywhich they know themselves in their own hearts.'

As we contemplate the future prospects of dialogue I think we had better take these last jolting thoughts to heart. Cox's words are sharp, but whether he was rude or brash is entirely beside the point. The world needs God, needs Christ, and, I also believe, needs His Church; but it neither needs nor will accept what is inhuman or dehumanizing, false and fantastic, authoritarian, arbitrary, hypocritical, useless, and self-serving. We shrink from the harsh charge of hypocrisy, as the Pharisees did when they felt its sting, but the disparity between profession and performance is undoubtedly the single most powerful obstacle to the Christian's winning the trust and respect indispensable as a condition for dialogue. There is nothing, certainly at this point in time, that can be said about dialogue that is more clamorous for the attention of believers, their intellectual appreciation, and their conscientious response. In conclusion, then, I find myself spontaneously recapitulating the theme of this final chapter, that is, relating intimately the problem of dialogue to that of renewal.

Conclusion

An adequate pastoral theology of unbelief recognizes the signs of the times in producing the elements of understanding and drawing guidelines for effective action. The present work has aimed chiefly at identifying its subject as a social as well as a strictly religious problem and at tracing, if only in rough outline, its extent, manifestations, and human significance. On reflection, as I struggle to find a key thread running through these vagrant musings, I am drawn to the disturbing realization, not of how adamantly so many reject the God in whom I believe but of how poorly we who believe present the faith-life and witness to its truth and power. The new values, human sensibility above all, have asserted themselves in place of religion and a theological ethic, with astonishing ease and naturalness. Whatever the future of religious adherence, these moral values will assuredly continue to demand recognition and respect on their own terms. This secularist value-orientation reveals, among other items, how widely atheists differ among themselves (although I am not identifying non-religious ethic with atheism as such) and the range of motives prompting them to their choice. A perspective eminently concrete and personalist is a prime desideratum for any pastoral-dialogal approach to the phenomenon of unbelief.

The reasons for unbelief are spread out across the spectrum of human interests and concerns and are often obscured or partially confused with the motives impelling an individual, who may not clearly grasp objective reasons, to opt for atheism. The principal reasons have been sorted out but call for closer analysis and penetration. Why, particularly at this point in Western history, is man so insistent that a transcendent God and a religion of transcendence are impermissibly out of touch with all that means and matters most in life? Why is evil at last so scandalous and its presence so unbearable that God must be rejected as an evil of the worst kind, so wicked that, if He existed, it would be the death of human dignity and freedom? Atheism is entailed, it is claimed, by man's responsibility for the total construction of his own destiny, in face of appalling evil and overwhelming physical odds. Echoes of Marx and Nietzsche resound in the writing of Sartre, who here focuses the most imperious currents of contemporary thought. The full thrust of this charge may have escaped us, because we seem thus far to have refused to acknowledge its seriousness or existential bite. In any case, and this is the last word, more than any other, religion in any of its major forms has proved nearly useless to provide solutions to the most serious problems facing mankind in this modern period. Scientific thinking no longer bothers to mount or support arguments disproving the existence of God or the authenticity of faith; the point is that life itself, as it is experienced and interpreted, has left no room for a God who is irrelevant to problem-solving. Enclosed in a world he regards as largely, or at least potentially, of his own making, the secularist has no need of God.

One would be guilty of a false and dangerous irenicism, indulgence in the grossest flattery, if one sought easy terms for dialogue by playing down or not facing up to serious substantive questions of faith and reason, religion and humanity. I have, I trust, avoided the egregious error of identifying atheism as a convenient pretext for ethical irresponsibility and self-indulgence. Atheism can be humanly satisfying in a variety of ways, and this whether the God who is rejected be the living God of Biblical faith or an idol. It is tempting, and perhaps legitimate up to a point, to depict the unbeliever as restless and unfulfilled, but this risks foreclosing the problem of God, on the ground that the unbeliever had already exhausted that possibility as uninteresting and unpromising. The atheism of today is not grossly out of touch with currents of authentic Christian thinking, so that one cannot get very far on the premise that unbelievers have really not known what faith demands, what the doctrine of God means. Christianity is anything but a novelty for them, an esoteric cult, and its very familiarity contributes to its unattractiveness: it neither interests nor excites. It may be that believers have nothing new to say, nothing that the world has not already heard, at least that part of the Western world to which unbelief is recently endemic. There is no reason to leave him in his serenity, should the unbeliever exhibit a smug complacency,

I

and reason enough, I should think, to shake him up, to disturb him and challenge him.

I have not done this, because I have felt this work of legitimate apologetic would be tackled in other volumes of this series. There are arguments for unbelief which have by no means lost their appeal, including those against the existence of God, and it will not do simply to dismiss them, without examination, as invalid difficulties or paralogisms. The traditional proofs or ways by which Catholics have undertaken to establish the rational foundations of religion require both extensive historical knowledge and considerable philosophical sophistication, but this holds, equally, for those who would claim to dispute the positive and metaphysical claims of faith. The atheist must ask himself, if he is to be an honest partner in dialogue, if his motives for embracing unbelief are sufficiently rational or if, in place of vigorous intellectual considerations, he has been influenced by particularly unhappy life-experiences. There is a dark night for the unbeliever, to be sure, for atheism can be excruciatingly traumatic, a devastating emotional wrenching leading to spiritual collapse. It would be a serious error to over-rationalize atheism—an error which I hope I have not committed and one to which, I fear, my own conception of faith, formed out of a solidly scholastic background, may have unduly exposed me. The rationalization of a position adopted originally is a hazard to which every man is liable, and it is far from clear that unbelievers as a group seize upon atheism chiefly as the conclusion to a carefully conducted process of pure reasoning. Unbelief is examined most appropriately in the categories of choice and option, that is, of conscience, of that existential decision which is para-rational rather than purely rational or irrational. There is evidence that arguments which lack probative force are accepted by certain unbelievers as establishing beyond question the invalidity of faith and the unreality of God. For such atheists, unbelief is itself a preferred value. They *believe* that God is not, that religion is disqualified on scientific and ethical grounds.

If God has lost both meaning and meaningfulness for the highly educated or spiritually alienated modern secularist, then the believer must find ways to arouse a well-founded interest in the God-problem; that is the task of witness—intellectually, of apologetic. But there is the more basic and equally legitimate obligation of understanding, of uncovering the reasons why God is out of focus and has no discernible relation with men's foremost concerns. When this question is faced in earnest and without prejudice, the result may be a reduction in the concern over technicalities and intramural squabbles which distract us from the present task. The response to unbelief is that God cannot be foreign to men's deepest needs and desires, that without Him human life loses its meaning and man becomes an insoluble problem and history an impenetrable enigma. The temptation here will be to claim too much, too easily, in a language inflated to conceal the lack of cogency in argument, for this point is extremely difficult to make or to sustain coherently and with conviction. The atheist today declines to accept God and transcendence precisely because, for him, human existence has an authentic meaning of its own, immanent and this-worldly, whereas he finds religion life-denying, unappreciative of secular values. The affirmation of these values by the churches may have been too late, or at any rate too hesitant and equivocal. A fawning and uncritical celebration of this world by naive churchmen finds a negative response from those for whom the misery and agony of life lead them to recoil before the triumph of the absurd, the irrational, the meaning-less in the world. Yet the disenchanted atheist seems, or professes, to be prepared to go on, an illusion cast in a measureless and in-different universe.

The unbeliever has to face death, the supreme test and an evil of which I have not taken specific account. As long as he has not overcome death, man cannot lay claim to a freedom or peace which will quiet desire, allay fear, encourage man in the long haul. An immense gain for the interests of truth and mutual understanding has been realized in the recognition that God is neither an explana-tory principle nor a remedial factor available to repair the world's mishaps and structural defects. With this insight we are afforded the opportunity to reaffirm that only things can be useful, in the proper sense, and never persons; on this basis we may wisely re-shape general thinking about personal and impersonal values and their interrelationship.

God cannot compete with the pursuit of scientific understanding, technological expertise, political stability, etc., because there can be no genuine rivalry between man's mundane existence and the One who gives ultimate meaning to things. Science is silent on the questions of man's life and death in their deepest significance, but the mind and heart persist in striving for light and the fullness of life, and it is in answer to this that a man affirms God or His surrogate, or relapses into sheer agnosticism. Reality as such, the universe as a whole, man as transcending and self-transcending spirit incarnate, these are all scientifically meaningless categories; a godless science is utterly powerless to reflect properly or in its own terms on its own godlessness, much less to offer explanations of which metaphysics and metaphysical theology alone are capable. For a believer, God is inextricably bound up with the human problem in its breadth and depth, so that there is no flight from experience or from the business of living in a faith which assents to a perfectly transcendent and perfectly immanent God. The unbeliever assumes, he does not provide either himself or others with compelling proof, that a godless existence makes a man more attuned to what is there, as it is, or more eager and better equipped to bridge the gap between what is, and what might or ought to be, closer to the heart's desire. A pastoral approach to the unbeliever, or, better, Christian witness (for it is a question of laymen even more than of clerics), should show him his own true face, while dispelling false and distorted notions of God. There may be a touch of hubris in this were the believer to confuse the light of faith and God's self-revelation, proper to belief, with that human wisdom about man's nature, condition and destiny, that he holds in common with the unbeliever. At the very core of modern unbelief, where its living nerve lies, exposed, there is the stubborn but powerful conviction that religious faith necessarily cancels out human freedom and responsibility and shrivels human personality to insignificance. Atheistic humanism denies God in order to affirm man, and man will be affirmed, whatever the cost.

It is a tragic development, the product of centuries of spiritual and cultural malaise, that men should come finally to regard the aggrandizement of God as the inevitable diminution of man. When this afflicts even intelligent, sensitive, and upright men, it must involve a seriously defective conception of man as well as of God. That is why a true Christian humanism is needed as desperately as a more adequate theology. The convergence of a profound re-examination of the themes of God, man, and faith should pass through a total dissipation of the Hegelian master-slave dialectic that has infested Western culture since the Enlightenment. To the challenge of unbelief, the God of Biblical faith has a response, if only in the halting and feeble word of one who, quite simply, believes. God only gives, He takes nothing; He is wholly Creator, generous, loving, gracious, concerned; the liberty He bestows He faithfully and scrupulously respects. God could not possibly resent or envy man's search for happiness, for He has made man to this very purpose and is concerned lest, going astray, he might lose himself in the pursuit. The greatness of man is his Creator's true glory, and every advance in man's self-understanding, self-giving, and mastery of nature expresses and reflects God's love for his creator. God's will is that man build his world and work out the potentialities of nature and history, not in defiance of Him or ignoring Him but in cooperation with His grace. It is, I think, tremendously exciting to reflect on the implications of the divine creative initiative: God Himself does not, by His unique and inimitable act, produce a universe complete and finished in every detail; rather, He empowers and invites man to collaborate with Him and put upon this world the stamp of human as well as of divine ingenuity and love. Teilhard de Chardin dwells repeatedly on this great mystery, the absolutely theandric character of world evolution, the mutual involvement of man and his Maker in the ongoing uninterruptedly creative and co-creative character of cosmic reality.

Whatever the purity of our intention, we must have been guilty of a misrepresentation of the God in whom we repose our faith, if so many of our fellows have turned from Him in revulsion as the supreme threat to their integral humanity. Worse by far, the lives of many of the faithful do not constitute a proof that God exists, meaningfully and with infinite value, or that He is transcendent and not reducible to anything in the world of experience, however noble and exalted, or to the totality of what man can possibly conceive or imagine or aspire to. Again and again the Christian must put his charity to the test, a consuming and purifying love which rises to the very goodness of God and from Him draws its strength and sustenance. To the defiant or humble 'I will not or cannot believe,' the effective reply is 'I know whom I adore; Him I serve, in love and fidelity.' Renewal, including the renovation of the heart, is for the sake of the world, as is the Church itself, not for its own sake. The entire being and purpose of the Church, the community of believers, is missionary, a witness and sign of Christ before the world. Failing this, we become a Pharisees' club that thanks God it is not like other men, faithless and unconverted. Our attitude toward 'the world' has in part been formed by the world's own self-interpretation, a forced impression calculated to boost its own morale. The secularists' self-advertisement tends to mesmerize others as well, who are thereby led to take at face-value his claims of optimism and self-confidence. The unbeliever does not admit that the world stands in need of God's mercy, and this is the key difference, in practice, between the world of faith and that of non-faith.

Can there be hope without faith? Where men are sensitive to the demands of truth and honesty, one cannot but infer that the Spirit of truth is blowing. When men adopt an attitude of serene contempt toward the grasping after money and the accumulation of property and refuse to esteem things, however lovely and valuable, more than persons, however squalid and unattractive, what really is asserted by the additional statement that they do or do not believe in God? I am not suggesting that the answer is 'nothing at all'; only that we take another long, hard look at the answer we give. Our interdependence as human beings ought to diminish drastically our individual anxiety over security or self-respect and the obsession of authorities with their power and prestige. When the unbeliever throws down the gauntlet, who can say that it is not God Himself putting faith to the test and allowing us to discern what is gold and what is dross in the belief we profess? There is a dimension to dialogue which I have not mentioned but which is of unequalled importance in the confrontation of unbelief and indeed in the life of faith. Prayer makes the difference.

Notes

Notes to Chapter One

1. Cf. the introductory address of Msgr. Veuillot, coadjutor archbishop of Paris, to the study days of Informations Catholiques
Internationales, in Veuillot et al., eds., *L'Athéisme, tentation du
monde, réveil des chrétiens?* (Paris, 1963), pp. 24–27 (hereafter cited
as Veuillot, *L'Athéisme*).

2. Among several fine studies published in recent years, two in particular have inspired the theology of faith summarily employed in this
section: Jean Mouroux, *I Believe* (New York, 1959), a splendid
exhibition of the eminently personalist elements in the doctrine
of St. Thomas, and Carlos Cirne-Lima's *Personal Faith* (New
York, 1966), an essay along phenomenological-metaphysical lines
highlighting in unique fashion the prepersonal and interpersonal
structures of faith. Valuable historical orientation and materials
are supplied in Roger Aubert's *Le problème de l'acte de foi* (Louvain,
1958).

3. Cf. Mouroux, *I Believe* (New York, 1949), pp. 41–64, and ST IIaIIae,
2.2 and 2.4 ad 3. Mouroux adds that God speaks to us as persons,
addressing Himself not to creatures in general and in the abstract but
to each soul. The signs of God's self-revelation are not only personal
in their origin, they are invariably directed to a person: pp. 17–21.

4. L. Patrick Carroll, S.J., has carefully traced the ecclesial dimension
of faith in an essay on 'Faith in the Church.' He prefaces a study
of the Biblical evidence with the observation that 'We, people,
meet and come to believe in Christ with a mature faith in and
through other believers, a believing community, a Church. And this
is no reoccurring accident. It is the plan of God that Christ his
son should continue to live and to be made manifest by the people
of God,' p. 291.

5. Henry Bars, *The Assent of Faith* (Baltimore, 1960), pp. ii–iii. The

conjunction of certainty and uncertainty, and unbelief as more 'natural' are discussed in Josef Pieper, *Belief and Faith* (New York, 1963), pp. 33–42; 47–51.

6. Karl Rahner, S.J., 'Thoughts on the Possibility of Belief Today,' *Theological Investigations* (Baltimore, 1966), 5: 3–22.

7. Cf. A. M. Henry, O.P., 'L'Athéisme aujourd'hui,' in Veuillot, *L'Athéisme*, pp. 31 ff.

8. D. Barthélemy, 'Les idoles et l'image,' in *La Vie Spirituelle*, mars (1962), p. 290.

9. Roger Verneaux argues forcefully to this conclusion, from the premise: '*La thèse générale que nous soutiendrons, parce qu'elle nous semble ressortir de l'ensemble de textes qui nous sont accessibles, est celle-ci; l'athéisme actuel n'est pas tant la négation de Dieu que le refus de croire en lui.*' *Leçons sur l'Athéisme contemporain* (Paris, 1964), p. 11. Étienne Borne sums up the case for the permanent possibility of unbelief, in virtue of the inescapable possibilities of human choice, by noting that '. . . the motives and movements which give rise to and encourage atheism exist less in this or that culture than in the nature and condition of man, man confronted at once by the success of his scientific inquiry into nature and the failure of his reflection on what exists, from which evil cannot be excluded. Science, the only mistress of his rational processes, accounts for more and more of the universe, fact after fact, phenomenon after phenomenon: so God is unnecessary. Evil is *a-theist*, godless or even exclusive of God, since by the very fact that it is, it forbids us to postulate an absolute Good: so God is impossible.' *Atheism* (New York, 1961), pp. 24–25.

10. Ignace Lepp, *Atheism in Our Time* (New York, 1963), p. 63. Lepp has succeeded in identifying accurately the multiple and diverse factors, personal and environmental, operative in several varieties of contemporary atheism.

11. Cf. Michael Novak, *Belief and Unbelief* (New York, 1965), pp. 13–14, prefaces what is indeed a splendidly reasoned disquisition on the problem of faith with a deeply personal expression of the basic human experience from which faith emerges. Novak calls it 'intelligent subjectivity,' p. 16, not minimizing the rational element but focusing on the personal *uses* which the free, self-determining subject makes of intelligence, in the life-long quest for personal identity and meaning.

12. It is, in the end, impossible to discuss unbelief without explicit reference to the faith or belief to which it is, by definition, in opposition. Martin Marty writes: ' "Unbelief" in its varieties and forms does not appear in a vacuum. It occurs as an event in history, over against "belief" in its varying definitions. This forces us to raise the question of the meaning of belief in the Christian tradition. If today there is a crisis of belief, if many are accused of departing from

it or opposing it, and if others are pictured as its defenders, we shall need to isolate some elements of the definition of belief.' *Varieties of Unbelief* (New York, 1964), p. 17 (hereafter cited as Marty, *Varieties*). Marty would, however, concede the inner originality and consistency of unbelief, as a positive act with its proper identity.

13. Marty, *Varieties*, pp. 27–34. Marty examines critically definitions of unbelief and disbelief suggested in New Testament writings and in the works of classical and more recent Catholic and Protestant theologians, including Calvin and Luther, Josef Pieper and Gustav Wingren, and the Jewish scholar, Arthur A. Cohen.

14. Karl Barth, *Church Dogmatics*, 3/1 (Edinburgh, 1952), pp. 7–8. Barth's influence has undoubtedly colored a great deal of subsequent Protestant thinking on the irreligious movements of our time; cf. Gustav Wingren, *The Living Word* (Philadelphia, 1960), pp. 92 ff.

15. In the section which immediately follows, unbelief is analyzed and its expressions classified according to the exactions of a formal logic to which historical actuality and its vagaries are extraneous. Cf. John Patrick Reid, O.P., *The Anatomy of Atheism* (Washington, 1965), pp. 5–6, on the different approaches, theoretical-abstract and historical-concrete.

16. Cf. Jacques Maritain, 'The Meaning of Contemporary Atheism,' in *The Range of Reason* (New York, 1952), pp. 103–105. Maritain prefers the designations, practical, pseudo- and absolute atheists, from the point of view of the person who professes to be an atheist, although it is difficult to see how, on this basis, one could speak properly of the practical atheist. Maritain's other division is into negative, or merely destructive, and positive, or militantly anti-theist. The types discussed in this chapter are realized, not always in pure form, in the many diverse areas and systems examined in the following chapters.

17. Speaking of the impact of Christians who do not take seriously the faith they profess, Garret Barden, S.J., insists that: 'There is nothing specifically irresponsible in Christianity; but Christians, like other men, can be irresponsible. And once they abdicate their responsibility, they can invent reasons to justify themselves. They can falsify the notion of the providence of God to suit their own laziness and greed. They can substitute a false notion of the will of God to cover up their lack of hunger and thirst after justice,' in an introduction to Jean Lacroix, *The Meaning of Modern Atheism* (Dublin, 1965), pp. 10–11. The Second Vatican Council's Pastoral Constitution on the Church in the Modern World declares, with respect to the prevalence of atheism today: '. . . believers themselves frequently bear some responsibility for this situation. For, taken as a whole, atheism is not a spontaneous development but stems from a variety of causes, including a critical reaction against religious beliefs, and in some places against the Christian religion in particular.

Hence believers can have more than a little to do with the birth of atheism. To the extent that they neglect their own training in the faith, or teach erroneous doctrine, or are deficient in their religious, moral, or social life, they must be said to conceal rather than to reveal the authentic face of God and religion.' *The Teachings of the Second Vatican Council* (New York, 1966), pp. 457–458. These strictures may be read as aimed at those we have called practical unbelievers.

18. Riccardo Lombardi, S.J., *The Salvation of the Unbeliever* (Westminster, 1956), pp. 148–176 (hereafter cited as Lombardi, *Salvation*), includes both a philosophical and a theological discussion of negative atheism, concentrating on the specific problem of the ignorance of God required for its possibility. Lombardi weighs the stated opinions of authors within the central Catholic tradition, with an interest especially in the question of personal responsibility. He concludes that the rational knowledge of God is possible to all, at least before death, but that a practically complete ignorance of God is not morally or physically impossible.

19. Henri Maurier has produced the finest and most comprehensive study of this subject, a work admirably organized and scrupulously documented, with judicious distribution of emphases, phenomenological, historical, dogmatic, pastoral, and scriptural, *Essai d'une Théologie du Paganisme* (Paris, 1965) (hereafter cited as Maurier, *Essai*). With a preface by Jean Daniélou, S.J. This work is oriented, as are most writings on the subject by theologians, toward the needs and demands of missiology, but without sacrificing objectivity and balance.

20. Valuable indications and suggestions for the construction of such a theology have been supplied by several reputable theologians, such as Henri de Lubac, S.J., Gottlieb Sohngen, Michael Schmaus, Karl Rahner, Joseph Ratzinger, and Max Seckler. Heinz Robert Schlette has outlined the general features and exigencies of a dogmatic understanding of paganism, in his *Towards a Theology of Religions* (New York, 1966). According to Schlette, the field is still largely theological *terra incognita*. Maurier complains that, even today, with all the resources made available in the past fifty years, theologians still fail to take the trouble to incorporate this immensely improved knowledge into their speculations on pagan and other non-Biblical religions, Maurier, *Essai*, pp. 24–26, with excellent bibliographical references.

21. Cf. the illuminating chapter on modern paganism, its causes and forms it takes, in Maurier, *Essai*, pp. 105–118, with good leads to further research. Maurier believes that some trace of paganism survives, as an archaic remnant, in all men, inseparable from the as yet unpurified experience of the human condition: p. 105.

22. For the quality and limits of the pagans' knowledge of God,

personal and impersonal, cf. the magistral essay of F. M. Bergougnioux and J. Goetz, *Les Religions des Préhistoriques et des Primitifs*
(Paris, 1958), especially pp. 64–95. Almost all of the writings of
Mircea Eliade cited in their bibliography offer valuable factual
materials and interpretation within the context of the history and
comparison of religions. On polytheism as a fragmented knowledge
of God, with abundant Biblical references, see P. Chalus, *L'Homme
et la Religion* (Paris, 1964), pp. 429–449.

23. Charles Hartshorne and William L. Reese present evidence of the
range and variety of classical pantheism, in both Oriental and
Western traditions, but do not substantiate their suggestion that
the earliest philosophy which functioned as a religion was pantheism.
They do admit that it is only in the Orient that pantheism has
become anything like the pervasive spiritual philosophy of a
culture. Cf. their *Philosophers Speak of God* (Chicago, 1953),
pp. 165–210, with selections of Hindu sages, Spinoza, Royce, and
the poet Robinson Jeffers. The authors themselves lean toward what
they call panentheism, the logic of which they analyze, pp. 499–514.

24. ST IIaIIae. The First Vatican Council promulgated a canon condemning the fundamental tenet of pantheism, the identity of the
substance and essence of God and of all things, and another
condemning the principal forms of pantheism. See Reginald
Garrigou-Lagrange, O.P., *God, His Existence and His Nature*
(St. Louis, 1948), 1:5–8 (hereafter cited as Garrigou-Lagrange,
God), on the meaning and import of these canons.

25. It is at least arguable that man today actually opts for pantheism,
rather than atheism. An Italian scholar, Giovanni Miegge, remarks:
'On the modern world-view God is everywhere and nowhere. The
two expressions may be regarded as synonymous. They do mean,
however, that it is by no means easy to reconcile such a world-view
with belief in God; it seems almost inseparably connected with a
pantheistic or atheistic understanding of things. It is, however,
possible to raise the question whether this pantheistic attitude is
in reality the corollary of a purely *scientific* interpretation of the
world; or whether it is in fact due simply to the fact that modern
man in the depths of his being has made a declaration in favor
of pantheism and against theism,' *Gospel and Myth in the Thought
of Rudolf Bultmann* (Richmond, 1960), p. 94.

26. There is not yet a major study of the early English deists. Leslie
Stephen's *English Thought in the Eighteenth Century* (New York,
1959) is a classic work which, however, tends to underestimate the
deists' philosophical acumen and their influence. His distinction
between critical and constructive deism has received general acceptance. Arthur O. Lovejoy's essay 'The Parallel of Deism and
Classicism,' in *Essays in the History of Ideas* (Baltimore, 1960),
pp. 78–98, is extremely suggestive and repays close study. For the

importation of deism into France, see Norman L. Torrey, *Voltaire and the English Deists* (New Haven, 1934).

27. The earliest deists, in England, were not avowedly anti-Christian. They were not, indeed, philosophical deists at all, as F. R. Tennant shows, in *Miracle* (London, 1927), p. 7. Toland speaks in accents representative of much of seventeenth- and early eighteenth-century deism, when he states as his program: 'I prove first that the true religion must necessarily be reasonable and intelligible. Next I show that these requisite conditions are found in Christianity. . . . I demonstrate, thirdly, that the Christian religion was not formed after such a manner, but was divinely revealed from Heaven,' *Christianity Not Mysterious*, etc., p. xxvii. Natural religion was developed in concept, as an alternative to Christianity, especially by the French, in the eighteenth century. On the English, French, and German versions of deism at this period, cf. Paul Hazard, *European Thought in the Eighteenth Century* (New Haven, 1953), pp. 393–434, and for natural religion, pp. 113–129.

28. Sir Leslie Stephen wrote that the word 'Agnosticism describes a form of creed already common and daily spreading,' *An Agnostic's Apology and Other Essays* (New York, 1905), p. 1. The heart of the agnostic argument, he continued, is epistemological; he notes that the word was coined by Thomas Henry Huxley, but the idea had been formulated by an earlier generation, by Auguste Comte and by the Mills and Herbert Spencer. Cf. Leonard Huxley, *Life and Letters of Thomas Henry Huxley* (London, 1888), 1:262.

29. The function and force of doubt in the suspension of religious belief are critically examined by Geddes MacGregor in *God Beyond Doubt* (New York, 1967), pp. 179–207. The author insists that both the mind and the bulk of experience are constantly up against what he calls the skeptical edge, but he asserts that this inevitable encounter may, and indeed should, issue in belief, rather than in agnosticism.

30. The alleged failures of every type of argument for the existence of God, and the unscientific character of theism, impel some would-be believers to a non-rational commitment. William Warren Bartley stigmatizes this as uncritical use of the rational faculty and a retreat from integrity, in *The Retreat to Commitment* (New York, 1952), pp. 88–133.

31. The First Vatican Council's definition on the ability of the human reason to know God with certainty had in view, among others, the error of fideism, 'the wide-spread error.' The *schema* declared, 'that the existence of God cannot be proved by any apodictic argument, and consequently that by no process of human reasoning can the certainty of it be established.' Cf. Vacant, *Études sur les Constitutions du Concile du Vatican* (Paris, 1909), p. 286, and Document VII, p. 610.

32. James Collins, in *God and Modern Philosophy* (Chicago, 1959), pp. 190 ff., concludes that Kant's position could not countenance any metaphysical basing of moral obligation upon the bond between man and God, for this would involve either an arbitrary assumption of God's existence or the restoration of the speculative demonstration of this truth. The best exposition of the Kantian contribution to agnosticism and its implication for atheism is the opening chapter of William A. Luijpen, *Phenomenology and Atheism* (Pittsburgh, 1964).

Notes to Chapter Two

1. John A. T. Robinson, 'Can a Truly Contemporary Person Not Be an Atheist?' *The New Christianity* (New York, 1967), ed. William Miller (New York, 1967), pp. 308–311. Robinson and others generally associated with the new theology and radical Christianity do not take sufficiently critical notice of the persistent tendency to transform worldliness into an immanentism in which transcendence is denied, or at least set aside. In any case the worldliness is out of joint with much of the venerated spiritual outlook and has yet to be examined soberly and sympathetically, except by theologians in the *avant garde*. For a useful survey of recent thinking on the subject, see Harry E. Smith, 'Secularization Defined and Refined,' in *Secularization and the University* (Richmond, 1968), pp. 67–93.

2. The Bible makes frequent reference to highly admired persons who witnessed to the truth and power of faith, thus: Abel, Enoch, Noah, Abraham, Isaac, Jacob, Joseph, Moses, Gideon, David, Samuel, the Prophets. These men are commended especially for their endurance in time of trial and deprivation, their obedience to God's order and command. The witness is necessary as long as man continues in his condition of believer, in *statu viatoris*. Unbelief, by immediate contrast, shrinks from a real but uncertain future, fails the trial, drops out of the race, surrenders in battle, and remains stunted and immature. The New Testament is not oblivious of temptations against faith or of faith's flagging, growing weary and becoming indifferent, and as Rudolf Schnackenburg observes: '... it is only in the New Testament that unbelief becomes something really disastrous, especially in the context of the gospels, where the divine message of salvation and joy resounds. Here it appears as the worst possible evil. Eschatological judgment threatens those who close themselves to God's last offer of salvation. In the preaching of Jesus this is the terrifying reverse side of the loving attempts to convert his people.' 'Biblical Perspectives of Faith,' in *Toward a Theology of Christian Faith,* ed. Michael Mooney et al. (New York, 1966), p. 51 (hereafter cited as Mooney, *Toward*).

3. This questioning is quite different from the type envisaged in our fundamental theology. In the Bible, when man sees his life threatened, his values challenged, then he is moved to ask what is the strength and reality of the faith he professes. But he can sustain himself in face of crisis if he has already known the joy of experiencing God's power and goodness. Anna, the mother of Samuel, reaffirms her faith, after her request has been granted: 'It is Yahweh who gives life and death, brings down to Sheol and raises up. . . . He raises the poor from the dust, he lifts the needy from the dunghill' (1 Sam 2.6). The elder Tobias cries out, in affliction: 'For the Lord strikes and shows mercy; he leads down to Hades and brings up again' (Tob. 13.2). St. Paul learns the lesson of trust, after being in danger of death: 'Yes, we were carrying our own death warrant with us, and it has taught us not to rely on ourselves but only on God, who raises the dead to life' (2 Cor 1.9).

4. God does not demand the impossible; confidence in His power and readiness to help the tormented soul is sufficient, even without doctrinal understanding. The Lord reprimands only lack of trust, faintheartedness, and despair (Mk 4.10; Lk 12.28); the unbeliever loses confidence that the power of God can accomplish all things (Mk 9.23; 11.23). But the faith that Jesus demands is not irrational; there is no danger, in the Gospels, of an excessively charismatic and emotional spirituality that would naively attempt to dispense with sound reflection. Our dogmatically developed conception of faith, as inquiring and seeking understanding, has a good scriptural foundation. Refining our notions of faith and bringing them the insights of dogmatic theology are legitimate and useful undertakings. The point is that faith conquers doubt and indecision by a power which is not that of rational penetration or deliberation, although reflection is not lacking. The stability of faith comes finally from God's grace. Cf. Alan Richardson's helpful essay, 'Faith and Presuppositions,' in *Faith, Reason, and the Gospels*, ed. John J. Heaney, S.J. (Westminster, 1961), pp. 68–88, esp, pp. 82–85, in which he illustrates the mutual influx of faith and reason from the spiritual development of St. Augustine.

5. Faith as liberation clearly defines the state of unbelief as one of bondage and the conversion to Christ as entry into freedom. This note is struck repeatedly in St. Paul's writings, that Jesus Christ lived, died, and rose again precisely to bring men to the freedom they needed but could not by their own efforts alone achieve: 'For freedom Christ has set us free; stand fast, therefore, and do not submit again to the yoke of slavery' (Gal 5.1). Again: 'Am I not free? Am I not an apostle? Have I not seen Jesus the Lord?' (1 Cor 9.1). A familiar theme: 'for the written code kills, but the Spirit gives life' (2 Cor 3.6), in which the unconverted are declared spiritually lifeless, 'Now the Lord is the Spirit, and where the Spirit of the Lord

is, there is freedom' (3.17). The Apostle hits on a prominent reason for remaining unconverted: unbelief provides an apparent refuge from the moral demands of faith. 'For you were called to freedom, brethren; only do not use your freedom as an opportunity for the flesh, but through love be servants of one another' (Gal 5.13). On the Pauline connection of conversion-faith-freedom and confusion in the secularist mind on the freedom of the believer, cf. John P. Keating, S.J., 'Faith, Slavery, or Freedom,' in *Faith in the Face of Doubt* (New York, 1968), pp. 49–70.

6. Besides Isaiah the Psalms speak often of man's faithlessness, and particularly of the proneness of Israel to sin against faith through lack of confidence in the God of the covenant, through murmuring and rebelling (Ps 78. 106). Unbelief is a deliberate and active turning away from God, not only or even primarily in thought but in action —an insolence toward God and a mockery of His law. The unbeliever can expect God's punishment; He will strike fear and confusion into their hearts, unsettle them completely and bring them to naught (Ps 14. 5). For the Old Testament writers, unbelief is not only the result of a personal choice; it is objectified, or at least universalized, as a sinister and evil power that will carry men to their destruction. Unbelief is very closely bound up with the mystery of iniquity for which men are responsible but which affects them in ways of which they are partially ignorant. One of the chief and most frequently encountered offices of the Prophets is to convince Israel of its faithlessness, to warn it of the terrible consequences of unbelief (Jer 5.17; 7.4, 8, 14; 13.25; 17.5; Am 6.1; Hos 10.13; Hab 2.4).

7. Cf. X. Léon-Dufour, 'The Belief in God,' in *The God of Israel, The God of Christians*, ed. J. Giblet (New York, 1961), pp. 130–132; Rudolf Schnackenburg, *The Moral Teaching of the New Testament*, pp. 37–38. St. John reports Jesus as asking for the same belief in Himself as He asked for the Father, with particularly strong emphasis on faith in His messiahship (Jn 11.25; 20.31), and a simple acquiescence on His part in such confessions of faith (6.44, 65; 20.28.)

8. On the Pauline doctrine of the operative presence of forces of unbelief in the world, cf. Fernand Prat, S.J., *The Theology of St. Paul* (Westminster, 1945), 2: 57–75; on faith as justification by God, cf. pp. 242–249; and on the redemptive death of Christ, cf. pp. 188–199. Faith as involving trial and coming to maturity only in the following of Christ is the theme of Heb 12.

9. None of the evangelists portrays more vividly and movingly than John the precariousness of faith, the perils to which it is exposed, its confirmation by trial and testing, and its degeneration and disappearance into a state of unbelief. Unless willingness to listen to God's self-revealing word is present, faith cannot grow (Jn 4, the Samaritan woman); but this good will serves faith well: 'Now we no longer believe because of what you told us; we have heard

him ourselves and we know that he really is the savior of the world' (4.42). But the demand for signs and wonders (4.48) debases faith and is the fruit of unbelief; a decisive step in the direction of belief is required, in a completely personal act, before faith can be an interior state. In John's Gospel, however, the disciples more than once demonstrate by their own actions that faith is always subject to the encroachment of unbelief (2.11; 6.6, 66–71; 11.8–16: difficulties and trials; 13.6–9; 14.4–11; 16.16, 29: inability to understand; men have to struggle for belief, zeal is no substitute for enlightenment: 6.70; 17.6). In 1 John faith is already beset by false and seductive teaching, a fanatical Gnosticism that preaches possession of God without moral effort (1 Jn 4.1–6).

10. The convert is not alone in the momentous step he takes, from unbelief-death to faith-life; he ranges himself alongside all those who, in following Christ, arm themselves to battle against the unconverted 'world,' the forces of hypocrisy (Mt 23; 15.1–20; Lk 18.9–14; Jn 8.42–6; Rev 22.15), respect of persons (Mt 22.16; Jas 2.1–9), and, above all, injustice, callous indifference, and unconcern for those in need (Mt 25.31–46; Mk 10.21; 14.5; Lk 3.10–14; 12.33; 19.8; Jn 6.15; 12.5; 13.29). Unbelief stands condemned in the first place as insincerity, selfishness, and radical dishonesty; for the Biblical, particularly the New Testament, sources, cf. Flor Hofmans, *Jesus: Who is He?* (Glen Rock, 1968), (hereafter cited as Hofmans, *Jesus*), pp. 73–78.

11. Jean Daniélou has distilled out of the New Testament passages a beautiful and illuminating explanation of the scriptural doctrine of faith as a conversion which leads to justification and sanctification, the setting out of the soul on a spiritual journey which moves ever farther from the pole of unbelief. Cf. the chapter 'The Inward Master,' in *Christ and Us* (New York, 1963), pp. 216–236.

12. St. John's favorite mode of expression for the conversion implied in believing is a turning away from the world, renouncing that world which refuses to acknowledge salvation through and in Jesus. The unbeliever prefers to turn to lying, to hold tightly to his standards, opinions, and certainties; he refuses that self-surrender to the invisible, over which he has no control (Jn 5.44), consolidating his 'world' and shutting it off at the top against God. He will not tolerate disturbance of his mode of life, especially when its legal or moralistic correctness salves and flatters his conscience (Jn 5.1–16; 9.1–34). For a further elaboration of these and other Johannine themes on the antithesis of faith and unbelief, cf. Rudolf Bultmann and Artur Weiser, *Faith* (London 1961), pp. 100–104.

13. Faith judges and is not judged by man; it examines all the forms of unbelief and deals justly with each and mercifully with men who act from weakness and ignorance. The sanctity to which faith ever

inspires the believer is an act of breaking away immeasurably more profound than all the rebellion and despair of atheism. Perfect faith, as the Gospels inculate it, supposes a non-acceptance of the world of things-as-they-are. This break with the world, or rather with the evil which is in the world, is free from all Manichean sympathies: the world must not be abandoned but preserved from evil, so that it may show forth more clearly the mystery of God. Thus Étienne Borne: 'The religious consciousness, and particularly that Christian consciousness which modern atheism has seen as the enemy to be attacked and destroyed, is faced with its ultimate trial, which it must bear and overcome: a trial of strength from which will result the total victory of the one and the total defeat of the other, and a trial of strength of mind also in a duel of intellects. Whichever comprehends the other is the conqueror, for to comprehend is to enfold, to dissolve, to pass beyond,' *Atheism*, trans. Tester (New York, 1961), p. 9. St. John returns often to the theme of faith overcoming the world, in truth and love (Jn 3.15–6.36; 6.40, 47; 20.31; 1 Jn 5.13); cf. the instructive commentary on the anti-Gnostic character of the Johannine concept of triumphant faith, in Bultmann, *Faith*, pp. 105–107.

14. Cf. the thoughtful essay, largely a meditation on the Scriptures, of Gotthold Hasenhuttl, 'Encounter with God,' especially the sections on Jesus as fulfillment of man's need for a gracious neighbor and His opening up to man of the possible communion with God as transcendent and immanent love: in *The Unknown God,* ed. Hans Küng (New York, 1966), pp. 91–158, esp. pp. 135–152.

15. Riccardo Lombardi, S.J., in his well-known monograph on *The Salvation of the Unbeliever,* trans. Dorothy M. White (Westminster, 1956), offers a lengthy and incisive theological commentary on the classical text of Hebrews 11.6, on the indispensability of faith, but little attention is devoted to the alternative, i.e., the lack of faith, or the nuanced degrees of faith; cf. pp. 69–74. For these interpretations one must turn to other Pauline passages and the writings of other Apostles.

16. The corpus of New Testament writings centers on the bond with Jesus, without which men are sunk in the misery their own sin has created. The references are too numerous even to begin to cite; one may profitably consult the texts assembled in Hofman's *Jesus,* pp. 98–102, and cf. the provocative and admirable discussion of the imitation of Christ as the heart of the Christian way of life, pp. 103–106. The attitude of unbelief, in its Pauline interpretation especially, is the refusal to recognize Jesus Christ as the 'Master for me' and to consent to an exchange of life with this Lord. Atheism is, in this perspective, a-Christianity, for faith, man's initial and irreplaceable communication with God, entails entrance into community with Christ (1 Cor 12). St. Paul can think of communion

with God in no other terms; cf. Ingo Hermann, *The Experience of Faith* (New York, 1966), pp. 23–27, on the personal relation to Jesus Christ, the inner form of the attitude of faith.

17. The rejection by unbelief of the Lordship of Christ is reflected in the continuing hatred of the Church across the ages, the shutting out of God's word by the prohibition of the Gospel. The presence of the Church, carrying out its divine mandate, is hampered by structures of social life which render masses of people impermeable to evangelization. Unbelief creates its own climate, to prevent the exercise of the freedom to consider the religious question and to shut out the effective witness of the Church. The unbeliever is alone, alienated, for there can be no authentic brotherhood in the denial of God; faith builds community and delivers man from his isolation. Cf. P. A. Liège, O.P., 'The Church, Milieu of Christian Belief,' in Mooney, *Toward*, pp. 262–282.

18. On the Biblical formulation of the problem of unbelief, cf. J. Daniélou, *God and the Ways of Knowing* (New York, 1957), pp. 94–138; and on the difference between this conception, derived from practical religious experience, and that of speculative philosophical inquiry, cf. Claude Tresmontant, *Toward the Knowledge of God* (Baltimore, 1961), esp. pp. 93 ff.

19. Some important studies of the evangelical theme of conversion and repentance as integral to faith-life are: N. Perrin, *The Kingdom of God in the Teaching of Jesus*, Rudolf Schnackenburg, *Gottes-herrschaft und Reich. Eine Biblisch-theologische Studie*; and A. Feuillet, 'Le Règne de Dieu et la personne de Jesus d'après les évangiles synoptiques,' in Robert-Feuillet eds., *Introduction à la Bible*, 2: 771–818.

20. *The Problem of God* (New Haven, 1964), (hereafter cited as Murray, *The Problem*). In the chapter on 'The Contemporary Problem of God,' p. 84, Murray deduces from this survey of Biblical types of the godless man the conclusion: 'The Bible clearly locates the ultimate root of atheism not in an erroneous judgment of the mind but in an act of choice, made somehow in the name of freedom, that launches the project of living the godless life, of freedom.' Cf. pp. 78–86, and Murray's heuristic essay 'On the Structure of the Problem of God,' in *Theological Studies*, 23 (1962), pp. 1 ff.

21. Murray, *The Problem*, p. 78. On the connection of the attachment to the basest forms of immorality with pagan unbelief, cf. the excellent analysis of a great number of texts from both Testaments in Henri Maurier, *The Other Covenant: A Theology of Paganism*, pp. 161–190.

22. Cf. Paul Heinisch, *Theology of the Old Testament, Essai* (College-ville, 1950), pp. 57–61, and on the Gentiles' vocation to abandon idolatry and acknowledge the one living God, pp. 285–288.

23. Paul's concern is not only with the fact of unbelief but with its

guilty character, its inexcusability, the attitude toward godlessness most common in the Scriptures. No distinction is implied between the well-educated and the vulgar masses, although the intellectual may be more blameworthy for having sinned against the light. It is to be noted that St. Paul affirms, several times and with remarkable clarity, that the pagans *knew* God and not merely that they *could* have known Him. They shut their eyes to the truth and 'keep the truth captive in injustice,' in his striking phrase (Rom 1.18): they know Him unreservedly but act in a way contrary to their knowing —and Paul speaks of this as something notorious in his own time. This searing Pauline text has not, I think, been read with full appreciation of the absoluteness with which the unbeliever is charged as guilty by reason of his rejection of God.

24. If God's word is to be taken at face value it is difficult to see how Christians (or believing Jews) can rule out the possibility of a knowledge of God arising from the experience and contemplation of the cosmos. In this passage (Wis 13.1–9), the author makes an act of confidence in the power and reliability of human intelligence, the finality of nature, and the knowability of God. The pagans held accountable for their godlessness are those educated enough to 'know so much,' and it is implied that the step from the material universe to God was not beyond their ability. The philosophical overtones are unmistakable but not altogether strange, given the time of composition and other circumstances of the Book of Wisdom.

25. Murray, *The Problem*, p. 85: 'Sartre, for instance, considers atheism to be the radical decision, the fundamental project. It is the original choice of one's self-in-the-world that is at the same time the discovery of the world; for the world from which God is absent reveals itself across the intention that he be absent. It is to the credit of Sartre's perspicacity that he does not even attempt to cast up a rational justification of the decision, the choice, and the ensuing project. They are by definition absurd . . . In a strange way, Sartre's view of atheism is hauntingly biblical.'

26. In the immediate context it is a question not so much of an unbeliever's ability to know God as of the fact that some pagans knew God, in some way (v. 21), but let that knowledge lie dead and unproductive in their lives and conduct. The failure is in not honoring God rather than in simply denying His existence. Where the author of Wisdom marveled that men should have been ignorant of the God whom they could have known, St. Paul complains of those who withheld from the God of whom they were not entirely ignorant the worship owed Him. The insistence, again, that nature is a medium of God's self-revelation is fully in the Old Testament and Jewish tradition. Over and above the divine existence mentioned in Wisdom, St. Paul adds certain divine attributes, including God's

invisibility, power, and eternity. This harsh indictment is somewhat balanced by what Paul says, in the next chapter, about the pagan who, even without the law of God, follows his conscience (Rom 2.14–16, 26–29). Cf. the comparison of the passages from Wisdom and Romans in Anthony T. Padovano, *The Estranged God* (New York, 1956), pp. 210–215.

27. In a book that appeared a few years ago, an English writer, Gerald Downing, expressed grave reservations about the propriety or continued helpfulness of speaking of God's self-revealing word as a 'deposit.' He argued, partly from Biblical sources and partly from an empiricist philosophical background, that Christianity might *be* a revelation, in the sense of a community of people who believe that God is ever revealing Himself and leading them forward. Downing rejects the concept of revelation as an object, possessed by men, not the truth God reveals but the truth through which He reveals. Cf. *Has Christianity a Revelation?* (London, 1965), and the critical remarks of Gabriel Moran, 'The God of Revelation,' in *Commonweal* (10 February 1967), pp. 499–503.

28. In consulting Denzinger's *Enchiridion Symbolorum*, 25th ed. (Barcelona, 1948), I have been aware of the inadequacy of such texts as are therein collected, usually incomplete and presented without full context or historical background. Denzinger creates a subtle but powerful impression that later centuries of ecclesiastical pronouncements did little more than reiterate and reapply the decisions and condemnations of earlier periods. This accords well both with a timeless conception of truth and with the doctrine of a fixed and permanently identifiable 'body' of revealed truth, deposited in a spiritual treasury once and for all and guarded zealously ever since. Hence the familiar and recurring procedure of examining statements pertaining to faith in the light of those already officially accepted as authentic, and in view of this comparison passing judgments of orthodoxy or non-orthodoxy. The prevailing mentality seems to express itself in the series of questions: 'Can this be said? Has it been said before? Has something contrary to this been said before?' If there is anything to the claim made in recent years that Catholic theological thinking has been dominated by an obsession with non-historical orthodoxy, it may be traced, at least in part, to the kind of naive complacency that will turn to Denzinger, by itself and just as it is, for purposes which are dubious and with results that evidence little real understanding of issues of complex historical and doctrinal significance. Denzinger has a certain limited value, I do not deny, but it has long been responsible for stunting the minds of uncritical students of theology. It is surely sobering to reflect that the Second Vatican Council declined to adopt the mode of discourse most highly respected among the various kinds of entries awarded a place in Denzinger.

29. W. H. P. Hatch, *The Pauline Idea of Faith in Its Relation to Jewish and Hellenistic Religion* (London, 1948), pp. 81–82. D. M. Baillie's *Faith in God* (London, 1964) has an excellent introductory chapter on 'The Idea of Faith and Its Historical Emergence,' pp. 37–80. The Biblical concept of faith, which underwent considerable development, is compared with analogous categories in ancient Hellenic sources. Faith emerges full-fledged into the light of day only with the dawning of Christianity. With the Christian consciousness, a firm and clear idea of unbelief also becomes, for the first time, a historical possibility.

30. Denzinger, *Enchiridion,* 808: Chapter 15 of the Decree on Justification of Session VI (Jan. 13, 1547) of the Council of Trent: by mortal sin man loses grace but not necessarily faith; by implication: only a sin directly against faith will expunge faith from the mind and heart. Chapter 8 explains how a sinner is justified by faith, a free gift of God, and chapter 9 rejects as empty and vain the heretical doctrine of fiduciary trust as equivalent to justification (Denz. 801, 802).

31. The defense of the reasonableness of faith and condemnation of the twin errors of anti-religious rationalism and irrationalist fideism preoccupies much of the nineteenth century. Names remembered only vaguely figured at the time in a series of pronouncements, such as the censures against Bautain (1840, Denz. 1625), the encyclical 'Qui pluribus' of Pius IX (1846, Denz. 1637), the chapter on faith in the dogmatic constitution on the Catholic Faith, of the First Vatican Council (1870, Denz. 1790 ff.), and on faith and reason (Denz. 1795–1800), the condemnation of Rosmini by the Holy Office (1887, Denz. 1915), and several others.

32. The authority of God revealing guarantees the certitude and unshakable infallibility of the assent of faith, which is not the mere concurrence of probabilities (Condemnation of Modernism, 1907, Denz. 2025), nor the fruit of any sort of religious experience (Denz. 2081), but shares in the wisdom of God Himself, as a grace entirely superior to anything reason could attain (the oath against Modernism, 1910, Denz. 2145). There are periodic statements affirming the trustworthiness and objective firmness of the assent of faith, from the early decades of the nineteenth century on.

33. On the necessity of faith for salvation, cf. the Constitution on the Catholic Faith of the First Vatican Council: 'The Catholic Church professes that the faith which is the beginning of human salvation is a supernatural virtue, by which we, with the inspiration and aid of the grace of God, believe those things revealed by him to be true, not because of an intrinsic vision of the truth of those things, obtained by the natural light of reason, but because of the authority of God Himself who reveals them to us, God who can neither be deceived nor deceive,' Denz. 1789. The Council of Trent had already

laid down as a first necessity for justification, faith in God's revealed promises, quoting St. Paul's 'without faith it is impossible to please God' (Denz. 798 and 801). Actually, the First Vatican Council was not directly concerned with the question of the necessity of the act of faith but engrossed instead with the necessity of faith as infused virtue, as distinct from the natural knowledge of God (Denz. 1811, and 1789, quoted above). On the theological elaboration of this pre-Vatican II authoritative teaching, cf. Lombardi, *Salvation*, pp. 54–65.

34. For a Catholic account of this controversy, cf. Maurice Nedoncelle, *Is There a Christian Philosophy?* (New York, 1961), esp. pp. 85–114, with an excellent survey of existing options on the question. Roger Mehl's *The Condition of the Christian Philosopher* (London, 1964) is a sound and representative Protestant statement of the interrelationship of faith and reason; cf. the chapter 'The Dialogue between the Theologian and the Philosopher,' pp. 194–207. Cf. also J. Baillie's *Our Knowledge of God* (New York, 1959); and one of the oldest veterans of the twentieth-century debate, Étienne Gilson, *The Philosopher and Theology* (Edgewood, 1961), esp. the chapters 'The Uninvited Handmaid' and 'Christian Philosophy,' pp. 154–199.

35. In the mid-nineteenth century Pius IX and the Roman Curia became alarmed at the widespread growth of rationalism and indifferentism and thereafter Church officials issued warnings and reaffirmations to guide Catholic thinking on the relation of faith and reason. Thus the papal allocution of 1854, insisting on the difference between sound theological method and the procedures of purely natural sciences (Denz. 1642), the condemnation of Frohschammer's teaching on the false autonomy of human reason (Denz. 1666 ff.), the letter to a German bishop in 1863, on dangerous and false notions of theological independence and progress (Denz. 1681), and Pius X on the false concept of reform in theological thinking attributed to the Modernists (1907, Denz. 2104), to cite but a few. More recently, Pius XII was concerned to lay down guidelines on the correct relationship of theological work to the Church's teaching authority and to point out certain erroneous and dangerous tendencies in the celebrated and controversial Encyclical *Humani generis* (1950). In the age after the Second Vatican Council, theologians have been reflecting on their function and place in the body of believers and re-examining the role of theology in the life of faith from a number of angles. Bernard Lonergan offers some sound suggestions in 'Theology in Its New Context,' and Yves M. J. Congar addresses himself to the same question in a different perspective in 'Theology's Task after Vatican II,' both in *Renewal of Religious Thought*, ed. L. K. Shook (New York, 1968), 1: 34–46, 47–65 (hereafter cited as Shook, *Renewal*).

36. The definition of faith in terms of a religious sense—much discussed and widely accepted throughout the nineteenth century after Schleiermacher—entered Catholic thinking in the first decade of the twentieth through that still obscure and confusing movement called Modernism. Pius X singled out this concept of the religious sense as particularly obnoxious and destructive of the transcendent and properly intellectual character of faith, reducing the Christian life to immanentist principles. The unique and divine origin of revelation is confused with the interior dictates of conscience and the person of Christ is stripped of its historical authenticity and salvific power. Cf. the excerpts from the Encyclical *Pascendi dominici gregis*, 1907, Denz. 2074–77, and for background and theological interpretation, the major article 'Modernisme,' by various authors in DictApolFoiCath 3: 612–630; and the comprehensive entry 'Modernism,' by J. J. Heaney, NCE 9: 991–995.

37. The Vatican Council of 1870 asserted, in a much-quoted text, the role of reason in the elucidation of supernatural truth, an assertion which has behind it many centuries during which Catholic theologians labored earnestly to work out a harmony of faith and reason, as part of the belief that grace perfects and does not destroy or compete with nature. Cf. Denz. 1796–1800.

38. The legal definition of heresy clearly distinguishes it from unbelief (CIC 1325.2); further, formal and material heresy are carefully identified, as the First Vatican Council recognizes (Denz. 1794). Today the difference between Catholics and other Christians, or even among Catholics, not all of whom share the same faith, is more difficult than ever to discern. Poor religious instruction, worldly influences of all kinds, a tepid and superficial spiritual life, all make the relationship of some Catholics to the Church, to the truth of the Gospel, as tenuous, unreal, and external as that of people who have never been Catholics. Cf. Karl Rahner, *On Heresy* (London, 1964), esp. ch. 2, 'The Traditional Concept of Heresy and the Heretic, and the Problems it Entails,' pp. 25–40.

39. The Council of Trent had to define more precisely the conditions under which justification is forefeited, in view of unacceptable doctrines touching on the nature and effects of original sin, concupiscence, and the relationship of grace to man's present state. Cf. ch. 15 of the fourth session (1547, Denz. 808). The Jansenists held that, when all love is lost, in grave sin, true faith is automatically lost and only its caricature remains: a proposition condemned by Alexander VIII (1690, Denz. 1302). Similar views, largely inspired by Jansenist thinking, had to be discounted again at the First Vatican Council (Denz. 1791).

40. Hans Küng traces the axiom back to Ignatius of Antioch, Irenaeus, Clement of Alexandria, and others, but ascribes its first complete

formulation, in negative terms, to Origen. Cyprian was the first to apply the axiom with juridical exclusiveness and its full consequences, and Küng notes that this extremist interpretation has consistently led to heresy and errors which the Church found it necessary to repudiate. Cf. the historical survey of the invocation of the formula in Hans Küng, *The Church* (New York, 1967), pp. 313–319.

41. Nels F. S. Ferré deplores the direction the rational defense of faith has taken, in pursuit of the modern mind led away from religion by the new world-outlook, the new secularist concepts of reason and nature. Much of Ferré's initial argument is for a more Biblical understanding of faith and a corresponding re-orienting of apologetics, toward the adequacy of a life fully responsive to the demands of the Gospel. His underlying claim is that faith fails so many who might otherwise be believers because they are put off by a massive façade of feverish, self-conscious apologetics behind which the reality of the faith-life is effectively hidden. *The Finality of Faith* (New York, 1953), esp. ch. 2, 'The Finding of Faith,' pp. 22–37. In the proximate future it is likely that theology will drastically reappraise the apologetic function, as part of an overall renewal of Christian self-understanding. Cf. Daniel Jenkins, 'Systematic Theology,' in *The Scope of Theology*, ed. Daniel Jenkins (Cleveland, 1968), pp. 96–110; and John H. Wright, 'Modern Trends in Theological Method,' in *Current Trends in Theology*, ed. Donald Wolf and James Schall (Garden City, 1965), pp. 32–57.

42. Cornelio Fabro, *God in Exile* (Westminster, 1968), p. 480. Fabro presents several examples of Catholic apologetical response to the irreligious philosophy of the French Enlightenment.

43. Session III, 1870 (Denz. 1782). In this formula the bishops of the Council were seeking to counteract two tendencies prevalent in late nineteenth-century thought, first that of a rationalism which made grace and revelation superfluous and unnecessary, and, second, that of traditionalism which held that man's power of reason was so weakened by sin that nothing could be known of God without revelation and grace. Cf. R. Garrigou-Lagrange, *God: His Existence and His Nature*, trans. Bede Rose (St. Louis, 1948), 1: 8–31. It was this mentality, prevailing at the Council, which met the challenge of Modernism in the first decade of the twentieth century. No tract in theology has undergone less real development, among Catholics at any rate, than that on God. If some Catholic theologians have begun, recently, to explore new ways of stating the problem of God, they are following a path, or paths, already beaten by others. The interest has shifted from establishing God's existence to the question of the meaningfulness of faith. Cf. Edward Schillebeeckx, 'Theology of Renewal Talks about God,' in Shook, *Renewal*, pp. 83–104.

44. Vacant, *Constitution du Concile*, p. 301, and Garrigou-Lagrange, *God*, pp. 10–11.

45. Cf. Jean Guitton: '. . . the characteristic mark of the epoch through which we are advancing now, and into which we have imperceptibly been moving for the last three hundred years, is that the faith is growing cold. There is today not enough religion left on earth to give rise to an explicitly religious heresy. One might think the end of the world is close at hand, if we are to attach a specific meaning to the moan of Jesus: "When the Son of Man returns, will he still find faith on earth?" ' *Great Heresies and Church Councils* (New York, 1965), p. 175. But Guitton, whose appreciation of the positive values of secular humanism is almost nil and whose confidence in the future of dialogue with non-believers is minimal, admits that it is difficult to tell to what extent faith has, in fact, disappeared. He observes, further, that 'we cannot readily determine how far the faith of preceding ages, when it coincided with institutions, was a true personal adherence or mere conformism. We shall never know. It is useless to ask ourselves these questions without answers: not even the men of the preceding ages whom we would have questioned could have given the answer,' p. 176.

46. I have made use of a number of historical and interpretative sources on the Council in general and *Gaudium et spes* in particular. Translations of the text of this Constitution are taken from the version published in Walter M. Abbott, ed., *The Documents of Vatican II* (New York, 1966).

47. *Gaudium et spes,* para. 3, in Abbott, *Documents*, p. 200. There points emerge in the Council's concern with the interdependence of sacred and secular: first, this is a concern of the People of God as such, fostered by their common co-presence and collective awareness; second, tension is bound to arise out of a courageous attempt to seek relevance, because too many have long been asleep or complacent, and third, faith includes the willingness to live in suspension between the lessons of the past and the demands of the future. This entire document should be read as the Church's understanding of its essential and intimate bond with the human family, in all its depth and amplitude. The problems of all men are, obviously, the concern of all believers, because they, too, are men and their faith must be lived in the one world.

48. The Pope continued: 'Never before, perhaps, so much as on this occasion, has the Church felt the need to know, to draw near to, to understand, to penetrate, serve and evangelize the society in which she lives; and to get to grips with it, almost to run after it, in its rapid and continuous change. This attitude, a response to the distances and divisions we have witnessed over recent centuries, in the last century and in our own especially, between the Church and secular society—this attitude has been strongly and unceasingly

at work in the Council; so much so that some have been inclined to suspect that an easy-going and excessive responsiveness to the outside world, to passing events, cultural fashions, temporary needs, an alien way of thinking . . ., may have swayed persons and acts of the ecumenical synod, at the expense of the fidelity which is due to tradition. . . .' Address of the Pope, public session, Dec. 7, 1965, in Xavier Rynne, *The Fourth Session* (New York, 1966), pp. 321–322. One need not puzzle as to the identity, in general, of those who expressed alarm at the Council's openness to the modern world. The Holy Father's language is guarded and sober enough to reveal at least a measure of similar concern and, more importantly, a concept of the world not altogether paralleled to that of the more outspoken realists and the renewalists at the Council. Good will and a sincere desire to make cordial and fruitful contact are beyond question.

49.   Pope Paul recognized from the first the importance of 'a completely new and disconcerting fact: the existence of militant atheism which is active on a world level,' a fact which he associated with the spiritual dialectic of the Council. Cf. the Apostolic Constitution *Humanae salutis*, Dec. 25, 1961.

50.   Abbott, *Documents*, pp. 215–220. These paragraphs distill the Council's definitive teaching on the subject of atheism, worked out and accepted overwhelmingly by the Fathers after considerable discussion, the highlights of which I shall report later in this section. Certain other conciliar texts contain briefer statements on closely allied topics; e.g., n. 22 of *Gaudium et spes* speaks of the need and duty to battle against evil through suffering and even death, and applies this not only to Christians but also to all men of good will in whose hearts grace works in an unseen way. Cf. also the Dogmatic Constitution on the Church, n. 16, which speaks of people who have not yet received the Gospel related in various ways to the people of God, and after mentioning the Jews, Moslems, and those who in shadows and images seek the Unknown God, declares that 'Those also can attain to salvation who through no fault of their own do not know the Gospel of Christ or His Church, yet sincerely seek God and moved by grace strive by their deeds to do His will as it is known to them through the dictates of conscience,' and more explicitly: 'Nor does divine Providence deny the helps necessary for salvation to those who, without blame on their part, have not yet arrived at an explicit knowledge of God and with His grace strive to live a good life. Whatever good or truth is found among them is looked upon by the Church as a preparation for the Gospel,' Xavier Rynne, *The Third Session* (New York, 1965), p. 309. Section 7 of the Decree on the Missionary Activity of the Church states that a man whom the Gospel message has not reached may have faith in some way. Preaching to unbelievers,

in a manner suited to their disposition, is urged as an important duty of bishops and priests, in the Decree on the Pastoral Office of Bishops in the Church, n. 11 and 13, and in the Decree on the Ministry and Life of Priests, n. 4.

51. Discussions and developments of the test of Schema 13 are fully recorded in the very valuable little work of Peter Hebblethwaite, *The Council Fathers and Atheism* (New York, 1967) (hereafter cited as Hebblethwaite, *The Council*), from which I have gathered a great deal of information, particularly on the interventions of the Council Fathers.

52. *Pacem in terris*, in Hebblethwaite, *The Council*, p. 18.

53. The Council clearly echoed Cardinal Silva's concept of a christocentric human vocation, a Christian humanism to answer the challenge of secularism. The ambiguity of social institutions was not always clearly recognized, unfortunately, in the sections of *Gaudium et spes* which dealt with social justice (n. 29), social ethics (n. 30), and responsible participation (n. 31). The shortsightedness was due in part to the Church's failure to appreciate the depth and extent of its own institutional involvement in the complexities of modern social life. The world, and not only that of the unbeliever, is more impressed by the Church's active witness to principles of man's dignity and freedom in society than by the reiteration of broad platitudes about the obvious facts of sociality.

54. This passage, from n. 16 of the document, has already been noted. The question of the salvation of the unbeliever is taken up in a later section of the present chapter.

55. In Hebblethwaite, *The Council*, p. 37. A major effect of Guerra Campos's intervention was to channel the thinking of the bishops toward finding the common grounds on which Church and unbeliever might meet. Emphasis would fall on legitimate aspirations, the deepest desire of all peoples for a decent, humanly satisfying existence, rather than on abstract ideas or systematic doctrinal differences. An empirical approach was adopted in the sociological survey of prevailing conditions which replaced a rather forbidding reassertion of orthodox principles of social ethics.

56. Alfrink's remarks were directed toward promoting solidarity among the family of nations (Article 25 of the schema) rather than immediately toward the problem of atheism. It was in this context that he turned to the subject of the Church's attitude toward Communism and urged a dialogue with all men of good will. No good could come from closing the doors to a dialogue, as would be the effect of the proposals of some of the Fathers who had demanded a restatement of former condemnations.

57. Karl Rahner, 'What Does Vatican II Teach about Atheism?' in *The Pastoral Approach to Atheism*, ed. Karl Rahner, vol. 23 of Concilium (New York, 1967), pp. 7–24. Rahner believes that the

Council could not avoid the question of a 'socially accepted, worldwide atheism' precisely because of its pastoral intent and desire to open itself to dialogue with the contemporary world. On the whole, nevertheless, and this is true even of *Gaudium et spes*, the bishops were neither so familiar with the actual mentality of today's unbeliever nor so avidly concerned with this problem that they managed to arouse a corresponding interest on the part of atheists. Reactions of the latter to the Church's new moves in the direction of openness will be discussed in the next chapter.

58. 'Too often—for example, when it is said that God is the only solution for all human problems—the language used seems to take for granted that every man today, whether believer or unbeliever, should obviously understand what is meant by the term "God," although the Pastoral Constitution itself declares that there are many people today to whom, in their own mind, religious language is wholly meaningless.' Rahner, 'What does Vatican II etc.?' p. 8. For divergent estimates of the present complex situation in this regard, cf. Leslie Dewart, *The Future of Belief* (New York, 1966); John Macquarrie, *God-Talk* (New York, 1967); and the chapter on 'Change in the Image of God,' in Thomas Sartory, *A New Interpretation of Faith* (Westminster, 1968), pp. 25–54. This is a small sampling of a literature growing to enormous size.

59. In an excellent epilogue to *God the Future of Man* (New York, 1968), Edward Schillebeeckx, O.P., reviews the major features of this problem and argues for a new approach to God as the One who is to come and who summons man to expend his own best efforts to build human community in this world, totally committed to the dignity which is his and to salvation here and now: 'Of course, this new concept of God implies a criticism of the earlier idea of God and of the concrete practice of Christian life that resulted from this idea of God. Anyone whose entire being is, culturally and religiously, oriented towards the past inevitably runs the risk of leaving the world as it is, of interpreting it, but not changing it. . . . Who could believe in a God who will make everything new "later" if it is in no way apparent from the activity of those who hope in the One who is to come that he is already beginning to make every thing new *now*, etc.,' p. 183.

60. Unbelievers are acutely conscious of their responsibility, personally and collectively, to fill the vacuum created by the loss of religious faith, in society and in the lives of individuals. The positive claims of unbelief are set forth in civilized, cogent terms by Karel Cuypers, a distinguished Belgian humanist: '. . . humanism must find ways to distinguish truth from poetic escape concerning the extensive mysterious areas of existence: the purpose of our birth and death, the absurdity of the destruction of one life to save another, the incomprehensible injustices and unfair distribution of misery in

human society. And is there anything more improbable than the existence of the universe? We can only accept the incomprehensible place of man in nature if we are totally impressed by what we feel as an immense overwhelming beauty. This is the purest form of religion, a religion free from authority, abuse, aggression, or presumption. It is found in varying degrees and forms in all people all over the world; it is responsible for man's tendency toward truth, beauty, and good.' 'The Humanist Response to the Problems and Aspirations of Men,' in *The Humanist*, 26 (Nov. and Dec. 1966), p. 185.

61. Ingo Hermann offers some 'utopian pointers between coexistence and pluralism,' an account of recent Marxist efforts to infuse a viable humanist ethos into Communist thinking and in particular of the confrontation of spokesmen for Marxist and Christian views at Salzburg (of which I shall have more in the next chapter), 'Total Humanism,' in *Is God Dead?* in *Concilium*, 16:157–178. More to the point are two other contributions to the same volume: Gaston Fessard, S.J., 'The Theological Structure of Marxist Atheism,' pp. 7–24, and Jürgen Moltmann, 'Hope without Faith: An Eschatological Humanism without God,' pp. 25–40, which is described as an essay toward a dialogue with 'esoteric Marxism.'

62. Jaroslav Krejci, 'A New Model of Scientific Atheism,' in *Concurrence*, 1 (Winter, 1969), p. 82. Krejci's outline is followed in the next two paragraphs and provides a useful statement of the latest and most sophisticated humanist-Marxist reasoning.

63. An apologetic that fails to persuade those toward whom it is directed, or at least that portion of men not already convinced by faith, can no longer be tolerated or propped up by periodic injections of topicality. Cf. Eugene Fontinell, 'Reflections on Faith and Metaphysics,' which calls for wholesale reform in the Catholic formulation of the problem of God and the defense of the reasonableness of Christian theism. Fontinell's is a carefully argued proposal for a radical change in our understanding of and relationship to the scriptural witness; his criticism of traditional apologetics is severe but not reckless; in *Speaking of God, Essays on Belief and Unbelief,* ed. Denis Dirscherl (Milwaukee, 1967), pp. 94–127. Schubert Ogden's criticism of apologetics is developed out of a twofold responsibility, to 'secure an appropriate interpretation of Scripture' and to 'mankind's search for an integral secular wisdom,' in 'The Strange Witness of Unbelief,' in *The Reality of God* (New York, 1966), p. 121.

64. A bright exception is James Collins, whose 'Tasks for Realistic Theism' begins with a hard look at human secularity and works toward an open religious humanism. Though he is very much at home with the traditional philosophical issues and fully appreciates the importance of what he calls 'the metaphysical difference,'

Collins proposes an integrative analysis of religion which is much broader in base than a speculative natural theology and takes seriously the dictum that all theology must be also anthropology. Collins' thoughts on a new theism are in his *Emergence of Philosophy of Religion* (New Haven, 1967), pp. 423–491 (hereafter cited as Collins, *Emergence*). On the humanist factor in religion, Walter Ong, S.J., comments: 'Instead of saying that this is an age when God is silent, it might be more accurate to say that it is an age in which man is silent about God, in great part because man has not assimilated to his knowledge of God the new knowledge of the physical universe which has been recently given him,' in 'American Culture and Morality,' Religious Education 58 (1963), p. 9. Further recommended reading on the subject: Martin D'Arcy, *No Absent God* (New York, 1962), on the mutual dependence of current ideas of God and of man; John Macmurray, *Persons in Relation* (New York, 1958), on religion as the celebration of interpersonal community among men and between men and God.

65. Daniel Callahan, 'The Risk of Faith,' *Commonweal*, 12 March 1965, p. 755.

66. Cf. W. H. van de Pol, *The End of Conventional Christianity* (New York, 1962), esp. chapter 10, 'Toward a Responsible Belief in God,' in which he draws six conclusions: (1) we are entering a new era of waiting for God in an eschatological sense; (2) belief in God will differ from that of conventional Christianity; (3) traces everywhere of the radical exclusivity of Karl Barth; (4) religion, Church, and theology will not escape transition in man's future-orientation; (5) in the post-ecumenical era a new and responsible belief in God is the issue; and (6) we are experiencing a collapse of a pantheon of all sorts of Christian and ecclesiastical idols, pp. 296–297. Van de Pol's work offers a convenient synthesis of much recent thought on the prospects of renewal in the light of rapidly accelerating cultural change. It covers part of the ground surveyed in Robert Adolfs' *The Church is Different* (London, 1966).

67. Introducing the problem which forms the subject matter of his work, an examination of the language and logic of theology, John Macquarrie writes: 'Theology is not only strange; it has become problematical in the modern world. What does it mean to talk about God at all? Impressed with the difficulty of returning a clear answer to this question, some theologians have proposed a theology without God. . . . Actually, much God-talk is probably dead. When we consider some of the theological disputes over which men got excited in the past, we find that perhaps most of them mean little or nothing to us. . . . We are more likely to wonder whether there are any correct answers at all, and our first step today would be to take a harder look at the questions themselves.

Are they genuine questions? Can we attach sense to the terms in which they have been formulated? . . . Can we find an intelligible sense for his [the theologian's] utterances? This is surely one of the most crucial problems in contemporary religious thought.' *God Talk*, pp. 11, 12, 13, 16.

68. Gabriel Vahanian, *The Death of God* (New York, 1961), pp. 194–195. 'Faith without works is dead—this is the way Christianity understood the relation of faith, of trust in God, with human obligations unto this world and its complex reality. Religion's existence was a mode of existence through which the world was *transfigured*, and with it all the pain as well as happiness it can offer. In the mentality of the revival there is an entirely different perspective. Religion is good, or faith is a good thing, because it works. And it works really only if the perplexing realities of this world are not transfigured but subjugated. Their subjugation is itself the test of a faith that works. . . . The recent temper of religiosity and the classical tradition stand at extreme opposites.'

69. The strongest and most typical thrust of contemporary humanism is toward the reconstruction of a world; it is active and creative, rather than contemplative or uplifting. Cf. Auguste Etcheverry, *Le Conflit actuel des humanismes* (Rome, 1964), pp. 5–20.

70. Charles Davis, *Theology for Today* (New York, 1962), in the chapter, 'With or Without Faith?' pp. 25–26. Davis himself offers an admirable response to this challenge in the chapter, 'The Mission of the Church,' in his excellent study, *God's Grace in History* (New York, 1967), pp. 89–124.

71. A generation ago, Joseph Wood Krutch, in the preface to *The Modern Temper* (New York, 1964), said of our age that one of its most distinguishing features was its inability to achieve either religious belief on the one hand or exultant atheism on the other. This ambiguity and indecisiveness seemed to continue into the late fifties, but I think that it is no longer the case. A line of major thinkers, including a number of prominent humanists, has accomplished precisely an exultant atheism, an atheism which competes with religious belief for the enthusiastic loyalties of the masses. Cf. Susan Anima Taubes, 'The Absent God,' in *Journal of Religion*, 35 (1955): 6–9.

72. Edward Hyams, 'Religion and Progress,' *New Statesman*, 11 February 1966, p. 189. Hyams concludes: 'How have those comebacks been accomplished? The clergy have an enormous advantage in a weakness nearly all of us share. *Timor mortis conturbat me*. . . . We remain afraid of death, and although most modern clerics are chary of making the extravagant promise about an after-life which used to be their best line, leaving such vulgar nonsense to the Spiritualists, yet the notions they propagate do still give a faint vague hope of continuance rather than extinction. On the day science

overcomes death you can probably shut the doors of church, chapel and synagogue; but not before.'

73. Thomas Merton, 'Is the World a Problem?' *Commonweal* (3 June 1966), p. 305. Merton strikes right to the heart of the matter: 'There remains a profound wisdom in the traditional Christian approach to the world as an object of choice. But we have to admit that the habitual and mechanical compulsions of a certain limited type of Christian thought have falsified the true value-perspective in which the world can be discovered and chosen as it is. To treat the world merely as an agglomeration of material goods and objects outside ourselves and to reject these goods and objects in order to seek others which are "interior" and "spiritual" is in fact to miss the whole point of the challenging confrontation of the world and Christ,' p. 309.

74. Quoted by Gary Schouberg in 'Secular Humanism and the Christian Faith,' *The Catholic World*, 51 (November, 1968): 69. I have made extensive use of the Schouborg article in defining the terms of confrontation between Christian and modern secular humanism.

75. Charles B. Ketcham has assembled materials from every branch of the contemporary arts and philosophy to document the extensiveness of this questioning and its increasing alienation from religious concern. In the chapter on 'The Revolt,' Ketcham identifies those who lead the search for an answer to man's profound self-questioning, and they do not include churchmen, theologians, or any spokesmen for institutional religion. The most articulate —perhaps also the most sensitive—are civil rights workers, peace marchers, radical student activists, anti-poverty workers, and a number of composers, painters, and literary artists. *The Search for Meaningful Existence* (New York, 1968), esp. pp. 19–57.

76. Samuel H. Miller argues for the religious responsibility for atheism with the assertion that the latter usually appears in the world as the void left by inadequate representations of God: 'When religion fails to give an adequate image of ultimate reality in the symbol God, then men, by reason of their honesty in the light of truth, must become atheistic and often in their atheism will affirm realities that are religious. God was not rejected in a satanic mood with unbridled gestures and profane heroics.' 'The Point of Religious Atheism,' *The Dilemma of Modern Belief* (London, 1964), p. 45 (hereafter cited as Miller, *Dilemma*).

77. There has been a keen interest in recent religious literature in the question of experience and reasons for believing and unbelieving. Cf. H. D. Lewis, *Our Experience of God* (London, 1959), esp. chapters 5 through 7, pp. 104–145; and, for an updated survey of the problem in its most important aspects, John E. Smith, *Experience and God* (New Haven, 1968), with a remarkably clear and incisive statement of the key issues, in the introductory chapter,

which concludes: 'It will never be possible in the end to argue and by sheer force of reason to settle a person in a religious faith. The ultimate roots lie deeper. But understanding has its own role to play and it is a role played by no other power in human life. It removes the sense of the strange and the untrustworthy, of the one-sided and the explicitly irrational. The major step in the recovery of God in the modern world will be taken when religion no longer appears to us as something foreign, embarrassing, and outworn, but rather as the ultimate fulfillment of human existence,' p. 20. Protestant thinkers have thus far shown a greater interest in the subject of religion and experience and its importance for the understanding of religious alienation than have Catholics. Robert Johann, S.J., is an exception, but he has not published a major work or collected his thoughts in a systematic article. One must hope for further contributions from Bernard Lonergan, S.J., besides the very brief piece, 'Openness and Religious Experience,' included in the volume *Collection,* ed. F. E. Crowe, S.J. (New York, 1968), pp. 198–201. Henri Niel, S.J., finds in Lonergan 'a combination of close contact with experience and an utter dedication to reason. He expresses fully the notion of theology as a confrontation with all other experience, with all the other sciences, in order to lead them all to God. What attracts him to St. Thomas is the discovery in the medieval theologian, admittedly in a very different cultural context, of the same openness to experience, the same confidence in reason.' 'The Old and the New in Theology,' in *Spirit as Inquiry*, ed. F. E. Crowe, S.J. (Chicago, 1965), pp. 180–181.

78. Michael Novak understands the role of personal encounter in making contact with the hidden God and the severe shortcomings of a theological approach which envisages God merely as the goal of our drive to understand, an 'impersonal "light,"' which betrays the essentially personal character of human understanding: *Belief and Unbelief*, pp. 107–109. Different, but not clashing, interpretations of the personalist character of faith are offered in Hans Urs von Balthasar, *The God Question and Modern Man* (New York, 1967), the first part of which outlines a new, personalist approach to religion, in preference to what he calls the 'cosmological approach' which has predominated heretofore, pp. 12–89; and Jean Mouroux, 'The Nature and Structure of Christian Faith,' in Mooney, *Toward*, pp. 68–104,

79. Gary Schouberg, 'Secular Humanism,' writes: 'Men commonly observe that one is never persuaded to love until he has experienced its reality through being loved first by another. Similarly, a human being will be persuaded to turn to Christ in prayer by two factors. The primary factor is the interior action of the Spirit. But this apparently never takes place totally separated from the secondary, social factor (a fact which is at the heart of the significance of the

K

Son's becoming *man*). One advised to pray will be reasonably skeptical to the extent that his counselor is himself dishonest, emotionally tied to his convictions, and afraid of truths that will possibly demand that they be abandoned; in short, if his life appears to be no better than those of people who deny any validity to prayer,' p. 74.

80. Schouborg, *ibid*.

81. Johannes B. Metz, 'The Future of Belief in a Hominized World,' in Mooney, *Toward*, pp. 300–320. Metz's article is a renewed reflection on the question treated in an earlier essay, 'A Believer's Look at the World,' in *The Christian and the World*, ed. Mooney et al. (New York, 1967), pp. 68–100. On the assumption that the believer must, by reason of the historical character of the Christian faith, seize each successive stage of history as a task, Metz finds the current world-awareness identical with a shift in man's thinking from nature to history, from the cosmos to man—a point alluded to above, in note 78. This personalism is inspired by the faith in the transcendence of God, in the redemptive Incarnation, and in man's responsible freedom. Faith has a future in a humanized (Metz's translators usually render this 'hominized') world, i.e., such a world-experience makes possible a distinctive faith-experience. One finds here further promising material for a theology of the religious significance of experience.

82. Arthur A. Vogel develops the theme that transcendence is not the bane of religion because it is the basis and not the nullification of the value and meaning of human existence and achievement. Behind, and responsible for, the inexorability of our drive beyond any given or conceivable state is the transcendent God, and in a well-developed argument Vogel contends: 'Contrary to popular expectation, many of the problems we have in religion come not from God's transcendence but from the fact that we will not let him be transcendent enough.' *The Next Christian Epoch* (New York, 1966), p. 87. Cf. the chapter entitled 'In Defense of God,' pp. 76–91.

83. The collection *Toward a Theology of Christian Faith*, ed. Mooney et al, from which I have quoted frequently, includes a fine trio of essays, the titles of which express clearly an appreciation of the ecclesial nature of faith-life: 'Credo Ecclesiam,' by Karl Rahner, S.J., on the role of the Church in the articulation of faith, pp. 134–152; 'Faith and Community,' by August Brunner, S.J., on faith as essentially formative of interpersonal community, pp. 244–260; and 'The Church, Milieu of Christian Belief,' by P. A. Liège, O.P., on the responsibility of the community in engendering and nourishing faith, especially in prospective and young believers, pp. 262–282.

84. David Jenkins' Bampton Lectures, published as *The Glory of Man* (New York, 1967), argues the thesis that our concern with the

dignity of personhood, respect for human rights, and the pursuit of personal fulfillment are all bound up with belief in Jesus Christ and the transcendent God.

85. Miller, *Dilemma*, p. 102, on the artificial situation created when religion concentrates unnaturally on being religious, posing and gesturing in its own mirror.

86. Rudolf Bultmann, *Primitive Christianity* (New York, 1961), p. 231. When a manifestation, a visible, experiential, showing-forth of the power and value of faith is demanded, it is borne home to the believer that his mode of existence is thoroughly paradoxical. Ronald Gregor Smith points to God's forgiveness as the supreme element in the subjective appropriation of faith, which yet leaves man in a condition which no purely natural phenomenology can ever penetrate: *Secular Christianity* (London, 1966), in a chapter on the non-empirical character of faith, pp. 56–57.

87. Cf. the contributions to a volume on new style in campus ministry, Albert H. Friedlander, ed., *Never Trust a God over 30* (New York, 1967), esp. the essays 'Religious Commitment on the Campus,' by Lyman T. Lundun, pp. 149–180; and 'The Silent Sixties?' by John H. Cushman and Lawrence Susskind, pp. 181–198.

88. The forms of irrelevance of the religious question on the problem of God are analyzed by Arnold Rademacher, in a section on the separation between religion and life, in his *Religion and Life* (Westminster, 1962), pp. 37–66. The history of the tension between religious and secular consciousness, developing eventually into the radical secularization of culture, is traced in several stages, with focus on the crucial century of Enlightenment. Rademacher exposes the inadequacy of a world-hating religiosity and an immanentist humanism, each of which, in diverse ways, promotes indifference to the religious question: pp. 100 ff.

89. On the strength of these empiricist restrictions, Ronald W. Hepburn intensifies and broadens a critique of religious language 'embarrassingly over-rich in metaphysical meanings and suggestions,' in *Objections to Humanism* (London, 1963), pp. 29–54. John E. Smith distinguishes three types of empiricism and charts the impact of each on the status of religious knowledge, *Religion and Empiricism* (Milwaukee, 1965). James Collins' remarks are directed to meeting the challenge of a restrictive definition of experience, *Emergence*, pp. 443–445.

90. Guy Swanson's article, 'Modern Secularity: Its Meaning, Sources, and Interpretation,' employs and analyzes the findings of several of the most competent sociologists to survey the extent and depth of religious indifference, particularly in American life. Swanson has amassed a formidable array of statistical information which he interprets largely as evidence of a wholesale decline of interest in the whole area of religious belief, practice, and affiliation. In *The*

Religious Situation, ed. Donald R. Cutler (Boston, 1968), esp. pp. 809–830.

91. 'Reflections on Religious Indifference,' in *The Pastoral Approach to Atheism,* vol. 23 of *Concilium,* pp. 61–63.

92. That is why the atheist sees an inseparable link between the denial of God and the affirmation of man in his new self-awareness. Man has used and exploited God, or rather faith in God, until He was of no use any more—until men saw through the farce of invoking God as a ready solution to perplexing problems. Cf. Nathan A. Scott, Jr., 'The Christian Understanding of Man,' in *Conflicting Images of Man,* ed. William Nicholls (New York, 1966), p. 28.

93. Cf. A. M. Henry, O.P., 'L'Athéisme d'aujourd'hui,' singles out the Marxists as untypical in this respect among contemporary unbelievers, both in the intensity of their preoccupation with religion and in the thoroughness with which they insert atheism into a comprehensive world-outlook, in Veuillot, *L'Athéisme,* pp. 45 ff.

94. This is a large part of the case made currently against a 'God of the gaps,' by those who call for a renovated Christian theism in a world in which men have managed to eliminate many sources of anxiety and to deal effectively, through natural means and the employment of secular resources, with other insecurities and frustrations. The literature on this subject is vast; cf. selections from Altizer, van Buren, Cox, Hamilton, Robinson, and Vahanian, in *Radical Christianity,* ed. Lonnie D. Kliever and John H. Hayes (Anderson, 1968), esp. pp. 126–151.

95. Girardi, 'Reflections,' p. 67.

96. Robert Adolfs, O.S.A., *The Grave of God* (New York, 1967), pp. 79–80. Adolfs adds: 'Of course, there are people who see through this ideological background to our life today, but they are only relatively few in number and are powerless as individuals to do anything about it. All these assumptions are accepted by the great majority of people as a normal climate in which to live. . . . This is the great strength of the social ideology of the Western world today—it is anonymous and hidden. A clearly defined ideology is much more vulnerable, because it is exposed to criticism,' pp. 80–81.

97. W. H. van de Pol defines 'conventional Christianity' in terms of faith-tenets, piety, morality, and general world-attitude, and bids it farewell in a series of analyses of the changed image of world and man. His conclusion comprises background, aspects, and prospects of a belief in God responsive to the needs and sensibilities of modern post-religious man, *The End of Conventional Christianity.*

98. This episode is reproduced, with comment, by L. Patrick Carroll, S.J., in his contribution 'Faith in the Church: the Modern Problem,' in *Faith in the Face of Doubt,* ed. John P. Keating, S.J. (New York, 1968), pp. 74–75.

99. Daniel Jenkins contrasts honest and dishonest doubt and in

answer to the question, what are the tests of honest doubt, writes: 'The first is that such doubt should be existential . . . genuinely engaged on the level of experience appropriate to the subject of his [the doubter's] enquiry. In relation to God, of course, this means the most fundamental level of all. His doubt will not be honest unless he finds himself fighting for his life. Not all the judgments which men are required to make concerning the Christian faith are of this character. But the closer man comes to the heart of the encounter of faith, the more existential does his engagement become. Yet this test is inadequate without the other. This is that the doubter must continue, in his doubt, to be sustained by a spirit of love,' *Beyond Religion* (London, 1963), pp. 64–65.

100. Robert Johann, in *The Pragmatic Meaning of God* (Milwaukee, 1966), reproduces the argument, commonly heard today, that godlessness is not the conclusion of a syllogism but arises primarily from a new and positive self-awareness on the part of contemporary man. It is a new way of life that is involved and not a philosophy or a deliberate decision. Johann analyzes the notion of quality of life, identifies what he takes to be the prevailing, felt quality and attempts to construct a theism in harmony with that quality.

101. Nicholas Berdyaev comments on man's awareness of a loss which makes his life seem essentially meaningless and of his longing for meaning: 'There is a craving for belief in modern man. . . . Faced with the futility of his own existence, the modern European finds himself stranded high and dry. The trouble is not, of course, political in the narrow sense. It concerns what are known as the bourgeois values of life. These values have created an appalling vacuum in the mind and heart of modern man. The vacuum is still there and, as it appears, historical Christianity, no less than politicians, fails to fill it,' *Dream and Reality* (New York, 1959), p. 326. Cf. the entire chapter on the restless and dissatisfied unbelief characteristic of a large segment of twentieth-century intellectuals, 'The Age of Longing,' in Franklin L. Baumer, *Religion and the Rise of Scepticism* (New York, 1960), pp. 187–229.

102. Cf. the outstanding article by Friedrich Wulf, S.J., 'Do the Churches Show the Future Joy of Christians?' in *The Gift of Joy*, vol. 39, of Concilium, pp. 99–111. Also the excellent chapter on 'Christianity: A Message of Joy,' in Albert Dondeyne, *Faith and the World* (Pittsburgh, 1963), pp. 26–63.

103. Peter Schoonenberg, S.J., offers a concise history of the concept of salvation, the varied experiences of men awaiting and expecting to be saved, and the series of events culminating in the fullness of Christ by which the union between God and man is finally accomplished. *God's World in the Making* (Pittsburgh, 1964), pp. 62–105.

104. 'Christianity is not the only message of salvation that the world has known. All great religions announce themselves as bringing

a message of salvation. The Christian believer must not take offense at the fact that there are other religions besides Christianity and that some are even older than Christianity. For they are expressions of that pre-Christian religious longing which Christianity needs in order that its message might find a resonant echo in the soul.' Albert Dondeyne, *Contemporary Christian Faith and European Thought,* trans. Burnheim et al. (Pittsburgh, 1958), p. 34.

105. Küng is not sanguine about the continued usefulness of the formula; he recommends: (1) commemorating the phrase in dogmatic theology as an expression of Catholic tradition; (2) passing it over in preaching, as little understood or misunderstood today, *Church,* p. 138.

106. Denz. 1647.

107. Dogmatic Constitution on the Church, n. 16, in Rynne, *The Third Session,* p. 309.

108. Küng, *Church,* p. 316.

109. The questions on the virtue, causes, and effects of faith, in the secunda secundae of the *Summa Theologiae,* are followed by three questions on the vices contrary to faith. Question 10 is on unbelief in general and includes articles on such topics as the relative magnitude of the sin of unbelief (the answer on this point is remarkably nuanced and laced with careful distinctions), the social status of the unbeliever, and his civil rights in a Christian community. Heresy and apostasy from faith are treated each in a single question (11 and 12); blasphemy is a sin against confession of faith (13); and ignorance and dullness of mind are opposed to the gifts of knowledge and understanding which perfect our grasp of faith (14). On the spiritual condition of the unbeliever cf. q. 10, art. 5: the presumption throughout all of these articles is that the Gospel has been sufficiently announced; otherwise, ignorance excuses or diminishes culpability.

110. Decree on the Missionary Activity of the Church (*Ad Gentes*), n. 7, in Abbott, *The Documents of Vatican II*, p. 593.

111. The Rahner sources are listed conveniently by Klaus Riesenhuber in his afterword, 'The Anonymous Christian according to Karl Rahner,' in Anita Röper, *The Anonymous Christian* (New York, 1966), which is inspired by Rahner's thinking but is an original essay arguing persuasively its own thesis. The bibliographical information is on pp. 172–173.

112. Maurice Eminyan, S.J., produced a synthesis of theological views on salvation in which an amazing array of authors was presented and their positions analyzed and tabulated. Eminyan's volume, *The Theology of Salvation* (Boston, 1960), distills the opinions of perhaps fifty theologians of recent vintage and some stature and concentrates on just two major issues in the problem of salvation,

namely, the possibility of faith among infidels and the relation of non-Catholics to the Church. The question involves a great many dogmatic and doctrinal points, some of which are still controverted; it is true that Eminyan's book antedates the Council, but one can see in the positions adopted at Vatican II developments, refinements, and in some instances rejections of the opinions which had accumulated over a period of many decades. It may be said that the Council did not ignore or override these theological efforts which contributed substantially to the enlightenment of the Church generally and of the bishops in particular.

113. The theology of salvation considers only the de facto order willed by God, which is that of man's vocation to eternal life through grace in Christ. A debate was carried on, not completely in the open or with full candor, because of severe ecclesiastical censorship and pressure, with regard to the possibility of a natural end, the natural desire to see God and the whole complex relationship of natural and supernatural. The controversy petered out but not many firm conclusions or generally accepted clarifications were reached; as it stands, there is no sound theological reason for discussing salvation in terms other than those which have been employed traditionally in official statements and theological discourse. Cf. the interpretation of this problem by P. Schoonenberg, *Het Gelook van ons Doopsel* (Nijmegen, 1966), vol. 3, pp. 90 ff.

114. Lombardi has the most comprehensive treatment of the indispensability and possibility of faith, comprising two-thirds of his volume on *The Salvation of the Unbeliever*. It will be difficult to surpass this extended essay on what is the central issue in the theology of salvation.

115. Cf. Karl Rahner, *Lexikon für Theologie und Kirche*, vol. 4, p. 998, and *On the Theology of Death*, pp. 96–104.

116. Theodore Steeman, O.F.M., examines man's existential need for moral purity, i.e., uprightness of conscience, and his relation to God: 'Psychological and Social Aspects of Modern Atheism,' in *The Pastoral Approach to Atheism*, vol. 23 of Concilium, pp. 49–52. Rahner has it that an implicit act of faith is made in 'the silent gentleness of patience in the performance of one's daily duty,' in 'the constant preference given to the good in any particular sphere of morals.' 'Thoughts on the Possibility of Belief Today,' in *Theological Investigations*, vol. 5, p. 17.

117. Rahner, 'What Does Vatican II Teach about Atheism?' in *The Pastoral Approach to Atheism*, pp. 18–19.

118. Rahner remarks that the Council, while teaching that there is a guilty as well as a guiltless atheism, did not spell out the sense in which the former can be really related to God. Nor did it make clear why salvation and faith are compatible with such an atheism. Rahner's distinction of categorical and transcendental elucidates

this aspect of the situation for which the conciliar teaching makes only a general and unspecified allowance. Rahner's position is expounded fully in 'Atheism and Implicit Christianity,' which is included in the special number of *Theology Digest*, February, 1968, pp. 43–56.

119. Eminyan identifies four possible interpretations of the doctrine of the possibility of faith among infidels, and reports the various versions of each adopted by leading theologians. The possibilities are as follows: (1) that there are positive supernatural values in false religions—this point is not extended to explore the analogies in non-religious moral commitment; (2) that a special divine intervention is granted the unbeliever, by way of an interior inspiration, a view that has not found wide support; (3) that a decisive moral-spiritual choice is made as the first mental act at the 'dawn of reason,' a view which has an impressive number of supporters of considerable distinction; and (4) that the grace of faith is offered at the sunset of life or at the moment of death: much has been made of the supreme importance of death, but Rahner's theory bypasses the question, although he has himself written movingly and profoundly on the subject in other contexts. Eminyan, *Salvation*, pp. 27–94.

120. Johannes B. Metz, 'Unbelief as a Theological Problem,' in *The Church and the World*, vol. 6 of Concilium (New York, 1965), p. 59. Metz's conceptualization of the problem has greatly influenced my thinking on the subject and suggested lines of development which I have followed in this section on the unbelief of believers. Metz refers to the writings of Lacroix, on contemporary man's a-religious self-understanding, de Lubac on those whose conscience will not permit them to believe, Rahner on the anonymous Christian, and Schillebeeckx on implicit Christianity. I have benefitted greatly from the thinking of all of these authors.

121. Cf. Jean Lacroix, *The Meaning of Modern Atheism* (Dublin, 1965); thematic atheism is today the presupposition rather than the precise object of unbelief, pp. 18–19. Metz links this a-theistic existence with the humanist projects of Feuerbach and Marx, in which philanthropy and class solidarity, respectively, are substituted for religious concern, 'Unbelief,' p. 60.

122. Henry Bars, *The Assent of Faith* (Baltimore, 1960), on the antinomies of faith, pp. 8–12. Cf. also Romano Guardini, 'Faith and Doubt,' in Heaney, *Faith*, pp. 24–41: faith must face crises because it is a form of constant overcoming, in face of change in environment, human concepts, personal tragedy, and scientific and moral difficulties, and the beautiful and powerful thoughts on God as the incomprehensible mystery of human existence, in Karl Rahner, S.J., *Belief Today* (New York, 1967), pp. 111–114.

123. A world where faith keeps the life of man open and resonant to

larger realities, to the past and to the transcendent, even a secular world is not without grace; it is, then, simply the world waiting for its full meaning. Resonance for the transcendent, which is the essence of faith, is the place where, if there is any meaning in freedom or in the future or in grace, it must occur. Samuel Miller, *Dilemma*, pp. 92–94, describes the victimization of faith, its enslavement, by a smooth but vacuous interpolation of traditional clichés and pious patter.

124. Gabriel Marcel is the great twentieth-century philosopher of fidelity; his sustained meditations on what it means to be faithful might serve admirably for a theological essay on this aspect of the believer's commitment and the unbeliever's moral resolve. Cf. Marcel's *Being and Having, Du réfus à l'invocation*, and the sources tapped by Kenneth T. Gallagher, *The Philosophy of Gabriel Marcel* (New York, 1962), pp. 68–73.

125. Cf. Paul Tillich, *The Courage to Be* (New Haven, 1960), in which he speaks of God above God in terms very much like those denounced by the Church at various stages of its history. The Gnostics spoke, in effect, of a god, or of several gods, beyond the God revealed in and by Jesus Christ. Mystics have often been fascinated by the 'beyond' in God, yet the real root of the insight lies deeply in the soil of Christian history, and it can be of the greatest assistance to the Church in trying to discern the will of God today, pp. 182–190.

126. Metz, 'Unbelief,' p. 68.

127. Catholic theology is able to rejoin certain streams of Reformation thought in a doctrine of concupiscence in which the radical nature and absolute interiority of temptation are given their full weight. Cf. Karl Rahner's essay on the theology of concupiscence in *Theological Investigations*, vol. 1 (Baltimore, 1960), pp. 347–382, and his interpretation of the threat of unbelief to faith already possessed as a Catholic version of *simul fidelis et infidelis, Gerecht und Sünder Zugleich*, p. 437.

128. Pope St. Pius V condemned as one of the errors of Baius, a Jansenist before the event, the contention that the stirrings or promptings of concupiscence are actually sins (1567, Denz. 1050, 1074). Cf. the perceptive comment of William F. May, *A Catalogue of Sins* (New York, 1967), pp. 11–12.

129. Assessing the responsibility on the part of Christians for the 'scandal' of unbelief, Samuel Miller complains that we have stripped God of His majesty, trapped Him in nets of ideas, cornered Him ecclesiastically, dressed Him in our vanity, and trained Him to acknowledge our tricks and bow to our ceremonial expectations. The iconoclasts cleared out a great deal of the rubbish of superstition, but they prepared the way for empty abstractions to take the place of a real God. *Dilemma*, pp. 45–49.

130. Carlos Cirne-Lima attempts a phenomenology of the interpersonal

L

structure of faith: *Personal Faith* (New York, 1965), pp. 20–60, and an analysis of its metaphysical nature, pp. 135–167.

131. Hans Urs von Balthasar states that the philosophical penetration of intersubjectivity has yet to be made, and this lag hampers the unfolding of the theology of the interpersonal character of faith, *Glaubhaft ist nur Liebe*, reproduced as 'Only Love is Believable,' in Mooney, *Towards*, pp. 126–131.

132. Paul Matussek, 'The Function of the Sermon with Regard to Repressed Unbelief in The Believer,' in *The Pastoral Approach to Atheism*, vol. 23 of Concilium, pp. 112–121.

133. Paul Hanley Furfey, *The Respectable Murderers* (New York, 1967), esp. the concluding chapter, 'The Strong Delusion,' which explains how prejudice and attachment to personal and group interests blind one to the moral demands inherent in authentic faith.

134. Matussek, 'The Function,' p. 119.

135. Gabriel Vahanian was one of the first American writers to make us aware of the depth and extent of our responsibility for the disaffection of masses from Christian faith. His contention has been that many nominal Christians are concerned with idols rather than with the living God and, further, that the rapidly spreading unbelief bears strongly, if not overwhelmingly, on idols rather than God. By idolatry Vahanian means inserting the personal ego at the center of religion, using God as a means, replacing God's unfaltering fidelity by human securities, such as a tradition, ecclesiastical authority, orthodoxy, convention, anything which can be easily ascertained and manipulated. God's grace alone can preserve man from succumbing to the allurement of idols—and that grace is not denied the sincere, upright unbeliever: *No Other God* (New York, 1966), esp. chap. IV, 'The Word of God and the World of Man,' pp. 37–63.

136. I turn again, gratefully, to Karl Rahner, for a splendid set of reflections on 'Intellectual Integrity and Christian Faith,' in *Belief Today*. 'One might say that a person of intellectual integrity wants to get to the heart of things, that he is impartial in assessing the difficulties inherent in a universal viewpoint today, and that he is ready to accord intelligence and good will to a person of conflicting opinions. He has the courage to change his convictions at times, avoids fanaticism, and seeks "coolness" and "objectivity" in his decisions. He examines his own position just as critically as the position of others. He takes into account the prejudices which he may have acquired through the spirit of his time, his social class, his education, his own profession, yes, even through his own innate or social advantages, and feels constrained to do his utmost to overcome them and the ideologies that go with them,' pp. 93–94.

137. Olivier A. Rabut has produced an essay noteworthy for its frank and bold coming to grips with an issue badly mishandled in the

history of theology. *Faith and Doubt* (New York, 1967) seizes directly the contemporary passion for verification and moves then to a patient, sympathetic inquiry into the place of doubt in the life of faith and of the doubter in the community life of believers.

138. Cf. the two essays by James A. Mohler, S.J., 'Thinking with Assent: the Theology of Faith of St. Augustine, an Interpretation,' and 'The Dynamic Faith of Thomas Aquinas,' in Dirscherl, *Speaking*, pp. 1–27.

139. Rabut undertakes a brief but quite able and conscientious examination of the responsibilities of a theological appraisal of the problem of doubt or suspension of belief, a task not yet undertaken in earnest, *Faith*, pp. 13–20.

140. Or, more to the point, the professional theologian seriously and conscientiously critical of prevailing 'official' doctrine. The issuance of the papal encyclical *Humanae vitae*, on the regulation of birth, aroused a storm of controversy unprecedented in the present century and led to an intense discussion of the rights and limits of theologians to dissent from magisterial positions in the pursuit of their discipline. Karl Rahner, as one would have expected, wrote a comment on the encyclical which spelled out with great precision the terms of this problem, an essay of far-reaching importance translated and reprinted in *The National Catholic Reporter*, 18 September 1968, pp. 6–7. One should consult an earlier article by Rahner, occasioned by a letter in the summer of 1966 in which a Vatican Cardinal complained of dangerous tendencies in contemporary Catholic theology, 'Theology and the Magisterium after the Council,' in *Theology Digest*, February, 1968, pp. 4–16.

141. The complete passage about faith and works from chapter 2 of James:

'What will it profit, my brethren, if a man says he has faith, but does not have works? Can the faith save him? And if a brother or sister be naked and in want of daily food, and one of you say to them, "Go in peace, be warmed and filled," yet you do not give them what is necessary for the body, what does it profit? So faith, too, unless it has works, is dead in itself. But someone will say, "Thou hast faith, and I have works." Show me thy faith without works, and I from my works will show thee my faith. Thou believest that there is one God. Thou dost well. The devils also believe, and tremble. But dost thou want to know, O senseless man, that faith without works is useless? Was not Abraham our father justified by works, when he offered up Isaac his son upon the altar? Dost thou see that faith worked along with his works, and by the works the faith was made perfect? And the Scripture was fulfilled which says, "Abraham believed God, and it was reckoned to him as justice, and he was called the friend of God (Gen 15.6)." You see that by works a man is justified, and not by faith only. In like manner was not Rahab the harlot also justified by works, when she welcomed the messengers and sent them out another way (Jos 2.4)? For just as the body without the spirit is dead, so faith also without works is dead.'

142.   Cf. the chapter 'Indirect Believing,' in the Biblical study by Ingo Hermann, *The Experience of Faith* (New York, 1966), pp. 96–104.

143.   Quentin Lauer, 'The Problem of Unbelief,' in *Thought*, 40, no. 4 (Winter, 1967), p. 511.

144.   I should like to quote again from another of Quentin Lauer's articles, 'Catholics and Freedom of Thought': 'The problem comes at a level of what we might call clerical or ecclesiastical thinking, which may or may not be genuinely authoritative. Concretely— if somewhat crudely—the question might be asked: to what extent can a good Catholic disagree with the party line? Is there room for independent thinking in matters theological, to say nothing of the philosophical, the scientific, or the artistic? The complaint is not entirely groundless that priests tend to do our thinking for us, even in non-religious matters, that they will make decisions for us, where our own consciences should be the arbiters,' in *Thought*, 38, no. 151 (Winter, 1963), p. 517. Father Lauer's complaint has a historical validity but is clearly outdated at a time, some six years after the appearance of his article, when priests are hard put to come to many firm, unclouded conclusions of their own, much less to impose them on others.

145.   Faith is historical in the dual sense that it arises as a consequence of certain events in history and in the sense that its shape and content are determined by these events. Faith has to do, certainly, with God's existence as inserted into and affecting the direction and meaning of human history; faith itself is, immediately and essentially, bound up with historical existence. The inescapably historical character of the believer's understanding of faith, and of theology's progressive development, stem directly from this faith-condition. Cf. J. McIntyre, *The Christian Doctrine of History* (Princeton, 1955), on the centrality of history in theology's self-understanding, esp. pp. 3–11, and the chapter, 'History as a Two-Phased Plan in a Divine Teleology,' in the scholarly monograph, *History, Time, and Deity*, by S. G. F. Brandon (London, 1965), a comparative study of the conception of time in religious thought and practice, pp. 148–205, with abundant source materials cited.

146.   Cf. Hans Jonas, *Gnosis und Spätantiker Geist* (Tübingen, 1964); also R. Mc L. Wilson, *The Gnostic Problem* (London, 1964), esp. pp. 132–135.

147.   Cf. the chapter, 'God and Mythology,' in Martin D'Arcy, *No Absent God* (New York, 1962), pp. 116–131.

148.   The section on morality in the chapter on 'Conventional Christi-

anity' in one of the finest in W. H. van de Pol's *The End of Conventional Christianity*, pp. 39–45. The author asks the provocative question: has not the great seriousness with which conventional Christianity has tried to bring *faith* into agreement with the testimony of the Bible been in inverse proportion to the slight efforts made to inculcate a life of faith in the truth of Jesus?

149. 'Properly understood, the responsibility of the theologian to speak understandably allows for offensive as well as defensive moves in his discussion with those who do not share his first duty to secure an appropriate interpretation of Scripture. What is required of him is not that he conform his claims to the secular thought of his situation, but that he establish their validity in terms of the same general standards of experience and reason to which that thought itself is subject. I hold that this requirement is more or less clearly implied by the very nature of the scriptural witness. In confessing that Jesus is the Christ, and, indeed, the very *Logos* of reality (John 1), Scripture implies that the truth he decisively re-presents is somehow of a piece with whatever truth men know anywhere,' Schubert M. Ogden, *The Reality of God* (New York, 1966), p. 121.

Notes to Chapter Three

1. Canon Jérôme Régnier links the choice of atheism to the exigencies of a fuller personal life, the overcoming of alienation, social integration, and finding roots in the cosmos, and concludes that the negative factor, the denial or rejection of God, has been considerably eclipsed in atheism's new look, 'Appelo et refus de l'homme moderne,' in the collection *Visages et approches de l'incroyance,* ed. H. Holstein, S.J. (Lyon, 1945), pp. 69–91.
2. On the distinction between security and certitude, to which reference has already been made, cf. Georg Muschalek, S.J., 'Faith, Freedom, and Certitude,' in *Toward a Theology of Christian Faith*, ed. Mooney, et al. (New York, 1966), pp. 181–182. Security is carefreeness, whereas certitude has to do with having sure knowledge. Faith is certain but struggles in the midst of threat, gains its knowledge in and from this struggle; the certitude of faith derives from a firm determination, a decision which liberates the believer from doubt but not necessarily from care and fear. Neither in the life of the individual nor in its movement through history is faith privy to a security with respect to its goal or to its own integrity. This is the clear teaching of St. Paul, in several places, e.g., Phil 2.12–16; 3.12–14; Eph 2.2; 2 Cor 5.7.
3. Henry Bars, *The Assent of Faith* (Baltimore, 1960), p. 17. These are precisely the aspects or features of Christian faith experienced most

intensely in the present age: cf. the perceptive essay of Vincent Ryan Ruggiero, 'The Fabric of Modern Faith,' in *The Catholic World*, 52: no. 3 (March, 1969), pp. 255–258; and two important conclusions in particular: first, that the believer may learn, from the unbeliever even, that formal assent to a body of doctrines is not necessarily to identify with Christ and His message, and, secondly, that to win the minds and hearts of men the Church must meet the world without pretending that all its pronouncements are final, without claiming freedom from human error. Ruggiero raises a real issue, without pursuing adequately its complexities, when he suggests that although denial of church teachings may in some cases represent a lack of love, in other cases affirmation of those teachings may represent substituting idolization of words for love of people. Is this a purely tendentious and false antithesis?

4. For a provocative and enlightening analysis of the varieties of belief, as interpreted from the results of careful demographic and sociocultural investigations, cf. Martin Marty, Stuart Rosenburg, and Andrew Greeley, *What Do We Believe?* (New York, 1968). Trends are noted, particularly those in which traditional orthodoxies are eroded; the most significant changes in recent years have involved relationships to and within the institutional churches, rather than flat-out denials of major doctrinal tenets. To me this suggests the importance of pursuing the question of the credibility of Christians, of their Church, and not only that of their faith in God and Christ, etc. This cooperative study is exactly the sort of hard research by social scientists of which the theology of unbelief can make such profitable use.

5. Thomas Clarke, S.J., searches the positive values which Christian secularity is finding outside the institutional Church: 'The World Is Already Christic,' *America* (29 May 1965), pp. 800–803.

6. The substance of these thoughts formed the main body of a paper prepared by the author at the request of the Vatican Secretariat for Non-Believers. I have been guided consciously by the provisions set forth in the conciliar Decree on Priestly Formation (*Optatam totius*), a document prepared with delicate concern for the true image of the Church.

7. Yves Congar, O.P., 'Theology in the Council,' in *The American Ecclesiastical Review*, 155, no. 4 (October, 1966), pp. 217–230. Congar surveys the actual situation, the directions theologians are likely to follow in the immediate future, in 'Theology's Tasks after Vatican II,' in *Renewal of Religious Thought*, ed. L. K. Shook, C.S.B. (New York, 1968), vol. 1, pp. 47–65.

8. Cf. Henri Bouillard, S.J., *The Logic of Faith*, esp. the introductory chapter on 'The Nature of Apologetics' (New York, 1967), pp. 11–36.

9. Charles Moeller, 'Renewal of the Doctrine of Man,' in Shook, *Renewal*, pp. 420–463.

10. In the essay cited, in Shook, *Renewal*, pp. 427–437, Moeller makes extensive use of the article by P. Watte, 'Êtes-vous structuraliste?' in *Revue Nouvelle*, 45 (1967), pp. 653–662, a very informative précis of the theories of Levi-Strauss and Lacan.

11. Moeller examines the categories of thought underlying the Christian theology of man, the Hebrew and Greek N.T., and explores the proper kerygmatic sense of anthropological themes in theology, Shook, *Renewal*, pp. 447–458. Within this framework he proceeds to sketch several perspectives important in the development of a Christian doctrine of man.

12. William A. Van Roo, S.J., 'Talk about God,' in *America* (14 May 1966), pp. 691–694. (Hereafter cited as Van Roo, 'Talk.') The author is recommending the witness of Scripture, insights gained in theological questioning, and a spirit of humility and understanding to those who propose to join unbelievers in dialogue.

13. In response to the question of how we can talk about God in a way that makes sense to modern man, Van Roo emphasizes that there is no one way, that our choice of which ways will depend on whom we are talking with and what we are trying to tell him, in 'Talk,' p. 692.

14. John Courtney Murray, S.J., *The Problem of God* (New Haven, 1964), esp. the section on the Thomist problem, pp. 66–76, where St. Thomas Aquinas is identified as consummating the process of intellectual transposition begun at the early Church councils by the Fathers.

15. 'For the signs of revelation to be understood for what they are, the subject must grasp that there is an intrinsic relationship between the mystery which they are said to manifest and our own existence. The subject must at least glimpse what the Christian faith contributes to the fulfillment of his destiny. No apologetic will touch him if it does not in some way achieve this.' Henri Bouillard, S.J., 'Human Experience as the Starting Point of Fundamental Theology,' in *The Church and the World*, vol. 6 of Concilium, ed. Johannes B. Metz (New York, 1965), p. 87.

16. Because God remains hidden and inaccessible, even in the depths of His revelation, Gregory of Nyssa takes the life of Abraham as a central *leitmotif* of the life of faith, the image and type of the exodus through which men must push forward ceaselessly toward a God who remains ever hidden. Perhaps the first lesson of unbelief, Jean Daniélou notes, is to remind us of the inaccessibility of God; cf. his *Platonisme et théologie mystique. Grégoire de Nysse* (Paris, 1950), pp. 90–91.

17. The study of atheism envisages both the person (phenomenological) and the doctrine (systematic); while the approach should not lose contact with the concrete, it is equally important not to lose sight of the different kinds of atheism, to classify the attitudes

that people assume in practice into definite thought-patterns, Moeller, in Shook, *Renewal*, p. 27. The sometimes startling complexity of actual forms of unbelief is brought out in Dorothee Sölle's provocative study, *Atheistisch an Gott glauben* (Munich, 1967), esp. pp. 77–96.

18. Cf. A. Vergote, 'Anthropological atheism,' in *Psychologie religieuse,* pp. 277–284, atheism today is as much the affirmation of man as the denial of God. C. Moeller, *Littérature du XXe siècle et christianisme,* in several volumes, and, more succinctly, 'Aspects de l'atheisme dans la littérature moderne,' in *L'Ateismo contemporaneo,* ed. J. Girardi; and Paul Ricoeur, *Finitude et culpabilité,* esp. pp. 218–243.

19. Charles Moeller has written a theological critique of Sartre's *Words,* in the ninth edition of his *La Foi en Jesus Christ.* Sartre's comments about God's staring at him are extremely revealing and are always linked with his passion for capturing a freedom from every transcendent norm; cf. *The Words* (Greenwich, 1966), pp. 100–103, and on this, Régis Jolivet, *Sartre: The Theology of the Absurd* (Westminster, 1967), pp. 32–34.

20. The quotation, from O'Casey's *Sunset and Evening Star,* is in Georges Morel's contribution to the section 'Les images de Dieu,' of the collection *Dieu aujourd'hui,* ed. Olivier Lacombe, p. 188. He reads this text as accusing Christianity of being one of the chief causes of the world's misfortune and unhappiness, in support of Freud's thesis that religion, and the Christian faith in particular, diverts men's energies to an imaginary realm of eternal salvation. Marcuse's complaint is spelled out in *Eros and Civilization* (New York, 1964), p. 71.

21. Cf. Cardinal Emmanuel Suhard, 'The Meaning of God,' in *The Church Today,* a collection of his writings, ed. Louis J. Putz, C.S.C. (Chicago, 1953), pp. 173–216. Suhard's pastorals and addresses, dating back to the early 1940's, are still brilliant and incisive commentaries on the most pressing spiritual problems. Bonhoeffer notes: 'There is no longer any need for God as a working hypothesis; whether in morals, politics, or science. Nor is there any need for such a God in religion or philosophy (Feuerbach),' *Prisoner for God* (London, 1965), p. 163. Bonhoeffer sees the abandonment of the 'god of explanation' as the result of man's acceptance of responsibility for the world and the sign of his 'coming of age.'

22. Karl Rahner, 'In Search of a Short Formula of the Christian Faith,' in *The Pastoral Approach to Atheism,* vol. 23 of Concilium, ed. Karl Rahner (Glen Rock, 1967), pp. 70–82.

23. In another article Rahner illustrates this point with the understanding of the word 'God' and the changes it has undergone from the New Testament age, to St. Thomas's day, to the present time. A short formula of faith today should not presume a common and universal understanding of what or who God is; this poses

the problem of discovering in actual experience the bases for such an understanding and for its existential expression: 'Bemerkungen zur Gotteslehre in der Katholischen Dogmatik,' in *Catholica* 20 (1966), pp. 1–18.

24. Paul Ricoeur's comment on the function of faith in the modern world is in the section 'Sciences humaines et conditionnements de la foi,' in Lacombe, *Dieu*, pp. 140–141.

25. Cardinal Paul-Émile Leger, 'Theology of the Renewal of the Church,' in Shook, *Renewal*, p. 27, quoting John H. Newman, *An Essay on the Development of Christian Doctrine*. Leger states that the Church is made to be remade, so that we go against the truth of Christ if we deny that it is subject to change, that it suffers division, sinfulness, limitation, faithlessness. So, he concludes, our task is to renew the Church each time its light becomes less brilliant in the night of the world.

26. Because I have not spoken of it explicitly, in the text, I am somewhat concerned that my point may not be taken in its full seriousness. Renewal means, calls for, and is measured by the *holiness* of the people of God; it is to this that we are called by the Spirit and the great lack of the contemporary world is nothing other than the soul's hunger for God, without which the person is bereft of hope and the return to barbarism threatens the most civilized society in history. An illuminating perspective on the question of renewal and holiness may be gained from Johannes Metz's *Poverty of Spirit* (Glen Rock, 1968).

27. Hans Urs von Balthasar, *The God Question and Modern Man*. The author's contention is that the metaphysical sense has been not completely effaced but buried, first beneath a cosmocentric physicism, and more recently by a subjectivist psychologism. The road back will start from where we find ourselves at the present moment, a project recommended by Heidegger and other leading thinkers. Along the way the contingent, historical character of a number of fixations and attachments will be discovered, and believers must be prepared to reassess the value and necessity of much of what has passed for Christian 'tradition'; cf. pp. 11, 118–142 ('Being Lost').

28. Louis Evely, *The Faith of Modern Man*, chap. 6, 'Charity' (New York, 1969), p. 79.

29. This is the thesis of a very important and basic essay by Hans Urs von Balthasar, one which has received far less than the attention it deserves: 'Immediate Relationship with God,' in *Opportunities for Belief and Behavior*, vol. 29 of Concilium, ed. Christian Duquoc, O.P. (Glen Rock, 1966), pp. 39–53. The question is raised by a challenge, by the suggestion that the right relation to God is nothing but the right relation to neighbor (and oneself). This implies that religion as closeness to God has lost its validity—if it ever was valid—or was always an error, from which the modern

age has delivered us. On this basis, of religion as ethics, some common ground is provided for the dialogue with atheism. Balthasar argues against this suggestion, allowing the measure of truth that it contains but arguing for both the possibility and necessity, historically and at the present time, of an immediate relationship with God. Balthasar concludes: 'From the Christian point of view, a human "thou" can *remind* me often seriously and actively of God's demand and make it present to me, but as such (i.e., as a created "thou") it can never be the measure of God's demand on me in Christ. Men are most often considerate toward one another out of a sinful connivance, and the sinner himself is usually most considerate toward the sinner. In his demand for love God is indeed kind and forbearing, but not considerate, and the real mission of the Christian is measured by the measure of divine love. It is therefore in its origin and lasting structure immediately related to God and above dialogue,' p. 52.

30. Robert Adolfs, O.S.A., *The Grave of God* (New York, 1967), p. 104.
31. Yves Congar notes that the word 'church' has taken on a diminished, distorted, and depersonalized meaning, indicating not so much the body of the faithful, as it should, as a system, an apparatus, a depository of complex rights, duties, penalties, primarily if not exclusively, the clergy: 'I would like to point out in this respect a problem which, as far as I know, has never been considered, namely the application of the directives of the Gospel, not only to individuals but to the Church as such. Is it the individual alone who must be the servant and not the master, who must forgive offenses, bless his enemies and not curse them? Have themes such as this any longer a place in an ecclesiology identified in practice with a treatise on public ecclesiastical law?' *Power and Poverty in the Church* (London, 1964), pp. 64–65.
32. Yves Congar, O.P., 'The Church: the People of God,' in vol. 1 of Concilium (Glen Rock, N.J., 1965), p. 10.
33. Karl Lehmann, Rahner's assistant at the University of Munich, worked out the elements of a practical approach, leaning heavily on Rahner's *Handbuch der Pastoraltheologie* (Freiburg, 1964). Lehmann's essay attempts to answer three questions: in what ways is a meaningful approach to the modern unbeliever theologically and pastorally possible? What are the necessary basic structures for the concrete announcement of the Gospel? and what principles of public Church action are particularly urgent today in the coexistence with unbelievers: 'Some Ideas from Pastoral Theology on the Proclamation of the Christian Message to Present-day Unbelievers,' in *The Pastoral Approach to Atheism*, vol. 23 of Concilium, ed. K. Rahner (Glen Rock, 1967), pp. 83–102.
34. The incarnation of unbelief in religious forms, unbelief as a permanent corollary of faith, the 'agnostician and atheism of religion'

are the dramatic terms in which William Stringfellow discusses what Martin Marty calls the 'religious varieties of unbelief': *A Private and Public Faith* (New York, 1964). Parts 2 and 3 of chap. 1, pp. 25 ff.

35. Cf. Karl Rahner's essay on 'Demythologization and the Sermon,' some reflections on the present-day need to translate forms of explanation and presentation of the Gospel in view of the alienation of so many men from traditional terms and categories, in *The Renewal of Preaching,* vol. 33 of Concilium, ed. K. Rahner, S.J. (Glen Rock, 1967), pp. 20–38.

36. It will be an apologetics with a profoundly anthropological perspective, clarifying the credibility of faith by uncovering the conditions making it acceptable to man, and its appropriateness, that is, the intimate relation between being man and believing. Formerly the emphasis in apologetics has been on the compelling authority of a revelation sufficiently identified as divine; in future the fact of God's addressing Himself to man will be stressed, to bring to the fore the necessary conditions relevant to man, which may capture his interest. Of special interest is Karl Rahner's 'Theology and Anthropology,' in *The Word in History: The St. Xavier Symposium*, ed. T. Burke (New York, 1966), pp. 1–23.

37. Lehmann, 'Some Ideas,' p. 91, n. 10.

38. Robert McAfee Brown, 'Faith and Learning: Antithesis or Partnership?' in *Concurrence*, no. 1 (Winter, 1969), pp. 43–54.

39. McAfee Brown, 'Faith and Learning,' p. 52. The author points out also that man is liberated to a receptivity to the truth that has already been offered to him by his belief that humanity is defined not by formulas or abstractions, not even solely by such meanings as he can discern unaided, but by the life of One Who walked the earth Himself, p. 53.

40. Daniel Callahan writes: 'Modern man lives in a world of vast and rapid change; the social stabilities which once helped to ward off cosmic terror are disappearing; the scientific certainties which once gave man the impression that he lived in a materially unchanging world are evaporating; the belief that progress was inevitable has been dealt some shattering blows. There is no end to changes of this kind. When the Catholic today asks that the Church find a fresh language to express old insights, or a rich language for new insights, he reflects the restlessness of contemporary man and the contemporary Christian. He, too, has been cast adrift by the tide of history and human development. The Church he sees about him, even the Church engaged in renewing itself, still has about its body the garb of other eras. He does not live in those eras. They are strange and alien to him. He is thus forced to begin all over.' 'The Risk of Faith,' in *Commonweal* (12 March 1965), p. 756.

41. In an informal talk at the Dominican priory of Latour-Maubourg

in 1948, Camus demanded of Christians an unconditional condemnation of evil, especially in face of the exercise of inhuman and oppressive force. He said that the world expects Christians to speak out clearly with a great voice, so that not the slightest doubt could arise in the heart of the simplest man. Camus begged churchmen to get away from their cherished abstractions and confront the bloodstained face of history: in *Resistance, Rebellion, and Death* (New York, 1966), p. 53.

42. Cf. the meditative short piece by Hans Urs von Balthasar, 'Only Love is Believable,' in Mooney, *Toward*, pp. 126–131.

43. Joseph Ratzinger has searched out the major scholarly accounts of the development of the Christian ideal of fraternal charity, from New Testament writings, in *Christian Brotherhood* (New York, 1966), pp. 20–40 (hereafter cited as Ratzinger, *Christian*).

44. Cf. K. H. Schelke, *Discipleship and Priesthood* (New York, 1958), pp. 44 ff., and his authoritative entry on 'Brotherhood,' in RAC I, 638 ff.; also Ratzinger, *Christian*, pp. 71–74.

45. *Concurrence* has translated and reprinted Cardinal König's informative essay on 'The Second Vatican Council and the Secretariat for Non-Believers,' vol. 1 (Winter, 1969), pp. 34–42.

46. The Cardinal's remarks are reproduced in Richard Barta, *Francis Cardinal Koenig,* in the series The Men Who Make the Council, ed. Michael Novak (Baltimore, 1966), p. 35.

47. König's interview is reported in an article, 'The Secretariat for Non-Believers,' no author, in *Herder Correspondence*, April, 1966, p. 108.

48. *Herder Correspondence,* p. 108.

49. On the uses of dialogal forms by philosophers and other thinkers, from classical antiquity to Alfred North Whitehead, cf. James K. Pierce, *Dialogue as a Mode of Inquiry* (New York, 1967), with a good bibliography, pp. 170–175.

50. The possibility and conditions of various types of dialogue are surveyed in an excellent article by Dominique Dubarle, 'Dialogue and Its Philosophy,' in *Concurrence,* vol. 1 (Winter, 1969), pp. 3–12, from which I have borrowed extensively in these paragraphs.

51. Dubarle, 'Dialogue,' pp. 3–4.

52. Mortimer Adler, *The Conditions of Philosophy* (New York, 1965), pp. 21–31, in which the first condition is that philosophy be knowledge in a moderate and realizable, not strong and unattainable, sense, i.e., testable by evidence, subject to rational criticism, and either corrigible or falsifiable.

53. The best philosophical treatise on the qualities of faith as knowledge is Josef Pieper's *Belief and Faith* (New York, 1963), with a keen and sensitive appreciation of the epistemological and ontological dimensions of the act of belief.

54. Dubarle, 'Dialogue,' p. 5.

55. *Ibid.*, p. 7.
56. I have used the English version of the document issued by the Documentary Service of the Press Department, U.S. Catholic Conference, distributed in October, 1968, to the consultors of the Secretariat in the United States.
57. ActApS 56 (1964), p. 644.
58. *Dignitatis humanae*, n. 3. In the statement on the appropriation of the truth as the inalienable right and responsibility of individual conscience, the Council is reiterating a theme close to the heart of Cardinal Newman's thinking: cf. A. J. Boekraad, *The Personal Conquest of Truth according to J. H. Newman* (The Hague, 1962).
59. *Gaudium et spes*, n. 92: a statement on 'dialogue between all men.' It has been said that, in summoning an Ecumenical Council, Pope John wanted as much as anything else to initiate and encourage a true dialogue within the Church. The bishops were to meet to begin what the entire Church would carry on; this is quite other than the bishops assembling to be instructed and enlightened by curial savants, to proceed thence to instruct unilaterally a passive and unquestioning laity.
60. J. Trutsch gives a good survey of some noteworthy recent endeavors along these lines in 'Glaube und Erkenntnis,' in *Fragen der Theologie heute*, ed. J. Feiner et al., pp. 53–58. For another, more systematic view, comparing an 'existential-faith' and a 'dogma-faith,' cf. U. NeuenSchwander, *Glaube: eine Besinnung uber Wesen und Begriff des Glaubens*. I cite these as providing guidelines to some of the major problems in the relationship of faith and reason, a relationship which demands re-examination as often as a new and different understanding of either term is achieved, or claimed.
61. Cornelio Fabro locates an immanentist truth-theory very close to the center of the huge ideological movement in which contemporary unbelief has found its greatest intellectual support; cf. all of Part IX, 'The Inner Nucleus of Modern Atheism,' *God in Exile* (Westminster, 1968), pp. 1061–1153. More succinctly, Fabro identifies immanentism as the root error underlying 'The Positive Character of Modern Atheism,' in *Concurrence*, vol. 1 (Winter, 1969), pp. 66–76.
62. *Pacem in Terris*, ActApS 55 (1963), p. 300, cf. *Ecclesiam suam* ActApS 56 (1964), pp. 652–653. In view of this allowance it is difficult to reconcile older papal or other official texts ruling out unequivocally all possibility of encountering Communists in any capacity other than intransigent opponents.
63. These notes on published comment in response to the Vatican document are based on the study by Gerald J. Phelan, S.J., 'Report on the Press Reaction to the Document on Dialogue with Non-Believers,' in the *Bolletino di Informazione* of the Secretariat for Non-Believers, vol. 4, no. 1, n. 1, pp. 29–52.

64. Don Vincenzo Miano, S.D.B., has prepared a report, 'La trattazione dell'ateismo nel sinodo,' included in the *Bolletino di Informazione*, vol. 3, no. 2, pp. 9–23, on which my own account is based.

65. The proceedings of this symposium, held at the John LaFarge institute on October 30, 1967, have not been published; the data included in the text are taken from a news story by Edward B. Fiske, *New York Times* (31 October, 1967), p. 41.

66. Background material to the Catholic-humanist encounter is taken from the article 'Scientific Humanism and its Anti-Christian Straitjackets,' no author, in *Herder Correspondence*, December, 1966, pp. 351–355.

67. A. J. Ayer, 'Humanism and Reform,' in *Encounter*, 20, no. 6 (June, 1966), p. 17. Ayer contended further that theological questions have ceased to excite the interest which they once did, particularly in the nineteenth century; that there were no new or convincing arguments for theism, but at most only an occasional attempt, by Christians, to find a new way, at last, to reconcile religion with science. Hence the exaggerated attention being paid to Teilhard de Chardin, a master mystifier. Ayer's understanding of the current situation reflects a positivist impatience with recent fits and starts in the direction of a revivified natural theology, a refusal to move with the linguistic analysts in search of a metaphysic.

68. Cf. H. J. Blackman's remarkably frank and irenic article, 'Why Talk to Catholics?' his report as a participant on the Amersfoort meeting and his effort to justify such encounters to his fellow Humanists, in *Humanist*, 26, no. 4 (July/August, 1966), pp. 123–125.

69. The negative sentiments outlined in the following paragraphs are expressed in an unsigned article, 'Communists as Discussion Partners: The Perverted Dialogue,' in *Expulsus*, 14, no. 3, 1966, pp. 10–15. This is a Catholic newsletter devoted to problems of refugees from and the Church in eastern European countries. The views expressed are humanly understandable, in the light of the bitter experiences of persecution suffered by those who publish and contribute to this journal.

70. This note of sober realism is unfortunately absent from the otherwise constructive article by Harvey Cox, 'Let's End the Communist-Christian Vendetta,' in *The Christian Century* (9 November 1966), pp. 1375–1379. Similarly optimistic and without advertence to the hard facts of political life is Leslie Dewart's glowing hymn to the future of Marxist-Christian dialogue, 'From Dialogue to Co-operation,' his Introduction to Roger Garaudy's *From Anathema to Dialogue*, pp. 5–23.

71. Cf. Irene Posnoff, 'Expériences de dialogue avec des athées russes,' in Veuillot et al., *L'Athéisme: tentation du monde, réveil des chrétiens?* (Paris, 1963), pp. 205–210; and J. Wozniakowski, 'Experiences de dialogue en Pologne,' in Veuillot, *L'Athéisme*, pp. 211–213.

72. Thomas Blakeley, 'The Impossibility of a Dialogue,' in *Pax Romana Journal*, n. 1 (1965), pp. 16–17.
73. This first major dialogue between Christians and Marxists is described by Donald MacLean, S.J., in 'An Opening Attempt,' in *America* (31 July 1965), pp. 115–117, and, from a Marxist perspective, by John Lewis, in 'Dialogue between Christianity and Marxism,' reprinted in *Dialogue of Christianity and Marxism*, ed. James Klugman (London, 1968), pp. 1–16.
74. These articles are collected in Klugman, *Dialogue*.
75. Cf. Paul Oestereicher, 'Christians and Marxists in Dialogue,' in *The Catholic Herald* (20 May 1966), p. 7.
76. The Santa Clara meeting is reported by James Colaianni in the chapter, 'Marxist-Christian Dialogue,' of his *The Catholic Left*, which he subtitles The Crisis of Radicalism within the Church, pp. 91–95. The dialogue was organized by the university's Center for the Study of Contemporary Values.
77. Colaianni, *The Catholic Left*, p. 95.
78. Cf. Daniel L. Flaherty, 'Christian-Communist Dialogue,' in *America* (17 December 1966), p. 805.
79. The proceedings of the Marienbad conference are recounted in an unsigned article, 'Convegno di Marienbad,' in *Bolletino di Informazione*, vol. 2, no. 3 (July, 1967), pp. 1–15.
80. As this work is being completed it is only days since the Rome conference was held. I have relied on reports in the press and in the April 4 1969 issue of *Time*, pp. 51 and 53.

Bibliography

BOOKS

Abbott, Walter, editor. *The Documents of Vatican II.* New York: Guild, 1966.

Adolfs, Robert. *The Church Is Different.* London: Compass Books, 1966.

———. *The Grave of God.* translated by N. D. Smith. New York: Harper & Row, 1967.

Aubert, Roger. *Le Problème de l'acte de foi.* 3d ed. Louvain: Presses universitaires, 1958.

Baillie, D. M. *Faith in God.* London: Faber & Faber, 1964.

Baillie, John. *Our Knowledge of God.* New York: Scribner's, 1959.

Bars, Henry. *The Assent of Faith,* translated by Robert Halstead. Baltimore: Helicon, 1960.

Barth, Karl. *Church Dogmatics* III/1, translated by G. T. Thomson. Edinburgh: T. & T. Clark, 1952.

Bartley, William Warren. *The Retreat to Commitment.* New York: Knopf, 1962.

Baumer, Franklin L. *Religion and the Rise of Scepticism.* New York: Harcourt, Brace, 1960.

Bergougnioux, F. M., and Goetz, J. *Les Religions des Préhistoriques et des Primitifs.* Paris, 1958.

Blackman, H. J., editor. *Objections to Humanism.* London: Constable, 1963.

Borne, Étienne. *Atheism,* translated by S. J. Tester. New York: Hawthorn Books, 1961.

Bouillard, Henri. *The Logic of Faith.* New York: Sheed & Ward, 1967.

Bultmann, Rudolf, and Weiser, Artur. *Faith,* translated by Dorothea M. Barton. London: Adam and Charles Black, 1961.

Burke, T., editor. *The Word in History.* New York: Sheed & Ward, 1966.

Camus, Albert. *Resistance, Rebellion, and Death,* translated by Justin O'Brien. New York: Knopf, 1966.

293

Cirne-Lima, Carlos. *Personal Faith,* translated by G. Richard Dimber. New York: Herder & Herder, 1965.

Collins, James. *The Emergence of Philosophy of Religion.* New Haven: Yale University Press, 1967.

———. *God and Modern Philosophy.* Chicago: Regnery, 1959.

Congar, Yves. *Power and Poverty in the Church,* translated by Jennifer Nicholson. London: Geoffrey Chapman, 1964.

Cutler, Donald R., editor. *The Religious Situation: 1968.* Boston: Beacon, 1968.

Daniélou, Jean. *God and the Ways of Knowing,* translated by Walter Roberts. New York: Greenwich Editions, 1957.

D'Arcy, Martin. *No Absent God.* New York: Harper & Row, 1962.

Davis, Charles. *Theology for Today.* New York: Sheed & Ward, 1962.

Denzinger, Henricus. *Enchiridion Symbolorum,* edited by J. B. Umber. 25th ed. Barcelona: Herder, 1948.

Dewart, Leslie. *The Future of Belief.* New York: Herder & Herder, 1966.

Dirscherl, Denis, editor. *Speaking of God.* Milwaukee: Bruce, 1967.

Dondeyne, Albert. *Contemporary Christian Faith and European Thought,* translated by John Burnheim and Ernan McMullin. Pittsburgh: Duquesne University Press, 1958.

———. *Faith and the World,* translated by Walter van de Putte. Pittsburgh: Duquesne University Press, 1963.

Duquoc, Christian, editor. *Opportunities for Belief and Behavior* (Concilium, vol. 29). Glen Rock, N.J.: Paulist, 1966.

Eminyan, Maurice. *The Theology of Salvation.* Boston: St. Paul Editions, 1960.

Etcheverry, A. *Le Conflit actual des humanismes.* Rome: Gregorian University Press, 1964.

Fabro, Cornelio. *God in Exile,* translated by Arthur Gibson. Westminster, Md.: Newman, 1968.

Ferré, Nels F. S. *The Finality of Faith.* New York: Harper & Row, 1963.

Foote, Peter, et al., editors. *World: Vatican II's Pastoral Constitution on the Church in the Modern World.* Chicago: Catholic Action Federation, 1967.

Garrigou-Lagrange, Reginald. *God: His Existence and His Nature,* vol. 1, translated by Bede Rose. St. Louis: Herder, 1948.

Giblet, J., editor. *The God of Israel, the God of Christians,* translated by Kathryn Sullivan. New York: Desclée, 1961.

Hartshorne, Charles, and Reese, William L., editors. *Philosophers Speak of God.* Chicago: University of Chicago Press, 1953.

Hazard, Paul. *The European Mind, 1680–1715,* translated by J. Lewis May. New Haven: Yale University Press, 1953.

Heaney, John J., editor. *Faith, Reason, and the Gospels.* Westminster, Md.: Newman, 1961.

Hebblethwaite, Peter. *The Council Fathers and Atheism.* Glen Rock, N.J.: Paulist, 1967.

Heinisch, Paul. *Theology of the Old Testament,* translated by William Heidt. Collegeville, Minn.: Liturgical Press, 1950.

Hermann, Ingo. *The Experience of Faith,* translated by Daniel Coogan. New York: Kenedy, 1966.

Hofmans, Flor. *Jesus: Who Is He?* Glen Rock, N.J.: Paulist, 1968.

Holstein, H., editor. *Visages et approches de l'incroyance.* Lyons: Editions du chalet, 1956.

Jenkins, Daniel. *Beyond Religion.* London: SCM, 1963.

———, editor. *The Scope of Theology.* Cleveland: World, 1968.

Jenkins, David. *The Glory of Man.* New York: Scribner's, 1968.

Johann, Robert. *The Pragmatic Meaning of God.* Milwaukee: Marquette University Press, 1966.

Jolivet, Régis. *Sartre: Theology of the Absurd,* translated by Wesley C. Piersol. Westminster, Md.: Newman, 1967.

Kavanaugh, James. *The Struggle of the Unbeliever.* New York: Trident, 1967.

Keating, John P., editor. *Faith in the Face of Doubt.* Glen Rock, N.J.: Paulist, 1968.

Ketcham, Charles B. *The Search for Meaningful Existence.* New York: Weybright & Talley, 1968.

Kliever, Lonnie, and Hayes, John. *Radical Christianity: The New Theologies in Perspective.* Anderson, S.C.: Drake House, 1968.

Küng, Hans. *The Unknown God?* translated by W. W. White. New York: Sheed & Ward, 1966.

Lacroix, Jean. *The Meaning of Modern Atheism,* translated by Garret Barden. Dublin: Gill & Son, 1965.

Lepp, Ignace. *Atheism in Our Time,* translated by Bernard Murchland. New York: Macmillan, 1963.

Lewis, H. D. *Our Experience of God.* London: Allen & Unwin, 1959.

Lombardi, Riccardo. *The Salvation of the Unbeliever,* translated by Dorothy M. White. Westminster, Md.: Newman, 1956.

Luijpen, William. *Phenomenology and Atheism.* Pittsburgh: Duquesne University Press, 1964.

Macquarrie, John. *God-Talk.* New York: Harper & Row, 1967.

Maritain, Jacques. *The Range of Reason.* New York: Scribner's, 1952.

Marty, Martin. *Varieties of Unbelief.* New York: Holt, Rinehart & Winston, 1964.

——— et al., editors. *What Do We Believe?* New York: Meredith, 1968.

Maurier, Henri. *Essai d'une théologie du paganisme.* Paris: L'Orante, 1965.

Metz, Johannes. *Poverty of Spirit,* translated by John Drury. Glen Rock, N.J.: Paulist, 1968.

———, editor. *The Church and the World* (Concilium, vol. 6). Glen Rock, N.J.: Paulist, 1965.

Miegge, Giovanni. *Gospel and Myth in the Thought of Rudolf Bultmann.* Richmond: John Knox, 1960.

Miller, William, editor. *The New Christianity.* New York: Delta, 1967.

Mooney, Michael, et al. *Toward a Theology of Christian Faith.* New York: Herder & Herder, 1966.

Mouroux, Jean. *I Believe: The Personal Structure of Faith,* translated by Michael Turner. New York: Sheed & Ward, 1959.

Murray, John C. *The Problem of God.* New Haven: Yale University Press, 1964.

Nicholls, William, editor. *Conflicting Images of Man.* New York: Seabury, 1966.

Novak, Michael. *Belief and Unbelief.* New York: Mentor-Omega, 1965.

Ogden, Schubert M. *The Reality of God.* New York: Harper & Row, 1966.

Padavano, Anthony T. *The Estranged God.* New York: Sheed & Ward, 1966.

Pieper, Josef. *Belief and Faith,* translated by Richard and Clara Winston. New York: Pantheon Books, 1963.

Rabut, Olivier. *Faith and Doubt,* translated by Bonnie and William Whitman. New York: Sheed & Ward, 1967.

Rademacher, Arnold. *Religion and Life.* Westminster, Md.: Newman, 1962.

Rahner, Karl. *Belief Today,* translated by M. H. Heelan. New York: Sheed & Ward, 1967.

———. *On Heresy,* translated by W. J. O'Hara. London: Burns & Oates, 1964.

———. *Theological Investigations,* vol. 4, translated by Karl H. Kruger. Baltimore: Helicon, 1966.

———, editor. *The Pastoral Approach to Atheism* (Concilium, vol. 23). Glen Rock, N.J.: Paulist, 1967.

———, editor. *The Renewal of Preaching* (Concilium, vol. 33). Glen Rock, N.J.: Paulist, 1967.

Ratzinger, Joseph. *Christian Brotherhood,* translated by W. A. Glen-Doeph. New York: Sheed & Ward, 1966.

Reid, John Patrick. *The Anatomy of Atheism.* Washington, D.C.: Thomist Press, 1965.

Röper, Anita. *The Anonymous Christian,* translated by Joseph Donceel. New York: Sheed & Ward, 1966.

Rynne, Xavier. *The Fourth Session.* New York: Farrar, Straus, & Giroux, 1966.

———. *The Third Session.* New York: Farrar, Straus, & Giroux, 1965.

Sartory, Thomas. *A New Interpretation of Faith,* translated by Martha Schmidt. Westminster, Md.: Newman, 1968.

Sartre, Jean-Paul. *The Words,* translated by Bernard Frechtman. Greenwich, Conn.: Fawcett, 1966.

Schillebeeckx, Edward, *God, the Future of Man.* Translated by N. D. Smith. New York: Sheed & Ward, 1968.

Schlette, Heinz Robert. *Toward a Theology of Religions,* translated by W. J. O'Hara. New York: Herder & Herder, 1966.

Schnackenburg, Rudolf. *The Moral Teaching of the New Testament.* New York: Herder & Herder, 1965.

Schoonenberg, Peter. *God's World in the Making,* translated by Walter van de Putte. Pittsburgh: Duquesne University Press, 1964.

Shook, L. K., editor. *Renewal of Religious Thought,* vol. 1. New York: Herder & Herder, 1968.

Smith, Harry E. *Secularization and the University.* Richmond: John Knox, 1968.

Smith, John E. *Religion and Empiricism.* Milwaukee: Marquette University Press, 1965.

————. *Experience and God.* New York: Oxford University Press, 1968.

Smith, Ronald Gregor. *Secular Christianity.* London: Collins, 1966.

Stephen, Leslie. *Essays on Freethinking and Plain-Speaking.* New York: G. P. Putnam's Sons, 1905.

Suhard, Emmanuel Cardinal. *The Church Today.* Chicago: Fides, 1953.

Tresmontant, Claude. *Toward the Knowledge of God,* translated by Robert J. Olsen. Baltimore: Helicon, 1961.

Urs von Balthasar, Hans. *The God Question and Modern Man,* translated by Hilda Graef. New York: Seabury, 1967.

Vahanian, Gabriel. *The Death of God.* New York: George Braziller, 1961.

————. *No Other God.* New York: George Braziller, 1966.

van de Pol, W. H. *The End of Conventional Christianity,* translated by Theodore Zuydwijk. New York: Newman, 1967.

Verneaux, Roger. *Leçons sur l'Athéisme Contemporain.* Paris: P. Tequi, 1964.

Veuillot, Mgr., et al. *L'Athéisme: tentation du monde, réveil des chrétiens?* Paris: Éditions du Cerf, 1963.

Vogel, Arthur A. *The Next Christian Epoch.* New York: Harper & Row, 1966.

Wilson, R. McL. *The Gnostic Problem.* London: Mowbray, 1964.

Wingren, Gustav. *The Living Word,* translated by Victor C. Pogue. Philadelphia: Muhlenberg, 1960.

Wolf, Donald, and Schall, James, editors. *Current Trends in Theology.* Garden City, N.Y.: Doubleday, 1965.

PERIODICAL ARTICLES

Barthélemy, D. 'Les idoles et l'image.' *La Vie spirituelle,* March, 1962, 288–294.

Blackham, H. J. 'Why Talk to Catholics?' *Humanist* 26 (July/August, 1966): 123–125.

Callahan, Daniel. 'The Risk of Faith.' *Commonweal,* March 12, 1965, pp. 755–758.

Congar, Yves. 'Theology in the Council.' *American Ecclesiastical Review* 155 (October 1966): 217–230.

Cuypers, Karel. 'The Humanist Response to the Problems and Aspirations of Men.' *Humanist* 26 (Nov./Dec., 1966): 183–186.

Dubarle, Dominique. 'Dialogue and Its Philosophy.' *Concurrence* 1 (1969): 3–12.

Fabro, Cornelio. 'The Positive Character of Modern Atheism.' *Concurrence* 1 (1966): 66–76.

Hyams, Edward. 'Religion and Progress.' *New Statesman*, February 11, 1966, p. 189.

König, Franziscus Cardinal. 'The Second Vatican Council and the Secretariat for Non-Believers.' *Concurrence* 1 (1966): 34–142.

Krejci, Jaroslav. 'A New Model of Scientific Atheism.' *Concurrence* 1 (1969): 82–96.

Lauer, Quentin. 'The Problem of Unbelief.' *Thought* 42 (1967): 505–518.

Merton, Thomas. 'Is the World a Problem?' *Commonweal*, June 3, 1966, pp. 305–309.

Moran, Gabriel. 'The God of Revelation.' *Commonweal*, February 10, 1967, pp. 499–503.

Murray, John C. 'On the Structure of the Problem of God.' *Theological Studies* 23 (1962): 1–26.

Ong, Walter. 'American Culture and Morality.' *Religious Education* 58 (1963): 3–11.

Rahner, Karl. 'Atheism and Implicit Christianity.' *Theology Digest*, February, 1968, pp. 43–56.

Schouberg, Gary. 'Secular Humanism and the Christian Faith.' *The Catholic World* 208 (November, 1968): 69–74.

Taubes, Susan Anima. 'The Absent God.' *Journal of Religion* 35 (1955): 6–9.

Van Roo, William A. 'Talk about God.' *America*, May 14, 1966, pp. 691–694.

Subject Index

Absence of God, 82–3, 172
Absolute unbelief, 14–15
Action dialogue, 208–9
Agnosticism, 22–5, 37
Alienation, 154–5, 172
Analogy of unbelief, 13 f.
Anonymous Christianity, 102 ff.
Anthropology, Christian, 54, 60, 130–1
Anthropomorphism, 82–3, 93
Apologetics, xiv–xv, 14, 46–7, 81–3, 94, 111–12, 116, 129, 150–1, 238
Authority, 165–6

Belief, 1, 5–8, 177–80
Believer, unbelief of, 33–4, 110–31
Brotherhood, 109–10, 114, 163–4

Christ, 4, 34 ff., 80, 86, 96
Church, xvii–xviii, 4, 5–6, 44 ff., 48–9, 92, 96–7, 100 ff., 109, 119–22, 132–3, 145–6, 160 ff.
Communication, 174–6
Concupiscence, 117–18
Conversion, 7–8, 33–4, 35, 143, 159–60
Counterparts of unbelief, 16–24
Creativity, 97–8

Credulity, 7
Culture, 77 f., 88–90, 95

Deism, 20–2
Dialogue, xiii–xv, 192–216
Disbelief, 12
Disobedience and unbelief, 33
Doctrinal dialogue, 203–8
Doctrinal renewal, 83–4, 144 ff.
Doubt, 15, 112 f., 173
Dualism, 17

Enlightenment, xii, 49
Evil, 40–1, 44, 46, 52, 68
Existentialist atheism, 63
Experience of God, 105, 107–8, 123, 172, 176

Faith, 2–8, 29–30, 32 ff., 72, 79–80, 81–3, 85 ff., 97, 106 ff., 111–16, 124, 128–30, 156–9, 176–90, 233, 244–5, 250–1, 252–3, 257–8, 259–60
Fideism, 24, 48–9
Freedom and unbelief, 43, 48, 53, 65–8, 78–9, 83, 98, 109–10

Gnosticism, 129, 141
God-language, 60, 81–2, 110, 147–9, 150–1, 231

299

Index of Names

302